ART AND POLITICS

The History of the
National Arts Centre

ART AND POLITICS

The History of the National Arts Centre

Sarah Jennings

DUNDURN PRESS
Toronto

Project Editor: Michael Carroll
Editor: Rosemary Shipton
Text Design: Kim Monteforte, WeMakeBooks.ca
Printer: Friesens

Library and Archives Canada Cataloguing in Publication

Jennings, Sarah
    Art and politics : the history of the National Arts Centre / by Sarah Jennings.

ISBN 978-1-55002-886-7

1. National Arts Centre (Canada)--History. 2. Performing arts--Canada--History. I. Title.

PN1589.C3J45 2009   791.09713'84   C2009-900097-0

1 2 3 4 5   13 12 11 10 09

We acknowledge the support of the **Canada Council for the Arts** and the **Ontario Arts Council** for our publishing program. We also acknowledge the financial support of the **Government of Canada** through the **Book Publishing Industry Development Program** and **The Association for the Export of Canadian Books**, and the **Government of Ontario** through the **Ontario Book Publishers Tax Credit program**, and the **Ontario Media Development Corporation**.

Care has been taken to trace the ownership of copyright material used in this book. The author and the publisher welcome any information enabling them to rectify any references or credits in subsequent editions.
                                                                                J. Kirk Howard, President

Printed and bound in Canada.
www.dundurn.com

Dundurn Press
3 Church Street, Suite 500
Toronto, Ontario, Canada
M5E 1M2

Gazelle Book Services Limited
White Cross Mills
High Town, Lancaster, England
LA1 4XS

Dundurn Press
2250 Military Road
Tonawanda, NY U.S.A.
14150

To Hamish

CONTENTS

PRELUDE

Canada's National Arts Centre (NAC) opened its doors to the world on Monday, June 2, 1969. It was unique. Built both to produce and to present music, opera, dance, and theatre, it was also bilingual, designed to reflect Canada's linguistic duality—the first, and still the only, arts centre in the world with such a complex mandate. A fortuitous crossing of the stars had brought it about. While rooted in the modest hopes of Ottawa's local citizens to build a good concert hall in their city, the project had expanded, thanks to Canada's 1967 Centennial, into a magnificent edifice. The building of the National Arts Centre had been the right project at the right time for Prime Minister Lester B. Pearson, who had wanted something special for Canada's capital to mark the country's 100th birthday celebration. In G. Hamilton Southam, the man who was now its first director general, the Arts Centre had the right executive, one with the vision, background, and connections to ensure its creation. But even as this glittering first night unfolded, a new constellation of stars was moving into place in Ottawa—men who would bring new ideas and objectives to the development of Canada's arts and culture.

After a weekend of splendid weather, the opening night was rainy and windswept. The mood, however, was exuberant. *Time,* America's most popular news magazine and the sponsor of the night's live CBC English-network television broadcast, declared: "Not since Expo 67's shimmering debut has an opening night stirred such an exhilarating sense of grand occasion." A First Nights Committee had struggled for months to cut back the guest list of nearly three thousand names of Ottawa's "notables" to fit the 2,100-seat capacity of the Opera hall. A third of the audience was to be government officials; another third, "artistic people"; and the rest, members of the general public. With the possible exception of the governor general, everybody was supposedly paying for their own tickets, yet *tout Ottawa* wanted to be part of this evening.

There were no speeches. The organizers had decided that, in each of the centre's three beautiful new halls, the curtain rising on the first performance would mark its opening. The formalities had taken place two days before at a ceremony filled with politicians and dignitaries. Standing before the tall, embossed bronze doors of the Salon, with a children's choir serenading the proceedings, newly minted Prime Minister Pierre Trudeau had handed over control of the site to NAC chairman Lawrence Freiman. All through that sunny Saturday musical groups ranging from bagpipers to rock bands, stationed on the building's multi-levelled outside terraces, had entertained the forty thousand citizens who had poured into downtown Ottawa to scramble around the brand-new building. Its final cost, a cool $46.1 million, had titillated, outraged, and bemused politicians and the public alike for more than six years.

At the outset, in 1963, the price tag had been set at $9 million, but that first estimate had spiralled rapidly upwards to what was now, to many, an astronomical sum. Throughout construction, and in the face of devastating attacks from political opponents and the press, Pearson had resolutely backed the Arts Centre. On this opening day there was no doubt, at least in the minds of its organizers and builders, that "the Canadian public had got a first-class building at a bargain price."[1]

Trudeau's new minister for cultural affairs, Secretary of State Gérard Pelletier, did not agree. Shortly after his appointment, he had made it clear that if he had been in office at the time the NAC was proposed, he "wouldn't have built it … at least not at the cost." He had also added that he did not want the place to be "snobbish."[2] Pelletier's remark had little effect on Southam, who ensured that the opening night was a grand social occasion. The handsome and sophisticated scion of a blue-blooded Ottawa family, he favoured full-blown elegance when the event called for it—and this triumphant evening was one of those occasions. As the rain poured down, chauffeur-driven cars rolled up to the main entrance to deposit their distinguished passengers—the men striking in white tie and tails; the women gowned and bejewelled with a glamour rare in Ottawa.

Nothing stirred more excitement than the arrival of Pierre Trudeau and his entourage, which included Pelletier and his beautiful and cultured wife, Alex. Trudeau looked resplendent in white tie, the usual rose in his lapel, and on his arm Madeleine Gobeil, by day a lecturer in French literature at Carleton University but tonight dazzling in a lime-green lace minidress and tumbling blond tresses. Their photo would dominate the country's front pages the following day. Gobeil, a long-time Trudeau friend, had already been appointed a member of the first NAC Board of Trustees.

Though not yet detectable, a pivotal moment was occurring in Canadian cultural affairs. The old *lèse-majesté* way of doing things was about to give way to a more proactive, practical use of the arts in the country's political and cultural struggles, especially in Quebec. The concepts of "democratization and decentralization" in cultural policy that Pelletier was about to introduce would be different from the traditional kind of government support which had led to the building of "arm's-length" cultural institutions and organizations such as the NAC, the Canada Council, and the CBC. Over the long term, the new policies would change irrevocably the place of the arts in national life in Canada and the way that national institutions operated.

The arrival of the "French fact" in Ottawa also ensured that a new set of "notables" would take over, changing the established practices of the generally anglophone (though often bilingual) elites that had run cultural affairs to that point. The old guard, many of whom had been educated abroad and had travelled widely, generally held an international perspective on the arts. The new voices coming on the scene would focus more intensely on Canada's own experiences and history and insist that the broader world view should be secondary.

The civil and outward-looking perspective of the Royal Commission on Bilingualism and Biculturalism, with its proposals for a bilingual, bicultural Canadian society, was about to be overtaken and changed by the narrow nationalism surging in Quebec and the struggle within the Quebec family between Quebec federalists and separatists. Arts and culture would become just another tool in the long dispute between these opposing views. While the NAC had been forged and created in the older context, the environment would quickly change as decentralized interests took power away from the centre of the country. In the years to come the Arts Centre would have to fight to justify its existence and, by the early nineties, would reach almost total collapse. Only by recasting itself, particularly in terms of its financial model, has it recently begun to regain a place at the centre of Canada's national artistic life.

Part One
THE SOUTHAM YEARS

GENESIS OF
THE DREAM

On November 8, 1963, G. Hamilton Southam, president of Ottawa's National Capital Arts Alliance, drafted a careful letter to Prime Minister Lester B. Pearson. It contained a formal request written in the most concise terms: "For consideration by the government ... the idea of the creation of a performing arts centre in Ottawa ... and complementary to it ... a festival of the arts in Ottawa each year."[1]

The genesis of this idea in Ottawa went back decades—indeed, it was partially rooted in the dreams of Southam's own family. His father and uncle had initiated plans for a similar centre in the 1920s and had even paid to have blueprints drawn to sketch out a proposal. But although major orchestras and theatre troupes continued to tour through Ottawa during the thirties and the war years, no further concrete action on the idea of building a performance hall had occurred until now.

In 1952 Vincent Massey, the first Canadian governor general and a great patron of the arts, gave cultural matters in the city a significant push. In a Canadian Club luncheon speech to Ottawans at the Château Laurier Hotel, he urged "an eminent festival"[2] for the capital along the lines of the newly created Edinburgh Festival. The idea of artistic festivals was flourishing everywhere in the postwar period, but in Ottawa it was clear that any such festival would need a place in which to perform, and Ottawa still lacked a significant facility. Many prominent citizens at that lunch took note. Now, ten years later and barely a year since Southam had agreed to head a civic committee in search of a performing arts centre, a plan was ready.

His carefully worded letter to Pearson, an old Southam family friend, was a prelude to a formal meeting later that afternoon. His proposal to the prime minister was that the construction of a performing arts centre be Ottawa's project to mark Canada's Centennial.[3] Pearson was actively looking for something special for the capital, and the idea came at just the right moment. Within days of the meeting, he wrote back to Southam's group fully embracing the idea and advising them that he had instructed his officials to prepare a memorandum for cabinet approval. It was the culmination of a whirlwind eight months of research and preparation. For Southam personally, it was the first step in what would turn out to be his central focus for the rest of his professional career: a life in, and for, the arts. It was also the prelude to an enterprise that would shift and elevate the performing arts in Canada in a way that would alter its artistic landscape permanently.

G. Hamilton Southam was the privileged son of an Ottawa establishment family. His Scottish great-grandfather had come to Canada as a stonemason and had initiated the family fortune by buying a printing company. In due course, this business expanded into the Southam publishing empire, the source of the family's wealth. By the time Hamilton Southam was born on December 19, 1916, the youngest of six siblings, the Southams were fully established members of Canada's gentry class. With that came their sense of leadership and of responsibility to give back to the community—a common attitude among late Victorian families at the top of the social ladder. Throughout his life, Southam ascribed to the *noblesse oblige* that wealth, good looks, and a privileged upbringing bestow. He also possessed a genuine openness and a love of all things artistic, particularly for opera and music. The arts were a civilizing force, he thought, and they should be acquired, practised, and supported.

This sensibility had been instilled in Southam from childhood, especially by his Aunt Lilias, his Uncle Harry Southam's wife, who lived next door. They had converted an indoor squash court in their house into a music room, where they installed both a piano and an organ. There he listened to his aunt as well as more famous musicians play. When the concert pianist Sergei Rachmaninoff came to town, he happily accepted an invitation from the Harry Southams. Wilson Southam, Hamilton's father, had "a wonderful Victrola," which he allowed his son to wind up for summer concerts on the veranda. Ultimately, Hamilton Southam developed a keen appreciation for music, rather than the ability to play himself, and that led to his unstinting support for music and opera at the newly created National Arts Centre.

In the 1930s, the Southams made frequent visits to London and Paris, where Hamilton discovered opera—"a romantic form of music ... I fed on," he said. They also visited well-connected family and friends in the English shires or the French countryside. There in the summer of 1938 he met Jacqueline Lambert-David, the daughter of a distinguished French family. Hamilton, always chivalrous and with an abiding affection for women, was invited to visit her family home, the beautiful Château de Ferney in the village of Ferney-Voltaire on the Swiss-French border, where Voltaire

A member of a well-connected family, young Hamilton Southam was a page to the governor general, the Marquess of Willingdon, in Ottawa. Photo © Southam.

had lived for nearly thirty years before its purchase by the Lambert-Davids. The following summer Jacqueline and her sister Claude, in the rituals of such families, came to Canada to stay at the Southam summer home in the Rideau Lakes near Ottawa. When they sailed back to England, Hamilton accompanied them, travelling on up to Oxford for the fall term at his chosen college, Christ Church. He had hardly arrived there before war broke out. He immediately enlisted in the army, and was at Aldershot for training by Christmas. He and Jacqueline would marry in London in April 1940.

He served first with a British regiment, then transferred into the 40th Battery of Hamilton, a Canadian militia unit that had been raised by his uncle Gordon Southam in the years before 1914. By 1943 he was "becoming bored" in England, so he leapt at the chance of taking part in an exchange of officers which had been arranged with the Canadian army fighting in Italy. Joining the forces just before the Battle of Ortona, he moved up the rest of Italy "liberating opera house after opera house" as they passed through cities and towns and "enjoying the opera—or at least the idea of it—in each of them." He also found himself working closely with professional soldiers under fire. "The core of the regiment was the non-commissioned officers," he recalled, and he got along well with them and their troops and learned from their experience—qualities he would exhibit in later years at the NAC where, despite his sometimes lordly manner, he had good relations with the stagehands and the other backstage crews.

Demobilized in 1945, he joined the London *Times* and did a short stint as an editorial writer before returning to Ottawa with his bride. There he joined the family newspaper, the *Ottawa Citizen,* again to write editorials. But it was not a task suited to his temperament. Assigned a topic, he would disappear into the library for a week to research a piece, while a quick 200-word comment written in a day was what his editors wanted. In 1947 he wrote the exam for the Department of External Affairs and, two years later, left on his first assignment abroad, to Sweden. His career as a diplomat would take him in and out of Canada over the next few years before his penultimate posting in Poland, where he first served as chargé d'affaires. There he helped to expedite the return of the Polish Treasures from Canada, where they had been stored for safekeeping during the war, and finally became an ambassador. He also began an affair with Marion Tantot, the vivacious and intelligent young French wife of a junior colleague in the embassy, Pierre Charpentier. Their tempestuous relations would continue on two continents for decades before she became his third and last wife nearly forty years later.

In the summer of 1962 Southam was reassigned to Ottawa as director of the Communications Division in the Department of External Affairs. "Not the most prestigious division," he said, "but the largest and one of the busiest." He soon reconnected with friends, family, and colleagues in the upper reaches of the capital's society and settled in to what he thought would be a diplomat's home posting.

Shortly after starting his new job, on October 4, 1962, Southam received an unusual visitor at his new office in the Langevin Block, a federal government building at the corner of Ottawa's Wellington Street and Confederation Square. His well-dressed guest was a local society woman, Faye Loeb, the lively wife of a local Jewish grocery tycoon. Mrs. Loeb came as spokesperson for a loose collection of civic interest groups that were determined to do something for culture and the arts in the capital.

The early sixties was a time of rising optimism in Canada. In Ottawa, various citizens, spurred on by the seeds planted by Vincent Massey less than ten years before, had been ruminating on the future of the city's cultural life. At least two local impresarios were kept busy bringing performances in music, theatre, and ballet to the city, but frustration was growing that the only venues in which to play were either high school gyms or a downtown movie house, the Capitol Theatre. Ottawa by now had an active Philharmonic Orchestra of its own, and both the Montreal and the Toronto Symphony would come to town every year to fill out the concert season. Arts festivals had also become the rage during the booming postwar period, but there was no way Ottawa could contemplate a festival without a performing arts centre. And so it was that several groups went to work, independently of each other. Even the owner of the local football team, Sam Berger, thought it was time to have a place for the arts.[4]

When Faye Loeb called on Southam that October day, she asked him if he would spearhead the quest for a concert hall. At first he demurred, saying he was "far too busy" to take on the task and requesting three weeks to find someone else. However, he was intrigued and, as soon as Mrs. Loeb left his office, he began to consult several of his high-level friends, including Arnold Heeney, a former top diplomat and public servant; I. Norman Smith, editor of the *Ottawa Journal;* and Louis Audette, a former naval officer who ran the Canadian Club and was president of the Ottawa Philharmonic. Clearly, the idea appealed to Southam enormously from the beginning—the dream that he had inherited from his parents. When no one else agreed to take the project on, he decided he would do it himself.

Southam knew exactly what to do. By early December, he had established the Preparatory Committee for an Arts Alliance,[5] seconding his colleague Pierre Charpentier, who had also returned from Poland, to be his volunteer secretary. His small but heavy-weight working group was filled with his friends—deputy ministers, prominent socialites, and well-connected individuals on the Ottawa scene. The immediate order of business was to develop a feasibility study. With Southam at the helm, and the times encouraging, all the portents were right for what happened next. Southam knew everyone worth knowing, including Prime Minister Lester Pearson, who, as a young man, had courted one of Southam's sisters and frequently visited the family home. Charming and fluently bilingual, Southam's work was beginning at the very moment when the idea of bilingualism and biculturalism was blossoming in Canada. Centennial Year was looming on the horizon, a scant four years away, and Canadians were starting to prepare for a celebratory mood. The fast-approaching anniversary would unleash funds and creativity on a scale never before seen in the country. The arts were burgeoning and were clearly accepted as a sign of any maturing society.

In the postwar period, Canada had modelled its cultural agencies on their British counterparts. The Canada Council had been created by the Liberal government of Louis St. Laurent some eight years before, and its grants to artists and arts groups were already beginning to bear fruit. Above all, Ottawa's leading citizens wanted to take advantage of this mood and were increasingly eager to put their city, the capital of the country, on the map.

From the moment Southam agreed to lead the campaign, it took off. Working from his home at 267 Buena Vista Road in Ottawa's upper-crust Rockcliffe Park, he threw himself into the task with passion and advanced on a vast range of fronts. He used every social occasion, from lunches at the prestigious Rideau Club to small dinners and other social gatherings, to press the case. He also undertook a vast letter-writing campaign to every interested arts party in the city.

On February 14, 1963, scarcely two months after setting up his first committee, Southam announced the creation of a new organization: the National Capital Arts Alliance.[6] It was made up of fifty-five local arts groups ranging from the fully professional and established Ottawa Philharmonic to the amateur but long-standing theatre company, the Ottawa Little Theatre. His diplomat's approach—charming, interested, flattering, and positive—worked magic and, with a politician's instincts, he made sure no group was neglected. Besides the Jewish faction in the city, he enlisted prominent local French Canadians, among them member of Parliament Oswald Parent, the Queen's printer Roger Duhamel, the powerful developer Robert Campeau (who was already changing the face of Ottawa with his high-rise office buildings), and other more modest figures such as Jean-Paul Desjardins, the city's leading pharmacist among the francophone community. By May there were few in the city with whom Southam and his team had not made contact, with one significant exception. That holdout was Ottawa's mayor, the fractious Charlotte Whitton, who had not responded to any of his letters and made it clear she was "not yet ready to receive the Alliance."[7]

Nevertheless, by the first week in May, the Arts Alliance was ready to put the feasibility study to tender, and donors were sought to pay for its estimated $12,000 to $20,000 cost. Supporters for what would become known as the Brown Book reflected Ottawa society of the day. Among Southam's friends was his cousin-in-law, lawyer (later Senator) Duncan MacTavish, who was not only active in politics as president of the federal Liberal Party, but had strong connections with the city's banks and trust companies. MacTavish had no hesitation in rustling money from them and also using them to network through the important local business community, including industrial interests such as the E.B. Eddy Company. Southam drew on his high-placed diplomatic contacts, asking the French ambassador to obtain details about similar complexes that were being built in Le Havre and in Caen. And he made sure that Sam Berger, who had his own Development Committee for a Performing Arts Centre, and Lawrence Freiman, another prominent Jewish businessman who was working towards a Centennial Festival, merged their interests with those of the Arts Alliance. He even wrote to Vincent Massey, who was summering at his country retreat, Batterwood, near Port Hope. Although the former governor general declined to make a donation, he sent moral support and advice: the committee should be sure to choose a good name for the new complex, he said, "something that will be hard to get rid of."[8] Naming would be a perplexing and much-discussed issue in the years to come.

Harking on the theme of the centre's national importance in the capital, Southam sent requests to Dr. Albert Trueman, the director at the Canada Council, and to Dennis Coolican, the chair of the National Capital Commission, soliciting $5,000 from each of them to help pay for the study. Clearly he was confident of success: on May 24 the contract was let to Dominion Consultants for a projected cost of $20,000. Within a few short months this group would produce the Brown Book, the tool that went on to secure federal government approval and became the conceptual blueprint for the National Arts Centre itself—the basis for the architectural drawings and other planning on which the centre would be built.

All through that summer of 1963, the lobbying process and the discussions surrounding the project continued. Peter Dwyer, the assistant director of the Canada

Council and a former British intelligence agent, played devil's advocate at informal dinners and drinks with Southam. Erudite and deeply intelligent, Dwyer, although a keen supporter of the new centre, felt compelled in a personal letter to Southam to set out his concerns that Canada should perhaps focus on assisting artists to develop their work before constructing a massive emporium in which to house them.[9] Despite this questioning, however, the growing momentum behind the project mounted. In late August, Southam had a "sympathetic" meeting with Maurice Lamontagne, the federal minister in charge of culture. Lamontagne, a suave and courtly French Canadian, had broad political influence as the Quebec lieutenant in Pearson's cabinet. Also at the meeting was John Fisher, a former broadcaster known for his boosterism as "Mr. Canada" and the man assigned to run Canada's Centennial Commission. By the end of the month, so much enthusiasm had been generated that Southam and Heeney were already contemplating possible appointments for the new centre's board of directors.

Word of the proposed centre quickly spread through the small Canadian arts community. The enterprising Toronto-based conductor and musician Niki Goldschmidt heard the gossip and checked in by letter from Europe. Southam responded by asking him to collect some material at the Edinburgh Festival while he was there and to pay a call on its director, Lord Harewood, an old Southam friend who was also the Queen's cousin. Meanwhile, the networking through the social salons of Ottawa continued. Yousuf Karsh, the international society photographer who would live with his second wife in a residential suite at the Château Laurier, was among those who entertained guests in order to support the idea.

In early September, Mayor Charlotte Whitton telephoned at last. She mischievously told Southam that she favoured the old Union Station as a site for the new centre because "it has an exact replica of 'the Baths of Caracalla' in it and would be perfect for staging Greek dramas."[10] More seriously, she warned Southam off the Nepean Point location that was being considered because "there are caves under part of the land which could collapse and the rest is solid rock which would be very expensive to excavate." She related to him "the shocking cost" to the city of having to run a sewer pipe under similar conditions into the French Embassy just down the street. What Whitton really wanted was to choose the site—and she had one in mind. Eventually she offered him a parcel of land at the heart of the city on Confederation Square, just diagonally across from Southam's own office in the Langevin Block. He was delighted.

The volunteer activities of these senior diplomats, Southam and Charpentier, had been noticed by their political boss, External Affairs Minister Paul Martin. When he nervously queried his deputy minister Norman Robertson about what these two were up to, Robertson replied in a wry memo that yes, they were busy outside office hours "in the cause of the arts," but, he added, "I am sure they will not embarrass us."[11]

The site selected for the centre was at the heart of the capital. Photo © NAC.

On October 24 the Brown Book, the feasibility study put together by Dominion Consultants, was delivered to the National Capital Arts Alliance. Southam made sure that copies were swiftly circulated to all the key figures who could influence the final decision. Pearson and George McIlraith, the minister of public works and so-called Ottawa minister in cabinet, received copies, as did civil servant Robert Bryce, the deputy-secretary to the Treasury Board, and John MacDonald, the deputy minister of public works. C.M. "Bud" Drury, now head of the National Capital Commission, was on the list, along with Governor General Georges Vanier. A copy was deposited at the Ottawa Public Library for the benefit of the local citizenry, but the frugal organizers insisted that anyone else wanting copies had to pay $4.50 each for them.[12] Five days later, the Arts Alliance organized a lunch in the Parliamentary Restaurant for all the region's parliamentarians.

Southam and his group were determined to lay the groundwork carefully for the moment when the plan would come before the government: they not only worked directly with the politicians but also solicited letters from high-powered individuals in banking, industry, and the arts world. In addition, a small nucleus of brilliant senior civil servants who knew the ways of government assisted Southam in preparing for his government dealings. They included Jack Harrison at Forestry and David Golden at Defence, who, after moving on to be the first head of Telesat Canada, would later become a feisty NAC trustee. Their arguments were persuasive: "The building will complete the Capital in a spiritual as well as physical sense," they said. "It will help recruitment to the public service in both languages." And, they added naively, "the initial price tag seems nominal at a mere $9 million."[13]

Peter Dwyer was the lone naysayer. Although he supported Southam, he continued to think, as someone associated with the Canada Council, that a massive subsidy of the arts should precede a costly building. He accurately pinpointed the fact that, in his opinion, "Ottawa has nothing of quality to offer" and that "the future would better lie in touring companies and attracting ballet, opera and orchestras from Toronto and Montreal where pre-paid expenses would assist costs."[14] Southam ignored the advice and continued to work with Golden and others towards the design of future operations, which would "include a small board ... to protect the government from artistic matters." He kept up a persistent and thorough correspondence with anyone who could affect the final decision, and he collected a dossier of courteous and optimistic replies, including letters from the opposition party leaders—John Diefenbaker of the Progressive Conservatives, Tommy Douglas of the NDP, and Robert Thompson of the Social Credit—as well as from prominent figures in Canada's arts world.

The preparation was impeccable, and when the invitation came from the Prime Minister's Office to meet with the Arts Alliance group in early November, Southam

National Capital Arts Alliance members David Golden, Hamilton Southam, and Louis Audette after their November 1963 meeting with Prime Minister Lester B. Pearson, which had the "happy result" of his full support for the arts centre project. Photo © Ottawa Citizen/UPI. Reprinted by permission.

wrote an enthusiastic note to its secretary, Jack Harrison, that "a ground swell of public opinion should carry us irresistibly through the Prime Minister's door." That moment came on November 8, 1963, when Southam and a small delegation were asked to make their way up to Parliament Hill late in the afternoon to meet with Mr. Pearson in his office.

Less than a week later, the members of the National Capital Arts Alliance were informed that the meeting had gone well. Pearson wrote back to Southam confirming his support and advising that the matter would go before Cabinet within days. In the Prime Minister's Office, Gordon Robertson, clerk of the Privy Council and secretary to the cabinet, prepared the minute for Pearson to present to Cabinet, and, over at External Affairs, Deputy Minister Norman Robertson briefed his minister, Paul Martin, suggesting that he be supportive in Cabinet when the matter came up.[15] From the Senate, the Conservative Gratton O'Leary sent Southam a handwritten note assuring him that he had taken care of the matter with Diefenbaker. A momentary flurry in the preparations occurred when the Canadian Legion confused the Ottawa plan with a similar project intended as a war memorial that was under construction in San Francisco. Once Southam replied to their letter, politely disabusing them of this notion, they too came firmly on side.

Word of the project ignited interest everywhere, and letters started to trickle in to Southam's office from theatre and arts professionals who were interested in a future at the new complex. One of the first résumés received was from David Haber, who was then engaged, along with several other future NAC staffers, in planning the six-month artistic extravaganza that would run at Expo 67 in Centennial Year. Haber would join the NAC as soon as his Expo duties were over and become its brilliant one-man programming department during its first several years.

Southam was at a social reception at the National Gallery on December 11 when he picked up gossip that the proposal for the National Arts Centre had been approved by Cabinet a few days before. On December 23 the Ottawa project was formally announced. The plan had gone from enthusiastic suggestion to formal approval in just nine months, and Southam recorded this "most excellent" Christmas gift in his diary. Immediately, he was inundated with congratulatory messages, but there was no time to lose and, on December 30, the first meeting of a government-sponsored Interdepartmental Committee convened to start work on the future complex. Southam handed over a variety of letters he had received from architects and others interested in working on the project. With Gordon Robertson in the chair, the new arts centre was now officially designated a "work in progress."

THE REAL
TASK BEGINS

In an effusive letter written January 1, 1964, from his family's home in Belgium where he was spending Christmas, Niki Goldschmidt, the man who would become known as "Mr. Festival" in Canada, was among the first to send Southam congratulations. He also, characteristically, offered himself as artistic director for the new enterprise and, if that didn't work out, as director of the national festival that was being proposed. Closer to home, Southam had discreetly suggested to the prime minister that someone should be appointed to run the project. There was no question in Pearson's mind who that man should be, and he offered Southam the job. Within a month, Southam had given notice to the Department of External Affairs, the Prime Minister's Office had announced his appointment, and he had moved into new offices at the Victoria Building on Wellington Street, across the street from Parliament.

Southam's new minister was the secretary of state, Maurice Lamontagne, a sophisticated Quebecer with a long interest in the arts and an earlier influential role in the creation of the Canada Council. Southam, assisted by his able secretary, Verna Dollimore, who accompanied him from External, plunged into the same whirlwind of activity that had launched the project in the first place. His imposing new letterhead and cards read "Office of the Co-ordinator—the National Centre for the Performing Arts." In reality, he would become the mastermind for all that ensued.

The document setting out the duties of the coordinator might have been written, and perhaps was, by Southam himself.[1] Silent but friendly advisers in the Prime Minister's and the Secretary of State's offices, such as Henry Hindley, Lamontagne's assistant secretary, who would eventually draft the NAC legislation, lent an elegant hand to the writing of the specifications for the oncoming work. The government approval had been twofold: to create a physical centre for the performing arts in Ottawa and, in addition, an annual national arts festival to occupy it during the summer months. This idea had grown directly from Vincent Massey's suggestion in his Canadian Club "festival" speech ten years before where he'd stressed that, without a building, there could be no festival. The plan now called for the first performance to be presented in Centennial Year, 1967. The position of the coordinator was to be the linchpin in planning. He would coordinate all the meetings through his office and receive and disseminate all the pertinent information. Southam was pleased to find himself as the benevolent ringmaster at the core of the proceedings.

The first decision Southam made was that he needed advice. He turned to his friend Peter Dwyer at the Canada Council and asked him to create a series of arts advisory panels comprised of leading figures from the Canadian arts world. They settled on four panels in all, one each for operations, theatre, the visual arts, and the combined interests of music, opera, and ballet. The visual arts panel resulted from a felicitous development in government policies at the time which called for any federal building project to spend at least 1 percent of its capital cost on art to embellish the structure. Southam was determined that the new performing arts centre would take full advantage of this initiative.

Advisory arts committee members were the leading artists working in Canada. From (left to right) theatre directors Tyrone Guthrie, John Hirsch, CBC's Robert Allen, conductor Nicholas Goldschmidt, NFB's James Domville, Jean Gascon, the COC's Herman Geiger-Torel, (unidentified man), and Interdepartmental Steering Committee chair Gordon Robertson. Photo © NAC.

The leading arts professionals that Dwyer selected were a roll call of who was who in Canada's arts world at the time. At the invitation of the Canada Council, they were asked "to advise the organizers how their art form should be accommodated in this new building,"[2] in both the physical design of the centre and the way in which it would be put to use. Many were already acting as advisers to Expo, where cultural activities were to have a leading role, and they all believed they were contributing to something unique and special in the growing cultural life of Canada. Their collegiality and pride in what they were about to do is recorded in the careful notes kept of their meetings. Renowned theatre director Jean Gascon set the tone for all the discussions when he declared at the outset, "The Centre must have a heart that beats." In short, the new building must not be just a roadhouse for travelling shows but a place where real artistic activity was created. This goal became the guiding creed for the work that followed.

Gascon took charge of the Theatre Advisory Committee, which included Michael Langham and Douglas Campbell, his colleagues from Stratford, Leon Major from Halifax's Neptune Theatre, and the talented and strong-willed genius John Hirsch from Winnipeg's Manitoba Theatre Centre. Quebec theatre was represented by Gascon himself and Yvette Brind'amour, the director of Théâtre Rideau Vert. Old hands including Toronto's Mavor Moore were also on the committee. For the Music, Opera, and Ballet Committee, the multitalented Louis Applebaum took the chair, with the distinguished and austere Dr. Arnold Walter of the University of Toronto's Faculty of Music to assist him. Also tapped were Jean-Marie Beaudet from the CBC, Dr. Frederick Karam from Ottawa University, Zubin Mehta as conductor of the Montreal Symphony, and Gilles Lefebvre as head of Les Jeunesses Musicales. Herman Geiger-Torel, the ebullient general director of Canada's only professional opera troupe, the Canadian Opera Company, saw future potential for his company in the centre and became a keen and active supporter. From the ballet world, Celia Franca of the National Ballet and Ludmilla Chiriaeff of Montreal's Grands Ballets Canadiens were selected, and they met for the first time on this committee. Southam ensured that a technical adviser was also present to record the discussions. He hired Wallace Russell, the expert from Dominion Consultants who had written the Brown Book, as the secretary to each of the committees, with responsibility for reporting back the technical implications of any ideas that emerged.

A flurry of meetings was held through early 1964 as the work of these advisory committees got under way. From the beginning, there was a noticeably different character and mood in the groups for music and for theatre.

In the Music Committee, Applebaum insisted from the outset that "they needed to create a program for the community" and that it would be useless "to have a large structure without roots in the community."[3] This philosophy guided the thinking of the music advisers in the kind of orchestra they would recommend and the outreach that the NAC would have, especially into regional schools and Ottawa's two universities. When the new orchestra was finally created, the solid connections it already had with interested people and organizations in Ottawa served as a foundation for its work and was critical in providing its audience. The question of building up a loyal audience was certainly worrying, but Southam had reassured the group that at least two independent private impresarios (Tremblay Concerts and Treble Clef) had made their living in Ottawa bringing in classical music. These private companies were about to be put out of business by the new NAC, but they had proved that there was an appetite for good music and performance in Ottawa.

In the Theatre Committee, in contrast, members found common ground only when they were discussing the physical needs for their particular art form. Without question, they agreed, the new theatre in the complex should be a "voice room" designed specifically to serve the spoken word. But right from the beginning they worried about the subsidies that would be needed to produce theatre in Ottawa and fretted that this cost would draw money away from the regional theatre groups across the country. John Hirsch, although he would soon join the new centre and be its theatre adviser for a time, was particularly vociferous on this point. On other matters, too, committee members were often divided: they debated whether the company should have a base in Toronto, from which it would extend to Ottawa, or even have its home in Montreal. Some thought that the Stratford Festival could form the core of the English-speaking company, but there was no agreement over what it could do with this mandate or where it should locate. Meanwhile, Stratford's director, Michael Langham, opposed any move to Ottawa, believing that his company's winter home should be in Montreal, where it would have ready access to the National Theatre School. Altogether, this committee mirrored the splits in Canada's theatre world in general: the simmering

The three theatre men (left to right), John Hirsch, Leon Major, and Jean Gascon, examine the model for the "voice room"—the NAC's proposed 900-seat Theatre. Photo © Capital Press Photographers/NAC.

rivalries among the various groups that were trying to establish theatres in all areas of the country. As a consequence, while the creation of an orchestra forged ahead, little progress was made in planning a resident theatre at the Arts Centre.

The Operations Advisory Committee included managers of the best performing houses and established organizations in Canada: Hugh Walker from the O'Keefe Centre and Walter Homberger from the Toronto Symphony.[4] It was chaired by Ottawa businessman Bertram Loeb, the senior brother and "brain" in the Loeb family (which included the founding organizer Mrs. Faye Loeb), one of the richest Jewish clans in Ottawa. Southam diplomatically placed a local citizen on each of the committees: Gilles Provost, a rising young francophone director, for theatre, and Lyla Rasminsky, the wife of Louis Rasminsky, the governor of the Bank of Canada, for music. Whether they were there to offer solid advice or merely to be used as "window-dressing" was a moot point.

Southam recognized the limits of his own knowledge, and he had no hesitation in hiring the best people he could find to fill the gaps. Soon into the planning process, he persuaded Bruce Corder, an experienced theatre manager who had worked for years at Covent Garden in London before coming to Toronto to run the O'Keefe Centre, to join the small team in the Coordinator's Office. Corder was suave and well-spoken, yet tough minded and determined. He would be the ideal colleague for Southam—the skilful manager of operations and enforcer of difficult decisions who enabled his boss to stay above the fray. Their partnership in the years to come would ensure that, through Southam's good connections, the Arts Centre was supported at the highest levels, while, thanks to Corder's wide knowledge and experience, the systems and operations practices laid down for the day-to-day running of the building were of an equally high quality. The excellence with which these two men built their "artistic ship" enabled it to continue sailing in later years, even though its masts, sails, and rigging, and much of its key personnel, would be blown away by government budget cuts and poor leadership throughout the 1980s and early 1990s. Similarly, the strength of the original systems made its recovery possible when the NAC again changed direction in the mid-1990s.

Southam gave considerable thought to the fundamental management principles he should follow: whether the future festival should be run by the centre, how various levels of government should be involved, and how the new centre should relate to the Canada Council for the long-term benefit of the performing arts. He had clear ideas about what he should do, and he made every effort to ensure that the structure of the planning system and the future organization would come firmly under his control during the development process. And there he met very little opposition.

Southam thought they should not delay construction of the Arts Centre by having an architectural competition, so he went again to see the prime minister. Pearson concurred that there was no time to lose and told him to "go out and find an architect."[5] At the time, few Canadian architectural firms had any experience in building theatres. The only one that had two to its credit was the Montreal-based firm ARCOP, whose clever design partners were doing some of the best public projects in Canada. Among them, ARCOP had designed and built the Confederation Centre in Charlottetown and was currently working on both Place des Arts in Montreal and the Queen Elizabeth Theatre in Vancouver. Soon after being named coordinator, Southam picked up the phone and invited the ARCOP architects to come to Ottawa to talk about the new Arts Centre.

The firm was generally run on an egalitarian basis among the partners, with projects divided up among them. After the proposed performing Arts Centre was discussed in-house, Fred Lebensold was assigned as the architect on the job. He was a strong-willed, opinionated Polish Jew with a well-known stubborn streak when it came to his work.

The Department of Public Works was the formal client for the development, and the man in charge of its building projects was the chief architect, James Langford. He had applied for and won the job in Ottawa just a few months before and, by all appearances, was an even-tempered, unassuming, self-described "Prairie boy." After a brief stint playing professional football with the Calgary Stampeders, he had started with a small architectural practice in Saskatchewan and then served as the province's deputy minister for public works. The job in Ottawa was a big step up, but he was talented and knew his way around the Canadian architectural world. At thirty-seven, he was now responsible for all the Canadian government's building projects, supervising a staff of more than 180 architects and engineers and taking care of such important and prestigious undertakings as Canada's controversial new embassy in Australia. He took his responsibilities as a public servant and his role to protect the Canadian taxpayer seriously.

Scarcely a few months into his new job, the proposal for the National Arts Centre landed on his desk. Langford knew the architects at ARCOP and liked the way they worked, meeting among themselves every week to criticize each other's projects. In an unusual move for a rank-and-file civil servant, he was called in to meet personally with the prime minister to affirm Southam's choice of architect. He had no hesitation in supporting ARCOP's suitability for the job, although he didn't discuss with Pearson that day what he was really worried about—the $9 million price tag that had been attached to the proposal. Langford believed that this cost estimate was far too small, and he was equally dubious that the complex could be built in time for the Centennial celebrations. He "knew for a fact," he told others, that Toronto's O'Keefe Centre, "while it had been built privately by a brewery company and the real costs swept under the carpet," had cost far more to build than what was being projected for the Ottawa building, yet the Toronto complex was only a third of the size of what was being proposed for the capital. No one at the Art Centre office paid any attention to

Architect Fred Lebensold conferred frequently with the patient chief architect for the Department of Public Works, James Langford (centre), examining the building model with Hamilton Southam. Langford ran interference with the politicians as building costs rose. Photo © NAC.

Langford's observations, particularly not Hamilton Southam. Later, Langford would be called on the carpet at parliamentary committees to defend his departmental bosses from complaints about delays and rising costs, although it had been clear to him from the outset that this was going to be a difficult job where "regular procedures were not to be precisely followed."[6]

From Southam's viewpoint, cost was a secondary matter. Although he believed that "no public servant should think of money as a detail," he was convinced that he was "doing the right thing" and that cost was not the prime concern. He had a clear vision of the complex, one that was already set out in the Brown Book. After an early meeting with the American impresario Sol Hurok, he had discarded the notion of a 3,000-seat opera/concert hall that would accommodate the travelling road shows of hugely successful American impresarios. He had sternly informed Hurok that "we are not in this for profit."[7] Instead, Southam favoured the European style of opera houses and theatres, with their intimate auditoria and superb acoustics. There was no model in North America for what he wanted, so, shortly after becoming coordinator, he sought and received Maurice Lamontagne's blessing to go to Europe to research ideas.

On April 17, 1964, the core design team of Hamilton Southam, Wallace Russell, Fred Lebensold, and Jim Langford left Canada for what would be a whirlwind, month-long trip across the continent. Langford, who had not visited Europe before, remembers a "fabulous trip" as they "went everywhere," visiting twenty-five different theatres and halls, seeing performances, and studying technical facilities from Prague to Munich to Copenhagen. While Russell, Langford, and Lebensold stayed in small hotels and pensions, Southam, at his own expense, booked into grander hotels and met with equally grand friends that he seemed to know in every city. Nevertheless, they experienced an enormous amount together—and Southam ensured that they saw the best. The memory of seeing Maria Callas singing at La Scala still lingered in Langford's memory over forty years later. Southam already knew Milan and Florence well, having "liberated" the opera houses as part of the Allied Forces during the war, although he never boasted to his companions about these experiences. As a Jew, Lebensold balked when it came to going into Germany so soon after the war, but he rejoined the group in Paris before returning home.

Russell meticulously documented their technical observations of each facility, recording everything from a hall's mechanical equipment to styles of seating and crowd control. Southam noted that Vienna's Staatsoper had the best orchestra pit in Europe, and he made sure that they obtained the exact dimensions to guide the NAC's architect. The Austrians tried to sell them mechanical stage equipment, which they rejected as being "too complex," but this exposure helped them later to find better and easier solutions in Ottawa. Europe's experience became their model: "good acoustics" were key and "everything was to be top drawer." Years later, Southam would often tease Langford whether Canadian taxpayers had received good value from their trip. Langford, who wrestled many times with Southam over costs and scheduling, would ruefully always admit that this excursion had been well worth the money.

On June 1, 1964, back in Ottawa, Southam was "exhilarated" as he fed the details of the advisory committee meetings to Lebensold, who then single-handedly worked up the design concept for the building. He did not take the advice of the advisory committees lightly. Like Southam, he attended many of their meetings and listened, although perhaps not as carefully. The intrepid Russell, as secretary, continued to record the technical implications of each group's discussion and provided them to Lebensold. There were long debates among the artistic advisers on the Music, Opera, and Ballet Committee over such matters as acoustics and the size of the backstage required for large-scale ballets, while on the Theatre Committee the advisers focused on the size and shape of the stage—the virtues of "thrust" versus "proscenium" stages—sight-lines, and other theatrical necessities. All the participants took their duties extremely seriously: they were working together on something new that they believed would be good for Canada.

Langford saw Southam and Lebensold as two of a kind—both single-minded, strong-willed men. Once Lebensold had settled on an idea, he was "unmovable." Even Southam found him hard to handle, but he enjoyed his company and went along with his suggestions. Langford found the development of the architectural process engrossing and, even though he was there to defend the client's interest, he was frequently included in the weekly meetings and debates at ARCOP's offices in Montreal. Southam didn't like conflict. Rather, he would "wine and dine" his way through problems, Langford said, often leaving the clever but less-sophisticated Public Works architect feeling like a "bumpkin" in awe of the coordinator's skills at "manipulating" people.

Langford had to review the project for his department and arrange the contracts and tendering, all the while trying to ensure that Canadian taxpayers got their money's worth. It was a tough task at times, often conflicting with Southam's grand and glorious ideas. When the first prices came in, as Langford had feared, they were far beyond the original estimates. Yet, in the minds of the organizers, there was no question of cutting back. They were aiming for the best—and that was going to be expensive. It fell to Langford to devise the solution that would allow them to proceed. Although previously unheard of in government circles, and against his better judgment, he broke down the total work into three separate contracts. Ensuring that "the tendering process was all handled correctly,"[8] the first phase would excavate the massive hole in the ground. Next would come the foundations and the garage, while the final contract would be the rest of the building. The first two would eventually come in roughly on budget, but the last contract would spiral well beyond estimates. Langford took the gamble that, by then, the job would be too far along to turn back. Eventually, he would be proved right, though not without gut-wrenching struggles along the way. Going into construction, the price had already risen to $16 million, and it would continue to rise, higher and higher, along with the political clamour around it.

From the start, the change of site from Nepean Point to Confederation Square presented huge additional costs and problems. The designers were determined to avoid the mistakes of Montreal's Place des Arts, where a single exit kept visitors sitting in their cars among exhaust fumes waiting to leave. The garage in Ottawa was to open in several directions; an exit on Slater Street, a block away from the centre, required a concrete tunnel for several hundred yards. Its excavation brought furious complaints about dust from the British High Commission, located directly overhead on Elgin Street. As the plans worked their way through various government departments in the traditional approval process, Dr. R.F. Legget, the National Research Council's building research director and a soils expert, warned that if the design team wanted an underground garage alongside the Rideau Canal, they were sure to have water problems. He was right, and the design for the 900-car garage required special shoring, which was prohibitively expensive. Lebensold also determined that having the building's main entrance open to the world, facing Confederation Square, would create massive traffic jams. Despite objections, he made the controversial decision to turn the back of his building to the city and to lead people down a long curving ramp to the front door facing the canal. The basic hexagonal shape of the building was taken, Lebensold claimed, from the shape of the site—and he made it the dominant motif throughout the rambling structure.

Southam was "so convinced we were doing the right thing"[9] that cost remained a

To kick-start the project, James Langford broke the job down into three separate contracts. The first was for the enormous excavation of the site. Photo © Ottawa Citizen/ UPI. Reprinted by permission.

secondary issue in his thinking. His relationship with Langford could be "abrasive" at times, as the two of them struggled to keep the project under control. Despite these efforts, costs began to jump upward in leaps and bounds.

The building was to be "an architectural and engineering marvel," well beyond anything that had been built in the city since before the war. The change in location from the more distant Nepean Point to the site along Confederation Square opened up possibilities for a cultural hub to the city which had been partially foreseen. On the land immediately adjacent to the south of the hexagonal NAC site on Elgin Street, the previous Diefenbaker government had already proposed a large museum. The working drawings by Vancouver architect Ned Pratt had been prepared for tender, and the old Roxborough Apartments on the corner of Laurier and Elgin streets, where former Prime Minister Mackenzie King had made his Ottawa home, had already been torn down in preparation for future construction. When Langford arrived in town as the new chief architect, he saw immediately that the two cultural buildings could be complementary to each other, and he set about trying to have Pratt and Lebensold talk to each other. Before he could make much headway, however, the museum project was cancelled by the new Liberal government. The land where it was to be built sits empty to this day.

As more construction problems cropped up, the price tag of the Arts Centre accelerated, moving rapidly from $16 million to $21 million and then to over $26 million. Each time Southam called on the prime minister to break the bad news, Pearson would say, usually after a reflective moment, "We shall do it all the same"[10]—and so inform his finance minister, Mitchell Sharp. As the price went up, there were cries of outrage in the House of Commons, and Pearson was called upon on several occasions to issue reassuring statements and progress reports to the parliamentarians. Later, Sharp would explain that, in Cabinet, "the Prime Minister was so for it that we did not feel it appropriate to oppose it."[11] Southam concurred: "We felt unassailable really. It was the right thing to do and the right time to do it."

For the independently wealthy Southam, the times were exciting: his parents had had a similar dream, and "now here we were given the opportunity." He was in his element. But for others involved in the job, it was not so easy. Langford's bosses railed at him for not controlling the development better, and at one point after the site had been excavated and the foundations put in, serious consideration was given to filling the hole in again or filling it up with water, to make it into a lagoon in the summer and a skating rink in winter. Langford worried constantly, but Southam remained calm. He had his personal pipeline to the prime minister and, through his own shrewd organization, he also had the best artistic people in the country behind the development. "We had enormous impetus," he recalled. "There were a lot of talented people behind it. This gave me the energy to meet with the prime minister."[12] In Canada, in the early 1960s, these connections were enough to get the job done.

Besides car fumes, dust, and water problems, the project presented a fascinating array of structural issues. Engineer John Adjeleian, one of Canada's leading structural engineers with Toronto's SkyDome later to his credit, became architect Lebensold's alter ego, taking the architect's concepts and translating them into structural reality. The lively and intelligent American-trained Adjeleian was of Armenian origin, and he meshed well with the headstrong Lebensold. The two wrestled constantly with the rising costs, as Lebensold called on the resourceful Adjeleian to come up with economical solutions to his artistic vision.

Good acoustics were a priority, and the mechanical-electrical systems would have to run silently to accommodate both music and the spoken word. Although not a theatre person, Adjeleian became fascinated with the paraphernalia involved in theatres and concerts halls: screens, pulleys, and backstage equipment, the sound baffles and special music shells that had to be planned for and incorporated into the building. The requirements for the elaborate curtain being created for the opera hall by artist Micheline Beauchemin—how it would be hung, where it would rise and fall—opened a new world to him. His most important engineering achievement was to create the column-free spaces that Lebensold wanted throughout the building. The three tiers of balconies in the opera hall cantilevered out seventy feet over the auditorium, and Adjeleian marvelled years later that "you could look up and not see a column anywhere. You could see three balconies of people without a supporting column! How," he asked, "did we do that?"[13]

He also saved money. One initiative, after much heated discussion among the consultants, called for the use of moulded fibreglass in the ceiling tiles, then an architectural precedent. Another of his more interesting challenges was the creation of the box seats, and especially the Royal (State) Box, a nicety that the protocol-conscious Southam had insisted upon. That particular conundrum was how to cantilever the box without having another box hanging over it in the tier above, as happened in the classic European opera houses. This thorny question occupied Adjeleian for weeks.

The hexagonal grid that dominated the building design deviated entirely from traditional right-angled solutions. Some critics would later say the building suffered from "hexagonitis," but this shape was a popular innovation in modern architecture. The most repeated form in nature, used by bees in constructing honeycombs, it had recently been applied in Canada by Buckminster Fuller in his design for the U.S. Pavilion at Expo 67. Everything was triangular, "more mathematical than material," Adjeleian recalled, and this shaping required "thousands upon thousands of calculations."[14] Computer-aided design was not yet in common use in architecture, and all the work was done the old-fashioned way with a slide rule.

Similarly, the use of concrete for the building, which "enabled the marriage of architecture and structure," was at the cutting edge during the sixties. The style would later become known as "brutalist," but it was considered then as "an expression of the time." Outside the building, an entire city street was rerouted to accommodate the construction.

Adjeleian, despite his later triumphs, always maintained that the National Arts Centre remained his favourite building. "They were fun times," he recalled. For Langford, despite his troubles, it was the same, and although it was against regulations, he would often ride up in the construction bucket on a Saturday morning to take photographs of the site as the building rose up out of the ground. Colleagues on this massive undertaking became friends for life and, like old war veterans, they continue to hold an annual reunion and golf tournament, known as the "Disaster Open."

One of the remarkable innovations dreamed up by Jim Langford and his deputy architect in Public Works called for 1 to 3 percent of the capital cost of any project to be spent on "artistic embellishment of the building." They made sure that the policy was imposed on federal construction projects, and Langford got a lot of flack for it, especially from his staff in regional offices across the country. The result, however, was that a lot of art ("not all of it good") was placed in new federal government buildings.

It did not take long for Southam and his associates to spot the new policy, and they immediately struck an artistic advisory committee of some of the most distinguished people in Canada's visual arts community to take it in hand. With the new building's budget standing at $12.8 million in July 1964, nearly $390,000 was earmarked to buy art for the new centre. Southam's family had always been strong supporters of the National Gallery of Canada, and this aspect of the work was close to his heart. He had convened the first meeting of the Advisory Committee on Visual Arts at his home in April of the previous year, and Donald Buchanan, the director of the National Gallery, who was also organizing the arts exhibitions for Expo, accepted the chair. Other members of the committee included Montreal's Andrée Paradis, an attractive "belle-laide" of a woman who was editor of the avant-garde Montreal magazine *Vie des Arts*, and Eric Arthur, a top architectural consultant from Toronto.

When the group agreed that "art and architecture should be married on this project,"[15] that basic principle meant that architect Fred Lebensold would play a controlling role in the selection of artworks for the building. Their first meeting set out some ideals, several of which would hastily be discarded, including the stipulation that all the art should be Canadian. These artistic proposals were to be channelled through Hamilton Southam, who would convey them to the Department of Public Works to foot the bill. Lebensold and one of his partners, Guy Desbarats (who would later become deputy minister at Public Works), attended the first meeting and agreed to provide the committee, within the month, with crucial information regarding the "spirit of the building." In the meantime, committee members would draw up a list of artists for potential commissions.

True to his promise, Lebensold soon returned to a meeting of the advisory committee, where he outlined the interior spaces for them. Four main inside units—the Salon, Theatre, Studio, and Opera—would need art. The "jewel of the entire place" was the Salon, which would also serve as a VIP room. The Theatre, he proposed, should be subdued, with interest focused on the performance. Lighting would be a major source of decoration there, and he had the lighting expert to do it. The Studio should be "bare and naked," and the artwork placed in it would be "its only decorative element." The Opera was to be different from all the rest. It would be subdued during performances, but at other times would "spill over with light, colour and luxury," lending a special atmosphere before performances and during intervals. The intricate opera house lighting, by designer Bob Harrison, gave a gorgeous elegance to the hall, but its thousands of individual light bulbs also imposed a lifetime of special equipment and maintenance costs on the centre. Skilfully sweet-talking the committee, Lebensold kept full control of the overall interior design of the building to fit his architectural vision. "The Architect's opinion was to have major consideration in *any* decision," read the minutes, a fact that was tersely reported to the government's Interdepartmental Committee, which was "steering" the project.

Lebensold soon returned to the visual arts group with a shopping list of "decorative requirements," setting them out in a detailed memo that called for a tapestry ($25,000) and tall sculpted doors ($15,000) for the Salon, and stage curtains for the Opera and the Theatre ($50,000 and $25,000, respectively), among other things. Names of leading artists swirled about—Jean-Paul Riopelle for the Main Lobby, and Alfred Pellan or Harold Town for a mural in the Studio lobby. (William Ronald would eventually get this job on Lebensold's say-so after the architect paid a visit to the artist's studio.) Southam had his own tastes and preferences and, on his European research trip, he had already visited the studio of sculptor Ossip Zadkine in Paris. He immediately "gave in to one of his desires" and ordered an exquisite bronze free-standing sculpture of *The Three Graces* to stand in the new centre's lobby. Southam liked the work so much that, later, he ordered a similar sculpture for his own home. As building costs rose, Treasury Board eventually set a ceiling of $500,000 on the visual arts budget—a colossal sum for the day. Among the better acquisitions was an exquisite tapestry by French artist Alfred Manessier, inspired, he said, by the light he had experienced during a visit to Southam's beautiful cottage on the Rideau Lakes. He would not be the only artist to claim inspiration from Southam's idyllic summer surroundings, but his commission came with a special Canada Council grant that permitted him to travel from Paris to Canada to install his wall hanging.

Canadian artists were not forgotten. There was the magnificent Beauchemin curtain for the Opera, a piece so large that no loom in Canada could weave it. On a commission that would rise to $75,000, the artist went to Japan for a year to create it. Sculptor Charles Daudelin won the competition for an enormous free-standing exterior work, which still adorns a major outside terrace and casts an elegant high shadow against the back wall of the building. In one of the foyers, artist Jean Hébert devised a glass and metal *Tree Fountain* designed to filter light through its colourful segments. He struggled with the colours and special moulds, and when Canada's glass companies could not meet his demands, he asked for additional monies for a special kiln to fire the glass tiles himself. His contract rose from $15,000 to $25,000 as the committee justified its decision on the basis that it was advancing technical knowledge for Canada's glass producers.

From the start, the visual arts were to play a big part in the NAC building. In Paris, Hamilton Southam visited the studio of the artist Ossip Zadkine and couldn't resist purchasing The Three Graces *for the NAC foyer. Later he picked up another version of the piece for his own house. Photo © NAC.*

By this time the Visual Arts Committee was in full cry and ready to propose another $300,000 worth of items to the Public Works Department, but, in an unusual move, Southam felt it prudent to draw the line. The beleaguered Langford struggled in vain to maintain the budgets, but Southam generally took the artists' side when issues arose and, with his wily diplomatic skills, usually got the commissions through. When the *National Arts Centre Act* was finally passed and a Board of Trustees was created to replace the Steering Committee, the visual arts team would be the only advisory committee retained by the board until the building was finished. Such was the importance placed on the visual and plastic arts in this period.

Southam and his colleagues had anticipated "the threat of gifts of art," and, from the start, they were determined to resist. In practice, they employed "a lot of smoke and screens to avoid gifts," and they accepted nothing without the Visual Arts Committee's approval.[16] Somehow, Southam managed to circumnavigate this policy on at least two occasions, accepting an Orrefors glass chandelier from the Swedish government for the Salon and a bust of Chopin from the Poles. "After all," he reminisced later, "I had served in both countries." The new National Arts Centre was becoming ever more "his house," which perhaps it had always been. In 1972, when the NAC was finally in full operation, an unexpected $30,000 turned up in the Visual Arts budget. Southam wasted no time in commissioning a puckish mural of football-playing owls from Vancouver artist Jack Shadbolt and orchestrating a grand celebration for its installation in the Restaurant during a popular run by the Vancouver Playhouse in the Theatre.

While his artistic advisory committees buckled down to work, Southam occupied himself with the fundamental issue of how the Arts Centre would function. A raft of files crossed his desk, ranging from questions on how the new centre would attract audiences ("good halls and theatres generate their own audiences," he claimed confidently) to how best to acquire a fine organ for the concert hall. Southam lost no opportunity to talk up his centre with the public, and his daily diary was crammed with speaking engagements ranging from the music teachers in the Ottawa area to Canadian Clubs all across the country. He maintained a huge correspondence as he sought support everywhere for the project.

His former colleagues in External Affairs kept him abreast of cultural affairs internationally. Ambassador Arnold Smith, wiring from Paris, reported lengthy conversations with the French culture minister, André Malraux, whom Southam would meet on his European tour.[17] The French already had a plan to retain their Expo pavilion after the world's fair so they could pursue their cultural interests in Canada. They wanted to turn it into a *maison de culture* for Quebec, which the federal government resisted as being "too local." There was also intelligence on Charles de Gaulle's forthcoming visit to Montreal for the Centennial celebrations. Federal concern over the growing nationalism in Quebec and the potential role of the French government is evident in these official telegrams.

But for Southam and his colleagues, the Arts Centre they were designing was to showcase a cooperative Canada, an ideal reflected in the work of the recently appointed Bilingual and Bicultural Commission. There was never any doubt that the new centre, like its new director general, would be completely bilingual and bicultural. Two issues were central to Southam's planning. The first was his decision that the organization would be "national" in character and scope. The local consortium, the National Capital Arts Alliance, had helped to secure the government's approval and, although the local organizations did not yet know it, Southam had bigger plans for his Arts Centre that would leave little room for them. He proposed that the new centre be "more than a complex of theatres in Ottawa" and also "address its activities to be truly national and even international in scope." Local developer William Teron, the president of the NCAA after Southam left the post to become full-time coordinator of the new project, later expressed bitterness and shock at the manner in which local arts groups had been frozen out.[18] When the music groups complained about their lack of real local representation on the arts advisory groups, Southam told them firmly that "this is national."

Second, Southam, along with a team of public servants in his minister's office, had to devise a management model for the new Arts Centre. Their negotiations were initially cooperative rather than adversarial. At the time, a small coterie of individuals, many of them with similar backgrounds (if not always socially, then in terms of their education), was at the core of government policy-making in Ottawa. Together they refined the design of the managerial structure of the organization and began work on funding models. These memoranda, usually intimate and informal in tone, formed the basis of the legislation that would officially create the new organization. Not surprisingly, Southam favoured from the outset a managerial model that placed an administrator in full control at the top, assisted by an advisory board of trustees appointed from across the country. In later years, as delays developed and costs soared, Southam was increasingly required to defend the organizational structure to his political masters and their officials.

By mid-1964 Southam and his team favoured the "Brussels" managerial model, based on the Palais des Beaux Arts that had been built in the Belgian capital in the early 1920s.[19] It called for tenant organizations in the building, including an independent orchestra and theatre companies in both languages, which would be subject to an overall artistic policy set by the centre's trustees and management. These arts organizations would have their own charters and boards of directors, raise their own funds, and pay fees to the centre for their use of the facilities. The attraction of this approach to Southam was that the new Arts Centre's board would not be required to "find the large amounts of money nor take the considerable risks involved in artistic productions or the presentation of artistic groups." Those risks would, rather, be "courted by companies resident or visiting the centre." The centre's activities would be confined to "the efficient management and financial maintenance of the Centre" in accordance with a defined set of artistic principles: "encouraging performances of the highest standard in music, opera in any language, dance, drama and poetry readings in English and French ... whether they were authored by Canadians or not." The centre would also arrange appearances of the best professional performing groups in Canada and encourage the development of a resident orchestra and resident English- and French-language repertory theatre companies.

A "national festival organization" would run the annual festival—the second part of the government's original commitment. Because the festival was to "grow out of the centre's activities," Southam wanted to run it as well.

Southam envisaged the future Arts Centre as the hub of artistic activity on the national scene. It would encourage the development of performing arts schools in the national capital area and also provide offices and administrative arrangements for the headquarters of a national performing arts organization, establishing a library and museum and providing other services that might prove useful for the performing arts in Canada. In addition, the early working papers contain several references to the place of film and the role of radio and television in the new centre's activities.

By October 1964 the artistic working groups were hurrying to complete their tasks, but the debate continued in government circles over the operational model the new organization should adopt. Southam's preference for the Brussels concept was resisted by officials both at the Secretary of State's Department and in the Privy Council Office who favoured some sort of hybrid arrangement that combined Southam's model with the arts-producing example of the Stratford Festival. Just how "national" the place should be was also under discussion, as was the question of where the money for the centre would come from. In January 1965 a seminal meeting organized by the Canadian Conference of the Arts at St-Adèle, Quebec, brought Maurice Lamontagne together with representatives from all the key cultural organizations in the country.[20] The objective was to discuss the broad picture of arts financing in Canada, but the organizers also used the occasion to obtain comments on the new arts centre before the government finalized the legislation that would create the NAC.

While the organizers hoped to have this new act mentioned in the government's next Speech from the Throne, it was not likely to be introduced into the House until the following September. In the meantime, the Interdepartmental Steering Committee would continue to deal with problems on behalf of the future Board of Trustees. Among these issues was resistance from the still feisty but now outgoing Ottawa mayor, Charlotte Whitton, who was refusing to let the city hand over the deed to the site so construction could start. The committee recommended expropriation, but, after

Secretary of State Maurice Lamontagne (centre), flanked by Fred Lebensold and Hamilton Southam, presented the NAC project to his parliamentary colleagues. Lamontagne, Lester Pearson's "Quebec lieutenant," was an elegant and erudite supporter and left Southam to his own devices. Photo © NAC.

Don Reid, a new and friendlier mayor, took office, it was able to negotiate a ninety-nine-year land lease with the city. Just to be sure, Prime Minister Pearson wrote personally to the mayor, reminding him that a deed to the property was still required so that work on the excavation could at last get under way. With Centennial Year only two years off, time was pressing.

With the excavation contract in place and the shovel finally in the ground, the Department of Public Works pushed vigorously ahead with tendering the next two phases. Southam and his colleagues were already discussing an opening festival at the new centre for 1967, but, early into the work, Jim Langford warned that this date would be all but impossible.

By the fall of 1964, as the artistic advisory committees were finishing most of their work, the Operations Advisory Committee was coming into its own. Under Bertram Loeb, a new name was added to the list of experienced theatre managers already in the group: François Mercier, a well-known Montreal litigation lawyer with strong Liberal ties and also chairman of Montreal's Place des Arts. (He was destined to become more closely tied to the NAC later, when he was appointed the second chair of the Board of Trustees.) The job for this committee was to supervise the legal and operational practicalities and to target and solve pending problems. There was, for instance, a shortage of trained stage staff in Canada, so most touring companies brought in their own teams.[21] It was no accident, then, that Joseph Mackenzie of the Canadian Labour Congress was on the committee as the group assessed future needs, ensuring that the NAC would be a union house.

The organ lobbyists were also pressing, contacting government MPs and insisting that they have a formal hearing during the planning process. It fell to the Operations Committee to resist a grand organ on the grounds that it would have little use or appeal to Ottawa audiences. They pushed back the proposal by saying there was nothing in the budget for it and that Public Works would have to find other monies to pay for it. The idea for an organ was dropped—until it materialized much later in a gift from the Dutch people in memory of Canada's service in Holland during the war.

Southam tracked all these particulars closely, with a masterful breadth of attention and eye for detail. After the 1965 election had again failed to produce a majority for Lester Pearson, his long-time Quebec colleague and friend Maurice Lamontagne was cut from the Cabinet, and the feisty Niagara MP Judy LaMarsh took over to manage culture. Lamontagne's competent undersecretary, Ernest Steele, stayed on under LaMarsh.

There was bad news on the construction front—completion would be delayed well past 1967, most likely until 1969. Southam also warned Steele that the budget ceiling, now at $26 million, was about to be exceeded. Despite Pearson's steady support, the runaway costs were causing a Cabinet revolt. A report reached Southam that one solution about to receive serious consideration was the postponement of phase three—the construction of the building itself. In the interim, the garage would be roofed over and the site on Confederation Square covered with sod. Langford later confirmed that plans and drawings had been prepared in case this option was accepted.

Southam fought back eloquently, stressing that this was "the Government's only centennial project in Ottawa." He was sure that the government, "for the $25 million already spent, would not want a silent, grass-covered slope covering the empty tomb of its own centennial project," and he argued that the new centre, "more than any other Federal Government project, was doing more to quicken interest in Ottawa among members of the small but influential group of creative Canadians scattered from Halifax to Vancouver." He stated that the centre was useful in "refurbishing Ottawa's image in the rest of the country" and urged Steele to inform the Cabinet that the new centre had attracted the interest of all the country's leading arts organizations and was perceived "as an important factor in developing theatrical and musical life of the country at the highest level." In a passionate conclusion, he said that "the Centre is more than a building," that any postponement would be "a victory for the forces of provincialism," and that the group of "creative Canadians" now supporting the project would "melt away." Because of the centre's site on Confederation Square, "this unhappy development would be exposed to the world's gaze."[22] Fortunately, Southam had allies in Cabinet, among them the Ottawa-based public works minister, George McIlraith. In the end, the project was spared the proposed delay, although the construction cost ceiling was fixed once again, this time at $31 million.

While the logistics of construction and future operations were being thrashed out, Southam was soon writing again to Ernie Steele, laying the groundwork for the centre's artistic life. He had hired a Canadian-born arts administrator, Henry Wrong, a nephew

Despite all the problems, the construction went steadily ahead. Photo © Ottawa Citizen/UPI. Reprinted by permission.

of his old External Affairs colleague, Hume Wrong, as his overall programming consultant. Wrong had been working in New York as an assistant to Sir Rudolf Bing at the Metropolitan Opera. Also engaged was John Hirsch (as a theatre consultant), Jean Beaudet from the CBC, and Louis Applebaum, as an adviser on music. Strenuous efforts continued for the development of an orchestra as well as English and French resident theatre, although Southam still thought of these groups as independent companies and tenants of the NAC.

For now, the chairmanships of these possible future companies were entrusted to three local volunteers: Louis Audette, the president of the Ottawa Philharmonic; F.R. "Budge" Crawley, for theatre; and Lawrence Freiman, who was heading a group trying to create a Canadian Festival of the Arts. Their task was to push the planning forward on programming, but, in Southam's words, "progress was slow." What Southam wanted from Steele were official appointments to head the Music, Theatre, and Programming departments, including the Festival. Either Beaudet or Applebaum would suit the first, he thought, Gascon or Hirsch the second, and he nominated Wrong to head overall programming and direct the Festival. No time should be lost, Southam urged, in appointing Bruce Corder as head of the administrative branch looking after the new house, box office, technical departments, and, of course, accounts. Detailed outlines of the duties of these officers, as well as a carefully worked out management chart, accompanied Southam's request. He wanted these individuals in place before a newly formed board become active. The consistent and methodical fashion in which Southam planned and implemented the many facets of this complicated new federal government institution ensured that it would have the correct support and proper structures for the important national role that lay ahead.

3

MAKING IT HAPPEN

By early 1965 the boisterous Judy LaMarsh had taken over the culture portfolio from the refined Maurice Lamontagne. She would stay in this job until the end of Prime Minister Pearson's tenure. A down-to-earth populist in style and heart, LaMarsh seized the NAC file and gave it her full support, guiding the legislation effectively through the House of Commons. Wags who had worried about the new Arts Centre being too elitist joked that if LaMarsh liked it, it must be good. On July 14, 1966, having cleared the hurdles of both the House of Commons and the Senate, the *National Arts Centre Act* received Royal Assent.

LaMarsh wasted no time in appointing the new Board of Trustees. Lawrence Freiman, a friend of LaMarsh and George McIlraith, the minister of public works and the "Ottawa minister" in the Cabinet, was made chair. A mercurial, intense man who ran the family department-store business, Freiman loved the arts, served on the Stratford Festival Board, and favoured big symphonies and grand theatres. Both he and Southam were Ottawa-born and wanted the best for their city, but their tastes were different and, for much of the time they worked together at the Arts Centre, they would be at odds with one another.

The Honourable Judy LaMarsh, Maurice Lamontagne's successor as secretary of state in Lester Pearson's Cabinet.

The other eight trustees were a broad cross-section of people with experience in the arts and business in Canada. The heads of important federal cultural agencies such as the CBC, the Canada Council, and the National Film Board were given ex-officio status on the board, as were the mayors of Ottawa and Hull. This was the first time that representatives of these other agencies were placed on the board of a sister organization, and these linkages would prove useful in the years ahead.

It was several months before the new board met for the first time, on March 8, 1967, in the Orange Room of Ottawa's Château Laurier Hotel, just across the street from the building site. In the interim, Freiman had set about developing his own vision of how the centre should be organized. He had many friends in theatre, including the English director Tyrone Guthrie, who had helped launch the Stratford Festival. Freiman consulted him about the appointment of an overall director for the National Arts Centre. An ad hoc committee that included writer Robertson Davies and Dr. Arnold Walter had already considered this question and concluded that the obvious choice was Southam. Although reluctant, Freiman was eventually persuaded by these "distinguished Canadian figures" to accept Southam as the new director general. Once the polite preliminaries were over, the first motion by the new board was to transform Coordinator Hamilton Southam into the NAC's first director general. Bruce Corder was also confirmed as Southam's second-in-command and would soon become his "right hand" in running the place.[1]

Southam prepared well for these first meetings, and a series of motions that he and his team had developed clicked effortlessly through the proceedings. At the heart of his message was Jean Gascon's idea that, "without resident companies, the building would be misbegotten."[2] He sketched out carefully the plans that had been developed with the help of the advisory groups for both theatre and music. While there were no plans yet for resident dance or opera, Southam already had his eye on the Summer Festival and recommended that the board ask the government for a separate $1 million per year to pay for it. He had hired the Canadian-born arts administrator Henry Wrong as his future director of programming. Wrong, the designated head of the future Festival as well, had been the special assistant to Sir Rudolf Bing at New York's Metropolitan Opera and, not surprisingly, was a man with big ideas. His suggestions for the Festival already included visits by European companies such as the Salzburg Opera, which, he said, "could drop by Ottawa on its way to Japan in 1970." The immediate task, however, was to persuade Cabinet to approve approximately $2.5 million for the Arts Centre's general operations. Judy LaMarsh, primed by Lawrence Freiman, readily lent her political support.

A big item on the first meeting's agenda was an upcoming visit by the Queen, a prospect almost as exciting to the trustees as the new centre itself. A $5,000 budget was allocated for this celebration, and an invitation sent to actor Christopher Plummer to host the ceremonies at the building site. On July 5, 1964, Queen Elizabeth II arrived in

First NAC chairman Lawrence Freiman with Lester Pearson and Queen Elizabeth II on July 5, 1964, at an unveiling ceremony of a plaque marking the Queen's visit to the unfinished site. Photo © John Evans.

Ottawa on her way back to England after attending a conference in Quebec City. It was a first big public moment for the National Arts Centre: on this sunny summer morning, the Queen took an hour out of a crammed schedule on Parliament Hill to come over to the chaotic construction site to unveil a plaque. A crowd of spectators enjoyed the brief but lively outdoor artistic show that was presented on a temporary wooden stage erected the previous night on a patch of green sod hurriedly laid down in the middle of the muddy grounds. A special fanfare for the occasion had been composed by Louis Applebaum, and a proclamation written by author Robertson Davies. The lines were to be delivered by Plummer in English and by renowned Quebec actress Denise Pelletier in French, although there were many arguments over the translation of Davies's words into the language of Molière. At the last moment Plummer cancelled, and another Canadian actor, Robert Whitehead, stepped in to replace him. Freiman was in his element showing the Queen around the half-built site to the cheers of the blue-helmeted construction workers. Dozens of dignitaries were also on hand to celebrate. As the excitement subsided and the July board meetings continued the trustees expressed relief that the visit was over and that thinking could turn once again to more practical matters.

Considerable debate was devoted at the first meeting to the organizational model. Freiman opposed Southam's preference for the decentralized "Brussels" concept, describing its associated independent companies as "too expensive and duplicating responsibility."[3] With LaMarsh supporting his position, the new trustees swiftly voted to adopt the "Stratford" approach, in which they, through the centre's own staff, would have responsibility for all the artistic work presented there. Southam, who had promoted the Brussels model for nearly three years, acquiesced without a murmur. Decades later, when hard times hit the Arts Centre, this early choice would be revisited and thought given again to separating the orchestra into an independent if resident company. This fragmentation did not occur and, so far, the original decision has been maintained.

Henry Wrong initiated plans for the programming of the Opening Festival, now tentatively scheduled for June 1969. The first regular seasons would not commence until the fall. The inaugural event was to be "Canadian, bi-cultural and artistically interesting." Southam nevertheless continued to travel widely in Europe, forming alliances and viewing performances that might be brought to Ottawa in due course. One trip took him to Prague, where he first saw the work of the great Czech designer Josef Svoboda. The regular annual Festival was targeted to begin in the summer of 1970 under the aegis of the Arts Centre. Wrong had been thinking big—hugely, in fact—about this event. Besides the visit from the Salzburg Opera, there were plans for four different opera productions in a two-week season, complete with soloists from the Vienna Staatsoper. Even a Parisian haute couture fashion show was mentioned. Unfortunately, a personal tiff between Wrong and Southam would mean that the programming director would not be around to see any of these plans to completion. Although Wrong had already moved to Ottawa and settled his family into a new house in anticipation of his position at the centre, he was shortly to be fired.

The trouble was triggered by malicious gossip instigated by one of the artists now making their way to the Arts Centre in anticipation of future work. Something unpleasant was reported to Southam about Wrong and, instead of checking his facts, Southam took it at face value. When he confronted Wrong, the latter made an angry comment about the breakdown of Southam's marriage to his first wife, Jacqueline. In the midst of his busy work life, Southam's personal affairs had taken a tempestuous turn, and his long-standing attraction to women had reasserted itself. Southam was furious and, in a rare pugilistic moment, threatened to strike Wrong if he did not take back his hurtful words. Wrong declined, and Southam responded by "boxing his ears,"[4] resulting in the threat of a messy lawsuit. To avoid any further embarrassment to the NAC, Southam made a financial settlement with Wrong and the two arts administrators parted ways. Years later Southam mused that perhaps he had not been fair to Wrong, but the scandal had an immediate effect on planning at the centre as Wrong's initial grand ideas for the 1970 Festival were dropped with his departure.[5]

Fortunately for Southam, David Haber, the phenomenally successful impresario for the cultural festival at Expo 67, was waiting in the wings. Although he could not join the Arts Centre until his work in Montreal was completed, he came to Ottawa, met with Southam, and agreed to join the staff in March 1968 for an annual salary of $20,000. His arrival brought the centre an invaluable asset. With a tiny staff of one assistant and a secretary, he functioned, with the exception of the Music Department, as a one-man programming department for the next five years.

�֍

As 1967 unfolded, newly appointed NAC staff members assisted the busy Centennial Commission with its artistic activities, helping it to tour shows across the country. They arranged some of the popular programming, including tours by the Quebec singers Louise Forrestier, Pierre Ferland, and Ginette Reno, who were seen only rarely outside Quebec, in other parts of the country. They also organized European tours for the Quebec dance company Les Feux Follets and for the Montreal Symphony Orchestra. Their success and expertise in moving artists around the country and overseas gave Haber an idea that he delivered to Southam shortly after he arrived in Ottawa: the Arts Centre could develop a National Booking Office, which would serve arts groups all over Canada. Southam immediately grasped that this initiative could contribute to the centre's national role. Around the same time, the board realized that it must begin implanting the idea of the National Arts Centre in the general public's mind. It authorized management to hire a public-relations director, Laurent Duval, and allotted him a $100,000 budget for a campaign to start putting the word out.

Most of the trustees' thinking in those early days was wide-ranging and ambitious. Lawrence Freiman had by now resigned from the Stratford Festival Board, but he was still keen to devise a plan that would make the Stratford Festival company the resident English theatre company at the National Arts Centre. He dreamed of having it tour the country under the NAC's aegis and initiated a voluminous correspondence with Floyd Chalmers, the chair of the Stratford board, who shared his thinking. Characterized by their intimate "Dear Larry/Dear Floyd" salutations, the two embarked on what would be a lengthy, sometimes tortuous, exploration to make Stratford part of the NAC. It was left to Southam to work out the prospects for French theatre—a decision that would soon lead to trouble after he willingly took the advice of the francophone theatrical community,

There were non-artistic matters to deal with as well. Southam had discovered during his time in Sweden that the best restaurant in Stockholm was at the Swedish Opera. Good dining and good theatre had always gone hand in hand in his mind, and he firmly believed that "more things were wrought by a good lunch than others dreamed of."[6] The local property developer William Teron had experience building hotels in Ottawa. He had helped Southam out by taking over the National Capital Arts Alliance when Southam had no further use for the organization, and by way of thanks Southam had assisted his appointment to the new board of the NAC. Teron was considered the "house" expert in restaurants and given the job of exploring the catering requirements for the centre. Here, again, Southam knew what he wanted. After a particularly delightful dinner at the famous Paris restaurant Chez Maxim's—an august operation that had also been part of the French Pavilion at Expo 67—he had fleetingly toyed with the idea of inviting this establishment to come to Ottawa to look after catering at the Arts Centre. Although the idea came to nothing, his ambitious thinking would lead to the inclusion of a grand restaurant at the centre. Unfortunately, provincial Ottawans would take a long time to develop the habit of dining at expensive restaurants, and the food service at the NAC became a millstone that dragged down the NAC's bottom line through the early years.

Another extravagant plan dreamed up in this first year and indicative of the trustees' eagerness to plunge into some artistic endeavour was the creation of a mobile theatre, a travelling truck known as Le Portage, which would tour through the Ottawa region. Modelled after the trailer-trucks that were touring Canada with Centennial exhibitions, this project would eventually turn into an expensive folly and end its days in a cornfield a hundred miles east of Ottawa. The problem was the ingenious but costly design that called for the side of the truck to fold down and become a theatre stage. Before the trustees could learn enough about costs, the price for designing and building this concept had run away with them. Still, during the year or two that it functioned, it toured theatre throughout the Ottawa Valley on both sides of the river, heralding the art that was coming soon to the permanent new stages.*

Towards this goal, the Arts Centre continued to hire talented staff, including some of the best and most experienced theatre people in the country. Many were ready to embrace a grand new initiative after their work on the hugely successful cultural festival at Expo, which, as it drew to a close, was generally agreed to be one of the greatest collections of artistic excellence presented anywhere in the world. In addition to David Haber, staff joining the NAC included Andis Celms, Expo's talented technical administrator, now hired to manage technical affairs in the NAC's theatres. Celms would stay on for the next thirty years, rising to become head of the Theatre Department and, finally, if briefly, senior artistic director. Box-office expert Ted Demetre, a quiet-spoken but front-of-house wizard, also signed on. He had saved the day at Expo when the fancy electronic ticket machines had broken down at the beginning of the festival, and he had doled out thousands of tickets by hand to ensure that people got into the early performances. He too would have a remarkable career at the Arts Centre, putting

Le Portage, the mobile theatre that was the new board's first venture into the actual arts, proved an expensive venture. Photo © John Evans.

*Later, the truck was lent out to some other provincial ventures before it was mothballed.

his talents to work for many years in the Variety and Dance Department, a consistent money-maker for the NAC coffers which helped subsidize the more esoteric art forms. Both men would spend the bulk of their careers at the Arts Centre, becoming indispensable team players.

Behind all the dreams and plans, vigorous efforts were ongoing to get the NAC's financial house in order and to make long-term arrangements to secure the necessary financial support from the government. Southam used his contacts at the cultural agencies and at senior levels of the Treasury Board to work on the budget, while, in-house, Bruce Corder wrestled with schemes to make both the parking garage and the commercial space allocated for shops along Elgin Street into sources of funds for the new centre. Southam and his board estimated that they would need at least $2.5 million from the government for each of the first two years' operations, plus an additional $1 million for the Festival, which they hoped to launch in the summer of 1970.

At the September 1967 meeting, board members finally settled on the official name for the centre. After three years of discussion, they rejected Southam's romantic notion of calling the place "Les Rideaux"—a name that evoked for him his summer estate in the Rideau Lakes—choosing instead the National Arts Centre. The name translated nicely, although Southam grumbled that it had "a dull, institutional ring." At the same time, the board threw out the potentially contentious idea of naming the various halls after famous Canadians, opting instead for the generic labels of "Opera," "Theatre," "Salon," "Studio," and even "Le Restaurant" and "Le Café"—names that would stick almost all the way through the NAC's first thirty-five years. In 2000, Southam "succumbed to the temptation" to allow the Opera to be named after him and it has since been known as Southam Hall.[7]

While government officials worked on the structure and organization of the new centre, other supporters were preoccupied with arranging its artistic content. It is impossible today to imagine a small group of citizens agreeing to work together to establish an arts centre of the scope and complexity of the National Arts Centre, and then to go on to build the orchestra, theatre, and opera that would perform in it. Yet, incredibly, that is what Southam and his colleagues set out to accomplish.

Nothing was more carefully thought out or pursued than the creation of the National Arts Centre Orchestra (NACO). Credit for this achievement must go to a handful of dedicated music professionals who mostly had their careers at the CBC, the National Film Board, or a university. These men were determined to improve the place of music in Canada, and in the postwar period their ideas were allowed to flourish.

For almost two decades, there had been a reasonably well-functioning symphony orchestra in Ottawa, most recently under the leadership of concertmaster Eugene

Kash, then married to the exuberant mezzo-soprano Maureen Forrester. In the late forties and fifties, the Ottawa Philharmonic had been the first orchestra in Canada to introduce a series of children's concerts, but the orchestra had foundered in 1960 over problems with the musicians' union. The resulting musical gap in the capital had been filled by seasonal visits from both the Toronto Symphony and the Montreal Symphony orchestras. As the National Capital Arts Alliance prepared its study on a possible future performing arts centre in the city, it presented little hope for a new symphony orchestra in the region. Perhaps "after the Centre was built and Ottawa's population increased,"[8] it mused, a new orchestra would stand a chance. In the meantime, the visiting orchestras could fill the gap.

This kind of thinking changed dramatically once the Arts Centre planners were ignited by Jean Gascon's early statement that "the new centre must have a heart that beats."[9] Although it was an audacious move in the eyes of the country's established musical community, the members of the music committee quickly decided that there must be a new orchestra. With Louis Applebaum in the chair of this stellar group, Southam was receiving advice from some of the country's most notable musical thinkers. The gregarious Applebaum had been a moving force in Canadian music from the early fifties, working extensively at the CBC and the National Film Board, composing music for productions at both organizations, and developing a broad and rich music program at the Stratford Festival. (Eventually he would even become a senior arts bureaucrat.) Now, in his May 1965 report for a music program at the new Arts Centre, he wrote: "A good orchestra is called for. A superb one would be more to the point."

The idea for a small chamber-sized orchestra had been initially suggested a year earlier by the CBC's Jean-Marie Beaudet—another consultant to the Arts Centre and ex-officio member of the music advisory committee. He played a crucial role in figuring out the practical details and, by October 1964, his thoughts had crystallized into a carefully thought-out proposal for a mid-sized ensemble. The plan called for an orchestra

Jean-Marie Beaudet came from the CBC to be the NAC's first director of music. Photo © John Evans.

that would "give year-round concerts, provide the musical backbone for a summer festival, serve as a pit orchestra for visiting ballet and opera companies and play an educational role in the community as well as, possibly, offering its service to the CBC."[10] There was also the possibility of "national touring." The speed with which these ideas emerged was remarkable, and the real task soon became how best to put them into effect.

Beaudet's contribution to the creation of the NAC orchestra would be hard to over-estimate. This balding, slightly foppish, late-marrying bachelor, who smoked cigarettes from an ebony holder and peered out beneath a deeply furrowed brow through dark horn-rimmed glasses, gave all his support to the creation of this new all-Canadian orchestra. Like Applebaum, he was completely dedicated to the growth and development of the Canadian musical scene. With his excellent experience in managing musical programs and their budgets at the CBC, he had, by October 1964, laid out the preliminary budget for a conductor and expenses for a forty-piece orchestra operating for a forty-eight-week season. Although the CBC had made no commitment as yet, Beaudet suggested that the corporation could contribute to the budget by taking weekly one-hour broadcasts from the new orchestra for the radio network, and he pointed to the potential for television work as well. When the Arts Centre later got down to real budgeting, Beaudet's numbers were found to be close to the mark. His vision for the orchestra read like a recipe for making a cake: "10 first violins … 8 second … 6 violas … 4 cellos … 3 bass … etc."[11] He also presented sound advice on contentious issues such as salaries, the role of the powerful musicians' union, and what should happen when the orchestra needed to hire local musicians to augment itself for larger works. Beaudet's "masterplan" memo became an invaluable tool for Southam for use with everyone—from the government's Interdepartmental Steering Committee to members of the local musical community. It provided the groundwork for future discussions on musical life in Ottawa.

Throughout the fall of 1964, Beaudet continued to pour out ideas to his committee colleagues. Writing in both English and French, he pointed out to Southam the cost problems of a big symphonic orchestra, the role of the National Youth Orchestra as a source of musicians, and the importance of professional experience to music students still pursuing their studies. When Dr. Frederick Karam mentioned that he was thinking about establishing a music school at the University of Ottawa, Beaudet wrote to Southam that the whole enterprise engendered a "spirit of hope" in him.

Faced with this enthusiasm, Southam followed the advice of another committee member, Dr. Arnold Walter, and wrote to Professor Ezra Schabas at the University of Toronto's School of Music, asking for his comments on Beaudet's ideas. Schabas not only backed up Beaudet's proposals but expanded on them.[12] As a former general manager of the National Youth Orchestra, Schabas was sensitive to Beaudet's suggestion of integrating young musicians into the new orchestra, and he wrote a long and detailed response to Southam. With this backing in hand, Southam took the next step, asking Applebaum and his committee to prepare a full in-depth report on how this plan could be achieved.

While awaiting this study, Southam organized a generous reception on March 1, 1965, for parliamentarians in the West Block on Parliament Hill. There, architect Fred Lebensold, using the latest models and plans for the project, set out for the assembled MPs, senators, and others the details of this artistic work in progress. The politicians were charmed. Like a juggler whirling a series of plates in the air, Southam moved easily back and forth in the following weeks on all fronts, keeping up the momentum. His diary notes confirm that he missed no occasion or opportunity to promote the centre. He also continued his hectic social life and attended performances of plays, music, and dance in every city he visited.

Applebaum presented his report in May 1965. It would become the official blueprint for the development of serious music in the capital region for the foreseeable future. While not all of his dreams and aspirations would be fulfilled, most of the report's key planks were introduced. At its core was the simple premise that "orchestral musicians must be involved in the community's life and in the education of its children."[13]

While compiling the document, Applebaum met with officials at both of Ottawa's universities. Davidson Dunton, the president of Carleton University, had expressed some interest in expanding its music options but was not interested in a full-scale Faculty of Music. At the Université d'Ottawa, however, Applebaum found a more sympathetic ear in its rector, Father Roger Guindon, and its PR director, Bill Boss. Both became enthusiastic cheerleaders for the new centre. Applebaum and Southam were invited to make a presentation to the university's Senate, and by February of the following year they were assured that the governors had found money in their budget for a School of Music. Applebaum also recommended a conservatory for primary music education and a special school for gifted children, although these particular dreams were not to be realized.[14] All Applebaum's suggestions were based on the importance of a good education in music.

In the early months of 1967, as the Board of Trustees met for the first time, the question of the new orchestra was among the biggest topics of discussion. The board was having a hard time making up its mind what to do. Applebaum's carefully prepared report advocated a regional approach to music, but the trustees dithered over approving the core idea of the orchestra. Their uncertainty was reflected in an anguished paper prepared by Toronto trustee A.C. McKim entitled "To Be or Not to Be—An Orchestra," which attempted to set out the different points of view.[15] Despite all the preparatory work, it was up to the new trustees to make the real decisions. By July, Dr. Arnold Walter and a number of the other musical heavyweights on the board were becoming impatient. Walter wrote Southam a stern note urging him to get on with things. He advised the new director general to get together with Beaudet to resolve such issues as union negotiations, auditioning musicians, and hiring a conductor. There was no time to waste.

Although the trustees had yet to give the go-ahead for an orchestra, this indecision did not stop them from discussing whom they might hire as a conductor. They were thinking big—Charles Munch, the former music director of the Boston Symphony, Cleveland's George Szell, and London's Sir John Barbirolli would be asked for advice. Perhaps one of them could be engaged on a limited basis, maybe with a Canadian conductor as an assistant and the possibility of succeeding him in due course. The importance of having a Canadian conductor was noted, but it was felt more important to have a first-class person who could develop the ensemble.

As the controversy over the existence of the orchestra continued, the civil servants inside the office of the secretary of state were feeling the heat. There were sustained protests from Montreal and Toronto, whose orchestras feared they would be robbed of both players and money, and who argued that they could provide all the music Ottawa needed. Southam tried to ease matters by arranging meetings, attended by Freiman, with the other orchestra boards, but these encounters were of little avail. Intense lobbying continued at the political level to forestall the creation of the NAC ensemble. Henry Hindley, a senior adviser to Judy LaMarsh and a behind-the-scenes friend to the new centre, urged Southam to write out a solid case for the creation of the new orchestra and to present it to the minister. The final decision to authorize the NAC Orchestra would be made by the federal Cabinet.

Other arguments raged internally at the Arts Centre, especially over the proposed orchestra's size. Despite the careful groundwork laid out by Beaudet and Applebaum, which examined every aspect and implication of a chamber-sized ensemble, Lawrence Freiman much preferred large symphony orchestras. He insisted that Southam travel to New York with him to meet with Leonard Bernstein at the New York Philharmonic. Bernstein urged the creation of a larger orchestra because of the vastly greater number of works it could perform.

Freiman's view reflected local opinion. The Ottawa Philharmonic had functioned well in the postwar period, and Ottawa's classical music lovers were still enamoured of large symphonic orchestras. Southam had to tread carefully to try to maintain their support. Gradually Freiman began to see that creating a larger orchestra in direct competition with Toronto and Montreal would present insoluble political problems, and he came around to Southam's view, but the other local supporters of the Philharmonic remained unconvinced. Despite Southam's efforts, including many lunches and informal meetings over drinks, the nervous members of what was left of the now-defunct Ottawa Philharmonic's board of directors still wanted a larger ensemble. That was a worry, given that this local musical cadre would be important to future audience support. Southam exercised all his wiles, introducing them to Beaudet and acquainting them with the budding plans for the smaller group. For once his entertaining efforts failed, and he determined finally to go around them but not without throwing a diplomatic olive branch by arranging for a special paper on "continuing relations with the local community," a task that was left to William Teron.

By early summer, the creative and far-thinking Jean-Marie Beaudet had been seconded from the CBC to the NAC staff. He joyfully took up the job and never returned to the corporation. He would become the Arts Centre's first director of music, thereby ensuring that the substance of the orchestra concept and many of the other proposals for music in Ottawa would come to fruition. With the decision on the orchestra looming, Beaudet's task was to prepare a persuasive briefing paper for the September meetings of the board. This carefully layered and detailed submission presented all the facts and figures that had been worked out in the previous months. While the Toronto/Montreal pressure continued, with regional MPs and senior Cabinet members now pulled into the fray, the NAC board's newly created Executive Committee was effectively doing its own lobbying.

Southam, following Hindley's advice, had forwarded a lengthy memo to Judy LaMarsh which set out in lofty and lyrical terms the case for the arts, and particularly music, in society. Leaving no reference untapped, he ranged across the role of various kings and princes, as well as that of more recent socialist and democratic leaders who had recognized and supported the value of artistic activity in human life. He made lavish references to French culture minister André Malraux and to the views of Mme. Ekaterina Furtseva, a Russian minister of culture who had recently visited Ottawa and dined with LaMarsh. To make sure the Canadian minister got the point, Southam included the interesting information that a socialist government in Austria had rebuilt the Staatsoper in Vienna after the war, even though it was bankrupt. The paper was persuasive, well documented, and clearly stated in Southam's inimitable style. Critics not on top of their "Ottawa game" found it impossible to refute. Despite her reputation as a populist, LaMarsh, with Prime Minister Pearson behind her, backed the orchestra plan.

Beaudet's briefing paper to the trustees set out a time-table for the creation of this "national orchestra." When the board's Executive Committee met once again in September, members finally faced the music. Although Southam's memo to the minister and its fulsome references to kings and princes had made some of the trustees nervous— "after all we are living a democracy"—the committee finally grappled with the arguments that favoured the orchestra's creation.[16] In a carefully drafted memorandum, dated September 18, 1967, the recommendation went forward to proceed with a forty-five-member orchestra. At the October meetings, the full board endorsed the plan and sent it on to the minister for Cabinet approval.

This decision became the seminal moment in the creation of the NAC Orchestra. It went on to become, in the later words of one critic, "not merely the best orchestra in

Canada but easily one of the best of its kind in the world."[17] Southam had set out to get the best advice he could from some of Canada's finest arts professionals—Arnold Walter, Louis Applebaum, and Jean-Marie Beaudet—and he relied heavily on Peter Dwyer of the Canada Council for wisdom and insight. Southam's own ability to listen, his capacity to see an overall vision, and his connections to key people in politics and in the bureaucracy allowed him to push forward one of the great success stories of Canadian arts and culture. By the end of October 1967 the orchestra had been approved by Cabinet, and the next target was to get it up and playing.

Southam was in his element that Centennial summer as he travelled back and forth to Montreal to savour the artistic treasures on offer at Expo: the Swedish Opera, a glorious La Scala production of *La Bohème* directed by Franco Zefferelli, and lavish lunches and dinners with the "notables" of the cultural scene from all over the world. His diary jottings made careful notes of everything that might have potential for the Arts Centre in Ottawa, and he forged several new friendships with international impresarios, including Albert Sarfati, a Tunisian-born French citizen who was responsible for bringing many of the great European orchestra, dance, and theatrical companies to Expo. He also cultivated an earlier friendship with Lord Harewood,* who had been the director of the Edinburgh Festival and had since taken over the English National Opera. Southam's dream was to bring not only the best work in Canada to the National Arts Centre but also the best from the international scene. His premise was simple: that exposure to the very best would inspire and develop the arts in Canada. It was a formula that had worked for him. Excellence meant Europe and not the United States, and he would start to work immediately with these two leading arts figures to plan for the 1970 Festival and the NAC's future. Despite all these exuberant plans, the date of the centre's opening still remained uncertain as just the latest in a string of delays—a steel strike—once again slowed down construction.

The orchestra might be launched to the satisfaction of all at the Arts Centre, but there was no similar enthusiasm or agreement in the theatre department. Rather, the quarrels and frustrations of the next few years seemed to fulfill playwright Wole Soyinka's observation that "the most interesting aspects of a play are the actual goings-on behind the scenes, which vary from the hilarious to the tragic."[18] To begin with, the

---

*Harewood became a close friend, serving as godfather to Southam's daughter from his second marriage—to Gro Southam.

discussions with the Stratford Festival over a possible agreement that would make Ottawa the winter home for the company were still contentious. Stratford's artistic personnel were unhappy with the idea.[19] Although the director, Michael Langham, had originally supported this scheme, he had later decided that he didn't want the company to go to Ottawa. Rather, he said, it should locate in Montreal, nearer to the National Theatre School. Nevertheless, a formal agreement was signed between the two parties calling for "joint activities" on at least two Shakespearean plays to be performed during the winter season in Ottawa, along with other classics. A joint planning committee of the two professional staffs was established to hammer out the details.

Despite Jean Gascon's leadership on the theatre advisory committee, Southam was having little luck in attracting anyone from Quebec to head up a French theatre company.[20] Vincent Massey had long ago stressed that Canadian sovereignty was at heart a cultural matter, and ideological stirrings in Quebec with the rise of the Quiet Revolution meant that culture there was already developing its Quebec nationalist streak. Quebec theatre was in an exciting ferment, and its leading practitioners were loath to leave Montreal at this time for the outpost of Canada's capital.

On a hot mid-August day in 1967, Southam travelled to Montreal's Dorval Airport to meet with Quebec's leading theatre directors in an effort to resolve the matter. In a private room at the busy airport, he told them in his elegant Parisian French that he was getting nowhere in terms of establishing a French theatre company at the Arts Centre and asked them what he should do. For all his formal airs, Southam always seemed able to strike a chord with artists when he engaged with them, and the luminaries gathered there that day, who, besides Gascon, included Yvette Brind'amour from the Rideau Vert, Jean-Louis Roux, the artistic director at Le Théâtre du Nouveau Monde, and others, considered his question seriously. Although Roux claims to have been tempted,[21] he decided he would prefer to stay in Montreal.

Finally, the group came up with the name of a lesser light in Montreal theatre, a director by the name of Jean-Guy Sabourin. He was seen as "a small fish" who, to the disdain of some, ran only a semi-professional company. He was, however, deeply interested in the role theatre could play in society and its potential for effecting change. He was fascinated by the emerging theories in France for the "democratization of the arts," which were focused on establishing local *maisons de culture*, designed to mix professional artists with the local populace to work together in communities.[22] Schooled on the old-fashioned traditions of the Comédie Française, Southam seems to have missed the implications of this thinking and, on the theatre group's advice, he interviewed Sabourin and hired him. The Quebec director joined the NAC staff in October 1967. Soon after he left for France for several months, at the centre's expense, to study the new French methods and to plan his new theatre company and his first season.

Prime Minister Lester Pearson, with communications officer Philippe Paquet and Hamilton Southam, seemed to be thanking the gods as the NAC building neared completion. Photo © John Evans.

Meanwhile, Prime Minister Pearson was keeping a close eye on proceedings at the National Arts Centre, and in December he met again with Freiman and Southam. He seemed interested in the creation of the resident companies and indicated that he agreed with the long-term financial plans that had been submitted, although he cautioned that the organization would have to live within its proposed budget, especially for Year One.[23] This stricture would soon present problems in the ongoing negotiations with the Stratford Festival. The two companies had different perceptions of the plan they were discussing: the Arts Centre expected Stratford to form its English theatre company with a nucleus of its actors, but Stratford wanted to keep its whole company of forty-five actors intact during the winter. The centre had approved $600,000 for English theatre and $400,000 for French theatre, but Stratford's plans alone carried a price tag of $1.5 million. The horse-trading continued between the two organizations throughout the spring of 1968. One new distraction had appeared on the scene: theatre director Mavor Moore had begun to lobby to have some Stratford productions in his winter season at the St. Lawrence Centre in Toronto, where he was now director.

The date of the opening of the National Arts Centre was still unsettled, but non-stop budget discussions continued among management, the board, and the government. It was becoming evident that the government would grant only $2.5 million for the 1969–70 opening year, so Bruce Corder advised that they delay taking over responsibility for the building for as long as possible to save money on its running costs. Most worrying of all, nothing had been said about the additional million dollars intended for the annual Summer Festival, and Southam urged the trustees not to forget to ask for it. Freiman wanted to nail down the funds for the Arts Centre's basic requirements before asking for more, so he resisted Southam's plan. The friction between the two men only increased when Freiman insisted on managing the issue on his own with the politicians.

Despite these pesky frustrations, Southam moved ahead enthusiastically with his Festival plans. His vision called for a celebration of both Anglo-Saxon and French culture in North America, so he issued invitations to theatre and opera companies in France and in England and put his friends Lord Harewood and Albert Sarfati on the payroll as consultants. It was to be a grand festival indeed. Among the tentative invitees were the Comédie Française and the Orchestre de Paris, Great Britain's National Theatre, ballet companies from Sadler's Wells and Covent Garden, and several other national companies from both France and England. Harewood's contract called for up to $7,000 in consulting fees plus his expenses, and both men were due to arrive in Ottawa in May to firm up the Festival schedule. Meanwhile, Southam continued to pursue his government contacts, calling on Treasury Board president Edgar Benson, who was "sympathetic," to champion the matter in Cabinet "within a few weeks."[24] But no money for the Festival would be forthcoming and, in August, the board at last insisted that Southam postpone the event until the 1972 or even the 1973 summer season. Write-off fees were discussed for the two high-priced foreign consultants, but there is no record of any payment being made. In the end, Sarfati would have seven years of valuable work with the NAC, supplying it with European companies and performers through his agency, and, in return, he would import some of the NAC productions to Europe. Harewood would later be paid by the Canada Council to prepare a report on Canadian opera.

With the opening now barely a year away, the pace of work quickened at the Arts Centre. The talented programmer David Haber had arrived from Montreal. In Haber, Southam had found a gem, and the intense bespectacled young man soon covered the walls of his small office with vast charts of the future schedule that would present artists of all types in the coming seasons—from the world's favourite pop singers to the most esoteric cutting-edge dance troupes. Haber's incomparable contacts ensured that much of "the best of the best" would be seen at the Arts Centre in the next few years.

The dedicated genius of David Haber, the programming director as the NAC got under way, kept all three halls filled with exciting and innovative work. Photo © Studio Graetz.

4

NEW REGIME
IN OTTAWA

When Lester Pearson left office in April 1968 and Pierre Elliott Trudeau succeeded him as prime minister, Judy LaMarsh handed over the secretary of state's job to the former Montreal journalist Gérard Pelletier—a shy, somewhat diffident Quebec intellectual. He had been born in Victoriaville, Quebec, the son of a hardworking railway station-manager and a mother who worked occasionally as a seamstress. Thanks to his good education and his activities in Catholic youth movements in the province, he had travelled to South America and postwar Europe, where he developed an intense interest in cultural matters and social change. He became a journalist, working first in trade union journals, then as a public affairs reporter and commentator for Radio Canada, and was eventually hired as the editor of the powerful Montreal newspaper *La Presse*. He resigned in 1965 to go into politics with his two close friends Jean Marchand, a prominent union leader, and Pierre Trudeau, a lawyer, essayist, and sometime dilettante.

Dubbed the "Three Wise Men," Marchand, Pelletier, and Trudeau had been recruited by Pearson's Liberals to run in Quebec in the upcoming federal election. Pelletier had been in the forefront of the fight against the "Great Darkness" of the Duplessis era in Quebec

Pierre Trudeau's secretary of state, Gérard Pelletier, brought ideas to Ottawa that clashed with Hamilton Southam's view of the world but which would have long-term effects on the practice of arts and culture in Canada.

(although some political opponents alleged that this iconic term was nothing but Liberal propaganda).[1] He had strong ideas about the role of culture in national life and, once appointed to a position of authority in the Cabinet, he would lose no time in putting them into effect. In the meantime, his opening gambit so far as the Arts Centre was concerned was to declare that it better not be "too snobbish."[2] He and Southam came from two different worlds—and they would cross like ships in the night, with only *de rigueur* formal contact and little understanding of each other. Pelletier was one of the few neither enticed nor persuaded by Southam's celebrated social skills.

While the political regime changed in Ottawa, the struggle continued between the NAC and the Stratford Festival over their agreement. In March 1969 they organized a window-dressing signing ceremony in the unfinished foyer of the Arts Centre which briefly turned the theatre company into the "Stratford National Theatre Company of Canada." The biggest stumbling block was money, but the agreement would soon start to unravel in other ways as well. Stratford had set its "irreducible" budget to come to Ottawa at $1,062 million, but David Haber confirmed that the NAC English theatre budget could not rise above $875,000 at "the absolute maximum."[3] Southam, who seemed to have a penchant for airport meetings, arranged another one, this time at Toronto's Malton Airport (now Lester B. Pearson International Airport) to try to thrash out the problems.

Now another impediment emerged—the prospect of the Stratford Festival appearing in Toronto and elsewhere under the banner of the National Arts Centre. The Canada Council had weighed in to say that if it was giving Stratford grant money, the company could not tour under the NAC label, and especially not to the Ontario capital. This turf war reached the highest levels of the government, demonstrating how political pressure comes into play when government monies are at stake. Finally, Ernie Steele, the undersecretary of state, concurred with the Canada Council's position. It would not be the last time that the NAC would lose out in a power struggle with the other federal arts agency. Board chair Lawrence Freiman, by now ill and in and out of hospital, declared himself hurt and betrayed by this breakdown in the Stratford arrangement, and Southam was equally upset. Touring Stratford as the NAC's English theatre company would have added great prestige to the NAC enterprise. Stratford's own ambivalence about the arrangements and some behind-the-scenes footwork by its resistant management had contributed to the decision. For once there were hard feelings, and Southam uncharacteristically accused his Stratford counterpart, general manager Bill Wylie, of bad faith.

On the music front, things continued to proceed far more smoothly. Jean-Marie Beaudet had been diligently forging ahead with his search for a conductor and now believed he had found his candidate in Mario Bernardi, a Canadian based in London at the Sadler's Wells Opera whom he knew from earlier stints in Toronto and Stratford. Except for a lack of experience conducting symphonic music, Bernardi seemed to have all the other attributes that Beaudet was seeking.

While the music world in Canada at the time was expanding, many of its better talents still went abroad to study and work, Bernardi among them, and they returned only occasionally as assignments came up. Opportunities in Canada were limited, and although there was work with the CBC in radio and television, all the orchestras had short seasons, never more than thirty-two weeks, and professional musicians had to scramble to find summer employment. The Stratford Festival created important new possibilities as the ubiquitous Louis Applebaum developed a lively music program there in conjunction with the drama productions. Musicians performed incidental music for the plays, a new chamber music orchestra presented its own concert series, and a short season of smaller operas had even been added to the season at the Avon Theatre. Because the pit was so constricted, there were never more than thirty orchestral players. It was tough to get hired, and the group attracted a high calibre of performers. One summer the concertmasters from the orchestras in Edmonton, Winnipeg, and Quebec all turned up for work. The operas produced included works by Mozart, Rossini, and, one year, even a small Britten opera. Mario Bernardi returned regularly from London each summer to conduct some of these productions.

In the summer of 1967 Beaudet brought Freiman and Southam to Stratford to meet briefly with Bernardi (though he had already introduced Bernardi to Southam in London). Beaudet knew the conductor from the days when the young musician served as rehearsal pianist for a CBC production of *Carman* and as the piano soloist for a concert that he had conducted in Montreal. (Years later Bernardi said that he "did not think Beaudet was a very good conductor," and he was not alone in this opinion.) The Stratford outing gave the NAC team little more than a fleeting introduction to Bernardi, and they left it to Beaudet to see about the hiring. In the fall he flew to London, where he had a long meeting with Bernardi at the Savage Club.[4]

While his Canadian birth was fortuitous, Bernardi had received his core musical training in the demanding and disciplined schools of Europe. Born in 1930 in Kirkland Lake, Ontario, he had moved to Italy at the age of six with his mother, living in the small city of Treviso, near Venice, where they remained throughout the war. He studied at the Venice Conservatory and, at just sixteen, two years under the age for matriculation, received special permission to travel to Rome to write his final examinations. There he achieved the highest marks. He excelled in the keyboard instruments of piano and harpsichord, and, when he returned to Canada in the late forties, he hoped to become a soloist. A man of many talents, he was considered among the best of

Canada's promising young musicians emerging in the postwar period—a group that included Glenn Gould. When Bernardi discovered that there were no postgraduate courses at the University of Toronto to suit his needs, he began to take private lessons and to carve out a career as a "musician around town," playing recitals either alone or with experienced musicians such as the violinist Katherine Parr. A skilled sight-reader, he also picked up work as a rehearsal pianist for the Canadian Opera Company and, by his mid-twenties, had begun to conduct.

One day at a rehearsal for the Canadian Opera Company, Walter Susskind, the benevolent orchestra conductor, turned around and handed his baton to Bernardi, urging him to "give it a try." Bernardi quickly caught the opera addiction and, with theatre director Leon Major, soon had his own opera production at the COC, Leoncavallo's *Pagliacci*. Despite its success, he was warned by general manager Herman Geiger-Torel that there would be nothing else for him in the immediate future. One day, after helping a friend to apply for a Canada Council grant for study abroad, he decided to try for one himself. Dr. Arnold Walter and the Canada Council's Peter Dwyer guided his interests towards England and, when the grant came through, he left Toronto after the second act of a performance of *The Marriage of Figaro* that he had helped to rehearse, taking the night flight to London with his beautiful young wife, the singer Mona Kelly. He auditioned for a job at the Sadler's Wells Opera and, within six months, became one of its resident conductors. He had been there almost ten years when Beaudet tracked him down.

At the Savage Club that late autumn day, they "talked for hours and hours in the drawing room, which had a lovely ambiance," discussing their hopes and dreams for the future.[5] The size of the orchestra dominated their conversation, and they were tremendously excited by the flexibility that a smaller group would present, both for touring and for teaching: Beaudet called it his "Haydn orchestra," while Bernardi thought it was more like a Schubert-sized ensemble, larger than a chamber orchestra but inspired

Even before the building was finished, Jean-Marie Beaudet (left) had found Canadian-born conductor Mario Bernardi and had him appointed the first conductor of the National Arts Centre Orchestra. Photo © John Evans.

by the classical orchestra model. Bernardi had scarcely conducted a symphony orchestra in his life. Even though he would be going to a far-distant place that his English friends would mockingly drawl out as "Ot-ta-wa," this new orchestra would present him with a golden opportunity.

For the National Arts Centre, Bernardi's Canadian citizenship made him ideal, and Beaudet seemed to have huge confidence in the younger man's abilities. Without further ado, he offered him the job and flew back to Ottawa. There Southam happily accepted this proposal, and Beaudet went straight on to the board to report, "I have found our conductor." Mario Bernardi was hired.

Another new staffer in Ottawa was Ken Murphy, a CBC Radio producer from Montreal and former orchestral musician. He had been hired by the NAC's first public-relations director, Laurent Duval, to become his bilingual assistant in promoting the new centre and in building an audience for its performances, especially in music. Shortly after he arrived, he became friends with Jean-Marie Beaudet, whose musical talents and insights he admired enormously. Early in 1968 Beaudet asked him to move to the Music Department, initially to help him create the orchestra and with the promise that he would become its first manager.

Beaudet had a clear strategy. They would not advertise the new musical positions but rely instead on the "musicians' grapevine" to spread the word they were hiring.[6] Auditions were to be held first in Canada and, if positions still remained open, then in the United States and Europe. This approach proved effective. Many of Canada's most talented young musicians, such as the bassoonist Michael Namer, had moved abroad to study, frequently with the help of the Canada Council, and, until now, prospects of work in Canada had been uncertain. When Namer and others heard about this new opportunity, however, they immediately applied, and between four and five hundred applications poured in. The audition team comprised Beaudet, Bernardi, and Canadian violinist Lea Foli, then associate concertmaster at the Minnesota Symphony and a prospective candidate for the position of concertmaster. Ray Still, a renowned oboist who held the first chair at the Chicago Symphony and who Bernardi had met at Stratford, sat in for all the sessions with woodwind players. Bernardi knew what he was looking for—young musicians who were good players and enthusiastic about joining the new orchestra. Experience was not so important. His preference was for "young enthusiasts who had not become jaded by too much professional experience."[7]

Another musician the NAC consulted was Robert Oades, then serving as personnel manager for the musicians at Stratford. This quiet-spoken trumpeter had emigrated from London, where he had played at Covent Garden. In Toronto, despite its core group of "highly competent musicians,"[8] he found it difficult as a newcomer to break in. Fortunately, his specialty as a "Bach trumpeter" called for more skill than the usual dance-band standard of playing then common in the city and, before long, he won a $1,000 Canada Council scholarship to play with the Bach Society, a group founded by singer Lois Marshall and pianist Glenn Gould. Before he could perform with the group, however, it collapsed. Finding work at Stratford had been a god-send for him.

Now, when Bernardi asked for suggestions of names for the new orchestra in Ottawa, Oades was surprised that few of the musicians he knew were interested in this steady well-paid work. To many, Ottawa seemed like "the end of the earth" compared with the lively musical scene in Toronto. Oades had played in the capital when the Ottawa CBC Chamber Orchestra, a largely amateur group led by Fred Karam of the University of Ottawa, brought him in for special trumpet works, and he was not so daunted. When he received a telephone call from Ken Murphy informing him that the audition team would be in Toronto the next day and inviting him to try out, Oades jumped at the chance. He was signed up immediately after the audition and agreed to move to Ottawa not only as a player but also as the personnel manager for the NAC orchestra.

Bernardi had played with a number of Toronto musicians at the Canadian Opera Company and had earned a reputation for being "not an easy conductor—very, very demanding."[9] When he invited several of these players to try out as section heads, they declined to apply. Even singers were sometimes put off by him and, while they loved going to Stratford to perform, they became concerned when they learned that Bernardi would be on the podium. Nevertheless, Oades, who had played for him several times as part of pick-up orchestras for the Canadian Opera Company, believed he was the right man for the Ottawa job precisely because of those strong qualities of discipline and toughness.

By the fall of 1968 it was evident that Lea Foli would not be joining the orchestra as concertmaster, so the NAC embarked on a strenuous search to find someone else. The spotlight settled on Walter Prystawski, a Canadian who had been abroad for the previous ten years and was currently living in Basel as co-concertmaster of the Basler Orchester Gesellschaft, a smaller-town version of the Vienna Philharmonic. The orchestra presented three series of symphonic music every year and served as the pit orchestra for the operas, operettas, and ballet performed in the Basel Theatre. Prystawski had become well versed in all the different roles filled by a resident orchestra. The Arts Centre was determined to hire as many Canadian musicians as possible, and finding one with international experience was a bonus. Prystawski and Bernardi had known each other from their Toronto student days, when Bernardi was already earning a reputation and Prystawski had played for him once in a concert with the CBC Orchestra.

By coincidence, Prystawski and his young family had returned to Canada for Christmas 1968 but had heard nothing about the new orchestra. Only after returning to Basel in the new year did he find a letter in his pile of mail inviting him to London to audition for Beaudet and Bernardi. Prystawski recalls having "a devil of a time" booking a flight that would give him time for the London meeting before he was due back in the Swiss city to play a series of concerts.

When he arrived in London he caught up with Bernardi at Steinway Hall, where, settled amid a group of pianos, they spent the afternoon making music together and sizing each other up. It was a pleasant afternoon, both men recalled, as they played through a series of sonatas. Bernardi liked the violinist a lot, and Prystawski had equally positive memories of playing "some Brahms, definitely a Mozart and a little solo Bach." By the end of the day the conductor told him, "You have the job, but you need a new fiddle!" Prystawski didn't mind the comment. He also wanted a better instrument.

The two musicians went back to the Dorchester Hotel on London's Park Lane, where Jean-Marie Beaudet was waiting. The trio ended the day over drinks in relaxed conversation while they talked on about their hopes and dreams for the new orchestra. Prystawski remembered the occasion as "one of the nicer afternoons of my life."[10]

The attraction of the job for Prystawski was starting something from scratch. He had loved his time in Europe and being part of a long tradition of music, surrounded by musical icons. In the blue markings on the musical scores from which he was playing he could trace the evolutions of music. When he took over at the Arts Centre, his first few years were spent "marking the scores." All the musical scores were new, and as Bernardi had too much else on his hands, left the task to the concertmaster. "It sounds like a mechanical job," Prystawski explained, "but it's important. It tells people how to divide up their bows, how to play certain notes from a bowing point of view," and the best way physically to make certain sounds. Marked scores become a history of how specific music was played with a certain conductor and a particular orchestra, and that was to become the case at the National Arts Centre as well. The attraction for Prystawski in coming to Ottawa was that he could have his own "creative input," that he "would not be bound or constricted" by those very traditions with which European music was imbued. In Ottawa, "the hallways would be so wide that you couldn't see the sides of them." And, on a personal level, his small daughter was just ready to start school.

The story of the beautiful Guadagnini violin played by the NAC orchestra's concertmaster has many versions. Mario Bernardi had made a new and better violin a condition of Prystawski's hiring and indicated that the Arts Centre would help with funds to acquire a new instrument. Shortly after Prystawski returned to Switzerland, he took a day off to contact "fiddle dealers" and borrowed several instruments to try out by playing them with the Basel orchestra. Unfortunately, the cost of the potential candidates was usually three times the estimated $10,000 budget, the sum that NAC planners had in mind for a good violin. One day when he went to have a bow repaired, the shopkeeper mentioned a "J.B. Guadagnini" violin that was already out on loan to a young violin student for her graduation concert. Prystawski attended the concert and agonized for nearly a week before he could get his hands on the fiddle. There was no question that this was the instrument, and the NAC advanced $12,000 to pay for it. Within a few years it was to become the subject of one of the first financial *causes célèbres* at the centre.

Prystawski's recollection was that the NAC would take a pittance from his salary in instalments over the coming years so he could slowly pay for the violin. Bernardi's remembrance was that a fine instrument had been purchased for the NAC concertmaster and would be available in perpetuity to that position. Whatever the arrangement, no details of it were recorded, although the magnificent violin appeared as a line item in the NAC budget as one of its assets. Some time after the launch of the new centre and when the organization was settling down to regular activity, the auditor general arrived on the scene to review the finances. The matter of the violin was untidy, with a few dollars taken from the musician's salary while the item itself still appeared as a valuable asset to the centre. The auditor general was especially annoyed that the payoff loan to Prystawski was interest free, yet the value of the violin was rapidly accruing. The trustees resolved to fix things and asked Southam to take care of the matter. After he left the board meeting, he called Prystawski to his office and asked him to "sell the fiddle back to us." By Prystawski's account, after a long pause, he refused. He left Southam's office and quickly arranged a meeting with his bank

The new concertmaster, Walter Prystawski (left), showed off the newly purchased, precious "J.B. Guadagnini" violin to fellow violinists and new orchestra members John Gazi and Joan Milkson. Photo © Helen Flaherty.

manager. When he returned with a cheque, Southam remained silent, although eventually the two men negotiated and came to an agreement.

The auditor general continued to be perturbed, both that the deal was based on the violin's unrevised value—its appraised value was now around $45,000—and that this "crown asset" was even being sold off. Southam stoutly argued that the NAC had the right to sell the violin, though he did get on the phone to see what it was really worth. With the board, he sought the help of the prominent Ottawa lawyer Gordon Henderson, who deemed that the sale was not illegal, but the price should take into account the violin's increased worth. Southam skirted this issue with the board by arguing the merits of "replacement" versus "real market" value—and he deemed the latter in the $15,000 to $18,000 range. Prystawski increased his obligation to the centre, including a further loan of $3,000 on which he agreed to pay interest. Southam, not for the first or last time, reached into his own pocket to top up the difference. While the NAC trustees weren't happy, Prystawski became full owner of the instrument.

The incident exemplified the changing times that were slowly starting to impinge on the NAC. The *droit du seigneur* by which Southam had managed to build the place and run it since its inauguration was tightening up as government officials began to pay closer attention to the centre's operations. Although it was something of a private fiefdom at the outset, certainly run as an independent theatre, that situation was to become less and less the case. The violin incident also illuminated the way Southam often functioned, from his immediate agreement that an excellent instrument should be purchased to his search for a diplomatic solution when the government put his Board of Trustees on the spot. His decision to let Prystawski keep the instrument and his insistence, both to the auditor general and his own board, that he had the right to make this choice was standard Southam practice. He always liked to get his own way, although he did not hesitate to smooth the process by helping Prystawski out with a loan from his own pocket and expediting the purchase at a reduced price. For Prystawski, the violin would become a valuable asset in his old age. By 2006 it was worth around $400,000.

By March 1969 Beaudet had an upbeat report on the orchestra for the Board of Directors. Applications had been received from all over the world, including Asia, and nearly two hundred musicians had been given formal auditions. While there were still a few places for string players, Beaudet was satisfied that the orchestra was being created with little damage to existing major Canadian orchestras. No musicians had been hired from the Toronto Symphony Orchestra, only one or two from the Montreal Symphony, and one each from Winnipeg and Vancouver.

Beaudet also gave the trustees a taste of the music Ottawa might hear in the coming years. Two subscription series were planned for the opening season, "a balance of classic, romantic and contemporary music" that would include an all-Stravinsky program, Mendelsohn's Italian Symphony, the Schumann piano concerto, and works by Britten, Bartok, Wagner, and Schoenberg. Bernardi would also run a chamber music series, and the first year would end with a group of pop concerts in June. The most exciting idea was the proposal for at least three new works to be commissioned from Canadian composers. In addition, the NAC had included children's concerts in its plans and had hired Ron Singer as head of Youth Programming. He was already working on a series of school matinées with the full orchestra, in collaboration with school boards on both sides of the Ottawa River. Day trips by the orchestra to local towns were in the works. The key to the orchestra's success would be its acceptance by the residents of the National Capital Region, and plans were under way to secure this bond.

The previous fall, another top arts professional had been persuaded to join the Art Centre team. Mary Jolliffe, an exuberant, red-haired, frank-talking, sometimes hard-drinking enthusiast, was one of the best public-relations experts in the business. She had built her reputation with companies ranging from Stratford and the O'Keefe Centre to New York City, where she had worked with the Metropolitan Opera on various projects, including tours of its national company, and she was an old friend of Bruce Corder's from O'Keefe Centre days. She was yet another of the arts veterans who was completing a brilliant turn as PR director for cultural affairs at Expo 67. When it became obvious that the connections of the first public-relations director, Laurent Duval, were too limited for the job ahead, he decided to leave, and Corder telephoned Jolliffe to invite her to Ottawa. In hiring Jolliffe, the pitching of the National Arts Centre would move from what had been a "modest small-town venture" into the international big leagues.[11] If Southam wanted to put the NAC on the map, he could not have found a better person.

By March 1969, with opening night just over eight weeks away, David Haber was now the head of programming and in charge of the opening festival. Construction of the building was at last edging to completion. The turnover date was set at May 31, 1969, with the first performance slated to follow two days later on June 2. Haber had Southam's support for his plans for the opening events: the real celebration would occur when the curtain went up on the first performance in each of the three halls.

OPEN
AT LAST

On the glamorous but rain-lashed evening of June 2, 1969, when Prime Minister Pierre Trudeau and the other splendidly attired guests arrived for the first performance in the National Arts Centre, they were treated to a new work commissioned by the National Ballet of Canada. Conscious of the honour accorded the company, artistic director Celia Franca had gone to great lengths to ensure a memorable evening. With the bilingual, bicultural nature of the Arts Centre in mind, she had called on her "favourite choreographer in the world," the Englishman Anthony Tudor, to contrive a ballet based on a story by Voltaire. After months

Newly minted Prime Minister Pierre Elliott Trudeau and his companion, Madeleine Gobeil, already appointed to the new NAC board, made a stunning and much-talked-about couple at the NAC's opening night, June 2, 1969. Photo © Ottawa Citizen/UPI. Reprinted by permission.

of tinkering, Tudor had informed Franca that he was uninspired and could not produce the work. With only a few months left before the opening, she had turned urgently to another friend in the dance world, the French choreographer Roland Petit. As Franca remembered, she felt out of ideas at this point, so she gave Petit a free hand to pick the work, the music, and the designer for this commission.[1]

The result was *Kraanerg,* an avant-garde ballet with discordant electronic-sounding orchestral music by Greek composer Iannis Xenakis. The kinetic set was designed by the Hungarian-born, French-based "wizard of op-art," Victor Vasarely. The dancers, clad in stark white leotards cinched tightly at the waist with wide belts, had struggled hard to learn the steps. No clear discernable melody marked the score, and American conductor Lukas Foss resorted to a metronome and stop-watch to keep the beat. The dancers intensely counted their way through the movements with the aid of their French-speaking ballet master, who stood in the wings calling out the beats: "une, deux, trois." Ballerina Veronica Tennant recalled the experience as "out of the space age, like being in *Star Trek.*"[2] Still, the elastic geometric manoeuvres would be hailed by the critics, including the demanding dance critic Clive Barnes of the *New York Times.*

Barnes had been lured to the first night audience by Mary Jolliffe's energetic international promotion of the new centre as well as the prospect of a new ballet. He later reviewed the evening as "the same sort of disaster as the first night of *Swan Lake,*

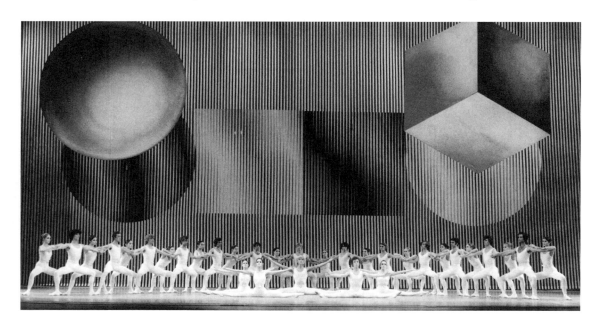

Kraanerg, performed by the National Ballet of Canada to ear-splitting music by Greek composer Iannis Xanekis, proved a challenge to the opening-night audience. Photo © Anthony Crickmay. Courtesy of the National Ballet of Canada.

Pierre Trudeau loved ballet and went backstage with Madeleine Gobeil after the controversial Kraanerg *to congratulate the performers. Dance star, later NAC board member, Veronica Tennant is on the extreme right. Photo © Ottawa Citizen/UPI. Reprinted by permission.*

shocking on first viewing but with music and dance that will endure."[3] As the two-week opening festival continued, Franca later recalled she could pinpoint the moment when at least thirty to forty patrons would rise in the middle of Xenakis's discordant music and leave the hall. But on this opening night, the audience politely sat it out. Whatever the aesthetic demands, "real culture" had arrived in Ottawa. This work went on to sporadic performances in the regular season of the National Ballet and became part of its repertoire. It would later be used by the Arts Centre as an example of one of the ways it should "assist the Canada Council in the development of the performing arts in Canada"--an essential part of its new mandate.

In designing the program for the two-week opening performances, David Haber had two key goals: to intrigue the audience by its diversity and to let the Arts Centre show itself off. Subsequent ballet performances included the sure crowd-pleaser *Swan Lake* and a sumptuous performance of *Romeo and Juliet*. On one of these evenings, a technical failure in the opera hall's grand new machinery took top honours. After a mis-touch of a button, the orchestra suddenly rose up out of the pit in mid-performance and travelled on past stage level to tower over both the performers and the audience. Franca, dancing the role of Lady Capulet in the ballroom scene of *Romeo and Juliet,* rushed to the wings and stopped the performance. As things settled and the platform descended again, a witty violinist tied his handkerchief to his bow and waved good-bye to the audience while the musicians sank back out of sight.

The rest of the programming unfolded relatively without hitch and mostly to critical praise. The Montreal and Toronto Symphony orchestras performed, and the Vancouver Playhouse brought a production of a new Canadian play, George Ryga's *Ecstasy of Rita Joe,* which portrayed the lostness of a First Nations girl in modern urban Canadian society. The production drew excited interest on Parliament Hill, where a Commons Committee on Indian Affairs was studying this very issue.

George Ryga's play The Ecstasy of Rita Joe, *about a benighted young First Nations girl, was also featured in the opening week. Then Minister of Indian Affairs and Northern Development Jean Chrétien and his wife, Aline, attended and met actor Chief Dan George at a post-play reception. Photo © John Evans.*

Le Théâtre du Nouveau Monde opened the Theatre with an outrageous and witty musical adaptation of Aristophanes's *Lysistrata* written by Michel Tremblay and directed by the sensational young Québécois director André Brassard. The Studio, the experimental three-hundred-seat space designed to function like a television studio, scheduled Jack Winter's *Party Day,* a three-dimensional work that had the audience sitting on all sides. Commissioned by the Arts Centre, the play revolved around the Nazi Party and the Nuremburg rallies. Even before opening night, this theme had elicited worried complaints from the German ambassador in Ottawa and the city's chief rabbi. Winter's message, a strong warning against government sponsorship of the arts, was received through gritted teeth by the first-night audiences and, after its NAC run, the play disappeared virtually without trace. Its inclusion in the opening festival signalled, however, that the new Arts Centre would be brave and audacious in what it presented.

Not everything on offer during these first two weeks was "high-brow." One of the NAC's basic tenets was to offer variety—and that would include a vast range of popular entertainers booked by the Arts Centre or by private impresarios who would rent the halls. Singers Gordon Lightfoot and Monique Leyrac were among the "popular" artists who played to sold-out audiences.

Despite the appearance of leading Quebec artists, Radio Canada was reluctant, given the nationalist sentiments stirring in Quebec, to report on these events in Ottawa. Finally, top CBC brass intervened and ordered at least some cursory coverage. CBC English television, in contrast, pulled out all the stops to cover the opening celebrations, with Bruno Gerussi on hand to host the proceedings. In the midst of a live broadcast on the first night, Gerussi chivvied Southam about his resplendent formal attire of white tie and medals. The good-humoured Southam gave back as good as he got. He was "on duty" this particular evening, he explained, so had to appear "in

The avant-garde Studio theatre set up for performances of Jack Winter's play Party Day, *which attacked the government's role in the arts. Photo © Studio Graetz.*

uniform," but when he later attended the Arts Centre for pleasure, he assured the interviewer that he would dress more like the tieless, wide-lapelled, bell-bottom-clad broadcaster himself, even asking the hapless Gerussi for the name of his tailor.[4]

Gerussi summed up the evening's events as "a mix of Carnaby Street and old school tie. Miniskirts and full-length minks … ruffled shirts and … the faint smell of mothballs"—in short, the Canadian scene on the eve of the 1970s. This mix of tradition with openness to the modern was at the core of Southam's approach, and it would be central to much of the programming at the NAC during his tenure. Combining the two would be his challenge in the years ahead as he moved to establish the National Arts Centre on the Canadian arts scene. The opening festival was meant to demonstrate

Actor Bruno Gerussi hosted a live CBC Television broadcast of the opening. Prime Minister Pierre Trudeau was interviewed. Photo © John Evans.

that the best and most challenging national and international work would be presented at the NAC.

The media response to the opening exceeded the organizers' wildest dreams. The press was filled with rave reviews for the building, the performances, and the very idea of a multi-performing arts centre of international standard on the banks of the Rideau Canal. Mr. Pearson's hopes seemed fulfilled; all eyes were focused on the capital. The international wire services AP and UPI, *The Times* of London, the *New Yorker* magazine, and the *New York Times* all covered the event, thanks to the prodigious efforts of Mary Jolliffe.

Amid the excitement of the opening events and the praise from the critics, a major crisis was brewing—the budget. Accustomed to the free-flowing expense accounts at Expo and the buzz needed to attract the hard-boiled international media, Jolliffe had realized soon after her arrival at the Arts Centre that there was insufficient money for the job she had to do. She told Southam right from the start that they needed at least $600,000 to promote the opening festival, but little more than half this amount had been approved for the entire first year's publicity budget. With only eight months before the opening when she arrived in Ottawa, she knew they had to "go like hell" and, while Southam worked on the financial side to try to increase the funding, she began to spend money as she saw fit. She found Southam an easy and amenable boss. When she brought him a draft of the first brochure, he inquired, laconically, "Am I supposed to approve this?" [5] He was never arbitrary in his decisions, she found, but usually deferred to the expertise of "the professionals"—Beaudet, Haber, Corder, and, indeed, herself. She thought Southam "a classy gent," equal to the leading arts czars of the era, men such as the Met's Sir Rudolf Bing and England's Tyrone Guthrie.

By May, before the Arts Centre even opened, not only had Jolliffe blown through most of the first-year PR budget but there were looming budgetary problems in other departments as well. Southam warned the Board of Trustees that there would likely be over-expenditures in some areas, including operations, and even in catering, where a row with the newly contracted concessionaire was spelling financial trouble. The problems were serious, the costs were already running $250,000 over budget for the year, and Southam appeared before a parliamentary committee to say that the new National Arts Centre really needed a budget of $3 million a year. He would later comment ruefully that his pitch "had not been a strong enough smoke signal." [6]

The board chairman, Lawrence Freiman, was deeply upset. He had promised Judy LaMarsh that the centre would live within the original $2.5 million budget, whereas Southam had blithely been pushing ahead. In several heated arguments with Freiman, he rationalized that public interest was much stronger than expected and, moreover, the basic costs had gone up. While the trustees urged senior staff to exercise better financial management, Southam argued in a memorandum to the May board meetings that they were dealing with artistic and theatrical temperaments—which functioned differently from those engaged in other activities. Freiman struggled hard to put better financial controls in place, even as he pushed to get the revenue-producing small shops along Elgin Street opened and the other commercial concessions paying some rent. The board floated yet another idea for fundraising in support of the NAC—a national lottery—but lotteries were still illegal in Canada and considered by many to be immoral. The plan was quickly rejected by the secretary of state's officials and then by the deputy minister of the Treasury Board as "an ineffective way to raise money over an extended period."[7] The dispute over money between Southam and Freiman continued through many meetings, with Freiman so distressed at one point that he left the proceedings and turned them over to his deputy, Claude Robillard. The effort would affect Robillard's already failing health, and, in October, he was forced to retire altogether from the board.

Jolliffe had worked hard to entice the Canadian and the international press to take an interest, and she introduced many of the leading journalists to Southam. He in turn beguiled them with lunches at the Rideau Club featuring the best food and wines, polished off with brandy and one of his Monte Cristo cigars. Whatever it took, the plan worked. Leading critics turned up to review the opening performances: Nathan Cohen, Canada's outstanding theatre writer; Clive Barnes of the *New York Times;* Courtney Towers from *Time* magazine; and Hilary Brigstocke, Ottawa correspondent for the London *Times,* all gave them extensive coverage. Many of the more thoughtful articles looked well beyond the gilded two weeks of the opening festival to ponder what this new arts emporium would mean to the Canadian public.

While Jolliffe had pulled off an international public-relations coup and the name of the National Arts Centre had appeared around the world in the quality press, she now had little left in the kitty to promote the first regular seasons of orchestra, theatre, and other performances that would soon be starting on the NAC stages. Southam had not discouraged her efforts for the opening, and she had achieved what he wanted. But now the bills were coming due, and that spelt trouble.

The first public signs of the problem came in an article by John Drewery, the national CBC political correspondent. On June 13, as the thrill of the opening peaked, Drewery reported that the brand-new arts palace was already running out of money. What was worse, the source of the story turned out to be the sometimes-bibulous Mary Jolliffe herself. Jolliffe developed close relations with her press clients and had let her hair down with Drewery, giving him a glimpse of what was going on behind the scenes. Alarm bells rang furiously on Parliament Hill, and Southam raced to assist the deputy minister, Jules Léger, to fashion a statement for the new Secretary of State Gérard Pelletier to deliver in the House of Commons. Peppered by the

Opposition, Pelletier spoke in the Commons on June 18, insisting that the real story was the "NAC's immediate success from coast to coast and the aura it gave off of being a permanent Expo." Léger kept the minister on message with a follow-up statement, that 65 percent attendance had been expected for the opening festival, but the event had gone way beyond that with an overall audience of 86.6 percent. This huge increase in unexpected visitors, the minister declared, had cost money.

Despite these public declarations intended to draw off the attackers, the board was facing a major crisis. The press leak had left the politically appointed trustees extremely nervous. At the July meetings, in the face of their chagrin, a sheepish Hamilton Southam delicately and dexterously brought about the disengagement of Mary Jolliffe. After the triumphant opening she had helped so much to engineer, she left with much praise and three months' salary. Southam met personally with Pelletier, apologizing for the fuss and assuring him that the Arts Centre would henceforth respect its budgets.

The financial crisis that had been allowed briefly to surface was real. An extended struggle had been under way between Treasury Board officials and the NAC management throughout the opening celebrations. Southam had written earlier to ask LaMarsh to provide supplementary funds before her departure as the minister responsible. He had requested an additional $300,000 to $500,000 beyond the base $2.5 million budget that had been approved, but the Treasury Board was stubbornly holding the line. Southam argued tenaciously that a performing arts centre could not be treated like other government departments—that performance bookings often had to occur years in advance and that budgeting had to allow for this fact. It was a problem that would rage over the Arts Centre's budget and dog its planning down through the years.

The trustees grappled with the problem and discussed how they should keep the government abreast of the gravity of the situation. Southam crafted yet another detailed memorandum for the minister to take to Cabinet, setting out reasons for the overruns that blamed everything from higher electricity costs than those projected by the Department of Public Works two years before to the expense of servicing the huge and unexpected increase in visitors. He also dropped a first hint that revenues for the proposed resident companies in the upcoming season might also be less than expected. The question of an audience for the real work to come had yet to be fully addressed.

As public tempests swirled around the fallout from the grand opening, inside the Arts Centre, intense efforts were under way for its real artistic beginnings. David Haber had carefully booked in a light season of summer fare for the tourists who poured through Ottawa in July and August. It included the Charlottetown Festival musicals *Anne of Green Gables* and *Johnny Belinda* as well as the Quebec folkloric dance troupe Les Feux Follets. One of the outstanding successes was a small in-house production,

Love and Maple Syrup, an amusing cabaret show presented in the Studio which was so successful that it had an extended run on into September. A witty and ironic look at Canadian foibles, written by Louis Negin, it played on a few bilingual themes, including a spoof on a Quebecer ordering "un hamburger" with "tous les works" over the telephone. One of its stars was Jean Gascon's brother, Gabriel Gascon, who had taken classical French theatre studies in Paris and then moved to London, where he trained and worked in English theatre with the famed director Michel St. Denis. The show proved so popular that it would come back again the following year.

While this first summer season kept the Arts Centre functioning as it prepared for the future, the trustees recognized that they had not yet devised a winning formula for the Summer Festival. It had been Part Two of the original approval for the NAC and was expected to attract and accommodate hundreds of thousands of tourists, both Canadian and American, to the capital each summer. By the end of the first year of operations, the tour guides had logged more than 117,000 visits to the Arts Centre. These encouraging numbers did not necessarily translate into audience members, but they did show a tremendous interest in the new facility.

The coming regular seasons in music and theatre were beginning to shape up. After lengthy negotiations, a final deal, although imperfect from the NAC's point of view, had been struck with Stratford. The company would become a year-round operation, with a "substantial portion" of the six months away from its summer festival home spent in Ottawa. The company would also tour extensively around Canada and into the United States, but not under the NAC banner. Despite the newly acquired "National" in its name, Stratford would not become the English-language resident theatre company at the Arts Centre. Instead, it was contracted to present a limited number of plays there, and company members would do school programs and tours in the National Capital Region. The balance of the full theatre season would be filled out with other companies from across Canada booked into the centre by Haber. This was a bitter blow, especially to Lawrence Freiman, who had believed so strongly in his close ties with Stratford. The intense behind-the-scene power struggles, which included intervention by the Canada Council and the Secretary of State's office, had eventually aided Stratford's desire to operate independently of the Arts Centre, and even Southam felt let down by Stratford's management. Still, the company would provide a core to English theatre for the first season.

The approach to French theatre was entirely different. Jean-Guy Sabourin had established the philosophy, structure, and repertoire for his company along with its name, Théâtre Capricorne (summer solstice), and the board had approved his plans. They called for a resident French company at the Arts Centre with at least six actors contracted on a twelve-month basis. This troupe would also visit schools and tour shows in the National Capital Region and neighbouring communities. However, Sabourin's proposal to mix amateur players, mostly from Université d'Ottawa, with his professional troupe was firmly rejected by the board, which instituted a "professionals only" policy for performers at the centre. Sabourin accepted the decision, but not before defending his ideas by reading long excerpts from French director Jean Vilar of France's Théâtre National Populaire into the minutes.

As for the orchestra, the final auditions were complete and, by the end of July, the last players had been selected and contracted. Years later the orchestra's union representative would marvel that the contract was no more than a short letter signed individually with each player, although a strong collective agreement would eventually emerge.[8] For Maestro Bernardi, his initial terms of engagement left him with a thirty-day dismissal clause if things did not work out. Although he found this clause unsettling, he signed the offer anyway because his wife "had purchased a lovely new house in Ottawa which carried a large mortgage."[9] In mid-August the musicians' names were announced. Claiming "no compromise over quality," fully three-quarters of the players finally selected were Canadian, and many of the others were already resident in Canada.[10] For budgetary reasons, the musicians were not put on the payroll until the end of August. They would have barely a month to get to know each other, and just two weeks to rehearse and learn to play together in time for the opening concert on October 7, 1969.

Finding the audiences that would attend all these new performances was one of the biggest challenges over the summer. When Mary Jolliffe had arrived on the scene months before, she had strenuously advocated "good subscriptions as the backbone of support."[11] This credo was already being drummed into Canadian arts companies by American box-office genius Danny Newman, who had been brought to Canada at the expense of the Canada Council to preach this gospel. His techniques would work wonders for orchestra and theatre subscriptions all over the country, but the National Arts Centre Orchestra, which would go from zero to 90 percent subscriptions in less than three years, was to become his star pupil. Ken Murphy, the orchestra's new manager, was well aware that finding an "instant audience" for the untried and unknown ensemble in the first season was its biggest problem. He turned for help to a young local music-lover who had lived all her life in Ottawa, Evelyn Greenberg—an avid musician with a warm and positive personality.

Like Bernardi, Greenberg played both piano and harpsichord and, although an amateur, she had appeared with the CBC studio orchestra in Ottawa from time to time. She had met the NAC audition team of Beaudet, Bernardi, and Murphy when she was recruited to play for the musicians who travelled to Ottawa for their auditions. These sessions had been held in a run-down movie house in Hull, the Montcalm Theatre, because no other space was available. Greenberg admired how quickly Bernardi was able to select the candidates who could be of value to his new orchestra. In early August, at one of the popular outdoor evening concerts run by the CBC at Camp Fortune in Ottawa's beautiful Gatineau Hills, an agitated Jean-Marie Beaudet had seized her by the arm and declared, "You're the one!"[12] He explained that Ken Murphy and he were very worried about creating an audience for the new orchestra and asked if she would take on the task of rallying the locals. Greenberg accepted with alacrity and was soon on the telephone to Southam, asking if he would attend a meeting of a new booster club she was devising. The Arts Centre's management understood from the outset the value of good volunteers, and Southam readily complied.

Using a model that today's pyramid marketers would envy, Greenberg invited five friends to bring ten others to the first gathering and, before long, this network had mushroomed into small parlour meetings all over the city. Greenberg remembers it was the early days of Chargex credit cards, and she urged her friends: "Ladies, now take out your credit cards and buy your subscriptions!"[13] It worked. Before long, the opening concert was sold out, and sales for the rest of the season rapidly picked up. Before long, these volunteers evolved into the National Arts Centre Orchestra Association, with Greenberg as its first president. This group would be responsible over the years not only for selling tickets but for setting up scholarships, looking after visiting artists, supporting orchestral tours, and providing other invaluable services in support of music at the NAC.

While the music association concentrated on the orchestra, another group of volunteers was created to look after the overall interests of the Arts Centre and promote it throughout the community. These Friends of the NAC named themselves Nine Plus—after all the lively arts—and drummed up attention with a whole range of social engagements, including the first of many grand balls that would be held in the NAC's honour.

Efforts to plump up attendance for the first performances were greatly assisted by management's decision at the outset to keep ticket prices low. This policy was most effective when the NAC was paying visiting companies all-inclusive fees, but more difficult to control when they received just a share of box-office revenues. It meant that audiences could see a Stratford play for $4.50, two dollars less than the cost for the same performance at the Shakespeare Festival's summer home in southern Ontario. Similar discounts and other enticements were used to attract audiences to the French theatre; group discounts were introduced and low-priced "stand-by" tickets provided to attract seniors and students to attend. The organizers were racing against time, but the results were good. When the doors opened to the first season, a respectable number of audience members were in the seats. For the orchestra, 60 percent of the seats were pre-sold by subscription for Series A, while Series B had reached 40 percent by the opening performance. By the end of the first year, the paid attendance at both main music series would reach 80 percent and 61 percent, respectively, a phenomenal start for a brand new orchestra. The National Arts Centre Orchestra Association, created to stimulate community support, was gratefully acknowledged for its share in this success in the first annual report.

The magnitude of the operations getting under way cannot be overstated. The resourceful Haber had to balance, on a year-round basis, the programs prepared in-house with visiting companies both Canadian and foreign. Although proposed performances by then-controversial shows such as *Hair,* with its on-stage nudity, were nervously debated at the board level, Haber, with only one assistant to help him, became the single impresario who booked in nearly all the artists for the Arts Centre's several halls. He quickly established a policy of "big name artists" which would bring entertainers as diverse as Marlene Dietrich, Ravi Shankar, Harry Belafonte, and Duke Ellington to the NAC in the coming years. The walls of his small office were soon covered with massive charts and schedules, and Southam developed the habit of dropping by from time to time to find out just what was going to appear.

On the programming and public approval fronts, the National Arts Centre was off to a very good start.

GROWING
PAINS

Soon after the elegant opening at the National Arts Centre, novelist Mordecai Richler quipped in *Time* magazine, "We now have our own Yankee Stadium but no Babe Ruth!" The reviewers thought otherwise, however, and, as the new season of performances unfolded, they were generally well received. All considered, *Time* concluded, there was no doubt that "the new showcase ... has immeasurably improved the choices of entertainment for Ottawa residents."[1] Fastest off the mark and most enthusiastically received was the NAC's orchestra.

The first notes to float out across the floodlights to the audience were a drum-roll played by the twenty-three-year-old tympanist, Ian Bernard. He had come almost directly from his final exam at Quebec's Conservatoire de Musique into the new orchestra. At the very first concert, before the rest of the ensemble joined in, he led with the opening bars of Haydn's "Drumroll" Symphony No. 103. The work would rapidly become one of the orchestra's "party pieces." The rest of the first night's program set the model of what the new orchestra planned to present. The evening's soloist, Ronald Turini, played Schumann's only piano concerto, and there were excerpts from Wagner and Prokofiev. Then came a new piece, "Divertissement/Diversion for Orchestra," commissioned by the NAC from Canadian composer Murray Adaskin. While reviewers gave the Canadian work a lukewarm reception, there were several parts for solo work that allowed the individual musicians to show off their talents. Above all it spelled out clearly the commitment that the new orchestra intended to have to Canadian music.

Within a month the orchestra had made its first tour, giving concerts in four Quebec towns as far away as Val d'Or and Rouyn, at the request of the Quebec government. In February it gave its first out-of-town concert in Ontario, playing in Deep River, as well as making its first foray into the United States, playing at Dartmouth

College in Hanover, New Hampshire. At the same time, the orchestra signed its first recording contract—a three-year deal with RCA (Canada) for distribution by the record company in the United States, and elsewhere around the world by the CBC's International Service.

Back in Ottawa, the players attended to their other duties, visiting schools throughout the region with weekly demonstrations, playing in the pit for two opera performances by the visiting Canadian Opera Company, and presenting the first of a series of six chamber recitals. With this musical introduction, the NAC embarked on a golden time in its artistic life. Everyone believed that this new orchestral venture was different from any other enterprise in Canadian arts. The youthful musicians—their average age was twenty-six—were quickly dubbed the "Ottawa Youth Orchestra."[2] They needed their energy as they worked furiously from week to week to learn new repertoire. Despite the earlier machinations from Toronto and Montreal to prevent the creation of the new ensemble, critics in the Montreal and Toronto papers now applauded "Ottawa's arrival on the orchestral map" and "yet another orchestra of distinction in Canada."[3] Only when orchestra manger Ken Murphy turned up with Evelyn Greenberg at an early meeting of the fledgling Canadian Orchestra Association and offered the other delegates a copy of the NACO's first recording were they brought face to face with how much privilege this orchestra enjoyed compared to others in the country. There was some envy that the new band had progressed so far, so fast, when other long-established orchestras had to work so much harder for similar success.

Dance played its part in that first season with appearances by all three established Canadian companies: the Royal Winnipeg Ballet, Les Grands Ballets Canadiens, and the National Ballet of Canada. The Toronto company presented the first of what would become an annual tradition—a Christmas presentation of *The Nutcracker*. In modern dance, the Groupe de la Place Royale and the Toronto Dance Theatre both appeared, and dance performances generally attracted a respectably sized audience. The Canadian Opera Company presented two operas, *Rigoletto* and *Die Fledermaus*, and announced itself so pleased with the magnificent new Opera hall and the new NAC orchestra in the pit that it could not wait to come back again. Houses running at 90 percent capacity confirmed Ottawa's keen interest in opera as well.

But could the city maintain this level of audience support? In addition to all the in-house programming by the National Arts Centre, the old ties with the Montreal Symphony Orchestra remained. During the first summer festival, this orchestra had given five popular concerts in the new facility, and, in the first regular season, it was brought back for six more concerts. The local impresarios who had kept the classical music scene alive in Ottawa were still trying to do business. Tremblay Concerts, which had been a mainstay on the Ottawa scene, brought the Santa Cecilia, Moscow, and Cleveland orchestras to the Opera hall as well as the Toronto Symphony. The Concert Society of Ottawa brought its own music series, which had historically appeared in the auditoria of local high schools, to the new Theatre. This embarrassment of riches proved problematic for both the schedules and the pocket-books of Ottawa music lovers. The city, used to eight or nine orchestral concerts annually, was suddenly faced with thirty-five such events.

At the November 1969 meeting, the board resolved that a Program Committee would henceforth review all requests for rentals of the halls by local impresarios in all areas, in the interests of providing "a balanced artistic program" to the public.[4] The idea was to prevent "the clashes and crushes" which had occurred with competing events during the opening season, but the effect was to lead to the demise of the local impresarios who had sustained the city for so long. The NAC was taking a practical approach to the control of programming in its halls to ensure its own well-being as a priority. The policy applied to all programming areas from music to variety, and it would create tensions between local interests and those of the NAC that continued through the years.

On the English theatre side, things proceeded smoothly, with the Stratford Company presenting its well-travelled productions of *Hamlet* and *The Alchemist*, and the rest of the season filled out by other visiting companies, including the Shaw Festival, which brought a well-reviewed production of *The Guardsman*. Stratford's participation, although well compensated, was provided reluctantly, as its management continued to resist becoming the NAC's resident company on any but its own terms. The relationship between the two theatres would not endure. As Haber remarked later, "In my time we never got around to producing theatre at the NAC, except offstage."[5]

The real drama in this first season, however, was in the resident French company. Le Théâtre Capricorne had started its regular season with a production of Friedrich Durrenmatt's *La Visite de la Vieille Dame,* which opened to critical success on September 29 in the Theatre. But from the outset the performers, mostly actors imported from Montreal, had clashed with artistic director Jean-Guy Sabourin and, by mid-October, they were in open rebellion, refusing to work further with him. It was clear that these artists, schooled in the Montreal theatres of Le Théâtre du Nouveau Monde and Le Rideau Vert, were not interested in the sociological theories of the theatrical art-form which Sabourin and his associate theatre administrator, Benoit de Margerie, were trying to impose on their work, and they had little respect for Sabourin's methods.

The NAC was already being criticized by the Canada Council for the large size of its French theatre budget. Southam countered that he needed professionals, and that meant bringing actors from Montreal. Besides, he said, Le Théâtre Capricorne was "the only French-speaking professional theatre company outside Quebec."[6] Southam met individually with the French company members and thought he had worked out a compromise, but the strife continued. Pelletier was made informally aware of the problems through contacts in the Quebec theatre community. In an effort to solve the difficulties and save the French theatre season, the board authorized the vice-chair, actor Paul

Hébert, to set up a special committee of French-speaking trustees—Hébert, Madeleine Gobeil, and Andrée Paradis—to work out a plan. While the actors fundamentally did not agree with Sabourin's approach, the fact that most of them had been shipped in from Montreal aggravated matters. Ottawa was still a social desert at this time with virtually no good restaurants and no place to go at night after performances. This lack of Québécois conviviality, along with Sabourin's requirement that the performers do community work as well as the mainstage plays, had ensured revolt among his players.

By the February 1970 meetings, the board felt compelled to terminate Sabourin as the artistic director.[7] Sabourin gave the trustees a spirited defence of his ideas and even appealed directly to Minister Pelletier to intervene on his behalf, but his tenure at the Arts Centre was effectively over. By May, the board instructed Southam to negotiate a settlement with him. The original idea of a permanent French theatre company was temporarily cancelled, with what was left of Le Théâtre Capricorne to play an impresario role in the coming season.

It was back to the drawing board on how best to present French theatre. Southam again consulted Jean Gascon and other leading figures in French theatre, including the renowned French director Jean-Louis Barrault, who was booked to appear at the Arts Centre. Along with the criticism over the budget for French theatre, Southam also had to contend with controversy over a tour by Les Jeunes Comédiens, a group of young players associated with the Théâtre du Nouveau Monde, which was travelling the country under the auspices of the National Arts Centre. It was a rocky start to the NAC's efforts.

Behind the debacle in the French theatre lay a fundamental conflict between two strands of thought vis-à-vis the development of the arts, both internationally and now in Canada. In Europe, as in America, there was a move to "democratize" the arts. In Britain, the self-styled "liberal elites" of Maynard Keynes and his colleagues had moved to revamp Covent Garden and create the British Arts Council and other cultural organizations to serve the public as a whole, not just a select few. This group aimed to make its own tastes available to a wider public.

A similar idea for taking art to the masses was germinating in France, but the French approach was more proactively socialist. There the thrust was to create grass-roots, populist *maisons de culture* to pursue the goal of cultural democratization. These organizations cast the artist as a social activist whose job it was to work together with the populace to produce art. The old-line classic companies such as the Comédie Française would continue to be the state-run exemplars of traditional French culture much as they had always been, but, at the level of the populace, there was a desire to make art of and by the people.

The tension and differences between these two philosophical threads would have a significant impact on the future growth of the arts in Canada. The National Arts Centre, like Canada's other cultural organizations such as the Canada Council and the CBC, had been cast in the mould of their British forerunners, with the overall idea of excellence as a key component of their work. But the seeds of these French-grown ideas, exemplified at the Arts Centre by Sabourin, would inform at the deepest level Secretary of State Gérard Pelletier's approach to culture, and, through him, they would have a huge impact on the development of the arts in Canada in the coming years.

Chris Young, the editor of the *Ottawa Citizen*, identified the problem early in the first season of the NAC when he wrote, "There is a lingering sense … that the public is not really welcome at the Centre."[8] The performances were fine, but there was something about the place, an elitism, that put people off. Pelletier agreed with this perception and was quoted in the press as saying that "magnificent art centres sometimes seem to serve the elite … poorer people might be afraid to enter, fearing that they would be out of their element or be laughed at."[9]

The course was set for a fundamental rift between Director General Southam's vision for the Arts Centre and Minister Pelletier's approach. Southam did not seem to take much notice of Pelletier's remarks. He had ensured that the spanking new restaurant was stocked with the finest wines, and he delighted in entertaining his elegant friends there. Much later he acknowledged that he did not get along with Pelletier, who, he said, "thought I was elitist—and I was."[10] But this word did not carry the same sense of class for Southam that it did for Pelletier. Southam's idea of elitism, he declared, was "not people who thought they were the best but people who wanted the best," and his idea of the national importance of the NAC was straightforward. He believed firmly in the "centres of excellence" approach and thought that the composition of the Arts Centre should "reflect the Canadian reality with the appropriate proportion of French and English content": "if we could make it work here," he said, "it was working for the country."[11] Although he was aware of the growing problems in Quebec, particularly through his close friendships with Quebec artists such as Jean Gascon and Jean-Louis Roux, he paid little attention to the new approach to the arts and culture stirring in Canada which Pelletier was initiating.

Pelletier had come to Ottawa with several ideas in mind, but key among them were two: he wanted greater access to the arts for ordinary people and, paradoxically, he believed in more centralized control of the cultural organizations at his disposal to achieve his "decentralization and democratization" policy. In Quebec, Pelletier and his colleagues had seen the independence at the French-language CBC co-opted by a growing separatist movement, and they were leery of having these institutions beyond the control of the government. The free-wheeling, "arm's-length" independence enjoyed by the dedicated but powerful individuals who ran the cultural agencies was about to be subjected to growing pressure for control at the political level, all in pursuit of the new government's national goals.

Meanwhile, tensions within the Board of Trustees at the Arts Centre were coming to a head over issues of money. These concerns would lead to a vigorous shakedown in operations, but not before board chairman Lawrence Freiman and Hamilton Southam had come to a final show-down. During the October 1969 meetings, a major explosion between the two men became so intense that Southam walked out and sat reflecting for a while in the Theatre over whether he should resign. He didn't, but soon after, Freiman, already suffering from ill-health, gave up his post. At the core of the problem were two men who both loved their city, the arts, and the Arts Centre, but were as different "as chalk and cheese."[12] At the heart of their incompatibility were their different views of the world: Southam, the privileged elitist, who was used to the best and accustomed to getting it, seemingly without effort; and Freiman, the bedrock businessman, who knew the dangers of financial imprudence and sought sound business practices in operations. Freiman's resignation lanced a boil, but the real problems remained. Most immediate was the fact that the government was still offering $300,000 less than anticipated for the 1970–71 season (a $2.5 million subsidy, not the requested $2.8 million). Before this particular rumpus settled down, the chief financial officer, Robert Montpetit, had also resigned in protest. Southam and his deputy, Bruce Corder, vowed before the board that they would mend their ways and take steps to improve their operations.

On November 14, 1969, François Mercier, a brilliant and politically well-connected litigation lawyer from Montreal, was named to succeed Freiman as chair. Both Southam and Corder put a good face on what had occurred by arranging to call in the government's Bureau of Management Services to help put their house in order. Among their difficulties were the arrangements for catering, which had been contracted to the food management firm Gabriel Management Ltd. and which were not going well. One of the reasons was confusion over who controlled the liquor licence for the NAC, particularly after Gabriel issued huge invoices to the centre after the opening ceremonies. The board eventually decided to take the food service in-house, but not before trustee Dr. Arnold Walter registered caustically in the minutes of the November meeting that he deplored the fact that the pending deficit of over $100,000 was being caused by non-artistic matters. Parking revenues and other potential commercial revenue streams were still struggling to get up to speed, but the main cause of the deficit was the food service. In one of his first acts, Mercier intervened with Gabriel's lawyer to minimize the costs of disengagement to the Arts Centre.

By the end of the year, both board and management had put a bright face on the problems. Just the normal growing pains of any new organization, they said.

Another blow was in the offing. Shortly after the opening concert, music director Jean-Marie Beaudet was felled by a severe stroke. After all the brilliant work he had done to help create the new orchestra, he was able to attend only one more concert and could not resume his duties at the Arts Centre. He finally resigned formally from the NAC on February 1, 1971, and died a little over a month later. Orchestra manager Ken Murphy, who was deeply devoted to Beaudet, carried much of the load during the first months of his absence, working to the point of exhaustion, but once it was clear that Beaudet would not return, the burning question became who should succeed him. Beaudet, with his huge knowledge of music, had played a key role in programming for the first season, and his departure left a serious gap.

Bernardi, although an expert in opera, had limited experience with the symphonic repertoire, and he was now being severely stretched by the constant demands of building an orchestra, learning new repertoire, and programming the multifaceted concert season, replete with all its guest conductors and soloists. With no other obvious candidate in view, Southam finally gave Bernardi the job of music director in February 1971, though with promised support. Bernardi chose Hugh Davidson, a former CBC music producer now living in London and working with the BBC, to join the NAC in the new post of music administrator. His prime role was to assist the maestro with programming, and he arrived at the centre in mid-June. Davidson had an immense knowledge of symphonic and most other kinds of classical music, including some training in opera. His appointment would turn out to be a godsend—for a time.

Going into the second season, the orchestra was booming. Subscriptions had almost doubled for Year Two to 95 percent and 81 percent, respectively, for each of the two main concert series, and visiting orchestras, including the Montreal Symphony and the Winnipeg Symphony, had been programmed into the series and obtained good audiences. The NACO had played in the pit for visits by the big three ballet companies as well as the Canadian Opera Company. A growing chamber music series quickly became so successful that it had to be moved out of the intimate Salon and into the much larger Theatre. In addition, the

Mario Bernardi was the new orchestra's gifted and hard-driving leader. Photo © NAC.

orchestra's outreach program into the schools and its matinee concerts for children were already a roaring success. All this, plus radio and television broadcasts, and tours and appearances out of Ottawa, were putting the orchestra on the map. Still, there was space in the musicians' contract for more services, and Bernardi and Southam determined that they would fill it up with operas as they devised their plans for the new Summer Festival.

Theatre remained a different story. The revised plan for the 1970–71 season called for two series in the Theatre of six plays each, one French and the other English, showcasing major and regional theatres from across the country. The Théâtre du Nouveau Monde and the Stratford and Shaw Festivals would make their requisite appearances, but others such as Toronto's St. Lawrence Centre Theatre Company would also bring shows. This outreach by the Arts Centre would be a great asset for these theatre troupes, most of which had little money to tour. The NAC would foot the bill when they came to the capital, and, if they managed to fit in other appearances along the way, so much the better. In short, the Arts Centre would have a significant role as a catalyst in getting theatre companies out of their own hometowns to be seen elsewhere, especially in Ottawa. In the first two years of its existence, the NAC brought an incredible array of artists to Ottawa as it strove to show Canadians the services and the exposure it could provide.

The resourceful and sharp-eyed David Haber believed implicitly in the importance of the NAC's national role. Acknowledging that "you couldn't tour a building,"[13] he constantly toured himself, looking for plays and productions that he could bring into Ottawa. In Calgary he spotted one entertaining work that would have a seminal effect on all sorts of theatre activity at the NAC, but not necessarily because of what it put on the stage. The show was Theatre Calgary's musical production *You Two Stay Here, the Rest Come with Me,* written and directed by Christopher Newton, who later became artistic director of the Shaw Festival. It starred Sandy Crawley, an actor soon to have a large impact on the national theatrical scene, ultimately as a leading light in the actors' union. The show's producer was Richard Dennison, the company's founding administrator and production director who had also worked at Expo. Haber negotiated with him to bring the show to Ottawa in late spring 1970, just after the regular theatre season had ended. Dennison, whose whole family was bilingual, jumped at the chance to come back east. Although the show was a lively and entertaining commentary on the history of Calgary, seemingly tailor-made to inform and entertain audiences elsewhere, it did badly at the Ottawa box office because of its late scheduling. NAC officials concluded that, in future, similar excellent productions must be presented within the subscription series.

Despite the debacles with the first season of theatre in both languages and the decision to turn the main series into a showcase for other companies, Southam had not given up on the idea of having the Arts Centre produce its own theatre. While the main Theatre would be booked with established plays and visiting theatre companies, the Studio, "with its wonderful experimental space,"[14] was available. Before long, Southam and his team made another effort to try resident work. They called it the Studio Project.

Southam was clear about what he wanted: to put two separate companies in the Studio and let them take turns mounting productions in Canada's two official languages. He hired two artistic directors for this venture. On the French side he chose the Belgian-born Jean Herbiet, a professor of fine arts at Université d'Ottawa with excellent local connections and an intelligent knowledge of French-language theatre. A small man in stature, quiet and shrewd, he had a poetic nature but knew how to keep his counsel and work within the system. His admiration for Hamilton Southam was boundless—"a gentleman scholar, civilized with classic and good taste,"[15] all the things that an educated European would admire. On the English side, Southam chose Michael Bawtree, a theatre director who had once worked at Stratford and, more recently, had been at Simon Fraser University in British Columbia. Southam felt he had the right artistic people in these two men, but he needed someone to look after the two companies. Haber recommended his new bilingual friend, the twenty-five-year-old Richard Dennison. After a quick interview, Southam hired him to be the administrator of the Studio Project—an experience Dennison would later describe as "the worst administrative experience of my entire life."[16]

Southam instructed the team to put together a season of three or four plays in each language and bring in the best acting talent available in the country. On the English side it proved relatively easy to attract good performers, and Bawtree had no trouble recruiting such outstanding actors as Jackie Burroughs, Neil Munro, Blair Brown, Richard Donat, and others. Herbiet had much more difficulty finding actors. Although he used as much local talent as he could, he once again had to hire in from Montreal because there was so little other work for francophone actors in Ottawa. Nevertheless, the results on the French side proved to be more supportive of the overall vision for the National Arts Centre.

Jean Herbiet, the quiet-spoken but brilliant guide who helped realize French theatre at the NAC. Photo © NAC.

While Herbiet set about in a relatively conservative manner to produce his requisite series of plays, building his series on themes of "Love," Woman," and other basic concepts, Bawtree decided to take literally Southam's suggestions that he wanted original work and that the Studio was an "experimental space." His own history was decidedly experimental. He had served as dramaturge at the Stratford Festival and been a close friend there of director Michael Langham. He had travelled in South America with the aid of a Canada Council grant and had worked there "with a subversive group who saw theatre as a political tool."[17] He was firmly attracted to the anarchist point of view, tended to believe that people were "warped by hierarchical tendencies," and had pursued these ideas in the Drama Department at Simon Fraser University, which was known during this period as the "Berkeley of the North." Once again, Southam was about to get more than he bargained for.

Bawtree decided to do a collective work, *How Many People Went to the Island, What Happened, and Who Came Back.* The production started with "a four-page binder of research on the Spanish-American Civil War, largely put together by Bawtree's personal partner. The text contained not a word of dialogue, but the production did have an expansive eight-to-twelve weeks in which to rehearse. "They needed it," laughed Dennison later, "because they had nothing to work with." The actors sat down with Bawtree and collectively began to "interact," with Bawtree resolutely refusing to take charge or direct. "The first two weeks were very exciting," he would recall. For the overall production, however, matters rapidly spiralled downward into chaos, with the troupe split between those who enjoyed the unstructured improvisation and others who demanded a script, some direction, and even a designer for the play.

As the opening drew closer, some of the actors still thought it was great, while others became desperate with the anxiety of appearing before an audience without knowing what they were going to do. While Bawtree held to his principle that "people should not want to be told what to do," Dennison went personally to Southam to warn him that a catastrophe lay ahead. In the end, the pressure wore even Bawtree down. Although suggesting later that he had been "fascinated by the horror of it all,"[18] he was on the edge of a nervous breakdown and, before opening night, suddenly fled from Ottawa with his lover for a Caribbean island. The cast, by now regressed to something akin to the survivors in *Lord of the Flies,* were at each other's throat and, sure enough, opening night was an unmitigated disaster. The reviews were dismal, and the show played to audiences of fifty or less in the three-hundred-seat Studio before it finally petered out after a couple of weeks.

Bawtree's next production, *Pericles,* with original music to be written by the Quebec composer Gabriel Charpentier, was cancelled, and Haber raced around to find a substitute, booking in a light-hearted and innocuous show, *The Evanescent Review,* to plug the hole in the schedule. Years later, Bawtree had nothing but praise for the manner in which Southam had tolerated his behaviour. He had been treated kindly by the director general, who had even invited him out to his cottage at the Rideau Lakes. Although he saw the NAC leader as "an establishment man," he also found him extremely "open and unjudgmental."

In truth, Southam had not been able to bring himself to deliver the *coup de grâce* to Bawtree. Instead, he arranged for Herbiet to deliver the news to Bawtree that he was fired, and for Dennison to wind up the English theatre company.

Southam was not prepared to give up on theatre at the NAC, however, and he now hired Richard Dennison to move over and become his assistant while they tried again. The idea this time was "to get some proper scripts and do the damn thing and present them to the public."[19] In short, get back to basics, even though "these cutting-edge collective creations" were being successfully produced elsewhere, such as director Paul Thompson's *Farm Show* that played in a country barn as well as at Toronto's Theatre Passe Muraille.[20] A lot of innovative work was going on elsewhere at this time in Canada, especially in English-language theatre, but so far none of it had been translatable into home-grown work at the NAC. Despite the tumultuous theatre experiences to date, Southam persisted. The decision, put forward and accepted by the board, was "to create a Theatre Department parallel to the Music Department and to charge it in future seasons with full responsibility for both English and French theatre productions."[21]

Fortunately, Southam had in mind someone who would be the right person to ensure that this objective would be met. Jean Roberts was a soft-spoken but clear-headed Scot who had come to Canada from a job as stage manager with the Royal Shakespeare Company in England to do her own theatre productions. A consultant to the NAC's early Theatre Advisory Committee, she had gone on to join the Canada Council as its theatre officer, recommending and administering theatre grants across the country. Both Canada Council chair Jean Boucher and Southam had maintained offices for a time in the same building and had got to know her as they rode up and down in the elevator together. Roberts had already

Jean Roberts, the first director of theatre, who finally put theatre on the rails at the NAC. Photo © Murray Mosher Photography.

decided to give up bureaucracy and was packing her bags to leave Ottawa and return to directing theatre when she received a call from Southam just before Christmas. He asked if they could get together first thing in the new year. She agreed.

When they met, Southam immediately offered her the job of running theatre at the Arts Centre. Before accepting, she consulted theatrical friends, including playwright Timothy Findley and his companion Bill Whitehead. After her English experience, she wasn't frightened by the size of the job, and both men urged her to take it on. When she got back to Southam, she indicated that she would accept, but under certain conditions. She wanted overall control of the theatre in both languages—programming, marketing, and budgets. Like Haber and her soon-to-be boss Southam, she believed that, "if the French/English thing was to work anywhere in Canada, it would be at the National Arts Centre."[22] Southam concurred and, fortunately, Herbiet was content to go along with the arrangement, becoming associate director of theatre. Roberts later remarked that she had once contemplated writing up job definitions for all her departmental staff, but she came to realize that the French side of things had an entirely different set of problems from those that the anglophones faced. In Herbiet she had the right colleague.

Roberts believed that Southam had hired her because, after her experience at the Canada Council, she would understand the bureaucratic processes with which the NAC had to deal. She did, but she also had a vision of what the NAC could do to develop theatre in Canada. Sometimes her views tripped over Southam's notions of the grand things he would like to see at the centre. Roberts had direct contacts with important English theatre figures such as Laurence Olivier, for example, and Southam liked the idea of inviting him to the NAC, although he thought he should do the asking. Roberts felt the big money that would require should be directed to Canadian theatre. In the end, Olivier was not booked.

In one instance, however, Southam's propensity for occasionally having his own way did affect what played at the Arts Centre. Herbiet and he had visited the Comédie Française in Paris, where Herbiet targeted a brilliant French production of *Richard III* that Paul Duke, then the head of the Comédie, wanted to tour in Canada. For Southam, however, the great French company meant great French works, and that meant Molière—and it was Molière's plays, at his behest, that were indeed booked to come to the NAC.

Overall, however, Southam was proving to be a "terrific leader" who, by and large, didn't interfere.[23] He had a clear vision, and he didn't lose his nerve when mistakes occurred. His best solutions happened when he finally landed on the right people for a job, gave them the tools and the money, and got out of their way. This policy had worked in music with Beaudet and Bernardi, and now was the time for theatre. In Jean Roberts and her associate Jean Herbiet, he had finally found the winning combination. Although Herbiet now had to report to Roberts rather than directly to Southam, he trusted her and believed her to be "fair."[24] In their respective domains, they would both build theatre at the National Arts Centre which would contribute significantly to the growth of the theatrical art form, in both languages, in Canada.

Roberts brought to the job an excellent bird's-eye view of the overall theatre scene in Canada gained through her time at the Canada Council. Now she set out to improve that world. Among other things, she began to build the theatre crafts at the Arts Centre, including set-building and costume workshops. Visiting companies would also be able to make good use of these facilities when they came to town. At the same time, she introduced real stage work for the competent stage crews who were slowly building their skills and earning a reputation as some of the best in the business.

At long last, theatre at the National Arts Centre began to proceed in a more orderly manner. The main venue for the work shifted back to the Theatre, although smaller pieces, and especially experimental work, continued to be produced in the Studio. The next six years would see the vision that Roberts wanted for theatre all over Canada developed at the NAC: the production of plays by Canadians, and steady work for the best Canadian talent. Her first season in 1971–72 sent a strong signal about her intentions. She knew that the regional theatres in Canada would think her situation "a bit rich," and she thought it essential for the NAC to be accepted by these theatres across the country. Entitling her first season "Theatre from Coast to Coast," she provided the funds to bring in "a judicious mix of invited theatre companies."[25] The bare outlines of an embryonic NAC theatre company also began to appear in productions such as James Reaney's *Colours in the Dark,* directed by Roberts's friend and companion Marigold Charlesworth, and *Tango* by Polish playwright Slawomir Mrozek, jointly directed by Roberts and Charlesworth. The play was hailed by the *Toronto Star*'s demanding theatre critic Urjo Kareda as "Ottawa's pride." He also ruminated on how this work could be toured and seen elsewhere—an idea which resonated close to home at the Arts Centre. The Ottawa public was equally enthusiastic, and Roberts felt proud

Jean Gascon in the 1978 production of August Strindberg's The Father, *directed by Donald Davis. Photo © Murray Mosher Photography.*

that her work "provided a kind of correspondence with the public." Certainly the new productions pulled in full and enthusiastic houses.

Both Roberts and Charlesworth had a strong commitment to developing audiences and reaching out to serve the "national" side of the NAC public, particularly in regard to young audiences. Although the Arts Centre was a long way from touring its own plays, the idea of the Hexagon/L'Hexagone was born at the start of the second season in 1972. Modelled on the Theatre Hour Company, a young people's company in Toronto with which Charlesworth was associated, the plan was to take the NAC's resources out to the public beyond Ottawa by sending a troupe of young actors on tour to schools. Travelling in a brightly coloured bus, these enthusiastic bands of troubadours, one in each language, would present excerpts, mostly from Canadian plays, in high schools wherever they could go. In the first season, more than 37,000 students saw their work, and it would only get better over the next few years. With this emphasis on youth, the project was warmly endorsed by the board, and Ottawa-based students were not ignored. Roberts set up a Student Young Company for those lucky enough to live close enough to see the NAC's regular plays. This group took selected local students a step further, behind the scenes, giving them workshops and apprenticeships in theatre craft.

The H/H Project, before it was ultimately cancelled for financial reasons in the early eighties, achieved a level of success with student audiences which, until now, had been rare in Canada. The French version, which outlived the English, at its zenith toured its company of young French-speaking actors all the way from Victoria, British Columbia, to the French islands of St. Pierre and Miquelon off the Atlantic coast. To Herbiet as well as Southam and the board, it showed that "this place could do a lot!"

In less than two seasons, Roberts had laid down a solid foundation. By the 1972–73 season, ten plays in each official language were scheduled, and eight of them were the NAC's own productions. Roberts's recipe for this putative "National Theatre in Canada" included presenting plays from the classic repertoire, supporting new Canadian playwrights, employing the best available Canadian talent, and using the laboratory setting of the Studio for experimentation and encouraging the work of new writers. By the 1973–74 seasons the effort was producing astonishing results: attendance figures for English theatre hit 94 percent, and an astounding 91 percent for French theatre. Within the organization, Roberts insisted that the civil-servant-minded culture also respect the fact that they now had a more or less permanent group of people rehearsing or working on the premises. She railed when there was no toilet paper in the bathrooms on Sundays simply because the building's cleaners were used to working five days a week. And she disabused the financial department that they could wait thirty days to pay the performers, explaining that actors were used to getting their money every Friday. She demanded respect for the theatre operation.

Herbiet's task in the French theatre was particularly tricky and depended on his careful selection of "a balanced cocktail of works."[26] He was interested in programming avant-garde European writers such as Ionesco and Brecht along with "the classics with a new take" and, of course, the new exciting Quebec theatre that was emerging. But the francophone community from which he had to draw his main audience was different from the fervent and increasingly nationalistic public in Montreal and elsewhere in Quebec. The local audience in Ottawa came largely from the well-educated ranks of Ottawa's and Hull's sedate bourgeoisie. They were interested in French theatre and delighted to have it readily available, but they were conservative and traditional in their tastes. When Michel Tremblay's first great success, *Les Belles Soeurs,* opened in Montreal to huge acclaim, Herbiet received a petition from the local community asking him not to present that kind of work in Ottawa. Only after Tremblay's work had been translated and successfully presented in English-speaking Toronto did he feel able to schedule such plays regularly into the French-language season.

Herbiet's own productions brought the Arts Centre some of its greatest credit and success, among them ingenious versions of Georg Büchner's *Woyzeck* and a bilingual *Dream Play* by August Strindberg. These productions were unique, using marionettes rather than actors on stage and created by the German-born master puppeteer Felix Mirbt, whom Herbiet had befriended at Stratford. The two artists collaborated on the scripts, with Herbiet doing the adaptations and writing. Nothing like this had ever been seen before in Canada, and *Dream Play* would later tour to Montreal's Centaur Theatre, the Edinburgh Festival, Belgium, and elsewhere in Europe under the NAC banner. Southam and the board put a lot of stock in the success of Herbiet's work, and described it in the 1971–72 Annual Report as "the cornerstone of our commitment to the ideals of bi-lingualism and bi-culturalism."

As the Theatre Department moved gradually forward, a well-grounded basis was laid and operations moved closer to

The partnership of the puppeteer Felix Mirbt (left) and Jean Herbiet, in rehearsals of Woyzeck, *produced some of the most exciting and successful early theatre at the NAC. Photo © Fernand R. LeClair.*

the resident companies that Southam had hoped for from the start. By 1973, Timothy Findley became the first occupant of a playwright-in-residence program, working closely with the company and learning about stagecraft. The following season his new play, *Can You See Me Yet?*, would be produced by the Arts Centre. In 1974 a mini-tour of John Hirsch's production of *The Dybbuk* was sparked by the NAC's invitation to bring it to Ottawa, and in 1975 John Coulter's 1950s work *Riel* was mounted with the astonishing Quebec actor Albert Millaire playing the lead. In the same season, Millaire crossed over to direct a Le Théâtre du Nouveau Monde production of the Federico García Lorca play *La Maison de Bernarda Alba* for the French theatre season. Roberts gave work to many individuals who would go on to have strong roles elsewhere in Canadian theatre. In 1972 she brought the English Shakespearean actor John Neville to the Arts Centre to play in the Restoration comedy *The Rivals*, and as Prospero in Shakespeare's *The Tempest*. This fortuitous casting would lead to Neville's being hired later as artistic director at Edmonton's Citadel Theatre. He went on to become an influential figure in the Canadian theatre world.

Within a few years, "a remarkable level of cooperation" had been achieved between the two theatre groups at the NAC, "each working from its own inheritance."[27] Roberts acknowledged that they had managed to establish a solid "resident production." Some of the players even felt secure enough to buy real estate in Ottawa—including the actor Edward Atienza, one of whose best roles to date had been to play a speechless dog

in a production of Findley's *Can You See Me Yet?* There was still no permanent resident company, however, and Roberts and others now began to push hard for it.

Left to right: designer Robert Prévost, Jean Gascon, Jean Roberts, and composer Gabriel Charpentier in rehearsal for the 1975 Riel. *Photo © Robert D. Ragsdale/NAC.*

FESTIVALS AND
FINANCING

Music, theatre, and dance were not the only items on Southam's vast agenda as the National Arts Centre moved into the early 1970s. He also negotiated with the Board of Trustees on the centre's financial affairs, kept up a stream of communications through memorandums and meetings with an assortment of government officials, and smoothed the way with the politicians by judicious appearances before the Parliamentary Standing Committee. Above all he turned again to one of his central interests—the Summer Festival—part two of the government's original approval for the Arts Centre.

The initial attempt at a festival had been slated for the summer of 1970, but had been stopped by the board in late August 1969 for lack of funds. That first plan had been hugely ambitious. The Festival would begin on July 1, Dominion Day, as it was then called, and run for a month in Ottawa. It was to have a wide range of attractions, some of which would be run by other government departments, such as the folkloric festivities on Parliament Hill to be presented by amateur ethnic dance and singing groups from around the country. Others, including a possible raftsmen's festival on the Ottawa River or excursion trips into the Gatineau Hills for outdoor concerts, were to be organized by the City of Hull or the CBC. The goal of all these activities was to make Canada's capital even more attractive during the summer when it was inundated with thousands of visitors from Canada and abroad. The inspiration for the idea was the Edinburgh Festival, and, like it, the key attractions would be the music, dance, and drama performances that, in this case, would be produced at the NAC.

In planning this first projected Festival, Southam had travelled extensively, visiting London and Paris and touring Europe from Paris to Prague to view performances that might find a potential audience in Ottawa, He had laid the groundwork meticulously for what he conceived as a major national and international event in Ottawa based on a suitable theme: "an exploration of the encounter and mutual enrichment of the cultures of the English- and French-speaking worlds."[1] Having ready access at the highest political levels in both France and England, he had met and dined with the most senior cultural figures, including French culture minister André Malraux and the minister for the arts in the United Kingdom, Jennie Lee. As a former diplomat, Southam knew how to pull the ropes, and his formidable and elegant presence made him an excellent envoy on behalf of the arts.

Particularly delicate had been his inquiry in Paris, where the fallout from President Charles de Gaulle's hasty exit from Quebec during Expo 67 was still fresh in people's minds. As his report to the board later revealed, he had beguiled the cultural ministers in both of Canada's founding countries by inviting them to become patrons of such a festival. Malraux, who perhaps saw an opening for further inroads in Canada in these politically volatile times, took special note, indicating that he would pursue it with his government and consider coming to the event himself if that was approved. Jennie Lee wrote Southam a friendly personal letter saying that though she would likely be out of office by the time the Festival happened, she would ensure that it continued to receive full support. She labelled her efforts-to-be "a friendly conspiracy" between the two of them, and assured Southam that he would likely get what he wanted from the British. Just to be sure, Southam had hired Lord Harewood, the former director of the Edinburgh Festival, in London, and Albert Sarfati in Paris as consultants to line up the European talent (see chapter 2). Harewood, one of the Queen's first cousins, would remain a lifelong friend, becoming godfather to one of Southam's children.

All these plans came to naught when the 1970 Summer Festival was cancelled, although some of the ideas would resurface in future festivals in Ottawa. In the aftermath of Expo, cultural spending was beginning to slow down, and officials in the Secretary of State's department and at the Canada Council gave a chilly reception to spending an estimated million dollar budget on bringing largely foreign talent to Ottawa—even if it was "the best."

Canada passed through a horrific storm in the fall of 1970 with the October Crisis. The imposition of the *War Measures Act,* which was quickly invoked by the Trudeau government to halt a possible civil insurrection, had seen the leafy streets of Ottawa's Rockcliffe Park, where Southam and many of the country's leaders and foreign diplomats lived, filled with army personnel in full battle gear. The aftermath of these events would have an impact on the way the national government would conduct its affairs in the future, especially in its deployment of cultural resources. In the immediate term, the crisis forced increased security around the NAC building, at a cost of $1,500 to the budget. More important was a sea change in outlook that Southam articulated later—that "something cracked" in this period.[2]

Just weeks before the crisis, the trustees had given Southam a cautious green light to explore the Summer Festival concept once again. He lost no time in getting together with Bernardi, and they began to devise a far more modest but still exciting plan that involved using leftover time in the orchestra's contract and tapping into Bernardi's wide experience with opera. Their decision was to build the Festival around what would be the NAC's first opera production. They selected Mozart's *Marriage of Figaro,* a work that was tailor-made for Bernardi. The maestro, proficient at the keyboard as well as on the podium, agreed to play the harpsichord for the recitatives throughout the opera. Together, they intended this first effort to be the template for bigger Festivals in the future.

Once again, Southam moved carefully to implant the Festival idea in people's minds, working up the same wave of enthusiasm that had helped to create the Arts Centre. On March 8, 1971, I. Norman Smith, the editor of the *Ottawa Journal* and a good Southam friend, editorialized that "Ottawa could be the Edinburgh of America" and that Mario Bernardi, as "a director of both music and opera," was "a man of the future." "We are young and gay," he proclaimed, as he urged Ottawans to enter into the spirit of the times and rhapsodized about the possibilities for Ottawa with the Festival. He envisioned activities ranging all the way from classical music at the Arts Centre to the raftsmen's event on the river, even as he endorsed bus tours and fishing events in the beautiful Gatineau Hills across the river in Quebec. It was not hard to detect the hidden enthusiast behind Smith's pen.

In April, board chair François Mercier proudly announced the details publicly. The Festival would be a "panoply of the arts," he said, with five performances of Mozart's *Marriage of Figaro* directed by Sir Tyrone Guthrie and with a Canadian cast that included Claude Corbeil, Allan Monk, Judith Forst, and Heather Thomson.[3] Four concerts by the Arts Centre orchestra were planned, featuring four new Canadian works, and the Royal Winnipeg Ballet would present a spectacular dance based on George Ryga's play *The Ecstasy of Rita Joe.* French theatre would be included by a Théâtre Rideau Vert production of Tremblay's *Les Belles Soeurs,* directed by André Brassard. Chanteuse Monique Leyrac and the popular duo Ian & Sylvia would satisfy popular culture fans, and the aboriginal singer, storyteller, and composer Alanis Obomsawin was also booked for her own show. These events were but a taste of the feast planned throughout July, and it was all to be followed by a "Young August" program at the Arts Centre aimed at younger people, featuring young artists, rock bands, and other popular groups.

This clever recipe for programming seemed to cover all the touchstones of a stirring Canadian identity that was receiving growing emphasis within the national government. Some 500,000 brochures were printed and distributed across the country and into the United States to entice would-be visitors. When Southam was asked by the press how much it would cost and who would pay for it all, he airily replied, "We have the money—we had a good year."

On July 1, 1971, all Southam's ingenious manoeuvrings to launch the Summer Festival and ensure its development paid off. The Art Centre's first in-house opera production, *The Marriage of Figaro,* was an enormous success, even though director Michael Geliot had been forced to step in as stage director at the last minute because of the sudden and unexpected death of Sir Tyrone Guthrie in March. The sterling, almost entirely Canadian cast of singers, Bernardi's exquisite playing as he conducted the orchestra from the harpsichord during Mozart's recitatives, and the splendid lavishness of the production combined to make it clear that the overall first-class standards already established at the NAC would also include opera on a grand scale. Designer Brian Jackson, assisted by Suzanne Mess, had created a gorgeous set and magnificent costumes. No expense had been spared. Among the many high points that delighted the audience, none was more exciting than the moment when the curtains parted for the final act to reveal a water-filled pond at centre-stage with an elegant troupe of live swans swimming in it. In later years, singers would recall with horror the menacing hiss of the swans when a performer came too close. A special swan-keeper, dressed as a

Claude Corbeil, Gwenlynn Little, and Heather Thomson here performing in The Marriage of Figaro *were among the first of many Canadian singers who bloomed in the operas presented in the Summer Festival. Photo © John Evans.*

peasant, remained on stage throughout the act to keep the lovely but threatening creatures under control. "They were vicious!" Bernardi would later recall, but the overall effect was audacious and thrilling.[4] Hugh Davidson, who arrived in Ottawa to take up his post assisting the maestro just in time for the opera, remembers it as a "glorious and brilliant production."[5]

Mozart's music was Bernardi's forte and, with this venture into opera, the Arts Centre, the orchestra, and the conductor himself began to come into their own in the rarefied world of opera. Mozart operas would become a cornerstone of the early summer festivals, and the quality of the work spread word of the Arts Centre far and wide throughout the musical world. Most of the orchestra players welcomed the chance to play in the pit for these performances, and, indeed, another dimension of communication was opened between them and their taskmaster maestro when he sat down to conduct and play at the harpsichord. "It was as if he was talking to us though the music in a way he couldn't when he was just on the podium," reflected one player years later.[6] The musicians admired Bernardi for this work, and the feeling was mutual.

For Southam all of the proceedings were a natural progression. Opera was the "sum of everything," he believed, and "you couldn't have a National Arts Centre without it."[7] He had persuaded the government to build the second finest opera house in North America after the Metropolitan Opera House in New York, and he intended to have it used. After this first successful summer, he was more determined than ever to create a full-fledged Festival in Ottawa with opera at its core. The plan was to make Canada's capital "Edinburgh-on-the-Rideau" and, to this end, Bruce Corder and several trustees travelled to the Scottish city before the next summer to pick up tips. Lord Harewood had been hired to prepare a report on opera in Canada, and, when it was published in 1972, it identified "Ottawa as key to opera in Canada." The success of the first summer, especially in uncovering so many opera fans in Ottawa, allowed a happy Southam to exclaim to a Canadian reporter during a Paris interview in June 1972: "I felt like a prospector wandering over the Canadian Shield, taking a crack at a rock and uncovering gold."[8]

There was more gold to come when the 1972 Summer Festival brought a repeat of *Figaro,* this time without live swans but sung in the original Italian, as well as a new production of Mozart's *Cosi fan tutte.* This event marked the debut of the noted Canadian-born dancer and choreographer Brian Macdonald as an opera stage director. Bernardi envisioned the work as "very balletic. After all," he said, "it's about three pairs of people. I could see some kind of choreographic nexus there."[9] Macdonald was the right man for the task, although it took him time to work out each scene, as he had first to learn and then become immersed in the technicalities of the music as rehearsals moved forward. The result was good, and the Bernardi/Macdonald duo would team up often on other operatic and musical works in the years ahead, many of them at the Arts Centre. Again, Canadian artists dominated the cast, the public was delighted, and the reviews were good.

The rest of the Summer Festival month was like "Expo year in miniature"[10]—a performance by the Royal Winnipeg Ballet, four orchestral concerts (one of them conducted by the distinguished British composer Sir Michael Tippett), recitals by classical pianist Harvey Van Cliburn and jazz pianist Oscar Peterson, a French play from Montreal, and two English plays: Shakespeare's *Taming of the Shrew* and Ben Jonson's *The Alchemist,* brought from London by the Young Vic Company. Added to this was entertainment on the lighter side—performances as diverse as the Québécois boy-singer René Claude and, in the Studio, the new Canadian satirical group The Jest Society. For the first time, chansonniers were booked into the Café to entertain patrons after dinner. Yet, somehow, this second Summer Festival fare did not quite gel. Tickets sold spottily, with only about 20 percent going to visitors from outside the region. The opera sold well, however, and, while overall attendance was down from the first year, revenues for the July summer events were up by 20 percent.

Despite the interest in youth, "Young August" had proved a hard sell, even with its rich all-Canadian menu. It featured everything from Canadian comedian Rich Little (who did play to packed houses), to Jeunesses Musicales, Toronto Dance Theatre, and plays in both English and French by students of the National Theatre School. Overall capacity for August, despite much favourable comment, hit just 60 percent. In the eyes of some observers, "ideal festival programming for Ottawa was still elusive."[11] Nevertheless, NAC management came out of the summer with the view that the Festival was now well grounded, and Southam immediately began ambitious plans for the third Summer Festival.

Meanwhile on the government front, a great deal was happening as Secretary of State Gérard Pelletier began to set in motion the initiatives that would dramatically affect cultural funding in the country. At his side was an astute bureaucrat, André Fortier, who, as a more junior official, had been associated with the NAC's beginnings and was now assistant undersecretary in the Secretary of State's department and a confidant of Pelletier. Together they initiated a formal Federal Cultural Policy Review, to be overseen by Fortier. Already, Fortier had been assigned to chair an interdepartmental "Canada Month" committee that would work to focus attention on Canada's capital during the summer. The NAC would have to manoeuvre skilfully to finesse its plans into this new broader picture being developed by the government.

Pelletier had strong views on the place of young people in society and had articulated a notion that "youth" was "an independent universal class, culturally and socially distinct."[12] At the same time, the Quiet Revolution in Quebec was becoming considerably less quiet, driven in large measure by youthful disaffected voices and sometimes reaching explosive proportions, as seen in the tragic events of the October Crisis. One of the federal government's responses was to launch the Opportunities for Youth program in 1970, followed the next year by the Local Initiatives Program. These plans not only enabled the government to get money more directly out to constituents but also tied in with Pelletier's objectives to "democratize and decentralize" culture. Many of the projects that received funding under these programs were in the artistic and cultural sector. The hugely successful Cirque du Soleil, for example, began with an Opportunities for Youth grant to two street buskers working in the lower Gaspésie.

These programs also had the effect of circumnavigating some of the grant-giving powers of the traditional funding agencies, such as the Canada Council and, more recently, the National Arts Centre, whose support was directed exclusively to professional artists. Both Southam and Louis Applebaum wrote to Pelletier expressing their concerns over the effect of these new granting programs and stressing their opinion that "federal support should be aimed at the professional level … and … support of semi-professional or amateur activities should be left to the regional or municipal levels of government."

Pelletier's department began to slash what were known as "B" budgets in these cultural agencies' financing, in part to underwrite, but also to have more control over, the new programs. "A" budgets were designed to establish the base operating budgets for the established cultural organizations, and "B" budgets were the additional wish list of items they would like to do if the Treasury Board granted them extra funds. These discretionary funds were not just left to bureaucrats to administer but could be the subject of some heavy discussion and horse-trading around the Cabinet table. Pelletier and his close colleagues now intended to use some of this money and these tools to effect social change—and to a significant extent they would succeed.

Pelletier also wanted a single unifying cultural policy for the country, to be set and run by the government. Until now, each of Canada's cultural agencies had a general mandate, and they had generally been left to operate as they saw fit. Starting with Pelletier, they would come under greater departmental control. The minister travelled to a UNESCO conference in Venice in 1970 where the concept of a national cultural policy was adopted by a majority of member countries, even though some doubters expressed fears that "cultural expression would be stifled under the weight of bureaucracy."[13] At a second conference in Helsinki in 1972, Canada drew closer to the European/French model of a Ministry of Culture, with its state (as opposed to "arm's-length") control of public funds for cultural affairs. In part, the goal of this change was to build a better bulwark against the cultural power of the United States, which was flooding Canada and other parts of the world largely through American television programs and film. Canada's more proactive stance in cultural activities abroad was intended to reinforce its differences from the United States.

Soon after, Pelletier instituted certain measures that broke with the tradition that Canada's arm's-length cultural agencies were responsible for administering arts programs.

The "capital assistance program," which made money available to build cultural facilities, was moved into the Arts and Culture Branch of Pelletier's department, where it remains today. The Canada Council had declined to take it on "because of the inevitable political implications surrounding the bargaining for and the selection of capital projects."[14] Giving this grant-giving power to the department itself contributed to the tensions that would grow between the ministry and the regular grant-giving federal cultural agencies.

Previously, the cultural agencies had not only set their own agendas but had also operated independently from one another. It was only with the establishment of the National Arts Centre that other agencies, including the Canada Council, the CBC, and the National Film Board, had been given ex-officio places on the board, so they could liaise with one another and try to work in consort where appropriate. Pelletier thought that there should be a common direction among the agencies, and that this objective should be established by the government. With the challenges of national unity mounting, the government wanted all the tools it could get at its disposal to fight separatism in Quebec. Pelletier firmly believed that all the cultural agencies should now be grouped within a national cultural policy under the government's control. The fight for freedom of cultural expression, how it was to be supported and who would control it, would resonate through the years into the present day.

To his credit, Pelletier wanted to engage the energies of governments at both the provincial and the municipal levels in his quest to spread the opportunities to produce art and cultural events. The ability to allow the provinces to undertake "educational" television was one of the early measures reflecting these principles—with André Fortier as one of Pelletier's chief negotiators.

So far as the National Arts Centre was concerned, Pelletier had shared his doubts about the institution and its director with Fortier. Their view of Southam was that "his attitude and way of doing things were those of an aristocrat," an elitist, and his style of living grated on them.[15] Most unfairly, they judged him as "doing something for himself and his friends at the Arts Centre, which looked more like an extended private club."[16] Southam, as we have seen, had a different view of elitism. He was not against democratizing the arts, but his vision was rooted in the concept of "centres of excellence," and he firmly believed that these institutions could not be created by governments but occurred where "the arts were started by people and then encouraged."[17] It had been broad-based coalitions of the general populace, after all, that had created institutions like the CBC and the Canada Council—headed, it is true, by leading citizens who were often, though not exclusively, anglophone.

There is no question that the two sides had decidedly different approaches, but the extent to which this conflict was affected by social rather than ideological factors—

the francophones' aggravation at Southam's "airs and graces" versus Southam's often patrician way of viewing the world—is hard to calibrate. Southam's mannerisms indeed put Pelletier's back up and, in his memoir published in the 1990s, he remarked on his distaste for the "long gowns and white gloves" approach that he thought the NAC represented.[18] Southam, in turn, would later describe Pelletier as "well educated but not a man of the world" and as a "scatterer of the wealth."[19] No love was lost between the two men.

While their differences were perhaps rooted in their individual starts in life, their views were also affected by their differing postwar experiences of providing art to the masses. Like Maynard Keynes in England, Southam had a view of what was "the best," and he thought it his duty to present these performances to Canada and so raise cultural standards in the country. That "best" should be not only Canadian but from abroad, such as the Comédie Française or England's National Theatre. He had been raised as an internationalist and believed that Canada had a larger role to play in the world, and not just within its national borders. In his mind, the NAC had been born into that international context. Pelletier, in contrast, subscribed more to the community-based French view, and he and Fortier privately thought the concept of the NAC "too old-school European."[20] By strictly theoretical standards, their position was more democratic and their charge of elitism stung Southam, although there was really no difference between the goals of the two camps—they both wanted to increase access to the arts for individual artists and the public alike.

Pelletier did not fully appreciate Southam's quick-witted and shrewd diplomatic skill at adapting to and managing the evolving political situations. In this respect the director general was the consummate politician on behalf of the NAC. As Pelletier's work began to build up steam, in March 1971, the NAC board, which held the power of appointment, renewed Southam's contract as director general for another five years. Southam said later that, had it been in Pelletier's power, he believed he would have been let go. Board chair François Mercier, with strong ties to the Liberal Party and the Trudeau government, liked Southam enormously, however, and he dealt with the reappointment expeditiously.

Nothing illustrated Southam's adroit management skills more than the financing for the early summer festivals. There, he picked up on the government's urgent new interest in issues of "national unity" and began to re-tailor his requests to fit this new paradigm. There might be less money from Treasury Board for "B" budget items, but there was going to be new monies for "unity" projects. The NAC had already sent in an impressive "B" budget shopping list that included the first mention of a possible resident dance company, based on a proposal from choreographer Brian Macdonald, as well as plans to bring Opéra Québec to Ottawa and to develop a National Booking Office that would service the whole country. Southam had no difficulty recasting the NAC as a useful player in the national unity cause. He had always believed strongly in Canadian unity–and the role that the National Arts Centre could play in bringing Canadians together.

In the fall of 1970, the NAC again proposed the Festival Canada idea to the government for the summer of the following year, this time fitting its own plans neatly into the national unity project. Southam took nothing for granted, and, in May 1971, he made a carefully prepared appearance before the Standing Committee of Parliament. There he stressed to the parliamentarians the NAC's role in the entire country, firmly rejecting the notion that it was a project only for the citizens of Ottawa. Rather, he sketched out for the country's representatives the good things that the Arts Centre could do, and was doing, for Canada, including "commissioning new works to perform at the NAC," "making the capital a centre of creation and attraction," and "developing itself as a 'national service centre' for the performing arts, as in the proposed National Booking Office being designed to serve the arts companies of the entire country." At the same time, he smoothly reminded the politicians that the NAC would need new money to achieve these goals. His message resonated with the authorities and, while the NAC generally funded the first Festival from its own funds, it implanted itself firmly as a major component of "Canada Month," a pet project initiated by the Secretary of State's Department.

By these means, the first Festival Canada, as it was called, went ahead at the Arts Centre. Produced on "a shoestring budget" of just $120,000, with $95,000 of that total dedicated to the new opera, it opened in July 1971 to great success. Overall audiences for the opera performances stood at 86 percent capacity, and a thrilled Bruce Corder reported to the board at its late July meetings that *The Marriage of Figaro* had "exceeded all expectations," received "rave reviews," and "played to capacity audiences." As planned, the Secretary of State's program on July 1st on Parliament Hill had attracted some 10,000 people, followed by a wide variety of other events in the region throughout the month. The long-dreamed Ottawa Summer Festival was off and running.

Encouraged by this success, the NAC moved quickly with its planning for a larger Festival Canada in 1972 and 1973. The 1972 budget was set at $393,000, over three times the first year's budget and a sum that included a special festival grant of $188,000 from the government's newly established "Canada Month" funds.

Southam also zeroed in on the new youth initiatives sponsored by the Secretary of State's department. The Arts Centre had always supported outreach programs for young people in music and the other departments, and the "Young August" program following on from the Summer Festival was specifically targeted to youth. Southam now made plans to help students from the National Theatre School, and the directors quickly cobbled together money from programming and theatre funds. The NAC offered the students the use of the dormant travelling theatre truck, Le Portage, although for the first year of this project, they chose instead to come into the NAC and work in the Studio. The following summer they did expand into the theatre truck and, with some money from the Opportunities for Youth program, travelled for several weeks around the Ottawa region.

The National Booking Office plan proposed by the NAC was also about to take off, although it would not be in the manner that the NAC instigators had hoped for or envisioned. Since its inception, the NAC had developed a useful role for itself in organizing and booking talent for other agencies in Canada. This initiative had first been noticeable during Centennial Year in 1967, when the centre had performed effective service for the Centennial Commission, booking and moving Canadian talent all around the country, working with all ten Canadian provinces on cultural projects, orchestrating over 694 performances from coast to coast with a sale of over 650,000 tickets as well as arranging some foreign tours.

This role had increased when David Haber, with all his expertise from Expo, joined the NAC staff. In 1971, at the request of both the NAC and the Canada Council, Haber prepared a detailed working paper on the concept of a centralized National Booking Office. Its objectives were threefold. After Centennial Year, there were a string of newly built auditoria across the country as well as flourishing arts companies that had gained impetus from the anniversary celebrations. Things had slowed quickly afterwards, however, and the Arts Centre hoped that a National Booking Office would help, first, to extend the seasons of these companies by touring them outside their homes cities and, second, to keep these fine new facilities active. In addition, it wanted to bring many of these arts groups to smaller centres that might not have smart new halls, but which, during the excitement of Expo, had developed a taste for the performing arts.

There were good reasons for putting these kinds of tours in Canadian hands. Haber's report estimated that, since Expo 67, approximately $1 million a year was going to American agents who were booking talent around Canada. The Canadian planners saw no reason why a National Booking Office should not take over some of these arrangements, including foreign tours that were coming into Canada. A similar service was already in place for outbound tours to other countries, especially to Eastern Europe. The Canadian Opera Company and the country's two main orchestras were competent to arrange their own tours, but the report revealed that while the Montreal Symphony and the Toronto Symphony had played in Europe and as far away as Japan, shockingly, neither had toured across Canada. The Toronto Symphony had never played in Canada outside Ontario. Even though the NAC Orchestra was only in its second year, it had already toured all the way to Vancouver, and was now planning an Eastern Tour that would reach to St. John's, Newfoundland. Through the latter months of 1971, the NAC engaged in a series of meetings with the Canada Council about the formulation of this important touring service.

The proposal, which Southam gave to his board in May 1971, envisaged the booking office as a separate department within the Arts Centre—a branch that would help to emphasize the "national" in the NAC's title. Unfortunately, this approach soon ran into stiff criticism from the Canada Council. At the core of the problem was the fact that the National Booking Office needed to be an independent operation, especially when it came to touring the NAC's own companies, to avoid any perception of conflict of interest in bookings. While the NAC could be a focal point for tours, its own companies had to be handled on an equal basis with the others. The Canada Council's managers and trustees gave the working paper's proposals a rough ride, and Robert Elie, its arts director, conveyed the objections to Southam.[21] To his credit, Southam replied firmly, correcting some of the Council's misperceptions, but this rebuttal was not enough to persuade the Canada Council to join with the NAC to endorse the centre as the agency responsible for this new touring office. The proposal still did not go forward to the government.

The matter was again thrashed out at a December joint dinner meeting between the NAC and the Canada Council at Hull's venerable Café Henri Burger, across the river from Ottawa. Also in attendance representing the Department of the Secretary of State was André Fortier. Although the others did not know it, he was about to accept an appointment from Minister Pelletier to become the director of the Canada Council. Fortier did not favour the NAC, and Southam was about to lose the bureaucratic battle to make the booking office a part of the NAC.

After a protracted debate, the question of the National Booking Office was finally resolved when the government finally gave the nod to the Canada Council as the agency to run it. Ironically, Haber himself may have played a role in this decision. When Southam sent him over to the Council for a time to help devise the plan, he had declined a suggestion that he become head of a new Touring Office, explaining that he would be "repeating" himself.[22] Southam had made a spirited case for the NAC, and he was deeply disappointed at the outcome. As the Canada Council Touring Office was formally created on April 1, 1973, among its first staff members were John Cripton and Yvon DesRochers. Both men were destined in the future to become directors general of the National Arts Centre.

As solace for his disappointment over the booking office and his slashed "B" budgets, Southam continued to pursue his interest in bringing the best international artists and companies to Ottawa. Cultural exchanges, especially between France and Canada, were deemed to have special importance, and a visit by the Compagnie Renaud-Barrault, led by the famous French actor Jean-Louis Barrault, was booked into the Arts Centre. It was part of a mini-tour that the NAC helped to arrange which would take the company to Montreal and also to Toronto, after the NAC promised to pick up 50 percent of the cost in the Ontario capital. Although internationally renowned, Barrault's work cut little ice with Montreal or Toronto audiences, but it had a fiery reception in Ottawa.

Barrault's stage effects included the use of live fireworks, something that the NAC's unionized stage crews refused to allow. They had just finished installing a magnificent new and expensive back-curtain into the stage in the Theatre, where Barrault was due to perform. Barrault was equally adamant that he would not appear unless he was permitted his rockets. He complained bitterly to Southam about his "mistreatment," and Southam made a rare intervention. Despite the stagehands' concerns over clashes with the Ottawa fire marshal, the show and the fireworks went ahead. For years afterwards, the stagehands took grim satisfaction in pointing out the holes that sparks from Barrault's pyrotechnics had burned in the brand-new curtain.

In January 1972 Mario Bernardi's contract as music director was renewed for another three years. Hugh Davidson's appointment as music administrator the previous June had proved to be an enormous help to the busy young conductor. Davidson had immediately set to work to help Bernardi build up subscriptions, plan programs, and book talent. Many important international solo performers, such as pianist Alicia de Larrocha, made their first appearance in Ottawa at this time and, as they returned year after year, they became household names with the Ottawa audience. Similarly they helped spread the word about the good work that was happening in Ottawa.

"What we were going to do, where we were going to perform, what Canadian music we would play" was Davidson's task to sort out.[23] Programming the season's several concert series was tremendously hard work, and Davidson remembered going over to the maestro's house in Ottawa's Glebe district and staying through the night until things got done. Soon the two men had developed a strong level of trust. "The orchestra was well managed and could play anything up to Wagner," he said, and he persuaded Bernardi that it had all the merits of "the 1844 Leipzig orchestra, which had been exactly this same size."

The orchestra's repertoire expanded rapidly and soon included works that Bernardi had not previously had time to consider, including all the Beethoven symphonies and Schubert's Ninth.[24] The maestro laughed later as he recalled his struggle to learn new repertoire to play week by week at a frantic pace. But visiting performers and conductors were impressed, and word soon got around musical circles outside Canada that there was a fine orchestra budding in Ottawa. This reputation played a role in the NAC orchestra making its New York debut at Lincoln Center's Alice Tully Hall on February 27, 1972. The review for this inaugural performance by the rigorous New York critics was warm and enthusiastic. "Young orchestra proves first rate," reported the *New York Times*.[25]

Ironically, just as Bernardi and the orchestra moved from strength to strength, backed by the musical knowledge that Hugh Davidson brought to the dossier, Southam made a decision that would break this flourishing musical partnership. With the summer operas firmly taking hold, he decided to create a separate formal Festival Department to manage the event. Instead of being an extension of the Music Department, it would come under the control and directorship of Bruce Corder. Bernardi would be the artistic director, a position that gave him a complete free hand in designing the programming. Southam had several reasons for making this change. Corder had proved himself a strong operations manager, good in all respects with budgets, and had negotiated the tough first union contracts at the NAC, including those with Actors Equity and the francophone union, Union des Artistes. With his background at Covent Garden and the O'Keefe Centre, where the Canadian Opera Company performed, he had considerable practical experience in presenting opera. He loved opera, and Southam's decision to put him in charge was perhaps coloured by his desire to give his loyal deputy, who did so much of the "bad cop" work at the Centre, something special of his own.

Whatever the reasons, both Southam and Bernardi knew they would have to handle the matter delicately with Davidson, who was not party to this important decision on musical programming. Bernardi was confident that his music administrator would accept the division, but he did not. Davidson, who was also trained and experienced in opera, took strong exception to this musical art form being moved away from the Music Department. When it became clear that he would not win the day, he resigned from his job in protest in the mid-autumn of 1972 to take up a post as music officer at the Canada Council, leaving Bernardi in complete charge of the artistic side of the NAC's opera productions. This severing of opera from the main Music Department would have serious consequences in later years when hard times hit the Arts Centre. Despite the turmoil that would follow, however, the opera seasons would become glorious landmarks in the final years of Southam's reign.

In his term as secretary of state, Pelletier had wrought significant changes in cultural policy and funding. Now, as 1972 yielded to 1973, Pelletier left to head up the new Department of Communications, a ministry that recognized the complex and growing world of communications technology. Southam and the Arts Centre would now have to deal with a new man in the Secretary of State's office—Hugh Faulkner.

8

ELEGANCE
AND OPERAS

Hugh Faulkner was another bilingual Montrealer, this time of anglophone origin. He liked the arts a lot, and he and his wife, Jane, soon became regular attendees at concerts and plays at the National Arts Centre. They were frequent guests at Southam's dinner parties before or after performances. Faulkner and Southam had much in common, even though the new secretary of state agreed with Pelletier that cultural activities had to be encouraged outside the big centres. Contrary to his predecessor, however, he believed in maintaining "the heart of the system"—the major national cultural organizations. He shared Southam's belief in "centres of excellence," in the importance of engaging the best talent and showcasing it.

Altogether he was a man "in tune with the performing arts" and had "always loved opera." One of the ways he thought he could assist opera at the Arts Centre was "to lean on the CBC to televise it."[1] There is no evidence he ever did so, but, from the centre's point of view, his heart was in the right place.

Faulkner had been Pelletier's parliamentary secretary, responsible for overseeing the grants for the Opportunities for Youth and Local Initiatives Program for his boss. In his view, these programs were strictly "political improvisations to deal with

The Honourable Hugh Faulkner, secretary of state.
Photo © Ottawa Citizen/UPI. Reprinted by permission.

employment problems across the country," not a new way of developing artistic practices.[2] When he became the minister responsible for culture himself, he said his task
was "to encourage the 'best and the brightest.'" If that happened in Ottawa and other
major cities, standards would rise across the entire country. While Faulkner acknowledged that cultural issues got only minor attention in Cabinet, he found that, if he made
"a good case for things, [he] usually received support." Prime Minister's Trudeau's quest
for national bilingualism had a practical bearing on choices. Although "western alien-
ation" was already a noted fact, ideas were invariably tested as to "how they would play
in Quebec." Not surprisingly, proposals that served the French-speaking public were
sure of a hearing and, as monies began to tighten, the ever astute Southam would note
this tilt and tailor his requests accordingly.

By 1973, artistic affairs at the Arts Centre had at last settled into a groove. The orchestra was flourishing, both English and French theatre were finally firmly implanted,
dance was doing fine by relying on visiting companies, and the Summer Festival had
two strong years behind it. The man who had brought matters to this point now entered
what was to be one of the happiest and most productive periods of his life. In 1968
Hamilton Southam had married for the second time and, within five years, he had
become a new father again, twice over. His life could never be described as straitlaced,
but he now began an intoxicating period of dinners, soirées, travel, and other entertainment centred on the endless flow of exciting artistic visitors and events streaming
to Ottawa to appear on the NAC stages.

It is easy to see why Gérard Pelletier and André Fortier could misunderstand and
reproach the way Southam used the facilities at the Arts Centre. He entertained his
friends and visitors handsomely and with style. A special alcove tucked in at the back
of the luxurious Le Restaurant did not quite constitute a private dining room but was
often reserved for delightful after-theatre supper parties that he and his guests enjoyed
after performances. These celebrations were seldom counted as business dinners.
Although Southam could always provide good theatre seats for his guests, he insisted
that the chits for these evenings go into his own "running" account in the restaurant's
books, with the accumulative bills scrupulously settled by his personal secretary at the
end of each month. Invariably, this account vastly outstripped the budget set aside for
his corporate hospitality.[3] He also lunched or dined in Le Restaurant's intimate velvet-
covered booths, which were well-designed for private or business conversations.
Southam delighted in his personal catch-phrase "that more was wrought over lunch
than men dreamed of."[4]

Ever the diplomat, he also took on, with ease, the government's request that the NAC
play an important role hosting "state visits": presenting special concerts, lunches, and

U.S. President Richard Nixon, Margaret Trudeau, Mrs. Nixon, and Prime Minister Trudeau. Nixon's visit to the NAC was a "first." The red telephone and hotline were startling additions to the state dinner. Photo © Studio Impact/NAC.

extravagantly elegant dinners for important foreign visitors to the capital. One of the first and grandest of these events was an enormous state dinner for President Richard Nixon, who came to Ottawa on an official visit on April 13, 1972. Helicopters whirled continuously overhead as Nixon moved about the city by motorcade. A special hotline telephone, set up by the White House secret service, became an unexpected adornment adjacent to the silver-laden, damask-covered table when the president sat down to dinner. The NAC's catering department continued to be a money-losing proposition, but no one in Ottawa could match the centre for the elegance of its dining room or the quality of its food, thanks to the style and taste imposed on it by Southam. The linen, flowers, and protocol were impeccable.

Perhaps there was a touch of the private club in these pleasures and an air of *noblesse oblige*, but the truth was that Southam never forgot the *oblige* part. His hospitality also extended to his private home at 267 Buena Vista Drive in Ottawa's upper-crust Rockcliffe Park, where the pleasant living room with its glowing fireplace and walls adorned with artwork that included a lovely Picasso and beautiful wall tapestries created a congenial environment for discussing the arts and great ideas generally. Many artists, from actors to composers to close friends like Mario Bernardi, recall with the deepest pleasure the hours they spent in Southam's company. In summer, the venue changed to his handsome cottage in the Rideau Lakes, a bucolic location that became a source of inspiration for many artistic endeavours, whether Alfred Manessier's woven tapestries or Franco Mannino's later musical composition "Rideau Lake Symphony." Southam fulfilled to the hilt the role of wealthy arts patron, vastly enjoying himself but also maintaining a firm and dedicated commitment to his country and the betterment of its arts. The arrangement was positive for the developing Canadian arts scene, which had never before experienced this kind of leadership. Southam's ability to harness his personal vision to his public commitment and to persuade others that it was right to have this enormous publicly supported artistic enterprise was the key to its early success. Though never claiming expertise, his personal delight and unwavering interest in culture informed and inspired those whom he hired as his artistic directors. His role, he said, was to create the environment where these creative people could do their best, and then stand back and get out of their way.

On the management side, the daily work of the centre had been established under Southam's oversight, but it was largely carried out by the able team he had built around him. His deputy, Bruce Corder, at first director of operations and then deputy director general, became the active field general for this generous but exacting field marshal. Although Southam did not suggest Corder as his successor, chiefly because he did not speak French, Southam would later confirm the indispensable support of his lieutenant. The outwardly suave British-born Corder played the "heavy" in the NAC's affairs, hammering out the union contracts as they were slotted into place, organizing the budgets, and overseeing store rentals on the Elgin Street side of the building in an effort to bring in commercial revenues. He managed everything in the front of the house, from the ushers' uniforms, to the cost centres of the box-office and the parking garage, to the lamentable revenues from the Restaurant and the catering department. It was a good balance: while Southam positioned himself above routine matters and took care of the social and political spheres, Corder paid close attention to all the details of the day-to-day operations.

Corder was particularly concerned with the new technology being introduced into the building. He turned up on a daily basis to check what was happening on the stages, and he had a close eye for spotting the most miniscule change. Staffers remember a man with a strong temper who could slam his fist on the table in a private meeting, but never display it in public. He let it be known when he was seriously displeased. One of his preoccupations was the architectural integrity of the building: when technicians changed any of the decorative details for their own convenience, he insisted on their reinstatement. Still, the technical crews could count on his support if they had problems. When the third balcony installation of the sound booth in the Opera didn't work well, Corder accepted their advice to move it down to the first level—and then insisted that the architects help to integrate the booth correctly into the new location. Southam and Corder complemented each other in their work. Inevitably, there were hitches and growing pains, but, overall, the Arts Centre developed in a way that was first class in all respects.

Some people thought that Southam carried on "like a king."[5] When he made the occasional sortie backstage, he was usually surrounded by an entourage. For all the originality and fearlessness of his vision, and contrary to appearances, he could be diffident when it came to free-wheeling artistic types. In his pinstripe suits with waist-coat and watch-chain, he gave off an aura of high-brow distance and stuffiness. It was an asset, therefore, when he moved Richard Dennison, the bright young theatre man from Calgary, into his office to become his executive assistant and, ultimately, the corporate secretary. Dennison had shown considerable courage over the debacle of Bawtree's English theatre experiment in the Studio, and, as its producer, he had spent many hours in Southam's office trying to find a way to sort the disaster out. Now, with his often scuffed shoes, pulled-back ponytail, and collarless shirts, he was being asked to step out of his world as "a theatre worker" to become Southam's assistant—part of the management bureaucracy. There could not be a sharper contrast between them, but Southam was astute in bringing the younger man under his wing.

Dennison played an indispensable role in connecting the chief executive with the artistic elements in his large staff. "For all his wisdom and wonder," he recalled, "Mr. Southam was not a walk-around kind of guy." He vividly remembered escorting his formally dressed boss through the backstage areas on many occasions: "We'd walk around the building, watch the ballet setting up, or go to the loading dock or scenery shop and I'd introduce him." Southam "always came to work dressed as if he were going to meet an ambassador or the prime minister—and he probably was!"[6] Southam took considerable delight in getting to know the mechanics of this place he had put together, but, on his own, he would have had difficulty making the connection between his office and the backstage world.

As he settled in to work directly for Southam, Dennison also became acutely aware of the importance of Southam's role: his constant dealings with the minister and the various government departments, his ongoing efforts to get funds for the NAC, his dexterous smoothing of the way, and his attention to the particular complexities in operating the Arts Centre. Over time, Southam did become fully informed on the back-stage workings of his vast emporium and, on official backstage visits with VIPs, he developed a habit of introducing dignitaries to the stage crews as well as to the per-formers. As a result, a marvellous theatrical culture and a real *esprit de corps* built up at the NAC which characterized and enhanced the activities on its stages. This culture would devise its own unique practices and ways of doing things, and in the early years it unquestionably bettered the artistic work.

Nowhere was this camaraderie more evident than in "Chez Claude," a backstage blind pig/speakeasy. The Claude of the title was Claude Desvoyault, another Expo "graduate." He had worked for Andis Celms at the world's fair as "assistant technical superin-tendent," looking after all the equipment used on its stages. Once the Centennial was over, this rotund, gravelly voiced stagehand had gone to work as a "fly" man at Montreal's Théâtre du Nouveau Monde—until he received an urgent call from Celms in Ottawa in the late winter of 1969. Struggling to get the centre's complicated new technical apparatus up and running, Celms sent out an urgent appeal for help, and Desvoyault and his colleague Wilfrid Pomereau, an experienced carpenter and millwright, were among the first who hurried to Ottawa to help the NAC's new technical administrator out. The crews worked day and night to fit up the Opera, and then the Theatre and the Studio, in time for the opening. When the building was finally launched, many of these workers remained—Desvoyault as head technician in the technically well-appointed but complicated new Studio; and Pomereau as head carpenter, setting up the workshops that would construct many of the brilliant stage-sets that helped to make the NAC famous.

At the core of this backstage world was the stagecraft union IATSE, the International Alliance of Theatrical Stage Employees. IATSE controlled everything that went on in this backstage kingdom. The National Arts Centre would become a full "union house" for all its employees, but no group, with the occasional exception of the American Federation of Musicians, was more powerful than IATSE. The role of its members was straightforward: they were "the guys who make the artists look and sound good."[7]

An international union with its headquarters in New York, IATSE had set up shop in Ottawa in 1902, many decades before the NAC came into being. It provided professional stage crews for concerts, theatre companies, and other professional performers touring through the city, playing at such venues as the old Capitol Theatre or on the stages of the de LaSalle Academy. Some of those early union members would come over to work at the NAC, but the huge needs of the new complex meant that this group could not supply enough people. Celms, under Corder's direction, set out to recruit more stage crew. Many came from Montreal, where, like Celms, they had gained valuable technical experience during Expo. The Arts Centre required their technical abilities—and bilingual crew members as well—to accommodate the considerable French-language productions that were planned. There was minor friction as some of the local members jockeyed with the newcomers, and a delegation was dispatched to IATSE headquarters in New York to sort things out. Finally, IATSE's head office reluctantly agreed to create a special chapter of the union which would be exclusive to the new building. IATSE Local 471 was born, charged with responsibility for everything that occurred inside the National Arts Centre and everything that toured out from it. The old union chapter, Local 95, retained jurisdiction over all the other events that played in Ottawa. New York always encouraged amalgamation of the two groups, but it was not until 1989 that they joined together, with the NAC forming the major hub of the work.

The different crews assigned to each of the three theatres also sometimes did not get along, and, to assuage this friction, Claude Desvoyault had the idea of setting up a small bar backstage where members could meet and talk over their differences. What came to be known as Chez Claude soon became an integral part of the backstage world. While Bruce Corder tactfully looked the other way, it was furnished with chairs and sofas and fitted up with a well-stocked refrigerator that included a healthy selection of alcoholic beverages. Unthinkable in a traditional office, and certainly illegal under the regulations of the Ontario Liquor Control Board, this facility helped to ease the tensions backstage. Rare was the artist in those early days, whether a Ginette Reno or a Harry Belafonte, who did not drop by Chez Claude at some point during a run to have a beer or a drink.

It became the place for many spontaneous production meetings where knotty problems that couldn't be solved in a formal stage rehearsal were worked out over a friendly drink. Even office staff were known to drop in, and Southam came for an occasional visit, all in good fun. It was no accident that Southam was made an honorary member of IATSE in his later years—the union's way of honouring him when the Opera was formally renamed Southam Hall. His confident respect for these industrious night owls who made his theatres function was evident from the outset. Everything about Chez Claude, like backstage life itself, was on the honour system, and Desvoyault, whose job it was to oversee bar supplies, affirmed that he had never lost "more than a case or two of beer through all the years."[8] For a backstage that became the centre for many uproarious after-performance parties and the focus for a whole social underworld as the years wore on, this record was remarkable.

The merry days of Chez Claude ended when things became "a little out of hand" and later management practices tried to get a firmer grip on these and other informal activities.[9] In the early days it was emblematic of an overall culture of recognition and respect for everyone on the NAC team which, in its turn, fostered the artistic life of the National Arts Centre and led to a remarkable bonding among those charged with its work. Many of those crew staff members were still "working the house" more than thirty or more years later. Their efforts and commitment assisted the work of the NAC to continue, especially through its most difficult years. No other performing house in Canada, and perhaps very few anywhere in the world, could claim the kind of staff loyalty engendered under the leadership of Southam and Corder.

The first two Summer Festivals had been a considerable success, especially in the opera performances. Indeed, opera seemed to hold a special place in Canadian cultural life at this time. Fuelled in large measure by the experience, values, and dreams of many Central Europeans who had immigrated to Canada in the postwar period and now populated much of Canada's musical life in Toronto and elsewhere, opera had established its place in the forefront for cultural organizers. Lord Harewood's report,

Baritone Claude Corbeil and the great contralto Maureen Forrester triumphed in a 1980 summer festival production of La Fille du régiment. *Forrester, a giant figure in Canadian arts, always championed the NAC. Photo © Fernand R. LeClair.*

commissioned in 1971 by the Canada Council and the Ontario Arts Council, provided a formal survey of opera in Canada. Although it lambasted the dull programming found in Quebec, Vancouver, and Edmonton, as well as the slow progress of the Canadian Opera Company in Toronto, it had high praise for opera at the NAC. It also commended the Stratford Festival's potential as a home for experimental opera, though an earlier attempt to hook up Bernardi and a few NAC Orchestra players and singers to do chamber opera at Stratford in 1970 had aborted, at some cost to the NAC. Harewood's suggestion that the COC might want to move its operations to the National Arts Centre in Ottawa garnered no takers, but the emphasis on opera generally led to immediate action on the part of several of the cultural agencies.

Franz Kramer, like Nicholas Goldschmidt an émigré, later destined to become music officer at the Canada Council, drafted a proposal for opera that included the possible creation of an Opera Institute. He thought, like Harewood, that it could be located at the NAC, and Southam presented the idea to the Canada Council for consideration. The Council's reply, once again penned by Southam's frequent nemesis, André Fortier, now director of the Canada Council, did not endorse a lead role for the NAC. Instead, he stated that the situation of opera in Canada was a matter of national discussion and that the idea of an Opera Institute was already under consideration at the Opera School at the University of Toronto as well as at the Vancouver Opera Association. In the end, the Opera Institute, conceived to train and supply singers to Canada's opera companies, was never created and, once again, Southam's idea that the NAC should have a more educational and development role was scotched. He was not deterred, however, and, with the able support of Corder, continued to build up Festival Canada with ever-expanding opera at its core.

In April 1973, then, when Southam set out his strategy for the Board of Trustees for the coming years, he called for a steady increase in the number of operas, to a maximum of four. He pointed out that planning for opera had to be done three or four years in advance, to secure the best quality of talent. But that level of control was severely hampered by the Treasury Board, which informed the cultural agencies every August of what they would receive the following year. Southam worked hard to secure "top-level cooperation and program coordination among the various federal cultural agencies."[10] To that end he proposed an overall coordinating committee for Festival Canada, under the leadership of the governor general, to mesh the activities and the budgets of the various departments and agencies involved in the month-long Ottawa celebration.

While initially his efforts produced few results, his constant campaigning and enthusiasm for the NAC's work produced at least one startling and positive declaration. The newly elected Ottawa mayor, Kenneth Fogarty, announced in his inaugural address on January 4, 1972, that the city would contribute $100,000 "to show the Government of Canada and the National Arts Centre that we in this city are prepared to make our contribution." Unfortunately, this good intention was not immediately followed up by his city councillors, but the idea of municipal support would later come to fruition. Over and over again, Southam reiterated the theme that the purpose of Festival Canada was "to strengthen national unity" by turning Ottawa into "a lively and entertaining place for all Canadians during Canada's birthday month."[11]

By the summer of 1973, Southam and Corder believed that they had devised the winning summer formula, and they established a healthy budget which was nearly twice that of the previous year to accomplish it. Unfortunately, the results of their programming were decidedly mixed. Central to the plan were three operas, one of them a French opera, Offenbach's *La Belle Hélène*. There was to be a single NAC Orchestra concert, devoted to French music, plus theatre, chamber music, film, popular entertainment, children's programs, and poetry readings. For the first time, too, dance would be produced in-house. Fresh from his success with *Cosi fan tutte* the previous year, Brian Macdonald put together a small company of sixteen dancers to give several performances of new Canadian works choreographed by himself and dancer Brydon Paige. Corder was dubious about the idea, but Southam pushed the plan ahead.

Besides the reprised *Cosi*, the opera program included two more new productions, a *Don Giovanni* conducted by Bernardi and directed by the brilliant British Shakespearean actor John Neville. Jean Roberts had initially brought Neville to Canada to work at the NAC Theatre, and now he was expanding into the general Canadian artistic community. The second opera, *La Belle Hélène*, conducted by the French-Canadian maestro Pierre Hétu and directed by the flamboyant Montreal theatre director Pierre Buissoneau, had started off as a Montreal Opera production and then transferred to Ottawa. All three operas took up thirteen performances in the nearly month-long Festival, and again they were a resounding success.

The dance initiative proved to be disastrous. Although Southam had encouraged Macdonald, the proposal had aroused stiff opposition in the established dance companies, which feared any competition from a resident dance troupe at the National Arts Centre on that grounds that the "already thin dance community" would be raided for both performers and money.[12] While strongly protesting that this was not the intention, Macdonald's main presentation, *Star-Cross'd*, a reworked version of the Romeo and Juliet story with music by Harry Freedman, fell flat at the box office and received negative reviews. As the management team watched the opening performance, which was clearly inadequately rehearsed and roughly danced, Corder turned to Southam and told him through gritted teeth, "I told you so." Years later, Macdonald conceded that the show had really needed a trial run in smaller centres such as "Belleville or Kingston, before being presented on the grand stage at the National Arts Centre."[13] The piece would go on to become an established part of the repertoire of Les Grands Ballets Canadiens, whose founder, Ludmilla Chiriaeff, saw it first at the Festival. The poor performances in Ottawa received a pasting in the press, with even the faithful *Ottawa Journal* editorializing against it. The response put paid for good to the idea of a resident dance company at the National Arts Centre or as part of Festival Canada.

When Southam prepared his report on the 1973 Summer Festival for the fall meetings of the Board of Trustees, he pinpointed both the successes and the problems. Opera had been the most successful component of the Festival, with the number of performances tripled and paid attendance doubled since 1971. Also in the plus category, though in a minor way, were poetry readings and children's entertainment. Dance had been catastrophic, with attendance even for the Royal Winnipeg Ballet presentation at the previous year's festival down by 40 percent from its first appearance at the June 1969 opening. Orchestral concerts had also done poorly, with a significant drop in audience at one point to an "unacceptable" 17 percent. Attendance for popular entertainment, although some individual performers did well, had, overall, plunged even more drastically, from 97 percent to a terrible 13 percent in just two years.[14]

The reason for this slump was not hard to pinpoint, and Southam deplored it in his report. Although Festival Canada was intended as a seamless month of integrated events, the different agencies, and especially the Secretary of State's Department, had failed to coordinate. In mid-July he had discovered that many of the top performers booked into the NAC for paying customers had also been contracted for free concerts during the Ottawa summer, either by the department at the outdoor Astrolabe Theatre, perched high on a cliff overlooking the Ottawa River just a stone's throw from the NAC, or by the CBC, for its open-air concerts at Camp Fortune in the Gatineau Hills. This programming disconnect would plague Festival Canada planning throughout the years, but Southam was furious and told the trustees he would complain to the minister. Other incidental programming that included some theatre presentations, and lunchtime art films and chamber music events at the NAC Studio, had simply languished.

This disappointing result for the third Summer Festival merely fortified Southam's determination to build on the NAC's strength. He advised the board to strengthen the operatic formula for the foreseeable future. "Our aim is to continue to set a national operatic standard of excellence in the interest of opera's future as a viable art form in the country," he declared.[15] Southam was correct about the trail-blazing path that the Arts Centre was forging. While setting out a future schedule of operas to be performed over the next five years, he drew attention to the interest that the NAC work was attracting. Both Montreal's Opéra du Québec and the Canadian Opera Company were proposing to put present and future NAC productions, complete with sets, costumes, and props, into their regular seasons—an idea that did, eventually, reimburse some of the operas' original costs.

The operas to be performed over the next several years were all "foreign," but Southam firmly pointed out that the Canadian content would be provided by "our conductor, orchestra, and by such Canadian singers, stage directors and designers who meet our standards."[16] He had no reservations about bringing in foreign talent if that meant higher quality, and this "mixed" policy would lead to some of the centre's most brilliant productions. There was plenty of work for good Canadian artists, especially singers, and there is no doubt about the benefits of their appearing in these NAC productions. Baritone Claude Corbeil, who played Figaro in the first 1971 production and appeared in several subsequent operas, spoke for many of the stars when he described his experience in Ottawa as being "the first time [he] felt at home as a Canadian artist." When he came to sing Figaro, he could barely speak English, yet, in the midst of the political troubles that were plaguing the country at the time, he found a camaraderie at the NAC that made him feel much more secure as an artist in Canada. The serious professional tone at the centre "validated the art form for us," he said, and it allowed other Canadian opera companies to see these artists perform there under superb conditions. Festival Canada became "an important reference" that led to bookings elsewhere, and, in Corbeil's case, took him to western Canada and other places in the country where he had never been before in his life.[17]

Equally important, the operas drew attention on the international scene to the quality of work in Canada—the singers, the designers, and the directors. Southam's vision and values permeated the artistic work and provided its underpinnings. For the future, he proposed to the board "an entirely musical festival from operatic to the broadly popular," with new creative productions, preferably musical ventures, in the Theatre and the Studio in both official languages. Canadian content was stressed, but only if it was good and sold at the box-office. Although he advised the board to approve a "restrained" budget of $550,000 for 1974, he was still aiming at $1 million—the original target for the Festival in 1966. The securing and rearranging of funds was Southam's own particular art form, and he would pursue it vigorously on behalf of his operas in his remaining five years at the Arts Centre.

While the Festival's plans developed, the other artistic departments also flourished. In 1973 the orchestra embarked on its first European tour, which took it in a grand sweep across the Continent to Russia and back, via England, including a visit to the Bath Festival. This appearance had been tacked onto the tour after Sir Michael Tippett conducted the orchestra the year before. As director of the Bath Festival, he had invited Bernardi to bring his musicians to the beautiful English Regency city. Everywhere they went their music was received with huge enthusiasm, especially in Poland and Russia, where the halls were full and people stood three deep in the aisles.* The programs always included a Canadian composition and featured Canadian soloists such as singer Allan Monk and pianist Louis Lortie. The journey filled the musicians with enormous pride and, though exhausting for the fifty players and their accompanying crew, this first European venture was a triumph for the Arts Centre.

In theatre, Jean Roberts and her associate French director, Jean Herbiet, were laying down a solid keel for that department. Roberts, though practical in her Scottish way, was deeply idealistic about wanting NAC productions to represent the best of what Canada had to offer. Her dedication meant that, as the years passed, she built up a solid repertoire of well-directed classical plays, interspersed by visiting companies performing their own best work. Although not yet able to form a permanent resident theatre company at the Arts Centre, she succeeded in setting up a stable of regular actors by giving them consistent work in her plays.

Roberts's creation of the Hexagon/L'Hexagone, which allowed small companies of young actors to tour out from the centre, was a *tour de force*, spreading the idea that the National Arts Centre would share its bounty in theatre into the far corners of Canada, just as the orchestra did. This solid and sensible approach earned Roberts a lot of support, not least from Donald MacSween, the director of the National Theatre School in Montreal, with whom she kept up a constant and positive exchange of ideas.

Meanwhile, Herbiet also delivered exemplary work. The French theatre company at the NAC had uncovered an enthusiastic audience for French-language works, to the point where, by 1974, the forthcoming subscription season was sold out long before the first play opened. Its productions were hailed as "some of the most original and

*The NAC was fortunate to have as its music press officer a former *New York Times* correspondent, Tanya Daniell. Fluent in Russian, she was a great help during the tour in the Soviet Union.

acclaimed theatre at the time in Canada."[18] Herbiet received well-deserved praise for his productions of the French classics, especially Molière, but nothing was more fascinating or unusual than his work with the German-born creator Felix Mirbt. They collaborated on several remarkable works, two of which were outstanding: Georg Büchner's *Woyzeck* and August Strindberg's *Dream Play*. What made these plays extraordinary was that they featured not live actors but puppets, created by Mirbt and manipulated by a hidden team of puppeteers. The two theatre men had first met when Herbiet travelled to Stratford for two weeks specifically to work with Mirbt. Ultimately, their Arts Centre productions, especially *Woyzeck*, would tour successfully under the NAC banner to Montreal's Centaur Theatre and then abroad, to France, Belgium, and the Edinburgh Festival.

In Ottawa, Herbiet was also able to present some politically provocative theatre, notably John McDonough's *Charbonneau et Le Chef*, which portrayed the struggle between Archbishop Joseph Charbonneau and Premier Maurice Duplessis at the time of the famous asbestos strike in Quebec in 1949. The action pitted the Roman Catholic clergyman against the authoritarian provincial premier in defence of union workers who had gone out on strike and were being pummelled by the provincial government. As the 1975 Annual Report quietly noted, some of the people involved in the play's events, including Pierre Trudeau and the former union leader, Jean Marchand, now Canada's leading politicians, were in the audience. The production was performed by Montreal's Compagnie Jean Duceppe, led by actor-director Jean Duceppe.* Trudeau went backstage after the performance to meet the cast, but, by Herbiet's account, many of the young actors had strong separatist sentiments and held back from the prime minister. Once assured that he was there to discuss the performance, not politics, they clustered around the federal leader.[19]

Herbiet made excellent use of the L'Hexagone and, like the English-speaking troupe, sent six young actors in a bus, along with their sets and costumes, on road trips of up to six weeks. He attained his greatest success in 1975, when he managed to book the French-speaking players all the way from Victoria, British Columbia, to the French-held Atlantic islands of St. Pierre and Miquelon. The whole exercise uncovered an unexpected appetite for theatre in both official languages right across the country—a concept entirely consistent with the NAC's mandate.

Behind this triumphant public face, the growing shadow of financial restraint was causing worry. The disappointing results of the 1973 Festival had put a dent in the NAC's

---

*Forty years on, Duceppe's son, Gilles Duceppe, would lead the Bloc Québécois, the federal Quebec separatist party, in the House of Commons in Ottawa.

finances, producing the first serious deficit in its five years of operations. Southam did not veer from his basic position that "the arts could not be churned out as if on some kind of production line," and he argued again that they required "large and growing subsidies—and this was true of every enterprise of this kind in the world." A failure of financing, he stated categorically in the Annual Report, meant the risk that the Arts Centre "could truly become the white elephant that some critics, now confounded, once mockingly predicted it would be."[20] It was a brave and unequivocal position in the changing world of finances in Ottawa, but, to Southam, it was unthinkable that the arts would not receive the support they deserved. It would now become the board's central task, and particularly the executive committee's, to try to control the NAC finances and avoid runaway deficits.

The man who would lead much of the jousting with management was the independently wealthy Arthur Gelber, an energetic, short, and bespectacled Torontonian with a generous reputation for philanthropy but a well-known aggressive temperament. He would eventually succeed François Mercier as chair of the board, but for now his role as a trustee was to keep a sharp eye on management's spending and machinations. His board colleague David Golden, an astute Ottawa player, was fully engaged in setting up and heading the new satellite communications company, Telesat Canada, but he maintained a love for the arts and, in particular, an interest in the National Arts Centre. When he first joined the board in 1971, he had been "struck by the grandiose ideas" and astounded at "how much money you could lose running a restaurant." He never questioned the centre's role as a first-class organization, however, and he gave it his full support.[21] Another seasoned Ottawa hand was Al Johnson, who, as president of the CBC, automatically became an ex-officio NAC trustee. He also had a passion for the arts and would be a precious ally in the struggles ahead.

These trustees had Ottawa experience, and they worked hard with management, massaging the NAC submissions to the government and assisting staff in working up the detailed Five-Year Plan required for Treasury Board analysis. The increasingly stringent practices of government financing were now impinging directly on the NAC's requests for money. In the fall of 1973 Southam asked for a subsidy of nearly $6 million, but he received a half-million less—a serious cut that would inevitably have an impact on programming.

There was some good news. Southam's continual lobbying had persuaded the Ottawa-Carleton Regional Government to commit a substantial $139,000 to the Arts Centre. In addition, some municipal money finally flowed into its coffers when another new Ottawa mayor, Pierre Benoit, delivered $100,000 to the centre. Unfortunately, when Treasury Board analysts got wind at least of the regional money, they reduced the federal subsidy by the same amount. This pattern would continue to assert itself in the coming period. Despite the new-found funds, it was clear that there would have to be programming cuts if the NAC was to meet its budget.

Wrangling over money and projects would now become a prime theme between the board and management. Gelber was the most aggressive activist on the board, taxing Southam about his costs, particularly those for Festival Canada. He razzed him over the number of opera performances, demanding to know why operas being produced by the Canadian Opera Company could not appear in the Festival. The board began to push hard for a reserve fund to guard against deficits, but Southam resisted on the grounds that it would eat into program funds. When it came to finding money, he and Corder opted for cutting across all departments instead of reducing the Festival's budget. When the board protested, Southam insisted that the high standards already established for the Summer Festival must be maintained.

Inside the Arts Centre, the reaction to these cuts was intense. Bernardi successfully resisted most of them for music by using the arguments of his music administrator, Guy Huot, that tampering with the success to date would have disastrous results. Ted Demetre in Dance and Variety, whose imported entertainers generated a lot of revenue for the centre, indicated that the cuts would have a deleterious effect on the indigenous dance program. Jean Roberts approached the cuts in theatre with a certain Scottish thrift and realized that the Hexagon/L'Hexagone touring companies would have to go. But she stood firmly against the proposal that the support facilities, including wardrobe and sets, be outsourced. Under her lead, the creative cadre in these admired disciplines had largely been developed, and she opted, eventually, to go off staff herself and become a contract employee rather than abolish them. Despite the belt-tightening, plans for the opera, the NAC's most expensive art form, went forward.

The 1974 Summer Festival again saw three operas mounted, including a rare production of Mozart's *Abduction from the Seraglio*. As pressures mounted, however, another financial crisis erupted over the operas scheduled for 1975. Offenbach's *La Belle Hélène* was to be reprised, but there were to be glorious new productions of Verdi's *La Traviata* and Mozart's *The Magic Flute*. Production costs shot up, with problems so severe that Southam was forced to bring the matter to the board. Each opera was seriously over budget: *Traviata* by $34,000, and *The Magic Flute* by a whopping $81,000. The cause given was "poor communication between directors and designers." Financial management had indeed been poor, and the operas' artistic staff had approached their task "as if the budgets were open-ended."[22] In the richly appointed *Traviata*, specially woven bolts of cloth had been commissioned to dress the choristers. The *Flute*, directed by Anthony Besch of the German State Opera, revelled in lavish Styrofoam sets devised by the renowned Covent Garden designer Peter Rice, who had been imported for the production. By the time the board heard about these overruns, it was too late to cancel the performances, but Gelber put his foot down, insisting that in future the opera productions must be more strictly controlled. Golden was equally tough-minded and backed Gelber, refusing to approve any new budgets until the $150,000 opera deficit was dealt with.

Southam moved swiftly to assuage the damage, thinking creatively on how the Festival, and particularly the operas, could be moved off the NAC books. Perhaps a separate agency could be established to produce them, he thought, and he engaged Niki Goldschmidt to prepare a proposal. Southam also put out feelers to some of his business contacts, including the insurance company Metlife of Canada and the family firm of Southam Press, for donations to defray the operas' costs. By July, Gelber was pushing to instill order, and the board devised a five-year Festival plan to take to the minister with "all future programming hinging on the outcome."

This outreach to the private sector for funds was the first serious attempt to look beyond government subsidy and the box-office to support the NAC's work. Apart from an unsolicited $5 donation in 1963 from a Miss Gisèle Bouvier of Ottawa, "to show my support for your idea," there had been no effort to raise non-government funds for the Arts Centre. On the contrary, trustees and management were convinced that if they pursued private fundraising, there would be an uproar, with the heavily sub-sidized NAC accused of competing for money with less-fortunate arts companies. Seagram's had been the only commercial name mentioned in connection with NAC activities so far, and another decade would pass before it would be permitted, after much soul-searching, to put its name on a NAC Orchestra concert series. Metlife finally turned Southam down on the grounds of "the unstable business environment." A sim-ilar approach to Bell Canada revealed that it would rather support touring the orchestra to small towns than high-brow stuff like opera.

The Festival idea itself, with its national unity overtones, was becoming more polit-ical. With input from the astute and well-connected Gelber, Southam devised a proposal that the Festival be shifted out of the NAC framework and into a special agency. He also recommended that the Arts Centre take charge of and run all Ottawa's Festival Canada professional activities—and that it be given the government budget to do it. This idea worked its way into a Cabinet memorandum over the signature of Peter Roberts, the assistant undersecretary of state, and went forward to Cabinet in late August 1975. In the meantime, as a diplomatic gesture designed to reassure the trustees, Southam proposed that the COC's artistic director, Lotfi Mansouri, be signed on as an opera adviser to the centre. He would be tasked to guard against opera over-runs. Mansouri had been contracted to conduct a new *Figaro* in the 1976 Festival season, so there were heated discussions about conflict of interest, but Southam assured the trustees that there would be no more commitments of this kind, and Mansouri was appointed.

In a further effort to defray costs, ticket prices were raised for the first time. High-end prices for most shows and concerts went up a dollar, to $7.50, and fifty cents was added to the lower-end $3.00 tickets. A subscription for the whole roster of three summer operas was $12.50, although it would shortly go to $15.00. There was no question that NAC audiences enjoyed first-class performances at subsidized prices, and, in return, they filled the seats. The 1975 Summer Festival was no exception. Despite the furor over production costs, both the critics and the public hailed the season. The stage was set for 1976, which would set a wondrous high-water mark in opera at the National Arts Centre.

As summer gave way to fall, Hamilton Southam informed the board that he would not be renewing his contract when it came due in less than eighteen months. The pinch of financial restraint was increasing, and the National Arts Centre was sharply criticized for a newly negotiated contract with its musicians. In this period of accelerating inflation, their salaries had gone up by 13 percent, while the number of services they gave to the centre decreased. Musicians in other major orchestras were angry and demanded to be at least on a par with their peers at the NAC. The Montreal Symphony members in particular were threatening to strike if they did not get as good a deal as the NAC players. Cultural officials generally, and specifically André Fortier at the Canada Council, were critical, and Fortier lobbied against the Arts Centre being given a larger subsidy. Nevertheless, the five-year plan called for a proposed subsidy of $11 million for the 1979–80 season.

The climate of the times was changing dramatically. In 1973, after the first shocking oil crisis in Western countries, inflation in Canada suddenly accelerated. The government "seemed uncertain what to do,"[23] and, while it indexed its expenditures, it de-indexed its revenues. As a result, the cost of government expenditures began to sky-rocket, by 23 percent in 1974–75 alone. Unemployment was rampant, and $1 billion of government funds was dedicated to job creation—many of the initiatives being little more than "make-work" projects. With the government unwilling or unable to curb expenditures, Treasury Board cost-cutting exercises became a routine fact of life in all government budgets. Arthur Kroeger, a leading public servant and deputy secretary at the Treasury Board in this period, remembered fourteen such cost-cutting exercises in just two years.

Some of the experienced members on the NAC board tried to persuade Southam that it was not a propitious time in which to find more government money, but they continued to use all their networks and connections to try to solve the centre's financial problems. By now the building itself was in need of serious maintenance, and Al Johnson, a former deputy minister at the Treasury Board, and David Golden fashioned a request to Gordon Osbaldeston, Johnson's replacement at the financial bureau. He helped to secure a special grant of $750,000 for building repairs and ensured that the money did not come out of the NAC's operating funds.

In-house, the deficit was growing, and Southam relied on a "special projects" fund that he kept under the control of his own office to try to bring the numbers down. A bilingual tilt to proposals unquestionably helped matters. An official in the Official Languages Office guided the centre's budget team in finding money to keep the French-language touring L'Hexagone project on the road while its English counterpart, the Hexagon, was cut.[24] By late fall, Southam heard that the NAC would be given responsibility for all the professional activities of Festival Canada, as requested, but there was no mention of any additional funds. He advised the government that the NAC could not undertake this responsibility for summer 1976 but would consider it for 1977.

As a result of these dire constraints, the NAC managing team kept planning for Festival 1976 to three operas, and no other theatre, music, or dance performances were commissioned. The board's executive committee protested, and Southam suggested that small musical ensembles be brought in to supplement the summer program. Financial discussions at the centre took on a tart tone as it struggled to deal with the government's Wage and Price Controls policy. Thanks to board chair François Mercier's close Liberal connections, guidance from Hugh Faulkner, and careful spadework by the trustees and management, the NAC's budget passed through Cabinet relatively unscathed. Mercier wrote a special letter to the minister to thank him.

In-house, Corder was juggling everything from fees in the parking garage to union settlements as inflation got out of hand and settlements were rung in at increases of 12–15 percent. He soon reported that the summer operas were "in terrible trouble."[25] Once again Southam approached his business connections, and this time both Metlife and Southam Press agreed to put in $25,000 each towards the summer budget.

Festival Canada 1976 reached a zenith beyond anyone's highest expectations. The backstage area was crowded with new scenery for a sumptuous all-new production of *The Marriage of Figaro*, directed by Lotfi Mansouri, which had a lavish baroque set and costumes. It was Tchaikovsky's *The Queen of Spades*, however, that put the seal on Ottawa's annual opera festival as a pre-eminent event on the international music

Czech artist Josef Svoboda, flanked by Hamilton Southam and Mario Bernardi, designed one of the NAC's most heralded opera productions, The Queen of Spades. *Photo © NAC.*

scene. Its five performances drew unanimous praise from critics who came to Ottawa from all corners of the globe.

The production was the work of two brilliant Czechs: the director Vaclav Kaslik and the scenographer Josef Svoboda, both artists who came to Ottawa from the National Theatre in Prague. Their work was already familiar to Canadians from Expo 67's *Lanterna Magika* at the Czech Pavilion, one of the most popular shows at the world fair. Southam was determined to get Svoboda for the Arts Centre, and he had visited him personally in Prague in 1970. At last he secured him for this crowning summer season.

The Queen of Spades galvanized audiences in Ottawa. As the program notes explained, the plot was based on a story by Pushkin: "The central character, Hermann, is an army officer, torn between his love for a young noble-woman, Lisa, and his obsession with gambling. Lisa's grandmother is an aged countess who knows the secret of winning at cards, and Hermann is determined to discover it. He succeeds, but with tragic results." A powerful opera, it was a daring leap forward for Festival Canada, which, until then, had been a rich but conventional mix of operas by Mozart, Rossini, and Offenbach. Instead of moving through the traditional scenes, Svoboda placed all the action in a single room in a mental institution, where the anguished Hermann either dreams or recalls the angst-ridden memories of his life. Svoboda's effects were achieved not through elaborate stage scenery, but through an intricate combination of lighting and multimedia devices. The staid NAC Annual Report would later describe the work as "a phantasmagoria of moments from the life of the insane hero, Hermann, seen by him, and the audience, through the walls of his hospital room." Essential to the production's success was the pairing of two of Canada's greatest operatic stars,

Maureen Forrester and the brilliant Canadian "heldentenor" Jon Vickers sang magnificently in the leading roles in The Queen of Spades. *Photo © Fernand R. LeClair.*

each with huge careers on the international stage: Jon Vickers as Hermann and Maureen Forrester as the Countess. They brought their powerful talents to bear on the tragic tale, and memories of this Canadian operatic event have resonated through the years.

Some of the most astute recollections of this memorable performance came from the stage crew members who worked on it. Unlike *Figaro*, *The Queen of Spades* had little in the way of constructed stage-sets. Its extraordinary effects, rather, came through the use of light. Heinz Roesler, a former U-boat crew member who had been appointed head electrician in the Opera hall, collaborated closely with Svoboda to achieve his brilliant effects. He had been at the Arts Centre since the beginning and had worked with every lighting director for every opera presented there. "Some of them were prima donnas who thought they had crowns on their heads," he remembered, but Svoboda was different. Roesler found him "beautiful to work with," quiet and diligent, and the two men laboured carefully for hours at a time, creating the scenic effects by focusing the lights, raising and lowering their intensity, and trying different colour schemes until they achieved what Svoboda wanted. During rehearsals, Southam would slip into the dark control room at the back of the hall where Roesler ran his lighting board and watch the evolution of the work with intense interest. The minimalist black-and-white décor brought a completely different view to opera than the ornate and lavish productions that then characterized most conventional opera. The work's powerful impact reached its peak with the performances of both Vickers and Forrester.

The temperamental Vickers had reluctantly arrived in Ottawa from his home in Bermuda, late for rehearsals and complaining of suffering from a bad cold. When he tried to persuade Bernardi to let his understudy step in for the opening performance, the maestro refused, saying they would "both be lynched" if Vickers did not appear.[26] The effort was worth it. Vickers, on stage for the entire opera, gave a stunning performance as the tormented Hermann, and Maureen Forrester was his equal in the difficult role of the Countess. This was opera of a different style, more European, and certainly in the vanguard of the best modern work.

No one was more delighted at the stark magnificence of the performance and the opera's success than Hamilton Southam. By sheer force of will, he and Corder had driven the Festival Canada productions to this triumphant peak. They had demonstrated, through their dexterous efforts, that Canada, and the National Arts Centre in particular, could produce opera of the finest international quality.

The last of the three opera offerings that summer was a revival of Rossini's *Le Comte Ory*. This vaudevillian opera, with its buffo scenes, was a complete contrast to the extravagant *Marriage of Figaro* and the austere *Queen*, but it also garnered excellent reviews, especially for its leading singers, the Canadian coloratura soprano Colette Boky and baritone Claude Corbeil. A new innovation, a specially arranged CN Rail Opera Train, ferried happy patrons back and forth from Montreal to view the performances throughout July.

�֍

As Southam prepared to take his leave of the Arts Centre, he could be satisfied that he had put in place Ottawa's long-dreamed of Festival. Little expense had been spared in achieving the desired goal, but the results spoke for themselves. More than anything else, the summer opera season was implanted in people's mind and had become an integral event on the summer festival route. The National Arts Centre and Canadian artists, at least musical ones, were becoming fixtures on the international circuit.

In official circles, however, Southam's success with opera was causing unease. Charles Lussier, another member of the Trudeau/Pelletier circle from Montreal, had now been appointed director of the Canada Council as André Fortier moved on to become the new deputy minister at the Secretary of State's Department. As the impending success of Festival 76 was unfolding, Lussier gave a cautious interview to the *Montreal Star*.[27] The interviewer, lauding the excellence to be found at the National Arts Centre, asked: "Couldn't we make this our Salzburg and attract tourists from all over the world?"[28] But Lussier was clearly troubled by the standards of "extravaganza in décor and costume" that the NAC had set, though he tentatively declared himself in full support of the "excellence" of the work. His dilemma, he said, was that the budgets at the Canada Council could not meet the demand for opera that was now bubbling up across the country. As Southam forged ahead with his opera festival, Council officials were working to try to save money by encouraging co-productions among opera companies, getting them to exchange productions, costumes, and sets. Lotfi Mansouri had been tapped to be the artistic director for the opera companies in both Toronto and Montreal, in an effort to create an economy of scale.

Lussier agreed with Pelletier over the democratization of the arts. Clearly, under his direction, the Canada Council would look more favourably on supporting small efforts throughout the country, such as the budding Guelph Spring Festival, which was producing smaller operas on a much more affordable scale than the National Arts Centre. The *Montreal Star* interviewer pointed out that nothing could be more democratic than the five dollar top ticket price that the NAC was charging for its performances. But the basic issue remained: To what degree should public funds be used to produce excellence in artistic work in Canada? This debate over how and where taxpayers' money should be spent in supporting the arts would remain a constant thread in political discussion in Canadian life.

The 1976–77 season would be the last under Southam's leadership, and the facts told their own story. From a first-year attendance of 494,169 in 1969–70, audiences had grown to 763,320 in this eighth full season of operations. Box-office revenues had risen from just over $1.1 million to nearly $4.2 million. The number of performances had increased from 645 in the first year to 827. In the previous season alone, performances had included fourteen different orchestras, chamber music groups, and choirs; main season performances by two opera companies; eight ballet and contemporary dance companies; eight English-language and eight French-language mainstage plays; and fifty "variety" shows, eighteen of them Canadian. The careful tabulations pointed out the level of support to Canadian talent: of the sixty composers present in the season's music program, eight had been Canadian; of twenty choreographers, half had been Canadian; seven out of ten playwrights in the English-language season were Canadian, and nine Canadian writers had plays put on in the French theatre season.

In terms of audiences, the work was achieving sterling numbers: well over 90 percent for the music programs, 96.8 percent for French theatre, and similar figures for the English theatre season. Jean Roberts's solid leadership had presented not only the classics but at least four original Canadian plays, including the production of playwright-in-residence Timothy Findley's *Can You See Me Yet?* Theatre London brought its production of James Reaney's *The Donnellys*, and Halifax's Neptune Theatre played *The Collected Works of Billy the Kid*, adapted from Michael Ondaatje's volume of poems of the same name. Under Roberts's own direction, the NAC had produced a fascinating run of Austrian playwright Peter Handke's work, *The Ride Across Lake Constance*, a play that was "stirring up excitement in the international capitals of the world" when Roberts presented it at the NAC.[29]

The benefits extended to arts organizations in other areas too. The Canadian Opera Company had made its usual appearances, as had the major ballet ensembles. And the Arts Centre had its own outreach programs too. The musicians had presented twenty-six demonstrations in thirty-one Ontario and Quebec schools, and the Theatre Department had also expanded outside to engage young audiences. Six players of the Hexagon troupe had toured for ten weeks into forty-seven centres with two Canadian historical plays, *Almighty Voice* and *1837: The Farmers Revolt*. L'Hexagone had also taken two shows, *Étincelle et Flammèche* and *Pile ou Face*, to 52,000 students in elementary and secondary schools in three provinces. All these tours were subsidized by the NAC, although the Annual Report signalled that this commitment could not continue in the growing environment of financial restraint. No wonder Southam declared that "it is unrealistic to expect the National Arts Centre to run at a profit."[30]

While Southam and the trustees argued for more cooperation with the electronic media, to extend the reach of the performances at the NAC through television and film, they made little progress with the CBC, the National Film Board, or the private sector. The early dreams for the NAC had been fulfilled beyond everyone's wildest expectations, but new dreams had come to replace them, and it was clear that the growing austerity meant that some of them would remain unfulfilled before Southam's departure. The goals included a Mozart-Beethoven Music Competition at the NAC, more opportunities for variety artists, greater accessibility to the Arts Centre work by the Canadian public through the electronic media, and the establishment, finally, of resident theatre companies at the centre which could tour as the NAC Orchestra did.

While none of these initiatives would occur during his term, Southam would continue to lobby the government for them—and his efforts would bear fruit after his departure.

While Southam prepared for his leave-taking in the spring of 1977, he remained firmly in command. Problems continued to pile up, many of them related to money. The operating costs of the building itself were becoming an issue. Concerns over energy conservation, not perceived at the time of construction, were now gaining importance, and Corder sought engineering advice on measures that could be taken to save money on heating and cooling the structure. The catering department had run at a deficit since the outset, and efforts to rein in its runaway costs by altering the restaurants' format were at last getting under way, overseen by Corder and overcoming Southam's earlier resistance. Southam's dream of a theatre-restaurant like the one he remembered at the Swedish Opera in Stockholm had not worked out in Ottawa, and he later confirmed that he had simply been "wrong" about the idea. Le Restaurant was now to be revamped to operate on a more economical and cost-effective basis. A move was afoot to build up the downstairs Le Café, which seemed more popular with the general public than Le Restaurant. By late fall these transformations were firmly proceeding, and Corder was able to report to the board that catering at the NAC "is on the right track this time."[31]

The Arts Centre also learned that the austerity program would apply to its activities as well as to other departments, and that the government was intent in rolling back some of the salary increases that, in some places, were running well over 30 percent. Salaries for everyone, including senior management, were not to exceed levels set out in the Wage and Price Controls.

John Roberts was appointed secretary of state to replace Hugh Faulkner in 1976. Southam took time to meet with him and brief him carefully on the NAC's affairs: because of the budget cuts, the Five-Year Plan had been reduced to a Four-Year Plan; there were joint opera initiatives with Toronto, Montreal, and Quebec; and the Arts Centre was interested in wider distribution of its work through touring and the electronic media. For the first time, the possibility of a Pay-TV system for cultural events was mentioned—an idea that finally came to be more than thirty years later when New York's Metropolitan Opera broadcast its first opera live on HDTV in cinemas around the world. At the end of their discussion, Roberts told Southam that he would be travelling widely on political business and that he intended to leave the day-to-day work of the department to his deputy minister, André Fortier. As regards the NAC, this would now be someone else's problem.

In his usual thoughtful way, Southam helped to arrange appointments for those close to him, including his able assistant Richard Dennison, whom he sponsored for

CAP, a public service executive development program. Others were also preparing for the change. Maestro Mario Bernardi wrote a long handwritten personal note to Southam from a hotel room in Winnipeg, reviewing the previous nine years of work together. He had no intention of resigning, but he proposed a year's sabbatical to refresh himself and his work.

In the meantime a search committee that included Arthur Gelber, Maureen Forrester, and David Golden had been struck to find Southam's successor. Although he did not sit on the committee, Southam was closely consulted and, by mid-fall, the decision was made. Donald MacSween, a bilingual Montreal labour lawyer who had been serving as director of the National Theatre School, would be the NAC's new director general.

Southam had prepared well for a time of ease and adventure ahead. He had ordered a ninety-foot, custom-designed sailing sloop from the British boat builders Camper and Nicholson, and, in the early fall of 1976, he graciously sent invitations to all the NAC trustees to join him in Southampton, England, for the boat's launch. On February 24, 1977, he met for the last time with the board, his monumental work for the NAC completed. While he sailed off to an adventurous new life at sea cruising the Mediterranean aboard *All Is Best*, the National Arts Centre was left behind to chart its future course without him—and in much more uncertain waters.

Part Two

THE DIFFICULT YEARS

9

NEW MAN
IN TOWN

On April 1, 1977, Donald MacSween formally took the reins as the new director general of the National Arts Centre. The tall "jocularly urbane" Montrealer would soon become known as a convivial bon vivant, a man-about-town in Ottawa.[1] His journey to the centre of Canada's arts world had not been by direct route. He had started his university education at McGill but had taken a side-trip during his legal studies to Laval University in Quebec City after failing his first year of law at Montreal. This move ensured his fluid proficiency in the French language, but he returned to McGill to complete his degree, graduating and beginning work as a labour lawyer at the prestigious Montreal law firm of Ogilvy Renault. There he toiled alongside Brian Mulroney, another young practitioner, before an unsettling marital split in 1972 set him off on a new career in pursuit of an old passion: the theatre.

By his own recollection, MacSween had loved theatre from the time he was a small child, writing his first play at the age of ten, "a bed sheets and lanterns affair" entitled "Mr. and Mrs. Riddle's Farm in Sutton Junction."[2] Too small to play on the high school football team, he remembered that he continued to pursue his interest in drama all through high school by participating in plays. Once at McGill, he joined the McGill Players Club, where he played minor roles while also writing humorous newsletters for the Arts and Science Faculty. There he also encountered, and become part of, a serendipitous group of artistically minded individuals, several of whom would go on to become key players in the creation of Canada's cultural policies and the practice of its arts. They included Timothy Porteous, destined to be a top Trudeau political aide and later director of the Canada Council; James Domville, later the commissioner of the National Film Board;*

---

*Both men by virtue of their positions later became ex-officio trustees of the NAC.

and Brian Macdonald, already making his way in the performing arts and soon to be famous as a choreographer and as a dance and opera director.

Although slightly younger than the rest, MacSween joined this seminal group of students, who famously wrote and performed the 1967 edition of *The McGill Review* under the title "My Fur Lady." An irreverent production, it took its inspiration from a British review of a slightly earlier vintage, *Beyond the Fringe*, written and performed by a group at Oxford, which went on to be performed on the professional stage.* Both shows typified the youthful debunking of staid tradition that characterized the 1960s, before the debunkers themselves went on to become firm members of the Establishment. "My Fur Lady" had a life of its own for almost two years, garnering rave reviews and standing ovations in a cross-country tour that included performances at the Stratford Festival. It was heady stuff for the young troupe, and no surprise that some of them would play prominent roles in the arts in Canada. Their interconnections continued in the years ahead.

By 1972, MacSween opted to give up law, where he could see "no other future than one of making money,"[3] and follow his passion into the arts. He was appointed director of the National Theatre School, a position he held for the next five years. Through his connection with theatre director Jean Roberts, he kept an eye on what was going on at the National Arts Centre, particularly in its Theatre Department. Given his theatrical background, linguistic skills, and excellent connections, it was no surprise when the Search Committee singled him out for the NAC job. MacSween later suggested that a Montreal friendship with architect Fred Lebensold had first put the idea in his head, but Arthur Gelber, a member of both the board of the National Theatre School and the NAC Search Committee, had observed MacSween first hand. Either way, MacSween was soon summoned to Ottawa for a meeting with the committee.

He had two concerns. First, he was about to become "a theatre manager" and felt he knew little about the "catchment basin" that would be his prime constituency for audience members. Second, he lacked experience with the workings of official Ottawa. When he queried whether these gaps in his résumé might be serious handicaps, David Golden quickly reassured him. After a good discussion, MacSween agreed to put his hat in the ring. On his return to Montreal, he sought advice from his mentor, Frank Scott, the distinguished professor of constitutional law at McGill who habitually "encouraged young lawyers to take an interest in things outside the law." MacSween recalled that, after a couple of martinis at the Scott household, his professor advised him that "there's one human right that everybody neglects: it's your right to fail."[4] MacSween took the advice to heart, along with Scott's assumption that, if things did go wrong, it

---

*Many of its key players, such as Jonathan Miller, Peter Cook, and Alan Bennett, all eventually found permanent places in the arts world in Britain.

would be the fault of those who did the hiring. When he was formally offered the director generalship, he took the job.

MacSween arrived in the capital in the spring of 1977 wearing what he would later describe as "rose-coloured glasses." The Trudeau era was in full swing in the national capital, and MacSween was "very impressed with the quality of people that were serving the country at this level." The Arts Centre building itself made a deep impression on him, its brutalist-style massive architecture striking him as "a natural outcropping" of the Canadian Shield—to use Lebensold's felicitous phrase. Although he knew it was sometimes also referred to as Fort Southam, he found that "it had a wonderful quality inside because of the way it was structured … the light filtering in through the windows … almost every time you passed through an area it looked different."[5] Perhaps a little dazzled by his new adventure, he believed that the NAC had been a huge success and, apart from a few minor problems, stood in good shape.

Southam's handover to him had been impeccable. The founding head went to great lengths to ensure that the new man was fully briefed and welcomed. One of MacSween's first official visits backstage followed a recital by cellist Mstislav Rostropovich, who had long been a friend of Southam. "Miracle! Miracle!" roared the Russian, as he enveloped the bewildered MacSween in a full embrace. "First time in arts I hear predecessor say good things about successor." Nevertheless, MacSween felt he had big shoes to fill, and years later he jokingly explained that shoes were often on his mind in those early days as he polished and buffed his own footwear, wondering whether Southam had ever had to do the same thing himself.

There were other contrasts with Southam too. MacSween was mindful of the small details and moved the director general's name from the top of the NAC house program to a line at the bottom of the page. Southam gently chided him for his modesty, but also wondered why he had not changed the founding director's voice on the tape inviting patrons to take their seats before a performance. Southam had a special reason for this inquiry: it had been his habit to have the favourite lady in his life voice the francophone portion of the bilingual message with him. He was now courting but not yet married to his third and last wife, Marion. MacSween responded that he had no intention of putting his own voice on the tape or of removing Southam's. Today, Southam's voice remains on the recording, along with Marion's, which was eventually added to it.

One of the most valuable assets that Southam bequeathed to MacSween was a good personal assistant. MacSween grasped a little of how things had been in Southam's time when she rushed into his office early one morning to apologize for not upgrading him from the standard government-authorized tourist class fare to a first-class ticket on a flight to Toronto. Southam's private wealth had allowed these luxuries to occur as a matter of routine, though they were never charged to the public purse. On more important issues, Michael Pitfield, Trudeau's well-connected clerk of the Privy Council, warned MacSween that Southam had always gone above the decision-makers when trying to get things done, and that he would now have to make his own connections. Southam had used his own money for much of his extensive entertaining on behalf of the Arts Centre, and veteran board members Gelber and Golden ensured that MacSween received an expense account that allowed him to continue this hospitality. Before long, the new director developed a reputation as a generous host and a con-vivial guest on the Ottawa social scene. Unfortunately, as he later noted ruefully, the crucial asset that Southam's independent wealth afforded him—of being "resignation-proof"—was a luxury he did not share.

For the first year, the portents seemed good, with the financial picture staying on the positive side in the Annual Report. All artistic departments were reporting success, and even the 1977 Summer Festival finished in the black. The festival had included a Banff Centre School of Fine Arts/NAC opera collaboration on two one-act operas, Wolf-Ferrari's *Secret of Susanna* and Gian Carlo Menotti's *Telephone*, as well as three mainstage operas: Strauss's *Ariadne auf Naxos*, which brought back the brilliant Czech team of Svoboda and Kaslik; Donizetti's *Don Pasquale*; and a reprise of *The Magic Flute*, directed by a Canadian, Jeanette Aster, though designed by the brilliant British designer Peter Rice. Overall, Canadian artists were doing well at the Arts Centre, according to the annual report directly earning more than $4.3 million as a result of NAC activities during the year, and with a further $11.4 million pumped into the system as a result of all the extensive NAC activities in the arts.

Although Donald MacSween claimed he had no great vision when he took over the job, in reality he had a big dream. His mind was set on accomplishing in theatre what Southam had done for music and the orchestra at the Arts Centre. While describing himself as a simple theatre manager "responsible for the life and happiness of the artists, technicians and support staff at the centre,"[6] his ambition was to create a resident theatre company in both official languages that was capable of touring the country and, perhaps, even internationally, just as the resident orchestra did. Coming out of the intense and lively ferment of the Montreal theatrical world, he was confident that, if he could establish a core company of actors, "within four or five years the NAC could develop a highly qualified performance ensemble, working in both languages, that could tour the country." He knew from experience that this kind of theatrical scene would also develop a rich pool of playwrights. The Montreal partnership between director André Brassard and writer Michel Tremblay had produced no fewer than twenty-six original plays, and MacSween dreamed of developing the same critical mass at the Arts Centre. At his core, MacSween was a passionate theatre man.

The solid work that had been going on at the NAC under the leadership of Jean Roberts and her associate, Jean Herbiet, had been moving firmly in this direction, but as yet there had been insufficient funds to put a full-fledged resident company in place. A lot of spadework had been devoted to the idea, Roberts said, particularly when Hugh Faulkner was the minister responsible. But he had left by 1977, and the new secretary of state, John Roberts, was preoccupied with other issues, particularly those of national unity.

The theatre scene was burgeoning all over the country, with a strong sense of nationalism pervading the work. The Stratford Board of Trustees had even been accused of a "colonial mentality" when the English-born director Robin Phillips was appointed to run the festival there in 1975.[7] Some new members of the NAC board, such as the distinguished Canadian theatre critic Herbert Whittaker, thought that the Arts Centre should be in the business of showcasing the best Canadian work, not creating it. MacSween opposed this idea forcefully, aligning himself with Jean Gascon's original idea that, to be successful, the National Arts Centre had to have "a heart that beats." Gascon would soon play a pivotal role in MacSween's plans for resident theatre at the NAC. MacSween convinced Whittaker that, while he might be "historically justified, he was creatively incorrect,"[8] and he soon won the board over to support his plans. He was able to demonstrate how the orchestra and the opera had given the Arts Centre credibility on the national and international scene, and now he hoped to achieve the same success with theatre. Within weeks of his taking up his new job, the board gave him its approval to proceed.

Years later MacSween would ironically observe that he should have known that the seeds of the financial problems that ultimately destroyed his dream had been sown long before, when the first oil crisis in 1973 began years of financial turmoil and damage to the Canadian economy. None of this impending disaster was clear at the time, however, and he blithely moved forward with his plans. First he tried to find ways to help John Roberts free up the money for the theatre project. That proved difficult to do, as the climate became ever more economically challenged and regional interests competed for increasingly scarce cultural dollars. There had long been a generalized resentment elsewhere over monies given to projects in Ottawa, and MPs from all parts of Canada were always ready to lobby for their local community. MacSween concluded that one way to overcome this opposition was to hire some "big" names.

The Honourable John Roberts, the secretary of state when Donald MacSween took the NAC's top job. Photo © Bill Brennan/Ottawa Citizen. Reprinted by permission.

First he had some tidying up to do at the Arts Centre. Jean Roberts had checked with him soon after his appointment to see if she was part of his future scenario, and he had initially implied that she was. Before long, however, it became evident that he had someone else in mind for her job. Rather than approach her directly, he arranged for friends to invite her to sit on a panel at the National Theatre School in Montreal and then, tactfully, try to persuade her to take over his old job there as director. Roberts realized what was going on as she travelled back to Ottawa by train, retrieving paper and pen from her handbag en route and jotting down the pros and cons of fighting for her NAC job. By the time she arrived in the capital, she had decided on her resignation. MacSween was glad to receive it although he later remembered the whole affair as "awkward, because I had a high regard for Jean Roberts."[9]

Her departure cleared the way for MacSween to proceed with his plan—to hire the brilliant and talented Jean Gascon to be his director of theatre. Gascon was a heroic figure in Canadian theatre life. As founder of Montreal's Théâtre du Nouveau Monde along with actor (and later Canada Council chair) Jean-Louis Roux, Gascon had blazed the trail for French-speaking Canadian theatre. In a memorable 1956 production, he took his actors to the Stratford Festival, where they played together with a group of English performers in Shakespeare's *Henry V*. He stayed on to become part of Stratford, and eventually its artistic director.

By the time the National Arts Centre had opened, his time at Stratford had come to an end and his personal life had taken a difficult turn. His first marriage to a French Canadian was over, and a remarriage to an anglophone had caused controversy among many of his old Montreal friends. Far more seriously, the theatrical world in Montreal had become severely radicalized. Many francophones in Quebec who had reached out to the Rest of Canada were considered in some circles to be *persona non grata*, even traitors to the Quebec nationalist cause. The dedicated Gascon, whose love was for the arts, not politics, was shunned in Quebec, and there was no work for him in Montreal or, indeed, anywhere in his home province. The National Arts Centre position seemed to offer the ideal solution.

MacSween moved quickly to put the pieces in place. He won over the board, including Herbert Whittaker, to his proposal for a three-man team: a single resident ensemble headed by Gascon, and French and English components each under their own artistic directors. These directors would each assemble a group of players to live in Ottawa and perform in repertory, with the potential of some crossover between them. Jean Herbiet decided he "could live with this new arrangement" and agreed to remain as director of French theatre.[10] On the English side, MacSween chose John Wood, artistic director at the Neptune Theatre in Halifax. Gascon would oversee their work, and direct or perform as requested. In addition, he would become an ambassador for the NAC, visiting other theatre companies across the country and providing his theatrical services free of charge—all part of the NAC mandate to assist in developing

A meeting with Pierre Trudeau ensued when Jean Gascon became the NAC's new director of theatre. There were high hopes, both theatrical and political, in Gascon's appointment. Photo © Murray Mosher Photography.

the performing arts in Canada. MacSween estimated that these changes would cost an additional one million dollars a year and, with the board's blessing, he took the concept to his minister, John Roberts. Dexterously, Roberts found the money: it came from a special National Unity Fund, a budget directly under the control of the prime minister and the Cabinet and not part of any departmental budget.

On May 5, 1977, MacSween and his theatrical team met with Prime Minister Trudeau and Secretary of State Roberts to formally announce the new plans for the Theatre Department at the NAC. Wood recalled later that Trudeau seemed most interested in chatting in French and at length with Jean Gascon. Wood, meanwhile, was distressed to realize that the photographs of the occasion would forever record the old brown corduroy suit he had worn that day. Not surprisingly, the announcement was met with cries of outrage from the Canadian theatre community, again angry at the large sum of money going to "Ottawa" and not out into the regions. Loudest among the critics was Robin Phillips at Stratford, speaking on behalf of his fellow regional theatre directors.

MacSween's choice of Wood was a calculated risk. In his three years in Halifax, this Montreal-born director had put together a strong company, and MacSween liked his work. He was, however, an "artist's artist" whose singular intent was to put on great theatre, and, in recent months, he had clashed seriously with his board at the Neptune Theatre. The suggestion to come to Ottawa was timely. In their one exploratory discussion, MacSween tried to convey his vision for theatre—to make it similar to the success that the NAC had achieved with the orchestra on the national scene, both on tour and in commissioning and performing Canadian music. Wood seemed to get the point and accepted the job, bringing with him from Nova Scotia key members of his theatrical cadre, including composer Alain Laing, actor/writer Neil Munro, and designer John Ferguson, who would in time become the resident designer and visual consultant at the NAC. Thereafter, MacSween refrained from interfering in Wood's artistic decisions, except during his annual performance review. Wood, however, had

Left to right: the new NAC theatre team of Jean Herbiet, Jean Gascon, and new English theatre director John Wood. The three would not mix well. Photo © Murray Mosher Photography.

his own ideas for English theatre at the Arts Centre, and they did not correspond to MacSween's concept of "a national mission."[11]

While Jean Herbiet set about assembling the best team of francophone actors he could persuade to come and work in Ottawa, John Wood embarked on an aggressive hunt to find the best English-speaking Canadian actors available—a mission that took him on a much criticized trip to England. Although the Stratford Festival had passed its twentieth anniversary and other theatre groups were blossoming all over the country, many Canadian actors still turned to England for training and performing opportunities. Wood wanted to bring some of this talent back to Canada. He placed an ad in the British show-business journal *The Stage*, then, accompanied by NAC theatre administrator Andis Celms, travelled to London and met with sixty-five British-based Canadian actors who had responded to the audition call. Five were hired immediately for the budding NAC company, including the young Benedict Campbell, son of the Stratford Festival actor Douglas Campbell.

Fifteen years before on his own pilgrimage to Britain, Wood had served as a dresser for the Royal Shakespeare Company. There he had seen his first performance of Shakespeare's *Troilus and Cressida*, and he dreamed of producing his own version of this difficult play and already had it in mind for his first season at the NAC. As Campbell auditioned, Wood decided he had found his Troilus and hired Campbell on the spot for the role. Before the two NAC staffers left England, Celms consulted with the Royal Shakespeare and other English theatre companies on suitable contracts and terms for actors playing in repertory. By the time they returned to Ottawa, arrangements were well under way for the first season.

The theatre audience was ready for something new. In what would be billed as "Jean Gascon's first season as the NAC's Theatre Director,"[12] that season would subsequently present a record number if 686 performances in both official languages to just under 295,000 patrons. The first English theatre season was eagerly anticipated and enjoyed a subscription renewal rate of over 70 percent. Wood bought time by opening in October 1977 with a New York Touring Company version of the Broadway hit *Same Time Next Year*, starring American actors. The play's sole connection to Canada

Graphic design was of a high standard. This poster is by Vittorio Fiorucci, 1977. Poster © NAC.

seemed to lie in its writer, Canadian-born Bernard Slade. Next on the schedule was Wood's own production of W.O. Mitchell's award-winning play *Back to Beulah*, which the Neptune Theatre had produced in Halifax the year before and now brought to the NAC. Jean Gascon directed the next English-language offering, an NAC production of Roch Carrier's play *Floralie, Where Are You?*, which featured some of French Canada's most distinguished actors, Michel Côté, Pierre Thériault, and Claude Faubert, and was choreographed by Brian Macdonald (who was now with the Grands Ballets Canadiens). Gascon saw the Quebec-authored play as important for English-speaking audiences: "*Floralie*, I hope, will tell English Canadians something about the soul of Quebec," he said. "I think it says something very deep about the people of Quebec during a certain period … about their lack of money and hard life, but also their marvellous, living desire for love."[13] The production elicited sufficient interest to draw out-of-town critics but received a tepid response: the *Montreal Star* noted "all the fine new facilities Gascon now has at his disposal" but lamented the play's "lack of simplicity."[14]

Nevertheless, the fall season for the new team was off to a good fast start and, with the holiday season approaching, all its key participants were talking optimistically to the press. Gascon took the high road with the clear expression of his own belief that culture, and theatre most specifically, was "a force of unity cementing the country together."[15] Apart from MacSween, he was the only one to express publicly the quiet political agenda behind the government's generous support for the theatre project and MacSween's own vision for the National Arts Centre and its role in national life. As Gascon explained to the *Globe and Mail*, he lauded the opportunity of bringing the great French-Canadian poets, writers, and dramatists to English Canada, and vise versa. "I think we may even discover eventually we are not so far apart and that we can learn how to respect and understand each other."[16]

Donald MacSween also hired a new publicist for the NAC—Mary Jolliffe, the PR genius who had been so successful, and expensive, for the opening ceremonies eight years before. Together they crisscrossed the country, speaking in cities from coast to coast and espousing the value of the National Arts Centre to culture everywhere in Canada. MacSween's persuasive pitch was captured in an article in Halifax's *Mail Star*, where his "winning boyish charm" was linked to his lawyer's "hard-headed sagacity." Willing listeners gave credence to his thesis that the prestigious invitation of a booking at the NAC had "functional and financial consequences for visiting companies by extending their seasons and their earnings." In his speeches he tactfully applauded theatre groups across the country, as well as his own, as being "all national assets." While disclaiming any power by the government to influence the NAC's artistic product, he completed his message by stressing "the importance of the arts as an agent of national unity."[17]

This neat view unfortunately did not fit into the pattern of what was happening in the arts at the time. Despite the confidence of the men at the NAC, and a huge flowering of the arts throughout the seventies, most other arts companies around the country were enduring severe stress under increasing government restraints. PACT, the national organization of Canadian theatre companies which Andis Celms and the NAC had helped to found, was in the process of organizing a letter-writing campaign to Minister Roberts to ask for more money for their members' operations, and especially more money for the Canada Council to enable it to provide theatres with adequate operating grants. Roberts was not impressed. He felt he had done well during times of severe restraint to come up with the $13.6 million in supplementary funds he had announced earlier for various federal cultural agencies. Over $2 million of these funds had been split between the National Arts Centre and the National Theatre School. In his view, this money was "demonstrating the government's commitment … to providing a stronger financial base for professional theatres."[18]

In truth, the arts were all flourishing at the artistic level, but were being severely undercut by the country's galloping inflation. Despite their success both in performance and attendance, deficits were looming everywhere. In the previous two years, Treasury Board had held the Canada Council's annual increases to 8 percent, well below the inflation rate of over 12 percent. By December 1977 Roberts had taken note of the problem and responded that the government would undertake a study in the coming year into "the effectiveness of federal cultural spending." As he explained to the *Globe and Mail*: "The explosion of public interest in the arts has occurred at a time of severe fiscal restraint and political crisis." The crisis had been precipitated by the election of a separatist Parti Québécois government in Quebec the year before. In Quebec, artists were concerned that directly accepting federal support would tie them to political efforts to "save Canada" and prevent independent voices. Elsewhere, the country was filled with unease.

While not calling for a study of the scope of the Massey Commission, Roberts wanted a quick six-month inquiry to pick up where Massey had left off, and he announced that he had appointed two arts consultants, David Silcox and Yvon DesRochers, to run it. Both men had solid track records in the federal arts bureaucracy and were familiar with the way the system worked. Essentially, he wanted them to examine how scarce cultural funds should be shared throughout the country. The political pressures to spread the wealth outside Ottawa were growing, and newcomers such as David MacDonald, a Conservative MP on the Commons Committee that studied arts and broadcasting, were starting to call for a more decentralized funding model for the arts which would also include improved tax breaks for private donors. For his part, Roberts specifically rejected the concept of "democratization and decentralization" that had been so popular with his predecessor Gérard Pelletier, calling it "a slogan that does not seize 'the reality of creativity.'"[19]

In this complicated climate, the NAC had set out to establish its new resident theatre companies. The two artistic directors immediately seized their chance. Although Herbiet would later laugh about his travails in trying to get francophone actors to move to Ottawa—"they wanted me to find them a marina to park their boats and pay the school fees of their kids!"[20]—the director nevertheless was able to build a stable of regular actors who came to live in Ottawa for an extended period and, above all, produced some astonishing French theatre. The first new French season had a 92.9 percent subscription rate and presented several of the classics, including Paul Claudel's *Partage de Midi* in a new production directed by Olivier Reichenbach and a double bill, *Le Médecin Volant* and *Le Médecin Malgré Lui*, directed by Jean Gascon and produced by Le Théâtre Populaire du Québec. There was also another new NAC production directed by Olivier Reichenbach, Chekhov's *La Mouette* (*The Seagull*), and a French translation of Brendan Behan's *Hostage* entitled *L'Otage*. The reviews were universally good, particularly for a unique version of August Strindberg's *Le Songe* (*A Dream Play*), which played in both French and English under Herbiet's direction, again using Felix Mirbt's remarkable marionettes. The work was seen in Ottawa and Vancouver as well as in Montreal and Toronto, co-produced with regional theatres such as Toronto's Tarragon Theatre, the Vancouver East Cultural Centre, and Montreal's Centaur Theatre. In early 1978 Herbiet/Mirbt's earlier production of Georg Büchner's *Woyzeck* toured to fourteen cities throughout France and Belgium under the auspices of the Department of External Affairs.

On the English side, Wood was gradually putting the members of his English theatre troupe in place. Besides Ben Campbell, he had attracted a young Jennifer Dale, the seasoned character actor Edward Atienza, Denise Ferguson, Joan Orenstein, Rita Howell, and others to take up residence in Ottawa. Their first chance to stretch their talents came with the new production, directed by Wood, of *Troilus and Cressida*, with the untried Jennifer Dale and Benedict Campbell in the title roles, and veterans Eric Donkin and Neil Munro also in leading parts. Opening in Ottawa on January 9, 1978, this lavish production featured much lusty athleticism, particularly among its male cast, and was a bold, brazen move by Wood that brought a mixed response from the NAC's patrons. The nearly four-hour play was a test for the audience, which was eager to know what the new company would bring them. One worn out critic suggested that Wood, too, had been "beguiled like many directors before him" with the abundant facilities available in the well-appointed Theatre. In this case, the several traps in the thrust stage had produced ponds of water, steam baths, and other lavish directorial gestures. John Ferguson's dramatic designs and composer Alan Laing's "eerie sound effects" included a chorus whose sound was compared to that of a "clock ticking or a beating heart."[21]

The other two NAC productions in this first year of the new company followed this same lavish style: Tennessee Williams's *Camino Real*, and an original Wood/Laing musical with the forgettable title *William Schwenck and Arthur Who?*, based on the work of Gilbert and Sullivan. As this ninth and final play in the season ended, Wood announced that it would be part of the NAC theatre tour planned for the following season.

Touring theatre across the country was at the heart of MacSween's vision for putting the "national" into the NAC identity. A substantial portion of the government's grant had been set aside for the tour, and much was riding on its success. It was unfortunate, then, that Wood decided to pin his chances on his own awkwardly entitled musical and his new production of Shakespeare's *Hamlet*—a work frequently performed elsewhere. At the last minute, a brilliant new Canadian play, John Murrell's *Waiting for the Parade*, was added to the mix—a poignant tale of the home front in Canada during the Second World War and featuring five women in the lead roles. It would prove ideal for "run outs" into smaller towns along the cross-country route while the big shows were being staged in the main cities.

Hamlet, with Neil Munro in the lead, had been well received when it opened in Ottawa. On the twenty-one city tour, the performances were generally well liked by the public and the local press, but the choice of plays raised the ire of envious theatrical colleagues everywhere. In Vancouver, director Christopher Newton put on his own competing version of *Hamlet*, and the NAC had to buy out a week of the Vancouver Playhouse's production of Arthur Miller's *The Crucible* to

Hamlet, *directed by John Wood and starring Neil Munro, received good reviews but was poorly accepted by other theatre companies across Canada when it went on tour. Poster © NAC.*

accommodate its travelling schedule. And there was a general feeling among the financially strapped regional theatres that this visiting rich cousin from the capital would overshadow their work and take away any potential funds. As MacSween complained later about Wood: "It wasn't what we had talked about. *Hamlet* is a great play, it's had a history of success ... but the programming that was offered was not the meal that the customer was likely to enjoy—the customer being the government. We could not put 'QED' under the experience."[22]

At the time, however, true to his own artistic principles, MacSween did not attempt to interfere with his English theatre director's choice of works. The whole experience of the tour left him feeling badly, however, not only for what he saw as Wood's lack of understanding but also because the NAC had not been able to demonstrate its value to Canada's theatre scene. Wood's perception of a "national theatre" was entirely different. "A national theatre," he said, "is something that reflects the country."[23] And in his mind that could happen wherever resources were available. His aim was to put on "a standard of theatre ... that would represent the best of the art form in the country as measured by international standards."[24] The political niceties of cultural funding in Canada held no interest for him. These very different views of the meaning of "national" in Canada, as compared with the straightforward approach to a national theatre in England or France, would inevitably cause a lot of angst in the months ahead.

The increasing downturn in the economy was of more immediate concern, however, and would contribute in a serious way to the decline in funds for the theatre project. NAC efforts to make some of the new federal grant a permanent part of the base budget were partially successful, but no similar cross-country tour would ever happen again. Some smaller tours were scheduled for the following season, but then they stopped altogether. The long-term contracts for the actors dried up, although some of the troupe were able to stay on for a time in serial engagements.

Although the touring vision was not to be, there was still a positive side to the Wood era in English theatre at the National Arts Centre. The work he did and the talent he developed there later helped to populate the best Canadian theatre with experienced artists, right up to the present day. Building on the strong foundation laid by his predecessor, Jean Roberts, Wood set about to build the repertory company that had been the dream at the NAC from the beginning. Beside the able team he had brought with him from Halifax, he added a roster of some of Canada's finest actors, many of whom were able to work, at least for a while, with the security of longer-term contracts for the first time in their lives. There was good evidence that the experiment was working when some of them, such as the itinerant actor Edward Atienza, bought permanent homes in Ottawa. Although it was soon evident that the original concept could not last, a core group of actors was established, and MacSween ran interference for it at the board level so it could get on with its work of producing a string of in-house plays. Much that was good was later forgotten or overlooked in the financial turmoil that ended the experiment, but there were important and lasting effects for Canada's theatre.

For the young actor Benedict Campbell, the new repertory theatre was the chance of a lifetime. After *Troilus and Cressida,* he went on to play a large number of major and minor roles during his time in Ottawa obtaining a solid grounding which became the basis for his career. Similarly, Neil Munro honed his skills as an actor and expanded his talents into directing and writing. Jackie Maxwell, who came to Ottawa to join her fiancé Ben Campbell, became assistant first to Wood and then to various visiting directors, until Wood put her in charge of a new performance space called the Atelier—a step that ultimately led to her appointment as artistic director of the prestigious Shaw Festival. Maxwell readily acknowledged that her time at the National Arts Centre was the key to her subsequent highly successful career.[25]

Wood's style was not to everyone's liking. His propensity to make sudden decisions, such as the impulsive hiring of Campbell as his Troilus, could add stress to an already difficult process. Campbell himself acknowledged that, as a young performer, he could have used a gentler hand than Wood's and, over the seasons, they clashed frequently, until Campbell reluctantly agreed to allow Wood full control. Wood, in turn, saw himself as flexible, saying that anything could happen as rehearsal began and that it was his responsibility to seize the moment when he felt it had arrived. He kept a large blackboard in his office where he chalked in plays and names of actors. Anyone could walk in at any time and see what plays were on and who was appearing in them— although the names and titles could just as easily be rubbed out and changed if the quixotic Wood changed his mind. Wood had a strong sense of his own freedom to do what he wanted. When he felt a play was not working correctly, he was not averse to stepping in, even after opening night or with another director's work—as the renowned director John Hirsch discovered with his *History of the American Film.*

Andis Celms, as the theatre administrator, grew close to Wood over the years but recognized the sharp contrast with his predecessor. Jean Roberts knew the Canadian theatre community well after her work as theatre officer at the Canada Council, and she had skilfully connected other companies with the NAC, bringing in the best of their productions. Wood, while a good director, was not known in the country and lacked communication skills.[26] According to Celms, when Wood attended PACT meetings with the artistic directors from all the other theatre organizations, he was "not outgoing." Celms sometimes wrangled with Wood over production costs, but found him intensely stubborn and supremely confident that what he was doing artistically was special, and it was for others to fall into line. Wood himself claimed to feel "embraced" by the trusted theatrical team he had brought together, and he focused his entire attention on the work that they were producing.[27] Unfortunately, matters became more difficult as the money began to dry up. "Basically," Celms recalled, "it was only two years, and then the idea of the resident theatre company sort of petered out."[28]

Still, under Wood's leadership, the English-language players became a tight-knit enclosed group doing something special. Plays included outstanding productions of the classics such as *Richard III* and, of course, *Hamlet.* Canadian work slowly made its way into the mix, both through visiting companies and the nurturing of a playwright-in-residence arrangement with writers such as Sharon Pollock, whose *One Tiger to the Hill* had its premiere in this way. Pollock's *Blood Relations* and *Walsh* had opened elsewhere, but obtained a rarely granted second production thanks to Wood. Leading directors such as John Hirsch were also invited to direct work. *Equus, The Caretaker, Billy Bishop Goes to War, Diary of a Madman,* and *Mother Courage* were all part of the mix of the visiting and in-house plays presented in this period. Wood also capitalized on other opportunities that his location in Ottawa offered. After attending a presentation of an Australia-Canada Literary Prize sponsored by the Canada Council, he promptly invited the Australian winner, John Romeril, to put on his winning play, *The Floating World,* in the NAC season. The performance featured a handsome Australian actor, Bruce Spence, who later would become famous as the gyro captain in the Mad Max movies.

Despite the excellence of some of this work, tales continued to leak out about the "lavish" budget—and some of them were true. Most notorious was the incident of "The Kid Leather Curtain Call."[29] The story stemmed from a wonderfully outrageous production of *The Tempest,* known in NAC lore as "The Calypso Tempest." Staged on a desert island, this version of the play came with shaved-head actors, a revolving volcano, several palm trees, and real sand—into which a boat disappeared. The production was generally deemed to be "full of fabulous ideas" and played to astonished audiences, but one final flourish turned out to be an expensive folly. In a reconciliatory gesture for the final scene, all the actors were to be dressed in the same costumes—rendered in white kid leather. Everything was fitted and made before it was realized that there was no time for the costume change before the play ended. Rather than ditch the leather gear, the cast donned it for the curtain call—making it perhaps the most expensive final bow in history.

At the same time, Wood was able to demonstrate that he could be just as successful with less as more. One play in the Studio which resonated in people's heads years later was his exquisite production of Chekhov's *Wood Demon,* performed with little more than a few chairs for a set.

An extraordinary amount of "subterranean work" occurred.[30] Among Wood's best initiatives, and one that had full backing from Donald MacSween, was the creation of a small off-site performance/rehearsal space that could seat up to two hundred people located in an old furniture factory in Ottawa's working-class Lowertown. With theatre in both languages and multiple other productions, there was heavy pressure on the in-house rehearsal facilities in which dance, music, and other events also had to be accommodated. Wood disliked the airless in-house rehearsal space intensely, and he and Celms set out to find alternative accommodation where the company could work on a more free and easy basis than in the union-regulated halls of the centre. With the establishment of the new performance space, which took on the perfectly bilingual name of the "Atelier/L'Atelier," some of the most creative theatre work in both English and French would occur.

MacSween agreed that the main theatres in the formidable Arts Centre and its unionized procedures could be constricting to performers. The move to the Atelier allowed them to experiment, using unrestricted generous periods of time to work on a piece. They could workshop new plays or arrange training sessions in theatrical technique, such as the Alexander Method in movement or the Linklater Technique for voice training. Actors Ben Campbell, Paul Gross, and Richard Greenblatt, director Jackie Maxwell, and others destined to go on to successful careers in Canadian theatre all had an unprecedented opportunity to develop their craft in this space. Neil Munro and Paul Gross had their first chance at writing and directing because of this NAC program. At the time, nothing quite like it was occurring anywhere else in Canada—and, unfortunately, the effectiveness of the program was hardly known outside Ottawa. Theatre people such as Bill Glassco at Toronto's Tarragon Theatre or director/critic Urjo Kareda were immersed in their own work. What was going on in Ottawa was "a little like working on the moon," Maxwell recalled.[31] Nevertheless, her experience there left her with a lasting impression of what the National Arts Centre could do for Canada's theatre.

On the French side, Herbiet's work was deemed exemplary. When the special theatre grant came through, Herbiet seized the opportunity. In the 1978–79 season, he managed to get three separate tours on the road, including two that together covered the country from end to end. L'Hexagone, cancelled on the English side for lack of funds, took the young francophone artists' company and plays out to communities in Ontario and Quebec. In a development that was unique in Canadian theatrical annals, the French company launched the NAC's entire theatre touring enterprise when it opened on September 28, 1978, in Vancouver with a production of Marcel Dubé's *Un Simple Soldat*. The play was presented to a full house—a norm that continued as the troupe moved through Calgary, Kapuskasing, and on into Quebec to places like Rouyn before switching plays and setting out to the eastern part of the country. In contrast to the English tour, the French company, with its twenty-eight actors and ten technicians loaded onto a bus, was a success wherever it went and, in Herbiet's words, "showed us the extraordinary vitality and sense of cultural identity of the French-speaking community beyond the borders of Quebec."[32]

The travelling French theatre troupe L'Hexagone took French theatre coast-to-coast. It outlived the English-language travelling company Hexagon, which succumbed early to budget cuts. Photo © NAC.

Once the French company returned to Ottawa, it dove back into its regular subscription series, presenting one of the hits of the tour, Eduardo de Filippo's social comedy *Madame Filoume*. It then moved on through a season that presented four more original productions, including *Des Frîtes, Des Frîtes, Des Frîtes*, a translation of Arnold Wesker's *Chips with Everything*. There were visits from other companies, among them La Compagnie Jean Duceppe, and the season concluded with a personal success for Jean Gascon, directing a magnificent production of Corneille's classic masterpiece *Le Cid*. After ten years on the job at the NAC, Herbiet felt that, in the 1978–79 season, "all of my dreams suddenly came true ... the finest and most exhilarating of my many with the NAC."[33]

Overall, the number of presentations in French theatre at the Arts Centre had increased fivefold in its first decade, with a paying public that had gone from 30,000 to 150,000 members. Performances for young children and students formed a large component of the total audience—a personal achievement for Herbiet, who believed fervently in introducing young people to theatre and whose work with L'Hexagone had been so successful. It was an astonishing achievement for the French theatre team, and, while Quebec theatre circles preferred to ignore the numbers, the NAC unquestionably put significant sums into their coffers by supporting other theatre companies and giving individual artists work.

As he savoured this success, Herbiet accepted an offer to leave the centre and go to Paris for four years to become the director of the Canadian Cultural Centre there. This move opened the way for MacSween to make a dramatic new appointment. The man he persuaded to come to Ottawa to replace Herbiet was André Brassard, the brilliant *enfant terrible* of Quebec theatre. Brassard, who was openly homosexual at a time when being gay was not as fully accepted as it is today, had been having a difficult time in Montreal, where his propensities for illegal substances, among other

André Brassard, the brilliant enfant terrible *from Quebec, succeeded Jean Herbiet as director of French theatre. A champion of modern Quebec theatre, especially Michel Tremblay's plays, Brassard's productions achieved the highest subscription rates in the NAC's history. Photo © NAC.*

things, were getting him into trouble with the law. He had been just twenty-three when the National Arts Centre had first engaged him and playwright Michel Tremblay for the 1969 Opening Festival.* In partnership with Tremblay, Brassard had been responsible for much of the most cutting-edge theatre produced in recent times in French Canada His return to the NAC in 1982 was a superb opportunity both for the centre and for this young, if mercurial, genius of the Quebec stage. At first, Brassard had hesitated "because I thought my friends would be mad at me," but the 1980 Quebec referendum was over and many of its artists had become disillusioned about its outcome. His colleagues now urged him to go to Ottawa, "if I could make a living there." While Brassard later claimed that living in Ottawa "rekindled my nationalistic flame," he also would nostalgically recall his years at the NAC as "the happiest of my life."[34]

Brassard joked that, when he came to the centre, he "had finally been given my choo-choo train"—meaning that he would have the tools and resources to expand his work to the full. Like many others, he placed a high value on what the NAC had to

---

*They had taken on the job of creating in the Studio the musical version of *Lysistrata*, which had featured many of Quebec's leading artists and included a musical score by Montrealer Gabriel Charpentier. A highly original version of Aristophanes's classic Greek play, it was produced in collaboration with the Théâtre du Nouveau Monde and had a further year of life after it was presented in Ottawa. Brassard recalled several luxurious months of rehearsal and lots of money, which had become "a kind of crazy adventure" with a cast and crew that mixed up old-guard actors with young *indépendentistes* who were getting up steam in Quebec. Brassard later took pride in the fact that he had been able to keep the peace between these two opposing generations to produce good work. James Domville and Jean-Louis Roux of the Théâtre du Nouveau Monde had helped engineer the production for the NAC, but Brassard confessed that, because of the nationalist trend in Quebec, he and Tremblay both tried to stay out of any photographs with Prime Minister Trudeau or other federal figures. As Jean Gascon would later learn, it was a dangerous time in Quebec to work for federalist interests.

offer him. "They had the greatest props and costume workshops I've ever met, with people who were very creative and helped you," he said. "The place was very alive."[35] And there was still money available to put on substantial plays.

Brassard opened his first season in 1982–83, characterizing it as "a return to sources"[36] which presented classic writers such as Racine, Chekhov, the modern Quebec classicist Tremblay, and Shakespeare's *Périclés*—a play rarely performed in English and never seen before in French at the NAC. Brassard laughed that he chose the lavish Shakespeare, which opened the year in the Studio, to "see what this big engine [the NAC] could do!" He directed four of the season's seven productions himself, two of them co-produced with Montreal's Théâtre du Nouveau Monde, with which he intended to continue working closely, and he also brought in other important Montreal directors such as Jean-Pierre Ronfard.* Brassard opened up post-play discussions with his audiences and, for a time, after the Monday night performance, cast, crew, and playgoers could share a meal together and discuss the evening. These were remarkable innovations at the Arts Centre, and the model became a template for the coming years. In Brassard's eight seasons at the centre, audiences reached and maintained their highest levels in the entire history of French theatre at the NAC.

In the midst of all this theatrical turmoil and excitement, Jean Gascon, the man who had originally attracted the government's support, was becoming an increasingly tragic figure. He had brought a legendary presence and an enormous artistic sensibility to his position at the National Arts Centre. He believed in the capacity of the arts to bring diverse interests together—that, through the French and English theatre, "these two artistic milieus that had been so separate" would be able to create together.[37] An uncomplicated man, Gascon was a visionary with a dream that included making theatre available to everyone. The NAC, with its generous flow of cash, seemed the place to provide the means. But the politics of the country were shifting in ways that would make the realization of this dream impossible.

Despite the public gloss put on his appointment, Gascon's real role in the NAC's theatrical operations had rapidly diminished. While carrying the title of director of theatre, he had under his nominal command two strong-willed, individualistic artistic directors in John Wood and Jean Herbiet. Wood was secretive by nature, and Herbiet, with an already established record at the centre, was not prepared to cede anything to Gascon. The senior theatre man became increasingly isolated in his office. Although he shared his artistry on occasion, as at the Citadel Theatre in Edmonton in 1982, and

---

*Ronfard directed a "wild and lusty" play, *La Mandragore*, based on Machiavelli's story of a foolish man and his young bride, which he had written himself.

he acted in various NAC productions and directed from time to time, his represen-
tational role was reduced to occasional reports to the Board of Trustees. Even there,
Andis Celms did much of the talking for the Theatre Department, allowing Wood and
Herbiet to concentrate on their artistic work. The result was a growing depression for
the theatrical giant. Cruel rumours began to circulate about his drinking habits, though
his assistant, Denise Robert,* was adamant that he never drank on the job. Wood
acknowledged that, when matters were coming to a head, he didn't help Gascon and
deliberately scheduled evening rehearsals when he knew his superior would have
enjoyed a full meal with wine.

A concerned MacSween worked hard to get help for the beleaguered artist, who
ultimately did seek it for himself. Negotiations to solve the problem simply stopped,
however, when the board was informed in July 1983 that Gascon had suffered a heart
attack. By then his time at the centre was at an end. The inability to take full advantage
of the great talent and experience that Gascon brought to Canada's national theatrical
scene in both official languages spoke volumes about the state of the arts in Canada
at the time.

Despite all, the overall artistic climate at the NAC in this period was extraordinary.
The atmosphere of creativity in both languages under one roof was unique in Canada,
and perhaps in the world. For those on the inside, the daily encounters in the backstage
Green Room, between the great international artists appearing on the NAC's stages
and its ordinary "workers," which included orchestral musicians, journeyman actors,
dancers, and other creative personnel, fostered a peculiar and valuable mix of talent
and ideas unmatched anywhere else.

---

*Denise Robert later went on to become a major film producer in Quebec, and she married
the renowned director/auteur Denys Arcand. She always credited her early time with Gascon,
as his personal assistant, as her first experience working directly in the arts and for educating
and inspiring her in the rest of her work.

A CULTURAL
INVESTIGATION

Theatre was not the only thing on Donald MacSween's mind as he settled down to the other tasks of his new job. He laughingly joked to friends who knew his sometimes earthy humour that Southam had advised him he was "running the biggest bordello in town"[1] and the whole point was to use the NAC's restaurants and tickets to woo important movers and shakers in the centre's interest. MacSween quickly got his social feet wet, cultivating important friends for the Arts Centre and establishing both himself and his theatre companies. In this pursuit he was fortunate to have the help of two able personal assistants, Sheila Marie "Gigi" Cook and, later, Sheila Watson, a Scottish-born, highly competent secretary who would stay to see MacSween through the darker times that were to come.

In his early days, Cook in particular was a great asset (in 2006 she became secretary to Governor General Michaëlle Jean). A vivacious woman with keen antennae for Ottawa protocol and mores, she would spend many hours with the director general working over the finer details of placement at his Ottawa table. Affable and easily liked, MacSween soon became an agreeable guest in official social circles around town, including the diplomatic set. There were occasional missteps in these early efforts, such as the time MacSween's staff organized a party for the renowned French-horn player Barry Tuckwell before the evening's concert. The fact that artists never eat before a performance had apparently been overlooked, and the embarrassed MacSween greeted the visiting musician with apologies when he arrived at the party. The laconic Tuckwell took no offense and ate a hearty meal before excusing himself just before eight to play his celebrated instrument in the concert hall.[2]

Stylish entertaining as a way to the hearts of the powerful resonated with MacSween. It was his policy to put politicians and public servants face to face with artists, and

Executive Chef Kurt Waldele put NAC catering on the map in official Ottawa. Photo © NAC.

he energetically set about doing just that. At the heart of his successful entertaining was the centre's excellent restaurant department, an area that had created some heartburn under Southam because of its propensity for losing money. MacSween decided to fix this problem by carefully micro-managing the department, assisted by his able deputy, Bruce Corder. He joked that "it was important to get the restaurant right so I could impress my Montreal friends."[3] He disbanded the banquet service, expanded the popular canal-side Café, and hired an ambitious young German-born chef, Kurt Waldele, to help remodel the NAC restaurant service and run the kitchens. The talented Waldele proved to be one of MacSween's best "hires"; he would not be able to stabilize the shaky finances of the catering services entirely at the NAC, but he at least gave them a new bloom.

MacSween's black-tie dinners for the senior mandarins in the city became a much-sought-after invitation. Waldele's imaginative dining ideas included an ultra-exclusive service available at a dining table in his own kitchen. Guests included many deputy ministers and other important people and their spouses, invitees who would remember years later the fun they had descending in a freight elevator to be feasted in Waldele's domaine.

The underground reputation these activities gained contributed to the government's continuing habit, established in Southam's time, of using the NAC for entertaining its visiting dignitaries. MacSween also entertained for every opening and for visiting stars. It became a habit as he welcomed guests at post-performance receptions to single out his "new young chef" for accolades for that evening's spread. It was a routine that continued even after the two had worked together for nearly ten years, and it served to draw attention to Waldele and his skilled team on the catering side. Whether all this socializing fulfilled Southam's earlier edict that "more is wrought over lunch/dinner than most men dream of" remained an open question. Certainly, the high and mighty in Ottawa would grow accustomed to having dinners and performances offered to them as part of their privilege rather than being proactive and financially responsible for the practice of the arts. A culture of "freebeeism" began to creep through the capital—and it did not serve the arts well.

The three "houses" of the NAC, with their ample backstage facilities behind. Photo © Malak Karsh.

The elaborate Opera house curtain by Micheline Beauchemin that was woven in Japan. Photo © André Dubreuil/NAC.

The Opera stage looked out to an elegant hall reminiscent of Europe. Photo © Fred Cattroll.

Lysistrata, *with a script by Michel Tremblay and directed by a twenty-three-year-old André Brassard, made a startling opening for the Theatre. Photo © André Le Coz. Courtesy of Théâtre du Nouveau Monde.*

Felix Mirbt's puppets in Le Songe/The Dream Play, *directed by Jean Herbiet, achieved huge national and international success. Performed in both languages, it had the longest run of any play at the NAC. Photo © Fernand R. LeClair.*

Riel *by John Coulter, presented in 1975, starred French-Canadian actor Albert Millaire in the title role and Métis actor Marrie Mumford as his wife. It was a landmark in NAC theatre. Photo © Robert C. Ragsdale/NAC.*

The so-called "Calypso Tempest" featured performances by (left to right) Rowland Hevgill, Neil Munro, Benedict Campbell, and Gordon Clapp. Photo © Murray Mosher Photography.

John Wood's first season production of Shakespeare's Troilus and Cressida *featured the young actors Benedict Campbell and Jennifer Dale. Photo © Murray Mosher Photography.*

Actors Neil Munro and Carole Galloway played in a strong Henry V *under John Wood's direction. Photo © Murray Mosher Photography.*

The opera festival brought leading designers from London's Covent Garden and elsewhere to Ottawa. Internationally renowned English designer Michael Stennett did the exquisite costumes and set for the 1978 production of A Midsummer Night's Dream. *Copyright © Michael Stennett/NAC.*

The French opera Le Comte Ory, *directed by Carlo Maestrini for the 1974 Summer Festival. Photo © NAC.*

The character Ann Whitfield in Man and Superman. *Costume design by Brian Jackson, 1976–77. Copyright © Brian Jackson/NAC.*

The character Jupiter in Amphitryon. *Costume design by the renowned Robert Prévost, 1981–82. Copyright © Robert Prévost/NAC.*

The character la Reine Elizabeth in a French-language version of Shakespeare's Richard III. *Costume design by François Barbeau, 1989–90. Copyright © François Barbeau/NAC.*

The character Julia in The Wood Demon. *Costume design by Susan Benson, 1982. Copyright © Susan Benson/NAC.*

The immediate attention would be useful to the NAC, but it also led to a potentially tricky conflict for MacSween when the new Mulroney Conservative government came to power in 1984. Chef Waldele had already formed a connection with Mila Mulroney, wife of the new prime minister. She had approached him earlier as the wife of the leader of the Opposition to ask for his help with their entertaining. The hostess and the chef liked each other and worked well together. Soon after the Conservatives came to power, MacSween received a visit from Mulroney's new chief of staff, Fred Duceppe, who complimented him on Waldele's work. Duceppe's suggestion, according to MacSween, was that Waldele, while remaining on the NAC payroll, should share his talents between the National Arts Centre and 24 Sussex, the prime minister's residence, where Mila Mulroney was expected to preside over considerable entertaining and also had a growing family to feed. MacSween pinpointed an essential drawback to a collaborative relationship: if there were competing events between the two locations, the Arts Centre would lose. He suggested that if the prime minister wanted Waldele, he should hire him directly, although the Arts Centre would be sorry to lose him. Waldele stayed at the NAC, although he helped out frequently on events for the prime minister and, for a time, the NAC provided a sous-chef to the official residence to help with the cooking.

The NAC would eventually become the official caterer for the government, with state functions in the city centralized and run by Waldele. Official dining and receptions at the National Gallery, the Museum of Civilization, the Department of External Affairs, and even at the House of Commons would eventually come under Waldele's direction for a time. Their style and management was moved out of the Government's Protocol Department into Mila Mulroney's personal office in the Langevin Building, across the street from the Parliament Buildings, where Waldele and the NAC Catering Department became partners in the team organizing what were now called Special Events.

As the MacSween era moved into the beginning of the eighties, there were warning signs that culture and its funding could be subject to radical change—cuts that would have a fundamental impact on the NAC as well as other federal agencies. The brief tenure of the 1979 Joe Clark Conservative government was the harbinger of things to come. Elected in 1979, the new government briefly installed David MacDonald as the minister responsible for culture. Previously, while in opposition, he had served on the Standing Committee for Broadcasting, Films, and Assistance to the Arts. In their first meeting with departmental deputy minister Pierre Juneau, MacDonald and his assistant, Fred Rumsey, brought with them a large thick binder setting out their views. Juneau, accustomed to being the one to set the agenda and maintain control, was surprised. But the Conservatives were to have only a brief, nine-month tenure before they

The Honourable David MacDonald took over the arts and culture portfolio in the short-lived Conservative government of Joe Clark.

lost a confidence vote in the House of Commons on December 12, 1979. In the election that followed, Pierre Trudeau and the Liberal government returned to power.

In the short time available to him, MacDonald had invited Toronto composer Louis Applebaum, who had been serving at the Ontario Arts Council, to chair a small group of experts to help prepare a "blue/white" paper (the colour depended on the government in power) with recommendations for Canada's cultural policy. MacDonald's idea had been to conduct a short but thorough examination of the current state of arts and culture, the first since the comprehensive Massey Report which had got the whole post-war cultural ball rolling.

After the Clark government's defeat, Francis Fox, the new Liberal minister taking over responsibility for both culture and communications, told MacDonald at a private lunch during the transition period that he was adopting several of the Tory minister's ideas, including this key investigatory committee. The mandate then expanded into a full-fledged inquiry into Canada's culture. Its official name became the Federal Cultural Policy Review Committee, with Louis Applebaum and the academic Thomas Symons among the members. Other prominent names were added to the group, including Trudeau's personal friend Jacques Hébert, who was named co-chair with Applebaum. The committee was formally announced by the Liberal government in June 1980 and soon became known as the Applebaum-Hébert Committee—or "Applebert" for short.

When Donald MacSween was invited to submit a brief, he seized the opportunity to make the case for the NAC in a detailed and comprehensive submission. He undertook the preparation and writing of this document, drafting most of it himself and pouring into the task his own strongly held views on how the arts should be practised in Canada and the role the NAC should have in expediting them. The finished document reflected the assiduous, exhaustive attention to detail of the lawyer he had trained to be. His preoccupation with the submission meant that the usually detailed annual reports between the years 1979 and 1981 were reduced to financial information and chronological lists,* while he poured his thoughts and ideas into the submission document entitled "A Climate for Creativity." This work would form the basis for all

---

*MacSween was also tidying up a long-standing anomaly whereby the NAC's artistic seasons had not overlapped with the annual financial year-end. This changeover resulted in a short interim period where there was a separate financial report and a truncated annual report.

MacSween's efforts on behalf of the National Arts Centre in the coming years. Expectations ran high that something of consequence was about to happen to the arts as a result of the Review Committee's work.

In the period leading up to the Applebaum-Hébert hearings, MacSween had plenty of other in-house problems to occupy him. When the feisty Arthur Gelber moved into the chair of the NAC board in 1978, issues of money once again came under close scrutiny. The theatre project was well and truly launched, but there were warning signs that the Arts Centre was moving into a financial box and that it would be difficult to sustain the resident theatre program as conceived. Reports on the 1979 Summer Festival showed a serious overrun on the new opera production, *Cendrillon*. The opera demonstrated a stellar artistic partnership between Maestro Bernardi and the beautiful American soprano Frederica Von Stade, but the cost led to questions from the trustees about the subsidy being provided to opera-goers—an amount estimated to be $35 per seat. MacSween vigorously defended the expensive art form, arguing that new productions always cost money, but James Domville, his former *My Fur Lady* colleague and now commissioner of the National Film Board (and thus an ex-officio NAC board member), expressed worries about the optics of the pricing. Discussions for the tenth-anniversary celebrations for the NAC were modest in scope, as the board approved a bursary for a National Capital Region music fund and a vote of thanks to Mario Bernardi and the orchestra for everything they had done in the first decade. Despite the chafing of some of his board, in January 1980 MacSween received a pleasant accolade with his appointment to the Board of Governors at McGill University.

American soprano Frederica Von Stade made beautiful music with Maestro Mario Bernardi, especially in a lavish but costly 1979 production of Jules Massenet's Cendrillon (Cinderella). Photo © Fernand R. LeClair.

On a broader level, the brief Conservative interregnum under Clark, although not in place long enough to have an immediate effect, had introduced ideas about the redistribution of cultural funds in the country which would have a severe impact on the Arts Centre in the future. For now, the NAC's trustees began to fret at the deficit financing that MacSween proposed. It was clear that the cost of touring could not be sustained without permanent funding, but MacSween was still confident that there would be sufficient money to continue a strong resident theatre program in Ottawa. He even assured the board and his other artistic managers that theatre would not be maintained at the cost of other programming. As the financial screws tightened, however, the trustees began to worry about "gambling on the future" by budgeting projects at a cost that still had no confirmed financial backing from the government.[4] MacSween's intentions were not dampened by austere comments from Deputy Minister Pierre Juneau to the effect that the NAC's financial requests, which were being channelled through the Secretary of State's Department, did not match up with what Treasury Board was contemplating—a difference of $250,000. At the very least, the original plan for the Theatre Department, especially touring, would have to be abandoned.

The NAC, like other federal organizations, was subject to interdepartmental competition for funds, and all departments of government would soon be subjected to heavy demands to help deal with the federal deficit. For now, MacSween continued to work with his hoped-for budget numbers. The NAC board resisted the idea of deficit financing, arguing that it could mean "mortgaging future fiscal years," but, in the face of MacSween's stubborn defence of the idea, it authorized, as "the worst position," carrying a deficit into the budget year for 1980–81.[5] Efforts were made to look everywhere for savings. Trustee Marie Lambert, along with other board members who were contemplating significant repairs to the building after ten years' use, suggested going back to the architects to nail them for construction deficits. This advice was sensibly ignored, but the substantial maintenance and repairs still needed to be addressed. Clever financial manoeuvring within the government added to the NAC's problems. Instead of the Arts Centre getting its annual subsidy outright to administer for itself, the government began to dole the money out in monthly instalments—depriving the NAC of more than $100,000 in interest that it had previously earned on funds in its possession but waiting on standby to be used.

Aggravating the financial situation were other in-house problems, such as declining programming revenues and catering costs. Despite all efforts, the operating deficit for food service by mid-1980 was dismal, running at over $115,000. The introduction of mechanical pourers for the bars had reportedly produced a saving of 30 percent in this sector, but Gelber remained frustrated and worried that the food department was again affecting programming. The diffident Ted Demetre, whose Dance and Variety Department had been a reliable money-maker for the NAC, reported dropping revenues even in his sector. Income from popular entertainment featuring performers such as Harry Belafonte, Nana Mouskouri, and Tom Jones was dropping as purses tightened and tastes changed.

With the Liberals' return, the Trudeau government was moving swiftly, for political reasons, to shift a significant portion of the civil service out of downtown Ottawa and into office buildings in Hull on the Quebec side of the river—a transfer that would take its toll on NAC revenues from the parking garage and even Le Café, where many public servants lunched. At the core of the difficulties were the fixed costs associated with the NAC's work. Whether it was unionized staff in the restaurants or administration everywhere else in the building, the organization had adopted, or had imposed on it, the standard practices and contracts of the federal government, including a stringent formal bilingual policy—even though it had operated on a bilingual basis from the outset under Southam. The Theatre Department reported that fixed administrative costs had jumped from 18 percent to 22 percent of its budget within the year.

The only flexible area where cuts could be made was in programming itself, and the vagaries of the box office left it vulnerable. As MacSween tried to explain, both to his own board and to the auditor general, programming was not an exact science. At times the best estimates could go dramatically off course, as in the case of a 1980 concert by the hugely popular Boston Symphony which resulted in a loss of $12,800. A close analysis prepared for the trustees of the annual subsidy and the allocation to programming in mid-1980 suggested that the direct subsidy to programming over the first decade had actually *decreased*, in favour of the fixed operating costs now integrated into the NAC.[6] Meanwhile, the indefatigable Bruce Corder continued to work away at deflecting the huge capital costs required for keeping the building in good condition. His efforts ultimately proved successful when a $750,000 budget for repairs was approved as a separate and special grant, and not part of the main annual NAC budget.

At the end of September 1980, as Gelber completed his term as chair, he handed over a somewhat uncertain situation to his successor, Pauline McGibbon. The 1981–82 theatre budget had still not been approved because of unresolved issues involving the future of both Jean Gascon and John Wood. Wood would ultimately sign a contract for two more seasons, but Gascon's time at the centre was winding down.

McGibbon, her long grey hair always tied up in firm braids that crossed over her head, was a highly respected figure in the non-profit sector. A passionate supporter of education and culture, and in particular of the arts, she had been appointed lieutenant governor of Ontario in 1974, before being appointed NAC chair six years later. Polite and gentle, she lacked the bullying acumen of Arthur Gelber when it came to financial matters and needed to have the details of operations explained to her. While the board continued to seek clarification on finances, MacSween and Corder stoutly defended the NAC's staff to the board over issues of shortfalls and overruns and always found reasons to excuse poor audience attendance, even blaming the weather.

Despite the uncertain finances, the NAC began to consider a suggestion from the Metropolitan Opera in New York that it send a production of one of its operas to celebrate the Met's 100th anniversary in 1982. Bernardi was keen to work with the singer Marilyn Horne, and the opera gift would allow him to make his conducting debut at the famous New York opera house. In collaboration with the Met, Handel's rarely performed *Rinaldo* was selected as the proposed production. At the same time, the Edinburgh Festival invited the NAC to send the Herbiet/Mirbt plays to Scotland. Both ideas received active support from management and the board—and the two invitations were accepted and carried out to great critical acclaim.

In March 1981 Ronald Reagan visited Ottawa. In the preceding weeks, MacSween received a call from the Prime Minister's Office requesting not only that he arrange a gala concert and dinner for the U.S. president but that he take over as coordinator for the visit. The request set in motion a series of events that MacSween recalled as among the highlights of his time at the Arts Centre and showed what could be done when the government unfettered the finances.[7] It also unleashed the talents of the artistic impresario that lurked inside the director general.

MacSween immediately moved into high gear, starting at the airport where Reagan would arrive, and followed step by step the route the president would travel through the city. The first stop was the airport's VIP "Billy Bishop Lounge," where Reagan would be received when he stepped onto Canadian soil. MacSween recalled that on first sight it reminded him of "the bar in a Cornwall motel." He called up Ottawa's leading interior decorator, Giovanni Mowinkel, who draped the walls in Italian damask fabric and replaced the furniture temporarily with a set of elegant Italian chairs and tables. On the way back from the airport, MacSween "began to get in the swing of things," spotting old lawn-mowers on bare grass patches along the route that he ordered to be whisked away. At Parliament Hill, the Peace Tower was under repair and the front lawn was stacked with construction materials. With the power of the Prime Minister's Office behind him, it took no time to direct the public works staff to hide the mess with an elegant royal blue and gold hoarding that, when properly lit, resembled the finest of stage sets. At a general meeting of the entire team involved in the visit, the delighted MacSween was hailed as "Monsieur le Chorégraphe"—a well-earned title for his imaginative solutions. The final touch came when he and his wife, Andrée, who managed the local branch of Holt Renfrew, remembered the American president's fondness for jelly beans. They ordered small bags of the store's own brand as a treat at a subsequent organizers' meeting, confirming to all that he had, indeed, thought of every detail. The visit culminated in a grand dinner and splendid concert in the Opera at the Arts Centre.

Prime Minister Trudeau was back in office when U.S. President Ronald Reagan made his first official visit to Canada in 1981. Photo © NAC.

MacSween never heard directly whether his efforts had been appreciated, though not long after the president left, Prime Minister Trudeau turned up at a special post-performance reception for the Peking Opera in the Salon of the Arts Centre. When MacSween introduced the PM, he commented on how well he enjoyed his own job at the NAC. In response, Trudeau wittily disparaged any idea that what MacSween was doing was "work." MacSween later observed that this favourable recognition might have helped to save the NAC from something much worse, but it did not spare it from the general cutbacks that were pervading Ottawa. No government agency or department would be exempt.

In one respect the cultural agencies were treated differently from other departments: they were able to retain their cherished arm's-length distance from the government. Southam had fought Secretary of State John Roberts when he tried to abolish this special status in 1975. The Canada Council had also refused to accept "designated funds" for projects which would define specifically how they should be spent—though the NAC showed no such qualms when it received the special grant for the theatre project in

Soon after Ronald Reagan's visit, China's Peking Opera Troupe performed at the NAC. Pierre Trudeau with son, Sacha, visited the performers backstage. Photo © The Canadian Press/Peter Bregg.

1977. Nevertheless, when the financial controls legislation resurfaced during MacSween's period, the goodwill he had built up with the government and with influential people may have helped him to shelter the arts organization from the full scope of the proposal.[8] In Ottawa, that was the way things frequently got done.

While the tectonic plates of culture funding began to shift with the advent of the Applebaum-Hébert Committee, other significant artistic developments were occurring at the Arts Centre. Dance had never been considered as a potential resident art form except for the preliminary feeler put out by Southam to choreographer Brian Macdonald in 1971. Macdonald's effort to introduce a small dance troupe into the 1972 Summer Festival went badly, and the idea was squelched. In any event, the general dance community opposed any residential company at the NAC on the grounds that it would take money and dancers away from the already thin resources of existing companies. The NAC therefore continued with its practice of booking, through its Dance and Variety Department, the major classical dance companies each year, the National Ballet of Canada, the Royal Winnipeg Ballet, and Montreal's Les Grands Ballets Canadiens, along with interesting Canadian and international contemporary dance groups. While the big companies usually made money, especially by taking turns in presenting a Christmas *Nutcracker*, many of the smaller companies resulted in a loss. Nevertheless, a loyal, well-informed audience for dance continued to grow in Ottawa.

In 1980 the Canada Council contrived to rescue two small and creative dance companies, Montreal's Entre-Six and Toronto's Ballet Ys. It combined the two and relocated them to Ottawa to form Theatre Ballet of Canada. One of the objectives was to continue to provide a platform for choreographer Larry Gradus, who was highly thought of by the Council's dance officers but whose work had been struggling since the death of his wife and muse, dancer Jacqueline Lemieux. The NAC made it clear it was not adopting the company as its resident dance troupe, but it did everything it could to ensure that the new company had a strong start and, when not on tour, played at the Arts Centre.

The launch of the new company on February 12, 1981, was marked by a grand "world premiere gala" at the Arts Centre. MacSween, with his flare for the theatrical, had worked closely with the women's organizing committee, chaired by Ottawa socialite Diana Kirkwood. At an on-stage party after the successful opening, he presented a "birth certificate" to artistic director Gradus which had been signed by all the "notables" present. They included NAC chair Pauline McGibbon, Chief Justice of the Supreme Court Bora Laskin (father of the Canada Council dance officer, Barbara Laskin), Canada Council chair Mavor Moore, and MacSween himself, the "attending physician" to this spectacular birth. Prime Minister Pierre Trudeau, known to have a penchant for dance, was among the appreciative guests, along with the leading dance critics in the country:

the *Toronto Star*'s William Littler, the *Globe and Mail*'s Stephen Godfrey, and *Dance Canada* editor Michael Crabb. Littler described "the clever idea" of "creating a chamber dance ensemble" that, while not being appointed the resident company, could still "call one of the best stages in the country its home."[9]

The Arts Centre next decided to host a Dance Gala in May 1981 to mark the twenty-fifth anniversary of the Canada Council. It was to be a grand celebration of Canada's dance, featuring the top classical and contemporary dance companies from all over the country, to be broadcast over both the English and the French networks of the CBC. As the event drew near, however, a strike by CBC technicians threatened the broadcast—and the issue had still not been resolved on the very eve of the gala. The NAC's IATSE crews were also threatening to down tools in sympathy with the CBC technicians' unions. When it became clear the night before the gala that the live broadcast would not go ahead, the NAC, in a remarkable *pas de deux*, managed to cleverly exploit some of its government connections. Despite its own arm's-length relationship from the government, it was able, with the help of Communications Minister Francis Fox and his deputy Pierre Juneau, to ensure that the gala was recorded for posterity. The National Film Board, set up during the war to make propaganda films, was a government department, not an arm's-length organization, so came under the direct control of the cultural ministry. The minister's office simply directed the NFB to send a film team to Ottawa, and, within hours, film directors John Smith and Cynthia Scott arrived in the capital with their crews and, that night, recorded all the gala performances on film.* The Canadian Dance Spectacular was captured in the extraordinary dance film *Gala*, perhaps the most comprehensive film ever made on dance in Canada.

At the end of Southam's term as director general, Bernardi had asked for a year's sabbatical from his heavy duties as music director at the NAC, and the board had granted this request. The Arts Centre would fill in with guest conductors for the 1978–79 interim season,

The Honourable Francis Fox became minister of a newly formed Department of Communications, which also looked after arts and culture. Photo © Drew Gragg/Ottawa Citizen. Reprinted by permission.

---

*Both filmmakers would go on to important careers, with Cynthia Scott later winning an Oscar for best documentary short in 1984 for her NFB film *Flamenco at 5:15*.

although Bernardi would come back to conduct three concerts and also maintain his connection with the opera festival. His absence would, however, allow certain frustrations that had been suppressed at the orchestra to surface. A sea change was about to occur.

After nearly twelve years of intense labour, which all agreed had produced magnificent results, the orchestra, like the proverbial adolescent, was in the mood to prove its independence. Bernardi had been a stern and authoritarian taskmaster, but had instilled huge discipline and musical values into the ensemble. For some players, his control had become burdensome. He had started with a dream: "We could be Canadian *and* really good."[10] Southam had empowered him in this quest and stood behind him, but by the time the maestro returned for the 1980–81 season, the plan was afoot to knock him from his pedestal.

MacSween was extremely proud of the orchestra, and had joined it on its European tour in the spring of 1978 as it performed in various German cities, including Bonn and West Berlin. Nevertheless, he was ready to put his own imprint on the Arts Centre. Orchestra subscriptions and attendance had begun to slip. As orchestra manager Ken Murphy told the board, "The novelty of the new orchestra was wearing off."[11] One of MacSween's solutions was to start hiring some fresh faces at the NAC, and a surprised Murphy, to his deep chagrin after his long years of service, was among several staffers who found themselves looking for new jobs.

Strictly speaking, MacSween had no direct formal relations with the NAC Orchestra musicians, but he let it be known that his door would be open if anyone wanted to talk to him informally about orchestra affairs. A delegation, later self-described as "a group of Young Turks," comprising concertmaster Walter Prystawski and, among others, principals David Currie and Robert Cram, soon took advantage of this offer.[12] MacSween lent a sympathetic ear to their gripes, much of which focused on Bernardi's authoritarian control over the orchestra, the demanding touring conditions, and the programming choices being made. Ultimately, the orchestra musicians felt they had grown and matured in their work and were ready to go farther, but Bernardi was not the person to take them there. Bernardi sensed the situation and, rather than fight it, tendered his resignation in May 1980, to be effective at the end of the 1981–82 season. David Currie, a spokesman for the orchestra, would later express regret, even guilt, over the "situational ethics" that brought about Bernardi's demise, but at the time they felt compelled to act. In the coming period, Currie would take on responsibilities for Youth programming for the NACO and also be involved in much of the orchestra's other programming.*

---

*Currie would later leave the orchestra to become a professor of music at Université d'Ottawa and, ultimately, a conductor himself as the leader of the Ottawa Symphony Orchestra. The OSO, a mixed amateur-professional ensemble that included some off-duty NACO members, aimed to play the large orchestral works that the NACO could not perform. Under Currie, it developed a strong and loyal following among Ottawa audiences.

Years later, Bernardi would recall philosophically: "It was time for me to leave … I guess they were tired of me and I was tired of them."[13] The legacy he had created in the orchestra's first thirteen years was formidable. Above all, the orchestra had become a finely honed, highly strung, deeply competent ensemble. It resembled nothing so much as a beautifully designed aircraft, revving its motors on the runway waiting to take off. MacSween would soon choose someone to take over the stick that would allow the ensemble to take flight and soar.

The NAC sent in its massive submission "A Climate for Creativity," drafted by MacSween, to the Applebaum-Hébert Committee and, on July 9, 1981, made a formal appearance before it in Toronto. During the public proceedings, there was a testy exchange between panel member Jean-Louis Roux, the actor and artistic director of the Théâtre du Nouveau Monde, and MacSween which quickly descended into what the press called "a verbal slugfest."[14] With his legal training, MacSween could sometimes be impatient, even pedantic, when others failed to hear him out while he made his point. This air of superiority unfortunately tripped in when Roux opened the questioning with the suggestion that the production of theatre, operas, and even music at the Arts Centre was "artificially imposed."[15] Perhaps it would be better, he continued, if the money was distributed instead to artistic companies elsewhere and the NAC's role restricted to showcasing these performances. MacSween snapped back at Roux, making personal references to the actor's money problems at the Théâtre du Nouveau Monde. His response drew gasps in the committee room and shocked comments in the press.

Whether the spat in the hearing room affected the final outcome is not known, but, unfortunately, for the final report, Roux was put in charge of the chapter on the performing arts. When the report was released in 1982, the National Arts Centre received only a few paragraphs in the massive study, which contained 101 recommendations and was heavily dominated by concerns over broadcasting, the role of the CBC, and the future impact of technology and the electronic media on culture. There was really only one recommendation relating to the work of the Arts Centre: that it should "forgo in-house production of theatrical and operatic works in favour of co-productions with other Canadian companies."[16] This Recommendation 43 came as a bombshell—and it would profoundly influence future decisions regarding NAC activities.

The entire Applebaum-Hébert Report was, in fact, soon overrun by the juggernaut of technological and ownership issues that would come to preoccupy the government, primarily in film, television, and other electronic media. In contrast, the live performing arts and other issues about Canadian content in culture were sliding down the government's scale of priorities. Applebert's work had been driven by a passion for the arts, but now other political forces were at the fore. While there was still a sense that a strong cultural life was vital to the country and that federal support was essential in allowing the arts to flourish, private commercial interests had begun to argue strongly that they could make both art and money.

When the Applebaum-Hébert Committee crafted its recommendations after nearly three years of work, it took as its basic idea "the central importance of human creativity."[17] Creativity was the theme of the report, and every recommendation addressed how it could, in one area of culture after another, be "strengthened and assured by federal action."[18] Pressures grew to put government muscle behind private sector initiatives in the media, filmmaking, sound recording, and publishing. Funds were far from unlimited, and there was a shift away from the arm's-length, publicly funded artistic institutions that had backed the arts in the post-war period. Complicating factors included the increasing fragmentation of the country, especially in Quebec, and the continuing financial restraint. The Canada Council's finances had, for example, been frozen for the previous five years.

The committee's work was also fundamentally altered by the change of government from the Clark Conservatives and back to the Trudeau Liberals. The format of the expanded Federal Cultural Policy Review Committee had called for widespread public consultations and a proliferation of briefs—all encouraged and assisted by the national arts lobby group, the Canadian Conference of the Arts, under the leadership of national director John Hobday (twenty years later to become director of the Canada Council). According to Walter Pitman, Louis Applebaum's biographer, the demands in time and energy of this unexpected change meant that much of the solid basic research that might have underpinned the committee's thinking was never executed. Instead, its perceptions and recommendations were significantly affected by the huge number of briefs from all corners of the country, most of which lamented funding that was pumped into and through Ottawa, rather than given directly to them. In this regard, Canada's cultural scene reflected the same decentralizing conflicts and shifts that were stirring in the country's political and economic life.

MacSween was affronted, even outraged, at the summary treatment of the detailed submission the NAC had sent to the committee. His careful enunciations had set out clearly the dual role of the Arts Centre as conceived in its mandate and interpreted by its boards and management since the beginning: its support of artistic activity across the country through financial assistance and in showcasing the best on its national stage, as well as the importance of in-house productions that could tour—as Jean Gascon had so eloquently described it, "the heart that beats." MacSween felt that the committee had completely missed the point. In the manner of a good lawyer, he set out a detailed response that again justified the Arts Centre's policies. Unfortunately, the shifting fortunes of the political times were not in his favour, and the NAC's place in the cultural life of the country would worsen.

CHANGE
AND LOSS

While Donald MacSween and his staff spent months preparing the NAC's submission to the Applebaum-Hébert Committee, changes continued to evolve in the Music Department at the Arts Centre. Bernardi's drawn-out departure, customary in the music world, gave MacSween the opportunity to construct an elaborate search committee for a new music director.* With the departure of Ken Murphy, he also hired a new young music administrator, Michael Aze, who had been working for Walter Homberger at the Toronto Symphony. Aze arrived at the Arts Centre in 1978 when Bernardi was away on his sabbatical and remembers meeting with the maestro "only a couple of times"

---

*NAC chair Pauline McGibbon, although a non-voting member, led the search committee, which included Walter Prystawski, Robert Cram, and David Currie from the orchestra and orchestra volunteer Evelyn Greenberg, as well as Montreal music critic Eric McLean, contralto and NAC trustee Maureen Forrester, and the Honourable Mitchell Sharp, who continued to maintain a keen interest in the orchestra. MacSween also contrived to obtain "special counsel" for the group by adding some high-powered international names: Wolfgang Stresemann, the *intendant* to Herbert Von Karajan at the Berlin Philharmonic; Carl Moseley from the New York Philharmonic; and Britain's Sir William Glock. These important musical figures were likely paid as consultants to the search committee, but the reputation of the National Arts Centre in the musical world had helped to secure their involvement and added extra lustre to the proceedings. The stated hope of the board was to find another Canadian, but they hedged their bets by stating that there could be no compromise over quality. The search would stretch out over nearly two years. In the meantime the Arts Centre had a list of guest conductors it could turn to, among them the reliable Montreal-based German Franz-Paul Decker, who maintained a long relationship with the orchestra over the years.

that first year.[1] Left pretty much on his own, he decided, first, to work on improving the NAC Orchestra's subscription sales in Ottawa. There he found "a smorgasbord of possibilities."

Somewhat to his surprise, Aze also discovered that the orchestra was "not really working as hard" as he had thought. Sometimes it had an entire week to rehearse a single concert. Aze examined the NACO contract and found he had surplus time available to develop new products. He therefore moved quickly to increase the number and the type of concerts. He liked the orchestra and thought it was playing well: "It was a nice machine," he recalled.[2]

He started by introducing a new Baroque Series to the orchestra's programming, followed by a Pops Series, something he had worked on at the Toronto Symphony but had never been tried in Ottawa. He also organized a new Great Artists Recital Series in the 2,300-seat Opera, along with the usual chamber music and special events concerts, which included the big-name visiting orchestras. In the marketing area, students were sent door to door recruiting subscribers, focusing on specific postal code areas in the city—a new technique for Ottawa.* The stage setup in the concert hall was also adjusted to bring the orchestra forward. This new configuration lost a few seats, but greatly enhanced the sound.

Aze had another sensitive task as music administrator: he became the buffer between the orchestra and management at the Arts Centre. He had been present at the seminal meeting between MacSween and the "Young Turks" group, and, as the messenger between the director general, the orchestra, and Bernardi, he helped to ease the maestro's exit.

While he later would marvel at his own inexperience when he took the NAC job, Aze was a dedicated and talented music administrator. With Bernardi's departure approaching, he set up an array of guest conductors to try out with the orchestra. These new faces included fast-rising artists such as the Mexican conductor Eduardo Mata; Romanian-born Sergiu Commissiona, who would hold music/artistic directorships in Vancouver, Baltimore, and Houston; and a German-based Israeli conductor Gabriel Chmura. Aze also remembered lunching at Ottawa's Lord Elgin Hotel, just across the street from the NAC, with the violinist Pinchas Zukerman while he was in town for a solo appearance with the orchestra. At the time Zukerman was conductor of the St. Paul Chamber Orchestra in Minneapolis, but already exploring possibilities at the centre.

Candidates like Commissiona seemed to epitomize what orchestra members thought they wanted next—"a senior European-trained conductor"—and, under Prystawski's leadership, "the orchestra's opinion carried a lot of weight over who that next person

---

*Using postal codes to identify higher income sectors of urban areas was a relatively new marketing technique in Canada.

would be."[3] Elaborate measures were taken to explore the possibilities of another Canadian as musical leader. MacSween engaged in extended correspondence around the country and drew up a long list of possible candidates. He had a "glimmer," however, that the likelihood of a suitable Canadian was remote and knew that the orchestra would never accept anyone who was not at least the equal of Bernardi.[4]

By 1981 Aze had wearied of the ongoing uncertainty and what he deemed "an insufficiently serious attempt" to find Bernardi's replacement. The search committee continued to deliberate and received representations from musical figures such as the flamboyant New York impresario Harold Shaw, who assured them, "You are going to take one of my people, and I manage only the best!"[5] Aze also felt out of stride with MacSween's overall management approach, which he felt sometimes had "a grandiose bent"[6]—as when MacSween proposed concerts by two French orchestras in the same season. Although Bernardi invited Aze to help him with the Summer Festival operas, Aze declined on the grounds that he had no expertise in this area. Before long and by mutual consent with MacSween, he decided to resign.

Aze's three years at the NAC had seen some good things: the orchestra's first appearance at Carnegie Hall in New York and at Washington's Kennedy Center; and an

The NACO performed before the General Assembly of the United Nations in New York with Pierre Trudeau and the shoe-loving Imelda Marcos, wife of Philippines President Ferdinand Marcos, in the audience. Photo © NAC.

appearance as guest orchestra at the United Nations when both the Philippines' Imelda Marcos and Canada's Pierre Trudeau were in the audience. Back in Ottawa, there had been some stellar concerts, including one under Bernardi's baton of Berlioz's *Beatrice and Benedict*, based on Shakespeare's tale. Despite a small audience, it was deemed "a sensational performance."[7] Using a script developed for the Boston Symphony, it was semi-staged and involved a rare collaboration between the Music and the Theatre departments. Berlioz's work had both sung and spoken lines, which had been translated into French. At the NAC, Bernardi arranged for the seven actors from the English theatre troupe to join the singers in the performances. They were arranged in large armchairs around the stage and spoke their parts in the original Shakespearean English while the singers sang in French. At the end, both actors and singers portraying the same role came together to symbolize the single characters. Besides a wonderful musical performance, it was an effective demonstration of the bilingualism that the NAC espoused. Another remarkable concert was a similarly semi-staged version of Poulenc's "La Voie Humaine." Those evenings, along with the visiting artists brought in by Aze, were as diverse as flutist James Galway, narrator Peter Ustinov, pianist Jon Kimura Parker (in his first appearance at the NAC), and the renowned Eduardo Mata—for whom Aze managed to find a new Mexican restaurant in eatery-challenged Ottawa. While his feelings were mixed as he departed the Arts Centre, Aze had many good memories of his time there.

The Music Department continued in a state of flux. The unusual structure that placed opera and the summer music program in a separate Festival Department, outside the Music Department, needed to be reorganized. And MacSween had spotted the person he wanted to do the job. The Greek-born Costa Pilavachi was young, ambitious, and smart, making his mark on the Toronto music scene and moving rapidly up the ladder of musical management that would eventually take him to the top as a vice-president of Decca Records and then as president of EMI Classics, two of the world's pre-eminent recording companies. His passion for the arts, and music in particular, had been minted in Ottawa, where his father had served as Greek ambassador for a decade at the time that the NAC was being built. Pilavachi had memories of walking past the NAC excavation on his way to school at Ottawa's Lisgar Collegiate. He also vividly recalled that he and his father had been forced to attend the second night of the opening festivities because Iannis Xenakis, the composer of the music for the first night's ballet, *Kraanberg*, had been exiled from Greece by the governing Colonels, and Greece's envoy could not be seen to officially recognize the renegade.* The piquancy of it all fired young Costa's imagination and led him to pursue a career in the arts.

---

*Years later as Greek ambassador to France, Pilavachi Senior was able to restore Greek citizenship to the composer after democracy had been reinstated in his country.

After graduating from Carleton University, Pilavachi, like Aze, had worked for the tough-minded, demanding Walter Homberger, followed by an invaluable three years with the NAC's first program director, David Haber, who had become a Toronto-based arts impresario.* By the time MacSween spotted him, Pilavachi had joined the widely experienced music producer Franz Kramer at Toronto Arts Productions, booking artists of world stature into concerts at Toronto's St. Lawrence Centre. Pilavachi was considered enough of a "whiz kid" that, at barely the age of thirty, Kramer had handed him the management of the company while the veteran music producer went off to Ottawa to become music officer at the Canada Council.

MacSween first invited Pilavachi in May 1981 to join him for dinner after a concert at the Arts Centre. Two months later, he followed with a longer interview at his rented summer cottage on an island in the Great Rideau Lakes, not far from where Southam had his summer property. Pilavachi later remembered a golden day and driving up to the lake in the company of concertmaster Walter Prystawski. After a good lunch and much discussion, the party was on its way back to shore when the boat they were riding in ran out of gas. Pilavachi seized the oars and rowed the craft to the landing—a gesture that MacSween took as a happy omen. Although there was as yet no formal offer, Pilavachi knew he had the job. MacSween said later that he thought he was taking a risk with the young man, but he saw it as "part of the NAC's job to foster talent."[8] With still no new music director in view, Pilavachi said "what MacSween wanted was a kind of 'music supremo'"—someone who would take overall responsibility for the NAC orchestra, all the Music Department activities, and the Summer Festival.[9]

While Bernardi had been the official artistic director of the Festival, he had mainly concerned himself with the operas, leaving the rest of the programming to a Stratford-trained arts administrator, Andrée Gingras, who had been hired by the Festival's general manager, Bruce Corder, as his number two. MacSween did not much like Gingras, perhaps seeing her as an impediment to his ambitions for more innovative programming in the summer. Although it would be a blow to Corder to lose responsibility for the Festival, MacSween saw Pilavachi's appointment as the key to making changes. The political machinations swirled largely over the head of the newcomer, and he was able to maintain good relations with Corder. To avoid confusion, MacSween invented a new title for Pilavachi—director of the Music Department.

From this vantage point, Pilavachi was able to observe the search for a new conductor. In general, he found the process "unwieldy," though it was obvious to him that the only people who had any real influence were the orchestra members, in particular Walter Prystawski. "They didn't have the actual authority to appoint the Music Director

---

*Underwritten in part by the Canada Council at a time when developing good arts administrators was seen as part of its mandate.

but they certainly had the authority to veto anyone who was suggested,"[10] Pilavachi laughed later. Eduardo Mata, who had appeared several times with the orchestra, was a popular front-runner. He brought a personal warmth to the podium, even though musically he was seen as a "cool' conductor, someone who "shone with a blue rather than a red flame."[11] Mata was finally offered the job but turned it down, explaining that he was prepared to be the orchestra's principal conductor but not its music director—the dual role would put too many demands on his flourishing career. Another candidate favoured by the Music Department was the Korean Myung-Whun Chung, who had "guest-conducted three marvelous concerts," but he was not popular with the orchestra.[12] With no obvious Canadian in view, the focus shifted after nearly two years of hunting onto Franco Mannino, an Italian conductor who had enjoyed two guest appearances with the orchestra. Those concerts had introduced an emotional component which had enthused the musicians.

Mannino, a demonstrative and romantic southern Italian, was the opposite of the cool and controlled Bernardi. His warmth and spontaneity had touched the musicians, who until now had lived a controlled and disciplined sort of life. With the orchestra's blessing, MacSween and Pilavachi set off in the beautiful spring of April 1982 for Palermo, Italy, to discuss the appointment with the maestro. Mannino had no experience as a music director. He was known primarily as a composer, often of Italian film scores. He had worked closely with the renowned Italian film director Luchino Visconti.* Although he had performed frequently with orchestras, these appearances were almost always as a guest conductor, often in programs devoted to his own music. The rest of his musical repertoire was not large. For these reasons, Pilavachi cautioned Mac-Sween against making Mannino the full-fledged music director. MacSween accepted the advice and, while both the orchestra and Mannino were upset at the decision, the Italian conductor

Donald MacSween and Costa Pilavachi, the young director of the music department, were pleased at their catch when they hired Italian Franco Mannino to be conductor and artistic adviser to the orchestra. Photo © Fernand R. LeClair.

*He composed the score for the film *Death in Venice*, starring the English actor Dirk Bogarde, among others.

agreed to become principal conductor and artistic adviser to the NAC. He was hired on a two-year contract.

From the moment that Mannino stepped into his new role, the orchestra was in heaven. As MacSween put it, "Bernardi was Northern Italy. He burned with a cold blue flame. Mannino was from Sicily and was hot red."[13] One veteran musician put it even more graphically: "It was like the change from the time of Oliver Cromwell in England to a vacation resort in Italy."[14] From the exhilarating opening concert under Mannino's baton, the musicians felt a sense of emotional liberation after the stern Bernardi years, and the Ottawa audience soon joined in the excitement too. Mannino's concerts "took everyone on a voyage … usually one of extremes," recalled the principle bassoonist, Michael Namer, adding that the maestro usually conducted from memory and, while he could write musical scores, he sometimes had more difficulty remembering them. His music making was full of feeling, but "the accuracy of the [orchestra] machine suffered" and, occasionally, there were "train wrecks."[15] Mostly the musicians did not mind; once Mannino realized he had made some grievous mistake, he flashed his "million-watt smile" and all would be forgiven.[16] To the relief of the musicians, he was equally forgiving of their occasional errors and fulsome with praise when they played well, signalling them with his hands or blowing kisses. Prystawski recalled that it was "not a time of growth for the orchestra, but a happy time," with the music they played together "full of nuances."

Mannino was not only an artistic talent, he was a shrewd businessman and, as his second year began, he entered into tough negotiations with MacSween for an extension. Still without a permanent replacement for Bernardi, MacSween renewed the contract for a further year, although he maintained that Mannino asked for, and received, "an exorbitant sum."[17] His musicians, meanwhile, were held to an increase of 1 to 2 percent in this time of financial restraint.

The maestro also secured a handsome commission for his own music. During a casual conversation with Hamilton Southam one day, the idea came up that a suite of music for Ottawa might be nice, something similar to "The Pines

*Concertmaster Walter Prystawski quickly struck up a friendship with Franco Mannino and enjoyed their adventurous concerts together.
Photo © Paul D. Hoeffler/NAC.*

of Rome." After yet another agreeable summer lunch with Southam at his cottage, they agreed that Mannino would consider a "little piece" tentatively titled "The Birches of the Rideau Lakes" for the orchestra.[18] To Southam's surprise, a substantial musical manuscript arrived in Ottawa a few weeks later which turned out to be a full-fledged symphony. Along with it came a healthy invoice for $25,000. This sum far outreached any amount paid until then for a Canadian work at the NAC, and it was a lot more than the generous Southam had contemplated. Concerned, he consulted MacSween. He was particularly worried that Canadian composers had not received any comparable commissions.

In the end, rather than quibble, Southam paid the bill, and the finished work, "Rideau Lake Symphony," was eventually premiered by the NACO "in the presence of the Southam family." The work featured principal tympanist Ian Bernard, for whom Mannino had written an extended cadenza. Bernard was expected to operate a wind machine as well as a thunder board to achieve the desired atmospheric effects, but when this combination proved physically impossible, a synthesizer was used instead. Later, Southam would wryly recall the piece as a "tone poem that could have been written about any lake," and he told the composer that he "should have added the song of the loon to the score, and then it really would have been about the Rideau Lakes."[19] "I was had!" Southam laughed, although the piece went on to be recorded by Mannino with the Leningrad Philharmonic and the maestro included it in subsequent concerts around Europe, always specifically thanking Southam for his handsome gift.

While the conductor secured a third season with the orchestra his constant money demands made it impossible for the financially embattled MacSween to renew him further. There were heated negotiations that involved much brinkmanship between the two men over Mannino's fee and, ultimately, as MacSween explained, money was the real cause for the end of the relationship. Other factors were Mannino's unwillingness to settle in Ottawa and be part of the community, and his perfunctory interest in Canadian composers. MacSween mused many years later that "some of the orchestra members never forgave me for letting Mannino slip through my fingers."[20] Others, like Namer, felt that Mannino's volatile style eventually raised doubts in the minds of the players and, while there had been many magic moments, it was time for something more stable in the musical leadership.

As the musical machinations with Mannino continued, the political and financial scene in Ottawa worsened. After the delivery of the Applebaum-Hébert Report in the summer of 1982, the NAC, along with every other federal government department and agency, received news that Treasury Board was taking even more drastic measures to improve the government's finances. The "6% and 5% program," which affected all wages and prices in the country and limited the increases in subsidies to all federal government offices, was extended for a further two years. The government also announced that it was redirecting $200 million in funds to a new job-creation program. The contribution from the Department of Communications' budget was to be $25 million—with a cool $1 million of that coming from the federal grants going to the NAC over the next two years.

These deficit reduction measures had an immediate impact at the Arts Centre. If no steps were taken, the NAC would have an accumulated deficit of $1,134,000 within a year, which would rise dramatically to $2,800,000 by the end of fiscal 1984. MacSween reminded the board trustees that during the major reductions in 1978, the centre had managed the process by "thinning out" expenses but generally had not touched programming. Now, he told them, programming would have to be cut if unmanageable deficits were to be avoided. The choice was to reduce in-house production in one of three areas: opera, music, or theatre. The Treasury Board edict also came with a rider: the cuts should have as little effect as possible on the labour force. The government wanted to avoid the spectre of mass layoffs in Ottawa. This factor would influence MacSween's choices. The summer opera festival had by far the largest budget of any programming department at the NAC, but a permanent staff of only three. MacSween therefore told the board in the fall of 1982 that "the most efficient way to reduce expenses with a minimum loss of jobs would be to abandon opera production for the next two or three years." Despite cancellation fees for artists already booked, he estimated that "the NAC could save nearly $500,000 … although some of this would have to be spent on alternative programming for the month of July."[21]

The renowned CBC Television producer Norman Campbell, whose television broadcasts of Canadian arts performances had won many awards and put a lot of Canadian talent on view, was now a board trustee. When he queried MacSween as to whether the staff of the Music Department had been consulted about this proposal to cut opera, he was told they had not, as this was "a financial, not an artistic, decision."[22] By the late fall of 1982, after lengthy discussions and much hesitation, the trustees gave MacSween the authority to cancel the opera productions if necessary. They agreed that, for now, the whole issue should remain strictly confidential.

A sensitive point with the NAC was how to respond to "Applebert" without appearing to bend to its direct recommendation that the Arts Centre eliminate in-house opera and theatre production. For MacSween, this was a point of honour, even though he was contemplating the opera's cancellation. Initially, he had considered a sharp retort to the report, but had held back. Now he reiterated his strongly held views on the NAC's "dual mandate"—that it was both a creative producing house and a presenting organization for Canada as a whole. To follow Applebert's recommendation would mean a fundamental change in policy in his view. He was determined that this redirection should not occur and persuaded his trustees to agree. It meant that making the required $1 million cut would be tricky.

People loved the operas and wondered why there weren't more performances of them. The ironic truth was that every time the curtain went up on an opera performance, it cost the National Arts Centre money. Although expensive, the productions on tap were gorgeous and continued to have great sales at the box office. Among them was a reprise in 1981 of a beautifully designed 1979 production of *A Midsummer Night's Dream*, first directed by John Copley from Covent Garden and now taken over by Canadian director Brian Macdonald. The summer of 1982 brought a brand-new production of George Frederic Handel's *Rinaldo* starring Marilyn Horne. Bernardi had long wanted to work with Horne, and *Rinaldo* would also be Canada's gift to New York's Metropolitan Opera on the occasion of its 100th anniversary in January 1984 and Bernardi's conducting debut there. Although *Rinaldo* was a great success in the 1982 Ottawa Summer Festival and had been selected by the CBC for broadcast, it was running seriously over budget, with upwards of $200,000 extra costs to be accounted for. MacSween defended the work, telling the board that "greater aesthetic considerations come at a higher cost,"[23] but, as finances became increasingly difficult, there was much agitated debate. In the meantime, Pilavachi, who had never produced an opera in his life, pushed ahead for an elegant production of Tchaikovsky's *Eugene Onegin*, scheduled for the summer of 1983.

The board's reluctant agreement that opera production could be abandoned if necessary was not a decision taken lightly, and it was revisited again and again in the following weeks. Discussions about overall reductions in programming continued. John Wood's Theatre Department was now compelled to line up

Canada's gift to the Metropolitan Opera on its 100th birthday was the NAC's lavish production of Handel's Rinaldo. *It starred Marilyn Horne and was conducted by Mario Bernardi. Photo © Fernand R. LeClair.*

outside plays for the 1983–84 season rather than develop new in-house productions. Ironically PACT, the Canadian professional theatre organization, had recently come out in support of original production at the Arts Centre, as part of its opposition to the Applebaum-Hébert recommendations. Undoubtedly the NAC's Andis Celms, who had assisted the founding of PACT, had helped to orchestrate this response. A similar initiative on behalf of opera was being sought from the Canadian Opera Association. These gestures of goodwill, however, had little impact on the Arts Centre's financial dilemma. NAC management led by MacSween made a scheduled appearance before the Commons Parliamentary Committee and it seemed to be a good chance to make the NAC's case. But it was soon clear that the committee's work was fully taken up with issues of broadcasting and film policy emanating from the office of Communications Minister Francis Fox. Instead, the Arts Centre itself was urged to become more involved in television projects. This advice was a harbinger of things to come.

There was a faint hope that the annual cut of $500,000 for the second year might be mitigated. The "6 and 5" policy was affecting not only in-house salaries and administration budgets but was noticeably decreasing the NAC's revenue-producing operations—from ticket sales to parking fees to restaurant meals. These reductions were in turn augmented by an inflation rate that was running far beyond the legislated amounts and by operating costs that continued to go up.

Nor was the NAC spared rigorous new government policies, for example those relating to official bilingualism in Canada. Although as an institution it had always operated in both languages, the centre was obliged now to do all its business in both English and French and to hire translators to produce a complete roster of documents in the two languages. One senior administrative officer recalled expensive simultaneous translation services being set up for board meetings, even though they were seldom used. Among the government's efforts to put a federal stamp on everything it supported in the continued struggle between Ottawa and Quebec, was a directive from Minister Fox's office that all federal projects should now come with a federal "brand," or word mark. This was one notion the NAC was able to resist. It insisted that it already had a beautiful logo in the hexagon symbol devised at its creation, and it was one of the few government agencies that managed to keep the clutter of the "Canada" motto off its letterhead and other promotional materials.

MacSween now had the authority to suspend the opera season, but in the early months of January 1983 he stopped short of making that decision. Ongoing talks with a seemingly sympathetic Francis Fox made it appear that the Art Centre's situation might be alleviated. The integral importance of the Summer Festival, and specifically the opera productions, to the reputation of the NAC, was not lost on either the director general or the trustees. They were also worried about the impact this suspension might have on the orchestra, still going through a dramatic period of change.

Plans for the 1983 Festival had now reached committed costs of approximately $500,000, and the board was advised this money would be wasted if the plans were cancelled. The situation put the NAC's financial fortunes in an awkward Catch-22. As MacSween warned, continuing the opera program inevitably caused the NAC's deficit to rise, while any relief for it remained only a vague possibility. The anxious trustees again delayed any final decision, and everyone concurred that the 1983 summer season should continue to completion. "Perhaps afterwards," they thought, "opera could be arranged every two or three years instead of annually."[24] As the money worries intensified, the NAC's financial staff monitored everything. Theatre staffers who had allowed contracted-in artists to use their telephone cards were called on the carpet.

At the Department of Communications, a new deputy minister had been appointed. Robert Rabinovitch began his government career in 1968 working in Gérard Pelletier's office and now had attained the top job at the Department of Communications. He informed the NAC that there might be funds for capital projects but not for operations. This advice led to an acoustical study for the Opera, with a view to having it fitted with new technology, and $52,000 was found in the Reserve Fund for a new Steinway piano. Still, the huge looming operating budget shortfall remained the prime concern. A major factor in that deficit remained opera production, now affected by *Rinaldo* being readied at considerable additional expense for its Metropolitan Opera performances. Rabinovitch recalled that when he tried to warn the NAC about what his department saw as excess, "They didn't get it."[25] Even so, MacSween continued to point out to the trustees that the anticipated deficit was more than the NAC could handle.

The moment for the axe to fall on opera was close at hand. Opera had brought the Arts Centre its greatest international recognition, but at a cost per patron subsidy that was the highest of all the art forms performed there. Finally, at the board's summer meetings, on July 15, 1983, as the plaudits for the NAC's latest new production, *Eugene Onegin*, rolled in, the trustees delivered the *coup de grâce:* further operatic performances produced by the NAC were suspended.* It was a decision that MacSween had encouraged even though "it was taken with much pain and regret."[26] He nevertheless was confident that the reasoning behind the move was sound. One of the oft-heard

---

Eugene Onegin was a spectacular production. Among its performers was the superb soprano Lois Marshall. Paralyzed in childhood by infantile paralysis, she was rarely offered the opportunity to appear in opera. In the role of Filippyevna, she stayed seated throughout the performance— and the experience proved to be emotionally fulfilling for both the artist and the audience.

complaints against the opera festival was that it was too elitist and had insufficient appeal for "Joe Public and his family" visiting Ottawa during the summer, a view for which MacSween had some sympathy.

But the director general had not anticipated the aghast reaction at his decision that now appeared in the press. Nor the black mark that people would remember in the coming years at the cancellation of the opera festival. The shock wave that greeted the news rolled up into Francis Fox's office, as some commentators speculated that MacSween's dramatic cancellation was a gamble intended to galvanize the government into easing the NAC's financial difficulties. If so, that was not to be the result. Private lobbyists, including Ottawa's Bertram Loeb and Hamilton Southam, ran their thoughts about some private fundraising to resuscitate the fallen art form past their government contacts, but to no avail. There was no acknowledgement from the Communications Department that it was the government's own financial policies that had created the problem.

While opera was not the only focal point at the NAC, its suspension symbolized a turning point in the organization's fortunes—which would continue to slide in the coming years. For Costa Pilavachi, the ensuing period became a time of "gloom and doom with no exciting programs left to develop."[27] A 1985 orchestra tour to Hong Kong and Japan, partially financed by the Department of External Affairs, remained on the books, but the disappointed Pilavachi began to look for new opportunities. When he received an offer to become artistic administrator at the Boston Symphony and work with the famed conductor Sejii Ozawa, he accepted it. The NAC's talented music marketing man, Gary Hansen, also left, accepting a good position at the Atlanta Symphony before moving on to a permanent position with the world-renowned Cleveland Orchestra. It proved, if nothing else, that time spent at the National Arts Centre was an excellent calling card for talented young Canadian arts administrators on the way up.

At the end of the 1983–84 season, with in-house theatre production at the Arts Centre at a virtual standstill, English theatre director John Wood declared he was no longer interested in just showcasing plays. With little money left for new production, he too gave his notice. What was needed, he told management, was not a creative artistic director but a theatre producer to manage other people's work. He suggested that Andis Celms, who had been associated with the theatre operations in both languages since the outset, was the obvious candidate. Jean Gascon had suffered a heart attack and was effectively gone from the scene. Left behind to cope with the difficulties was Donald MacSween, although the energy began to seep out of his tenure as mounting problems besieged him. For the record, he ruefully reported in the annual report that "1983 had not been a good year for arts organizations in Canada."[28]

THE REALITY
OF THE PLIGHT

At first Donald MacSween had held back on a formal response to the Applebaum-Hébert Report. Then he used the Art Centre's 1982–83 annual report to attack what he labelled "Applebaum-Hébert Errors."[1] In classic legal style he systematically listed and then firmly rebutted what he saw as the committee's misconceptions of his organization. It was a forceful defence of all the principles that had underpinned the NAC's work until then—goals that were now being altered, he stated, by "new issues and policies of regionalism in the country." He fervently believed that this approach was misguided.

As Trudeau's Liberal regime moved towards the fall 1984 election, it again made efforts to bring the cultural crown corporations more tightly under the terms of the *Financial Administrations Act* and to allow government more direct control over their activities. At the Canada Council, director Timothy Porteous was warned by departmental officials not to speak out against the proposal, but the chairpersons of the Canada Council and the National Arts Centre, Mavor Moore and Pauline McGibbon, respectively, made a spirited joint appearance before the Standing Committee on Broadcasting, Film and Assistance to the Arts, which was studying the matter. They threatened to resign if more restrictive financial measures were imposed on their cultural institutions.

The Liberal government finally fell, and an election was called for September 4. As campaigning got under way, the possibility of a regime change loomed into view in Ottawa. The records indicate that meetings of the full NAC board simply lapsed, although the Executive Committee continued to provide oversight, fussing over the NAC's bleak financial picture.

In the summer of 1984 MacSween finally closed the money-losing Le Restaurant. It would never reopen. In its place, a revamped Le Café overlooking Ottawa's Rideau

Canal provided the main food service to the public at the Arts Centre. With opera gone, the Summer Festival was radically rearranged and scheduled to run throughout the summer, not just in the July festival period. While it still lost money, MacSween pointed out that, although a Canadian Opera Company production of *The Merry Widow* had not done well, the other summer programming, "which included a number of ethnic dance and popular music groups … and other lighter fare seemed to have been enjoyed by the public."[2] He took grim satisfaction that he was at last making some progress in cutting costs in the Catering Department and, during the summer season, had managed "to provide twice the number of tickets for half the cost in subsidy."[3] But he would get little credit for it.

On the eve of the election, the issue of some private fundraising to support activities was tentatively raised again, this time to help pay for the orchestra's planned tour to Japan. MacSween continued to tell his trustees that what the NAC needed was more money and that the government's restraints, including those on ticket pricing, were drastically limiting the centre in the straightened times. His arguments were scarcely noted. Henceforth he would become increasingly isolated on the Ottawa political scene.

The election swept a new Conservative government under Brian Mulroney to power, one with an overall vision for cutting government costs and reducing Canada's deficit. MacSween, who had once been a colleague of Mulroney in the same Montreal law firm, perhaps thought that their personal acquaintance might help the beleaguered NAC. This would not be the case: Mulroney's focus was a long way from culture and the arts.

Marcel Masse, a Quebec nationalist and hard-driving political operative, was appointed to take over the Communications portfolio from the outgoing Francis Fox.

Masse had strong views about culture, especially when it came to Quebec. He warned his officials that he intended to be a hands-on minister and that it would be their heads which would roll if mistakes were made, especially ones with bad political fallout. A shrewd man who enjoyed crackling intellectual debate, he travelled widely across the country. He wined and dined with cultural notables, picking up valuable intelligence on how the arts community outside Quebec operated. These encounters included a dinner with author

The Honourable Marcel Masse, the new minister responsible for culture in Brian Mulroney's Cabinet. Photo © Rod MacIvor/ Ottawa Citizen. *Reprinted by permission.*

Margaret Atwood and her husband, writer Graeme Gibson, at their home in Uxbridge, Ontario, where they discussed cultural matters late into the night. Although his officials found him tough to work with, his stance earned him surprising kudos in the English-speaking arts world.

A prime plank in the Conservative agenda was to wrestle the ballooning federal deficit to the ground. Masse recalled that the new finance minister, Michael Wilson, pushed the Cabinet hard from the outset to come up with cost-cutting measures by Christmas, so he could put them into his budget. In due course, Erik Nielsen, a phleg-matic MP from the Yukon (and later deputy prime minister) whose brother Leslie was a Hollywood actor, was assigned as the chief axe-wielder. His Task Force on Program Review was created specifically to slash government spending at all levels and to iden-tify which government programs should be eliminated or privatized. Nielsen immediately set to work with coolness and diligence. Years later, Masse would recall that the initial target for the Conservatives was a $4-billion reduction. The projected cut in the com-munications and culture portfolio was $85 million, a seemingly small sum set against overall government spending.[4] However, it would have severe effects in a department where funding was extended over a wide range of subsidies and included organiza-tions such as the CBC, the Canada Council, the national museums, and the National Arts Centre.

With considerable political acumen, Masse found ways to delay Nielsen's most dra-conian measures while he figured out what he wanted to do. He set up his own series of task forces mandated to "study matters" before cuts were concluded and arranged meetings, dinners, and receptions with arts executives and officials all over the country. For a time he had to step out of office when questions over his election finances were raised,* but, by then, he had his allies in the Canadian arts community and, once cleared, he returned to the department to continue the fight.

The weakest part of the portfolio, he said, was that "cultural policies were not part of the public debate because many people perceived the arts as elitist."[5] Masse did not necessarily share this opinion. He was interested in cultural affairs, although he always put Quebec's cultural and political point of view first. He therefore chal-lenged MacSween when he came to his office in the fall of 1984 to plead the NAC's case. Masse went on a broad attack, even citing a budgetary line-item for flowers at the centre. MacSween explained that every leading artist who performed on an NAC stage received a bouquet. It might be a small matter, but the manoeuvre proved that the minister had access to detailed information about the centre and that MacSween and the NAC could expect tough handling from the new administration in Ottawa.

---

*A unilingual former Quebec school principal, Benoit Bouchard, was appointed as minister to fill in for Masse. His term was too short to have any impact.

Masse was able to put off many of the cultural cuts that the Task Force on Program Review wanted to implement. Among them was Nielsen's recommendation that the National Arts Centre be privatized. The idea stayed in the shadows for the present, but it would not be dismissed. Culture and the arts, in contrast to industrial communication policies, were simply not on the government's agenda.* And this overall lack of interest in arts organizations was repeatedly demonstrated in the way the government made appointments to the different arts boards.

The change in the federal government also meant major changes in board appointments at the Arts Centre. The culturally conscious Pauline McGibbon was replaced as chair by Pierre Boutin, a Quebec lawyer who had worked in the backrooms of Quebec's Union Nationale Party and, more recently, had been a political fundraiser for the federal Conservatives in Quebec. Masse would later comment that "the government did not do right by the guy! He would have preferred something like ambassador to Holland, where his brother had been killed in the war. Instead, he got a job where he had to come to Ottawa every month and had nothing but problems."[6]

These and other new appointments to the board "came from the top, the Prime Minister's Office," said Masse. "It was a bad process, but it was part of politics." The Conservatives had been out of power for several years, and there were a lot of political debts to be paid. The criteria for these new appointments did not include any aptitude in the arts, though they invariably had a connection to the party in power. In short, the first role of boards now was to reward political favour. Years later Masse himself would decry the system: "It was not a good practice. The minister did not have a single word to say, although these appointments came with his signature. There should have been more dialogue with the Prime Minister's Office."[7] Only much later in the government's mandate did this consultation occur, after political debts had been paid and it became possible to consider the qualifications for an appointment more closely.

For an arts advocate like Donald MacSween, this policy meant that he would have few kindred souls among his trustees. "Who did I have left to talk to?"[8] he mused later, as the long-serving Dr. Emmanuel Finkleman from Winnipeg left the board after a dozen years of loyal service. The new chair would not take office until January 1985 and, in the meantime, vice-chair Claude Frenette stood in, dealing with thorny questions such as Maestro Mannino's payments—which the conductor wanted divided up and paid into three Swiss Bank accounts. The board's executive committee prudently suggested that this plan be requested in writing.

---

*For more discussion of this larger question, see Ryan Edwardson, *Canadian Content: Culture and the Quest for Nationhood* (Toronto: University of Toronto Press, 2008).

By early 1985 half-a-dozen new names had been announced for the NAC board, including Gina Godfrey, wife of Toronto Tory Paul Godfrey; Toronto bandleader Johnny Lombardi; Montrealer Paule Tardif-Delorme, whose husband had been appointed head of the powerful communications company Teleglobe Canada; and Thomas Assaly, a hard-dealing Ottawa property developer. The new faces seemed to have little knowledge of the principles of the NAC's mandate, which MacSween had been so firmly espousing, as evidenced by their questions at early board meetings. Many, like Assaly, would prove themselves much more in tune with the privatizing cost-cutting ideas of Erik Nielsen.

The previous clarity over the NAC's dual role as both a creator of art and a showcase for the best talent available in Canada would become submerged in the changing financial and political times now at hand. Although the balance of MacSween's time at the Arts Centre would have its high points, it would mostly be a period of cuts and cuts again for a wearying senior management. They projected that a whopping $9.1 million would have to come out of the NAC budget over the next three years. For MacSween it would be an utterly demoralizing process, and he began to rely more and more on his senior team under Bruce Corder to find the money.

Although deeply disappointed at not being appointed to the top job, Corder had continued to serve loyally in the post of deputy director general. He was devoted to the arts and, by any standard, was the consummate theatre management professional in the NAC's administration. As the centre's financial situation grew more imperilled, not only by direct government policies but also by accumulative overruns in its own internal budgets, the cuts needed over the next three years would have to involve programming. Corder did not flinch from the task and worked intensely with his senior management colleagues and the

Bruce Corder, flanked by Governor General Roland Michener and prima ballerina Celia Franca, was always an experienced and gracious second-in-command. Photo © NAC.

department heads to find savings wherever they could. Inevitably, though, there had to be cuts, and the first to go were the summer opera festival and in-house theatre production.

Meanwhile, at the Department of Communications, deputy minister Robert Rabinovitch soon ran afoul of Masse and was replaced by de Montigny Marchand, who had been schooled in the Machiavellian ways of the Department of External Affairs and was able to work more flexibly with the minister. Among other issues, MacSween was now faced with a long series of labour negotiations with the unions at the NAC, including the orchestra. The Montreal Symphony Orchestra was the new pace-setter in financial contracts for musicians in Canada, and, while MacSween struggled to keep the musicians' pay raises within the 3–4 percent range, there was strong pressure to bring the NAC Orchestra players up to Montreal's gains. The other unions at the centre were agitating too, including the stage crews, who were threatening to go on strike. Of all the unions at the Arts Centre, IATSE had the power to close down the building if it wished.

Some of the new board members began to question what was appearing on the NAC stages, sharply cross-questioning MacSween at board meetings over performances with poor ticket sales. A 16 percent attendance at a concert by the usually popular itinerant singing group the Swingle Singers, famous for doing swing versions of Bach's music, produced incredulous comment from the board. Bandleader Johnny Lombardi even offered to assist in booking talent, and other board members thought they too should be actively involved in programming. In early 1985, with programming running at nearly a million dollars over budget (largely because of Maestro Mannino and other artists' fees), the trustees established an Artistic Advisory Committee designed to give management advice on content. The move forced the director general to spend even more time defending the situation as management tried to cope.

The Variety Department, which normally could be relied upon to make money, found itself saddled not only with the failed Swingle Singers but with three other money-losers, including an ill-starred production of *Duddy*, a musical version of the Mordecai Richler novel *The Apprenticeship of Duddy Kravitz*. The show had been championed by MacSween against the advice of his theatre producer, Andis Celms. It closed after just four performances. Despite these failures, the director general defended his artistic team to the board, explaining frequently that it was the NAC's obligation to present Canadian content—and that did not always mean big sales.

Some board members, particularly Thomas Assaly, aggressively pursued the government's idea of privatizing parts of the operations. The ticket service Teleticket, which the NAC had instituted in the early 1970s, was sold off to private interests. Assaly also argued for selling off the Catering Department to a concessionaire. Corder was able to demonstrate that outsourcing food would spell disaster for all parties. Board member Paule Tardif-Delorme, a Montrealer who had done some writing for radio and television and even authored the libretto for an opera presented at the Arts Centre, clashed with MacSween over finances as well as artistic matters. Much later she would say that the director general had not worked closely enough with the board. Whatever the reasons, there was a growing schism. It was a long way from the years when Hamilton Southam had helped to choose his own board members and relied on their staying on for long terms, providing stability to the organization.

Despite the worsening environment for the arts, there were some surprising, even heartening things still happening on the NAC stages. MacSween's solace in these difficult times, he would later explain, was the performances. Unlike many people who came to work in Ottawa, MacSween lacked enthusiasm for the overt political partisanship of the city. Instead, he rejoiced in the fact that part of his job included "going to hear that music, see that dance ... it was just totally uplifting."[9] He liked the people who worked at the Arts Centre, "their dedication, their competence," even though the circumstances around the NAC's operations caused him a great deal of worry.

The attacks on the program budgets notwithstanding, a vast array of Canadian talent continued to appear at, or with, the Arts Centre. The 1984–85 season included stellar concerts by singers Jon Vickers and Maureen Forrester, pianist Angela Hewitt in her premier appearance (she would go on later that season to win the International Bach Competition), and jazz great Oscar Peterson, who performed with the NAC orchestra in Toronto for the celebration of Bach's 300th anniversary. In both the French and English theatres, there were also impressive results. With André Brassard in his fourth season as director of French theatre and Andis Celms managing theatre overall and programming the English side, theatre subscriptions actually rose substantially.

Michel Tremblay's
Albertine en cinq
temps *featured (left to*
right) Rita Lafontaine,
Paule Marier, Murielle
Dutil, and Huguette
Oligny. When the play
was translated, the same
actresses performed in
the English version.
Photo © Guy Dubois.
Courtesy of Archives du
Théâtre du Rideau Vert.

In the French program, audiences were running at 92 percent for a mix of classic and modern work, including the premiere of a new Michel Tremblay play, *Albertine en cinq temps*, and another new play by Jean-Marc Dalpé. Robert Lévesque, the distinguished theatre critic for Montreal's *Le Devoir*, visited Ottawa and wrote afterwards that "the NAC is an important theatre centre."[10]

The English season that Celms arranged relied heavily on co-productions, but they proved popular both with the audience and with the regional companies that came to Ottawa. The season included an important new Canadian play, *New World* by John Murrell, which also marked the NAC debut of director Robin Phillips and actress Martha Henry, who co-starred with William Hutt. The play was co-produced with Toronto's CentreStage, and went on to play at Toronto's St. Lawrence Centre after its Ottawa opening. Several regional companies made their NAC debut that season—Regina's Globe Theatre, Winnipeg's Prairie Dog Theatre Exchange, and, in the Studio, Toronto Free Theatre with a new play, *Doc*, by Alberta playwright Sharon Pollock. Unfortunately, some central services were sacrificed in the effort to protect programming. The NAC Archives, a budding resource for the Canadian arts community, was cut to bare-bones' status after the death of the first archivist, Dr. Anthony Ibbitson.

The 1985–86 season followed a similar pattern. The NAC Orchestra at last made its successful tour to Japan and Hong Kong, taking with it a program that included works by two Canadian composers, Harry Somers and R. Murray Schafer, and presenting two Canadian soloists, violinist Peter Oundjian and cellist Tsuyoshi Tsutsumi, along with the American cellist Garrick Ohlsson.

Recording and broadcasting also enjoyed some success. New York's *Village Voice* magazine had already hailed the NAC Orchestra recording of Italian overtures, conducted by Franco Mannino, as "one of the three best classic recordings of 1983,"[11] and the next recording under Mannino's baton was again well received. Radio and television broadcasts included a TV Gala with the CBC, conducted by Eduardo Mata and featuring Felix Mirbt's puppets. And the fall of 1985 also saw the premiere of Mannino's Symphony No. 5, "Rideau Lake," which Southam had inadvertently commissioned.

Theatre continued to thrive. Twenty-five of the forty-six productions in English theatre came from elsewhere, and subscriptions soared to 88 percent capacity. Prominent among the plays was Tremblay's *Albertine*, again directed by André Brassard but now translated into English. Five of the six actresses who had played the leading roles in the original French-language production (co-produced with Montreal's Théâtre Rideau Vert) now returned to perform the play in English. Such was the peculiar co-lingualism that was possible within the framework of the Arts Centre, as nowhere else in Canada.

Brassard's French-language season, described as "searing," included a trilogy of historical works and another new Tremblay play, *Bonjour Là, Bonjour!* Again, special emphasis was put on French theatre for young audiences. Outside Ottawa, the NAC's Development of Regional Theatre Program assisted companies as far away as the

Théâtre Populaire d'Acadie in Caraquet, New Brunswick, the Cercle Molière in St. Boniface, Manitoba, and the Actors' Showcase in Winnipeg to mount quality productions in their own regions. It was no surprise that, at the end of the season, Brassard's contract was extended for another two years.

Dance was coming ever more into its own, with Ottawa noted for its discerning audience for modern dance. As the dance program continued to grow, *Dance in Canada* magazine called the Arts Centre "the best showcase for dance in this country."[12] The introduction of the Ottawa International Dance Festival at the beginning of the season brought "an eight-day feast from six countries"[13] and the richest of all dance programs to date, opening with the New York company of Merce Cunningham and concluding with the Tanztheater Wuppertal of Pina Bausch from Germany. In between were renowned Canadian groups such as La La La Human Steps from Montreal. Theatre Ballet of Canada celebrated its fifth anniversary in the capital, and Le Groupe de la Place Royale, which had been put together in Ottawa with help from the Canada Council, celebrated with works by its director Peter Boneham. The Kirov Ballet and La Scala Ballet of Milan rounded out the season.

Even the Variety Department seemed to have a new lease on life. Besides the usual headliners, it was a great year for musicals: *La Cage aux Folles*, *Man of La Mancha*, and *A Chorus Line* all found ready audiences in Ottawa, along with a revival of *South Pacific* starring the Canadian singer Robert Goulet, who now lived in the United States. There was plenty of multicultural programming as well: a dance troupe from Israel, Indian sitarist Ravi Shankar, and Ireland's singing group the Chieftains. The Catering Department even reported a 12 percent increase in gross revenues and a 56 percent increase in business at Le Café, though it was not documented how this success translated into more money for the NAC's coffers. At least the food service was no longer bleeding red ink.

Perhaps the best news was a decision on the next music director. After the exhaustive multi-year search, the Polish-born Israeli conductor Gabriel Chmura was selected. Approved by the board in November 1985, the news was announced to the public on January 7, 1986. As the winner of Berlin's 1971 Herbert von Karajan Conductor's Competition, Chmura seemed to be what the orchestra wanted: a solid European-trained leader steeped in the romantic repertoire. He had already performed twice as a guest conductor with the NAC Orchestra, and he was prepared to move his young family from Germany to Ottawa and become part of the community. The move would not actually occur until he took over full responsibility for the music program in September 1987. Joanne Morrow was moved up to replace Costa Pilavachi in the newly named post of music producer, and things seemed to augur well for music at the NAC. Sadly, MacSween would be gone from his post before Chmura began his first full season.

The 1986–87 season also read well artistically. The annual report claimed that a remarkable series of Easter concerts by the NAC Orchestra with the Gaeschinger Kantorei of Stuttgart, performed at New York's Carnegie Hall, Washington's Kennedy

Center, and in Montreal under the direction of German conductor Helmuth Rilling, marked "perhaps its [the NACO's] artistic high point to date."[14] Another recording landmark occurred when Maestro Mannino led the orchestra in the works of some of Canada's best-known composers: Norm Symonds, André Prevost, Harry Somers, and Jacques Hétu. And, when violinist Sir Yehudi Menuhin came to town to perform in the Great Masters Series, he participated in a first-ever master class for young students at Université d'Ottawa.

In theatre it was a "monumental juggling act" to accommodate everything being presented in Canada's two official languages.[15] The logistics of scheduling both rehearsals and performances in the two theatre spaces, the Theatre and the Studio, was an art form in itself. It was Brassard's fifth season, one notable not only for the mainstage productions but also for the high priority again given to young people's programs.* The English season, despite all the angst over in-house production, still saw "the largest audience ever for English theatre at the NAC."[16] The reason, claimed Celms, was "a combination of professionalism and solid entertainment."[17]

June 1987 would bring the first Canada Dance Festival to Ottawa, co-produced by the NAC, with dance producer Yvon St. Onge at the helm. It would ensure once again what *Dance in Canada* habitually described as "one of the big seasons now predictable at the NAC." While audiences for the Dance Festival averaged 55 percent (a figure that was later questioned by the board but defended on the grounds of support for new art), the attendance for the NAC's regular dance season was excellent, at 79 percent occupancy. Critics described the season as demonstrating "the extraordinary range and riches of dance in Canada today."[18] As well as Canada's top classical and modern troupes, Ottawa audiences saw some of the best and most eclectic of international talent, including the Feld Ballet, Béjart's Ballet of the 20th Century, and the Nederland Dans Theater—which had already earned a reputation in Ottawa from its first performances in 1971, when it presented an entire ballet in the nude.

Paid attendance at the Arts Centre for 1986–87 continued to exceed 640,000 for approximately 900 performances, or 2.5 performances per day throughout the year. It was not quite the average 700,000 persons annually of the Southam years, but close. And, given the circumstances, all this success was astonishing.

Behind the scenes, the picture was far from rosy. As the director general noted in his regular statement in the 1986–87 annual report, "not since the opening, seventeen

---

*Considerable credit was due to the work of Brassard's assistant, Jean-Claude Marcus. When Brassard finally left the NAC, Marcus would later take over for a time and run the French theatre.

years earlier, has the NAC known so much public scrutiny or undergone so much change."[19] A significant proportion of the time of senior management was now spent preparing for, responding to, or parrying outside studies of what the National Arts Centre should be doing. This "sport" was becoming increasingly popular in political Ottawa as officials jostled for money and power, and it reached its zenith in studies of the CBC.

It was part of the continuing struggle over which body would control cultural policy and decide how the arts would be practised in the country. The central federal ministry was taking more control into its own hands, as the Department of Communications and its officials wanted to decide who received federal money, how much, and for what. Constant questioning of the mandates and the efficiency of the arm's-length arts organizations was an effective way of diminishing their independence and putting their usefulness in doubt.

Marcel Masse was unhappy with the confidential Nielsen recommendation that the NAC building be handed over to the National Capital Commission and its contents privatized. He responded by announcing yet another task force to study the matter. It was exemplary of the friction between the two Cabinet ministers, Marcel Masse and Erik Nielsen, and reflected their different cultural backgrounds—a detail that was reported as gossip to his fellow trustees by NAC chair Pierre Boutin. With the help of a new assistant deputy minister, Jeremy Kinsman (another foreign service officer destined to go on to plum posts), Masse set up the Task Force on the National Arts Centre and appointed Toronto playwright Tom Hendry to chair it.

Hendry started his work in a conciliatory manner by arranging to meet with the full NAC board in January 1986, but MacSween seemed dubious about the process and had little confidence in the government's real intentions. The organization was now under almost constant scrutiny and the subject of two major government reviews—the Hendry study and a Comprehensive Audit Report by the Auditor General's Office. On the NAC board, as ex-officio members, were two long-time cultural bureaucrats—Peter Roberts, now director of the Canada Council, and Pierre Juneau, now serving as the president of the CBC. Both veterans of Ottawa cultural policy wars, they were wary of the auditors' definitions of what constituted "artistic evaluation." The auditors proposed comparing the NAC with the O'Keefe Centre in Toronto and the Kennedy Center in Washington, both run on entirely different lines as semi-commercial booking houses and not producers of creative work. MacSween told the board that the auditors would get a more accurate idea of how the centre functioned if they compared it to similar performing arts centres in Europe. He was correct in harking back to the NAC's beginnings, when it was modelled on European experience and not American practices in the arts. The potential outcome of both studies was a continuing source of debate and concern for the NAC board and its senior staff, and there was constant discussion but little consensus among the trustees about what should be the NAC's future. Some trustees like Thomas Assaly were pushing for more privatization; others on the board wanted better financial results from performances.

The record shows that MacSween could be testy in his remarks: he pointed out to the trustees that "even if the NAC sold off all its capital assets, it still could not pay its debts."[20] His own position was becoming more untenable as he tried to explain that the NAC was caught in mid-flight when austerity measures were suddenly imposed in the early eighties, and it had never been able to catch up. The arrival of the Tories had only exacerbated matters as their solution seemed simply to get the organization off the government's books. It was absurd, MacSween argued, to think of getting rid of the National Arts Centre.

There was no agreement inside the NAC over what it should present to Hendry. MacSween argued for the principles set out in "Climate for Creativity," the report he had written five years before for the Applebaum-Hébert Committee, and he hired a consultant, Richard Tait, to help him prepare documents for Hendry's group. Rumours of another $500,000 cut, and the need to find common ground, led to a special board meeting at the end of April. In early May the board's Executive Committee met again to discuss problems, including the fact that the NAC Orchestra musicians would have to stop playing at the centre for seven weeks because it could no longer afford the set-up costs. The mayor of Hull, Michel Légère, who had joined the board as an ex-officio member after being elected, immediately suggested that they should come across the river and play in his city. The situation was indeed becoming absurd.

MacSween's contract would expire in March 1987 and, at a meeting in May 1986, the executive agreed that his appointment would not be renewed. Thereafter, the weary and frustrated MacSween began to hand communications with the board over to his assistant director general, Ron Blackburn, the senior financial man at the centre. Soon further cuts followed, with another $210,000 taken from the NAC's parliamentary appropriation. Clearly there was tough in-fighting within government circles over scarce resources and the stubborn national debt.

By the time Hendry delivered his report in September 1986, Masse had left the Communications portfolio and been replaced by Flora MacDonald, the MP for Kingston, Ontario. Hendry later acknowledged meeting with Minister Masse "every three weeks for breakfast"[21] while his work was in progress. His report, "Accent on Access," was a severe blow to the senior directors at the National Arts Centre. It contained 103 recommendations, but two struck at the core of NAC activities. The first, on the grounds that "the country's theatre community has now matured," supported the Applebaum-Hébert Report and recommended that the NAC give up in-house theatre production completely and allow Canadian theatre companies to supply the content at the NAC.

Both Brassard and Celms were extremely upset at this suggestion, and Celms warned, correctly, that it would lead to the French director's departure—like John Wood before him. The second affirmed the place of the resident orchestra at the Arts Centre but, contrary to "Applebert," recommended that the NAC bring opera back to the Summer Festival. This notion stemmed in part from the private lobbying effort that had been going on behind the scenes from the moment the opera had been cancelled. It was backed energetically by Hamilton Southam and other local supporters, including Bertram Loeb, whose daughter Diane Loeb was a rising young opera singer and had appeared in *Eugene Onegin*, the NAC's last fully staged, in-house opera production.

The idea of reviving opera in the Summer Festival coalesced with another plan the government had in mind. Two new national museum buildings were to open in Ottawa in 1988—the National Gallery and the Canadian Museum of Civilization. In government circles, a grand Summer Festival at the Arts Centre seemed in keeping with these other events. The idea was that some of the funds for the summer could come from the disappearing budget for theatre production. MacSween, who had worked hard to make the summer programming both populist and more financially viable, now found himself in a situation that would take funding away from his core programming in favour of festival project financing. A new struggle ensued with the board over this issue.

Hendry's third big thrust was that the NAC should expand its touring, both physically and, even more important, electronically. "Electronic touring," the report declared, "is the pre-eminent tool through which the Centre can fulfill its national mandate."[22] The idea of taking the NAC out to the country through broadcast media had been on and off the agenda for years. Hendry's report now grandly proposed that the programs and the budgets of the Canada Council Touring Office and the Department of External Affairs touring program be turned back over to the NAC—to consolidate all touring at the federal level at the centre.

There was no way this recommendation could be fulfilled. The Canada Council's Peter Roberts quickly pointed out that the Touring Office could not be shipped back to the NAC on the whim of a minister or department; rather, it would require the agreement of the boards of both organizations and perhaps even a change in legislation. That proposal slipped off the table, but the concept of "electronic touring" was now becoming firmly rooted in the government's mind and was receiving serious study at the Department of Communications. Before long the National Arts Centre would have a new director general who would drive this concept relentlessly.

RUDDERLESS
MONTHS

As Donald MacSween's term as director general ebbed to a close, the last months were described by one observer as "bleak."[1] Problems mounted, and he worked more and more from his home in Ottawa's Sandy Hill, appearing only rarely at the office. Much had been hurled at him in his latter time at the NAC. In his two terms at the helm of the National Arts Centre, he had steadfastly maintained that the arts should be "leveled up, not leveled down," everywhere in the country, and he believed that governments should provide more money, not less. He particularly disliked the way that politicians moved the same money around for the benefit of one organization and at the expense of another. In the current harsh economic times, however, his ideas had little basis in reality.

The nature of arts funding continued to shift. Pelletier's concept of "decentralization" had found a literal echo in Clark's 1979 Conservative notion of Canada as a "community of communities." In that short interregnum, David MacDonald had suggested distributing the money for culture on an equal basis throughout all the country's constituencies. Increasingly, federal ministers in charge of culture, and their officials, endeavoured to strengthen their control over the way federal money was distributed and spent. The style and manner tipped towards the European, and particularly the French, model of a central minister of culture, although no such title existed in Canada. The spending discretion that had belonged to the arm's-length agencies in the sixties and seventies was diminishing, despite their protests, and the leash was tightened by stemming the flow of money that went to those organizations. It was a very different environment from that in which the Arts Centre had been conceived and first operated.

The Nielsen Task Force was but another version of this democratization. How, it asked, could the greatest number of Canadians benefit from public funds? It expressed no interest in any degree of excellence. In the cultural sector, performances of a high standard that were largely contained in Ottawa, or even toured out from there, were no longer satisfactory. The work of the talented artistic leadership that MacSween had brought on board, theatre's André Brassard and John Wood, and, later, dance producer Yvon St. Onge, had provided significant benefits around the country, but consecutive government studies such as "Applebert" and now the Hendry Report challenged the NAC's role in creating productions. Many arts organizations in the regions were now at a stage where they, too, wanted to tour. And several of these groups had complained to the Hendry Task Force. Why shouldn't they tour, come to Ottawa, rather than the other way round? The political pressure on the central government to support what was going on in cities and towns across Canada, rather than in Ottawa, was growing.

At the same time, regional arts funding bodies such as the Ontario Arts Council, as well the increasing number of municipal arts-funding bodies in many Canadian cities, were having a significant impact. "Why would we spend money bringing people across the country when we can develop our own theatre company right here?" they asked.[2] The initial stance of Quebec—that it needed something different and distinct from the rest of Canada—had triggered this change in perception elsewhere. Other jurisdictions were learning from the Quebec example: that it was useful to stand up for their own place and to demand the money for their own use. Who or what performed at the NAC had been largely based on the old-fashioned notion of straight artistic merit, rather than on "demographically, democratically or per capita driven principles."[3] The unspoken competition between "centres of excellence" and "art by and for the masses" lay beneath the surface of this struggle.

The key consequence for the National Arts Centre, as for other national cultural institutions, would be a fundamental change in the nature of its financing, although this critical sea change was still over a decade away. In the mid-eighties, it remained unthinkable that the NAC should solicit or accept large private donations, mainly because it was felt that doing so would be detrimental to other arts organizations which did not receive similar amounts of public funds. But the gap between what the NAC's mandate required and the public funds available to fulfill it was widening. And, in this situation, MacSween's position was fast becoming untenable.

MacSween continued to attend the meetings of the Board of Trustees. Ironically, his debates with the board in his last months in office focused on the trustees' determination, in response to the Hendry Report, to bring back the Summer Festival and opera—the very project that MacSween had cut in his efforts to save the Arts Centre. Marcel Masse had earlier demanded a swift response from the NAC to whatever Hendry recommended, but now, after a Cabinet shuffle, Masse was moved over to the

Defence portfolio. When the arguments ended, the board would be reporting to the new Communications minister, Flora MacDonald.

MacSween told his board "that a renewed summer festival cannot be done at the expense of regular programming."[4] He received some support: Francis Macerola, the NFB's film commissioner and an ex-officio trustee, insisted that "government must support its public institutions," though he acknowledged that governments now seemed to prefer funding ad hoc projects rather than providing sustained funding for arts institutions.[5] He was correct in his fear: although there might be funds for government-favoured and politically profitable programs, there would be little new money for general core funding.

The board's Steering Committee worked up three separate scenarios for proceeding. The NAC Orchestra, whose resident place at the NAC had been confirmed in all the reports, was to remain relatively untouched. The thrust of the various plans all favoured the Festival at the expense of Theatre's in-house production budget. At meetings on January 27 and 28, against MacSween's strong resistance, the trustees approved the revival of the Summer Festival and authorized $600,000 to be switched from Theatre to help pay for it. They anticipated that the balance of an estimated million-dollar plus Festival budget would come from the government. Theatre producer Andis Celms fought hard in the meetings to come up with another plan, knowing he would lose his best creative talent if the initiative passed, but when he stepped out of the board's all-day meeting to consult, the trustees passed the motion. They asked the staff to prepare an action plan on implementing the new policy. Before anything concrete could be done, MacSween's term of office expired.

On March 31, 1987, exactly ten years after his joyous arrival at the Arts Centre, MacSween's time was officially over. It was a deflated end for the man who had arrived full of hopes and dreams of establishing resident theatre in the Arts Centre in the same way that music and the orchestra had been established under Southam. As a tribute, the trustees decided to present him with the handsome Inuit sculpture that adorned a shelf in his office. In their own austerity measure, they had already decided that outgoing board members should now receive sterling silver cuff-links, not gold ones as had previously been the custom.

With MacSween gone, a turbulent period ensued where many of the NAC's affairs were actively overseen by a steering committee of trustees and staff who strove to keep the centre operating. Whatever the political dramas going on behind the boardroom doors, almost every night brought a new performance of music, dance, or theatre which had to be delivered on the stages. It was essential to hold things together while the organization awaited a new director general. Board members, supported by senior staff, remained in close contact with the Department of Communications and its deputy minister, now Alain Gourd, particularly in pursuit of the additional money that would be needed for the Summer Festival. Gourd had a strong personal interest in the NAC and did not flinch from taking a proactive hand in dealing with its problems.

Although the Communications Department had proposed $500,000 to make up the million-dollar estimated budget for the Festival, it hesitated now to grant the whole sum if opera was to be part of the mix. "Still too elitist," argued one faction among the senior bureaucracy. The long-suffering Bruce Corder, who had stepped in as acting director general, fought hard for the opera component. He insisting that the NAC was at arm's length from the government, that the money for the Festival should not be "earmarked" by the department—and, in any case, that Hendry had recommended, among other things, the return to opera. A production was already in the works under the guidance of music producer Joanne Morrow, in collaboration with the newly arrived music director, Gabriel Chmura.

Even though the government initially handed over only half the promised money, a respectable production of *The Marriage of Figaro* was mounted in July 1988, with a sterling cast of young Canadian singers and stars, including soprano Edith Wiens and base baritone Gaetan Laperrière. Chmura conducted, the sets and costumes from a 1976 production were used again, and the opera was directed by one of Chmura's German colleagues who had extensive experience in television. The lively and provocative scenes included one set in a Turkish bathhouse. Although not everyone's idea of Mozart, the opera received good critical reviews and an enthusiastic reception for the return of this genre to the summer stage. By season's end, the Department of Communications still had not handed over the balance of the money needed to cover its costs. Corder was left to press officials for the amount that had been promised, but again arguments broke out over elitism in the arts. Totally exhausted and disgusted, he resigned from the Arts Centre on September 15. The debate over money continued.

Corder's departure meant an end to the continuity that had existed in the NAC's top leadership since its inception. He had not attained the top job himself, and his latter years at the NAC had been largely unhappy. During the MacSween era he missed the partnership he had shared with Southam, although, in his secondary role, he had continued to do his best in the key areas of administration and programming. It would be hard to overestimate the work of the indefatigable Bruce Corder during his years at the Arts Centre, especially when it came to making the hard decisions. His resignation contributed further to the leadership vacuum rapidly developing at the NAC.

One of MacSween's most important legacies was the appointment of the new music director, Gabriel Chmura. Besides his immediate help in bringing opera back to the

German-trained Israeli conductor Gabriel Chmura was selected to become the third music director. Photo © Murray Mosher Photography.

Summer Festival, Chmura's first season of 1986–87 was launched with much enthusiasm and interest in the wake of the dramatic Mannino years. The solid German-trained young conductor brought all the discipline and formality of that school of music to the job. He was mortified when the marketing brochures advertising his first season to the public showed him wearing an open-necked striped shirt at rehearsal. "It made me look as if I was wearing pajamas!" he moaned. Subsequent brochures had him in proper white tie and tails as befitted the way he saw his role. He also went out of his way in his first weeks to learn what was available in Canadian music, travelling to Toronto to meet with members of the Canadian League of Composers and working on plans to include Canadian music and artists in his programs.

Although there would later be grumbles about his approach, Chmura brought much needed stability to the orchestra. Harold Clarkson, a former musician with the Hamilton Philharmonic, had been appointed orchestra manager in 1984. A youthful and confident appointee,* there was no doubt in his mind that the orchestra was "the jewel in the NAC's crown." He had worked fearlessly to protect that position, filling a vacuum after Costa Pilavachi's departure and working with Joanne Morrow to ensure that Music's substantial annual $5 million to $7 million budget was kept relatively intact through the turbulent financial discussions. This money included the salary budget for the forty-six contracted players as well as the programming and PR budgets—the latter running well over $200,000 a year.

Clarkson thought that Chmura was the right man for the position. The new music director was well trained and knew both his scores and the repertoire. Although his experience had been mainly with large symphonic orchestras, not chamber orchestras, he appeared ready to learn. Above all, Chmura brought the discipline the musicians needed after the Mannino years. Clarkson felt that the orchestra and the maestro were

---

*Clarkson, like other NAC staff members, went on to achieve a senior international position in classical music—in his case as European manager of IMG Artists. He had no hesitation in saying, "the National Arts Centre Orchestra made my career."

well matched in terms of their relative statures. The real gap in the maestro's experience and knowledge, Clarkson would later remark, was in the area of orchestral intrigue—a lack of awareness that would bring Chmura much grief. For now, though, the work went ahead with a first season of well-attended concerts that included some fine Beethoven and an opera teaser—a concert version of *La Bohème*.

Back in the boardroom, this period was punctuated by an episode worthy of Sherlock Holmes. It could well be called "The Curious Episode of the Director General That Wasn't." When the Executive Committee had decided at its May 1986 meeting not to renew MacSween's contract, a select group of board members—chairman Pierre Boutin, Montrealer Paule Tardif-Delorme, and a relatively new Toronto member, Leon Kossar—was assigned to conduct an executive search to replace him. Given the country's sharpened political climate, it was deemed of prime importance to consider a francophone for the job, and the group turned to the professional head-hunting firm of Coopers & Lybrand. Beginning with a list of some fifty potential candidates, they finally presented nine names to the search committee. By May 1987, however, all nine had been rejected for various reasons.

The trustees then turned to another management consulting firm, Wood Gundy, which brought a further three names to the search committee. The selection group opted for one candidate to put to the full board: the veteran public servant and career diplomat Ian Christie Clark. Although not francophone, Clark was fluently bilingual and an avowed francophile, with a long history in cultural affairs and diplomacy in the French-speaking world. His last post in Ottawa had been as secretary general for the National Museums Corporation. The approach by the search committee was timely: when he was contacted in Paris, where he was serving as Canada's ambassador to UNESCO, he had just learned that he was to be displaced by the political appointment of former Montreal mayor Jean Drapeau. Clark readily agreed to fly back to Canada to be interviewed. An experienced manager, he was confident about the administrative aspects of the NAC position, but knew he had "limited credentials when it came to the artistic aspects of the job."[6]

After discussions with the trustees, the idea developed that Clark should be supported by a strong artistic director. The brilliant Stratford artistic director, Robin Phillips, was targeted for that position. Clark met with Phillips in Toronto, and they agreed that they could work together. Pierre Boutin prepared to bring Clark's nomination forward for formal approval at a special meeting of the full board scheduled for November. Before that happened, however, the story broke in the press. The leak reported the pending Clark appointment as director general as a *fait accompli*. The news spread swiftly and received widespread positive comment, especially in the

English-speaking press, where the proposal for the Clark/Phillips team was greeted enthusiastically.

Internally, however, a handful of trustees were furious. The dissenting faction was led aggressively by the francophone mayor of Hull, Michel Légère. A French-speaking lawyer, Légère had worked as a public servant in the federal Privy Council Office before going into politics, and he would later run as a candidate for the separatist Parti Québécois in Quebec. He was vociferous in his criticism that all the top jobs in the cultural agencies were at present held by anglophones, and, even though these officials were all bilingual, he argued that a francophone candidate should be put forward for the NAC position. At a minimum, he insisted that the board have at least three candidates to choose from, and not the single recommendation that the search committee was putting forward for ratification. Marcel Masse had previously put on record that he wanted more francophones in key positions in Ottawa, and the Hull mayor fully agreed. "I cannot accept that a candidate with francophone roots who is competent and right for the job cannot be found," he declared to the press.[7] The November meeting, officially without a quorum, dissolved in chaos, with no appointment made.

While the debate raged, Clark and Phillips continued to plan for the future, exchanging formal letters of intent on the terms of their agreement, making arrangements to hire a business manager to assist them, and planning how they would proceed once the furore died down. On December 11 the board met again in Ottawa. Trustee Thomas Assaly, who by now had joined the dissenting faction, telephoned Ian Clark before the meeting to ask him some cursory questions about his plans to work with Phillips. By the time he presented the information to the board, however, the arrangement between the two men had been labelled "Clark's unacceptable conditions." Clark's nomination was promptly rejected. Without further ado a new search committee was struck with both Assaly and Légère as members, along with trustees Diana Lam from Vancouver and Louise Giguère from Montreal. It was agreed they would not start their work until the new year.

The NAC's chief financial officer, Ron Blackburn, had stepped in as acting director general after Corder's retirement the previous September. He was struggling to cope in the face of constantly changing budget figures and virtually no experience in arts management. Key issues continued to mark the daily life at the centre: plans for theatre, music, dance, subscription sales, and the next round of the Summer Festival— all arrangements that had to be made months and preferably years in advance—were now hampered both by time and by the ongoing uncertainty of how much money would be available. There were continued discussions over debts for past events, such as the Canada Dance Festival, with Air Canada and a local hotel, the Beacon Arms, still owed nearly $100,000. Arrangements for a celebratory gala concert to mark Israel's fortieth anniversary were under way in the Music Department, with input from the Communications Department, but with little knowledge or involvement by NAC senior

The search for a new director general to replace Donald MacSween took bizarre turns and twists, which puzzled the press and the public. Cartoon © Alan King.

management. It is a tribute to the professionalism of the staff that much of the work continued to be done despite the storm at the top. In an atmosphere of general confusion, arts consultants David Haber and Muriel Sherrin were brought in by Blackburn to coordinate the programming. In the haste to get the summer program organized, an uncertain board continued to question and to interfere with all areas at the centre. The NAC had now, in effect, been without a strong and permanent leader for nearly a year.

In February 1988 the NAC trustees were ordered to appear before an agitated Parliamentary Committee on Communications and Culture that was responding to continued press reports about the "circus" at the Arts Centre. A Canadian Press news story captured the MPs' mood: "NAC search for new director leaves MPs aghast."[8] Opposition Liberal culture critic Sheila Finestone berated Pierre Boutin: "This infighting is, I find, a total disservice to this country and to the job you hold."[9] Her remarks were echoed by others on the committee, including government members. A stinging letter was sent to the NAC, signed by the Conservative committee chair John Gormley, criticizing the board for its failure to agree on a suitable candidate and its confusion over the qualifications for the job. Légère's "racism" over the appointment also came in for some criticism. Ottawa Conservative MP David Daubney declared that, "to insist … that a particular position be filled by a francophone or anglophone and not on the basis of merit, and further, that bilingualism, the law of the land, is not good enough, amounts in my considered opinion to racism."[10] The parliamentarians were assured that matters were in progress for a new appointment, and that it was hoped "to have him in place by April 1988." Behind the scenes, the government's officials were working hard to try to make that happen.

The Clark appointment debacle led to Pierre Boutin's final disaffection with the job of chair at the NAC. Although his term ran until November 1988, he resigned in March, leaving vice-chair Thomas Assaly to stand in for him. Assaly's own term would expire on April 18, 1988. As Masse had predicted, it had been a lousy job for the Quebec City political fundraiser. He would not be active in further NAC meetings and was not interested in a reappointment. As for Clark, he found himself jobless and finally left Ottawa to take a post as president of the Nova Scotia School of Fine Arts. Four years later he returned to Ottawa, recruited by a new Liberal government to become chairman of the Canadian Cultural Properties Review Board—a cultural agency for which he had helped draft the legislation. Meanwhile, in government circles, all efforts were being made to end the embarrassing situation at the National Arts Centre.

14

TIMES GET TOUGHER

"It was the worst bloody job I ever took in the voluntary sector, and I've had a lot of them," exclaimed Robert E. Landry, who was appointed chair of the National Arts Centre on March 25, 1988.[1] A bilingual electrical engineer educated at McGill and St. Francis-Xavier universities, Landry was already well-known on the Ottawa political scene as vice-president of government relations for the Imperial Oil Company. As chief lobbyist for the powerful energy company, he had good connections with both of the main-line parties. The suave and smooth-talking executive was also known for his long association with artistic organizations. When the call came from the Prime Minister's Office, he was the incumbent chair of the National Theatre School. He swiftly resigned the position in favour of the NAC. His other arts activities included stints on the boards of the Toronto Symphony, Théâtre Ballet of Canada, and the Edmonton Symphony. He had also been appointed to the Applebaum-

The Honourable Flora MacDonald took over the culture portfolio and set out to stabilize affairs at the NAC. She was proud to announce Robert Landry, a vice-president of the Imperial Oil Company and its Ottawa lobbyist, as the NAC's new chair. Photo © Wayne Cuddington/ Ottawa Citizen. Reprinted by permission.

Hébert Committee, where he had listened to the complaints, grumbles, and desires of the arts community as that group toured the country in 1981.

Communications Minister Flora MacDonald was pleased with her catch and said so at a press conference to announce the handsome Landry's appointment: "With his unique qualifications and broad understanding of the arts scene, I am confident we will receive the dynamic leadership so necessary to this position," she said.[2] The ongoing soap opera at the NAC had ballooned into a national news flap, with wide coverage in both the local and the national media—press, radio, and television. There was much criticism of the poor patronage appointments at the trustee level by well-known columnists as diverse as the outspoken Claire Hoy, the competent Southam national arts reporter Jamie Portman, and the local Ottawa music critic Jake Siskind. They and others universally condemned the mishandling of the situation by the politically appointed NAC board.

The main charge in the press was that widespread patronage appointments by the government had led to incompetence in the governance of its agencies. In the cultural sector, MacDonald moved to put a lid on the situation. The announcement of Robert Landry was followed two weeks later by four new appointments to the NAC board, all of them women and most with impressive arts credentials. Marie-Claire Morin came from Montreal's McCord Museum, Dr. Reva Gerstein had been a senator of the Stratford Festival, Adele MacLeod-Seaman filled an Atlantic Canada slot on the board, and Madeleine Panaccio came with extensive experience in music and a position as assistant director general of the Montreal Symphony. Panaccio replaced the rough-spoken vice-chair Thomas Assaly, who was not reappointed, and, in the time ahead, she would play an influential role.

The new strategy seemed to work. "Arts Centre appointment continues a recent trend away from patronage" was the headline to an article by national reporter Hugh Winsor in the *Globe and Mail.* "Mr. Landry did not consider himself a political appointment," he wrote, adding that the new chair said he "did not take sides in Ottawa." "It might interfere with my job," he quoted him as saying. "I deal with governments, not political parties."[3] Landry told reporters that he was taking over personally the search for the new director general. It was imperative that the NAC improve its national image, particularly with the presentation of Canadian works by Canadian artists. As for a francophone in the job of chief operating officer, he declared that the first need was to find the right person, and then hope that this individual might also be a francophone.

Behind the scenes, the outgoing Pierre Boutin had thrown the search for a new director general over to the government for help. Mayor Légère kept up steady pressure in the press and elsewhere, including calls to the Prime Minister's Office. Bernard Roy, Mulroney's chief of staff, telephoned Alain Gourd, the deputy minister in the Communications Department, to ask him for some suitable francophone names. In his role as adviser, Gourd had already suggested several francophone candidates, including the relatively non-partisan arts official Yvon Guérard, who had been serving in Paris as director of the Canadian Cultural Centre. Even Jean Herbiet, who had also occupied the Paris job, was urged by Mayor Légère to throw his hat into the ring. Gourd advised Roy that he had only one name left, Yvon DesRochers, but because DesRochers had once worked for the Liberal communications minister Francis Fox, he had not proposed it.

Roy swept aside this detail and urged Gourd to contact Boutin and other members of the board to brief them on DesRochers. Gourd was aware of the overall administrative problems at the NAC and had some knowledge of other serious matters awaiting attention—the crumbling infrastructure of the building, which was being badly damaged by winter salt; outstanding issues with the unions; and difficulties with staff in the parking garage. "One thing Yvon had, in my opinion, because I had known him a little, was rigour--administrative rigour—and I felt he would bring that to the management of the National Arts Centre," said Gourd.

It seems certain that DesRochers's name was at the top of the list when Robert Landry brought the question of the director general before his first meetings of the board. The skilful chairman ensured his appointment by engaging his entire board as a "committee of the whole" and, after an elaborate process, the decision to appoint Yvon DesRochers was made unanimously. Landry was pleased with the choice: "He was a very interesting guy, a visionary … but he had sharp elbows too," he reflected later. "This would alienate a lot of people."[4] But he was also francophone. At last the long and anguished search for MacSween's successor was over.

DesRochers's background was the antithesis of Hamilton Southam's, and widely different also from the not-so-affluent Donald MacSween, who had nevertheless been raised and educated in comfortable circumstances. The tall, ginger-haired DesRochers was born into a poor, hard-scrabble family in Montreal, where his father was a garage mechanic. He was painfully separated from

Yvon DesRochers became the third NAC director general. His francophone background helped cement his appointment. Photo © Lynn Ball/ Ottawa Citizen. Reprinted by permission.

his parents as a young boy and eventually sent to boarding school in Cornwall, Ontario, to learn English. Then he went on to Université d'Ottawa to study law. After graduating in 1969 he was hired directly into the Department of Communications, where he was an aide to assistant deputy minister André Fortier. This job was his introduction to the cultural milieu. Fortier took him under his wing and became the young man's mentor, imbuing him with the same values of democratization and anti-elitism in the arts which had informed his own work. Both were conscious of the need to be "responsive to the public's needs."[5]

When Fortier left Communications to become director of the Canada Council, DesRochers went with him and, in 1973, became associate director of the new Touring Office. There he worked alongside another future director general of the National Arts Centre, John Cripton. In subsequent years, he continued to work in the arts sector, returning to Montreal to handle the arts component for the 1976 Montreal Olympics, moving in and out of other arts consulting jobs, and landing prestigious board seats with the symphony, the opera, and various dance troupes. He also became actively involved in partisan politics with the Liberal Party. By this route he was appointed as senior policy adviser to Communications Minister Francis Fox when the Liberals returned to power in 1981. His place next to the minister gave him wide exposure to new developments in both technology and policy in the burgeoning broadcast and communications sector, and he was heavily involved, sometimes as a negotiator for Fox, in the television and international communications agreements that the Liberal government was making to accommodate the expanding communications universe. This background informed his ideas when he came to direct the National Arts Centre. Unfortunately, behind the confident and open manner that he could show in public lay a complicated and conflicted personality. It expressed itself in a management style that was both abrasive and impatient.

Landry was determined that the announcement of DesRochers's appointment would not be leaked to the press, and, on April 28, 1988, in an elaborate series of secretive arrangements, the entire NAC staff was ordered to assemble in a rehearsal hall to be the first to hear the news. Delivered to the stage entrance in a chauffeur-driven car, DesRochers made a dramatic entrance through a side door, appearing suddenly in the midst of his new staff. In a back-slapping display of *bonhomie* he made his way through the throng to the front of the room, where he stated categorically: "My priority is to listen, and then I will listen again, to make sure I heard right the first time." Subsequent events would belie this ostentatious and seemingly benevolent beginning, as DesRochers brought an intensely authoritarian style to the office of director general.

When Landry agreed to become NAC chair, he had a poor view of the Arts Centre as a national institution. "I did not consider it a national institution at all," he reminisced. "In times of diminishing government resources there was only one way to become national and that was through television."[6] This was the key ingredient that had made DesRochers so appealing to the board. With his experience in the Communications Department and his knowledge of new technology, he was certain that the way ahead for the Arts Centre lay in "electronic touring"—a concept heartily endorsed in the Hendry Report and other studies and perceived by many as "the wave of the future." The cultural television channel, C-Channel, founded by Hamilton Southam and others, had obtained a television licence, but it foundered because it did not have a sufficient cash flow. Nevertheless, the possibility for an arts channel in the emerging "100 channel universe" of satellite technology was again capturing attention.

DesRochers's vision incorporated an additional dimension with entirely new technology—high-definition television, or HDTV. Although still in the experimental stage, HDTV offered images and colour definition of the highest quality, giving it seemingly enormous potential for delivering live performances and interactive educational arts activities. This concept, which he had set out clearly in his first interviews with the board, was to be at the centre of his work at the NAC, and he and Landry would pursue it in close alliance. The chairman committed himself fully to DesRochers's ideas and stuck with him, even after the catastrophic developments that lay ahead.

Even though Landry later maintained that he was not briefed on the financial shortcomings at the Arts Centre when he became chair, DesRochers had no illusions about the institution's difficult financial straits. Presenting himself as an opera fan, he welcomed the revised Summer Festival performances of *The Marriage of Figaro* in July 1988, but he told William Littler, music critic of the *Toronto Star*, that, "financially, this institution is dying. We don't have the means any more at the National Arts Centre to be producers."[7] He would continue to present opera at the Arts Centre, he said, but would do so by bringing in productions from the Montreal Opera, the Canadian Opera Company, or even the Vancouver Opera. He intended to dispel the notion that Ottawa productions, with their subsidized tickets, were just for the privileged few. "The whole country says those fat cats in Ottawa produce expensively subsidized shows for only a few people to enjoy, and I can understand their viewpoint," he stated forcefully. Everything would change, DesRochers assured Littler, by establishing "an electronic touring network based at the National Arts Centre and taking advantage of the High Definition Television technology being developed in Japan."

Although DesRochers did not mention it to Littler, he viewed the NAC Orchestra—the one remaining resident company at the Arts Centre—as the biggest obstacle to his plans. The orchestra's large share of the NAC's subsidy was an issue that all incoming directors general had to confront. However, the harsh and aggressive manner in which DesRochers set out to "fix the problem" was to have seriously bad consequences.

In the hectic months before DesRochers's arrival, negotiations had commenced for a new three-year orchestra contract. Among its clauses were significant wage increases for the players designed "to bring them into parity with the other orchestras, the TSO and the MSO"—a principle that had already been sanctioned by the board.[8] As orchestra manager Harold Clarkson, who was party to the negotiations, later noted, the orchestra had, by adroit management and a strong union, throughout this period, avoided most of the stringencies of the cost-cutting that afflicted the other departments, especially Theatre. In some quarters at the Arts Centre, this record created outright resentment because the orchestra appeared not to have "shared the pain that other departments were enduring."[9]

During the interregnum, Clarkson himself had brushed off suggestions that there should be any cuts to the Music Department budget. In the leadership vacuum that acting director general Ron Blackburn had tried so hard to fill, Clarkson had brashly argued, in a manner that he later admitted was "outrageous," that "you can't possibly cut the orchestra."[10] He got most of what he asked for, thereby helping to maintain Music's large budget for programming and publicity as well as the massive salary component required for the forty-six musicians. When DesRochers arrived, he pulled the proposed contract off the table and insisted that everything start over again. The manoeuvre opened an immediate rift in orchestra-management relations. Initially, DesRochers did not indicate what he had in mind for the orchestra, and an uneasy short-term settlement was struck. The musicians accepted a one-year contract and agreed to a "cooling-out period" to see what the future held. Clarkson had little doubt about DesRochers's intentions. "Yvon wanted to break the orchestra. It was clear from the negotiating of the first contract."[11] Whatever his goal, DesRochers was unhappy with the orchestra and its cost and wanted to find ways to use it differently. Various ideas began to emanate from the executive offices: the orchestra might be a training ground for young conductors; it might be used for taking risks on new music that other less well-supported orchestras could not; and it could be a place for young musicians to play alongside seasoned veterans. Much of the detail was alarming to members of the music community across the country. They began to track what was happening at the Arts Centre more closely.

Music director Gabriel Chmura's second season opened in September 1988 with good subscriptions and generally enthusiastic audiences. A series of solid early fall concerts ensued as the NAC Orchestra prepared for a forthcoming tour to the Maritimes and Labrador. Before its departure, DesRochers opened up another piece of unfinished musical business—the two-year extension that had been built into Maestro Chmura's contract. He offered the extension to Chmura and demanded an immediate response. Chmura explained that he did not attend to his own business affairs and must first give the contract to his agent for review. He then left to travel with the orchestra. For the moment DesRochers remained in Ottawa, complaining bitterly about the orchestra situation. In an interview he gave to CBC Radio, he made no secret about what he saw as their overindulged place at the Arts Centre.[12] Meanwhile, the musicians played their way through a twelve-day, thirteen-concert tour in Maritime Canada that took them to remote and extraordinary places, including Labrador City, where a special plane was chartered for the instruments to keep them warm as they were flown into the frosty town. There was another first-ever classical music concert in the hockey arena in the mining town of Sydney, Nova Scotia, and a diplomatic showing at Prime Minister Mulroney's hometown, Baie Comeau, on the north shore of the St. Lawrence River.

When the orchestra arrived in Halifax, a junior member of the music management team, Chris Deacon, received a telephone call. Unbeknownst to orchestra manager Clarkson, the director general ordered Deacon to set up a meeting with the orchestra's principle players because he was flying down to see them. His real purpose was to ask the orchestra leaders how they liked their maestro. After conversations with Prystawski and the other section heads, which included the usual orchestra *kvetching*, DesRochers returned to Ottawa with the idea that the musicians were not so crazy about Chmura. Landry, who also visited the orchestra on tour, later confirmed this impression.

Then, just as the orchestra returned to Ottawa, the ushers at the centre were threatening to strike and, one evening, the maestro made a disastrous mistake. As he made his way to conduct a concert, he was enjoined by the ushers to sign a petition in their favour—and he did. When DesRochers found out, he was apoplectic and called the conductor to his office for a savage dressing down. The bewildered Chmura, who had enjoyed little contact with his boss to that point, could not fathom the depth of his crime. Soon after, he left Ottawa for some concerts in Europe. In an unprecedented move, DesRochers decided to discard the maestro when his three-year contract expired at the end of the 1989–90 season, and he phoned Chmura in Spain to advise him. He caught the conductor in his dressing room, preparing to go on stage for a concert. Chmura was shocked, then devastated at the news, and he called his wife in Ottawa, imploring her to ask the concertmaster, Walter Prystawski, to intercede. A rumble of shock swept through the music community as the word spread. The local press, particularly the *Ottawa Citizen*, expressed its dismay in successive reports and editorials that soon spread into the national media.

DesRochers's deteriorating relations with the orchestra and his forceful moves created enormous disquiet, but his budgetary problems were real. Marcel Masse had been shuffled back into Communications at the end of January 1989 and, in the wake of the Hendry Report, he was now touting a harsh line for the Arts Centre that basically followed the Nielsen proposals he had stalled when he first held the portfolio in 1986. He suggested to startled NAC officials that they should simply cease operations, that the centre's assets be turned over to the National Capital Commission, and that the orchestra be privatized. While the department considered these proposals, officials scrambled to clarify that the minister was wont to throw out one idea after another to test the reaction and that nothing was definite. In fact, private interests, led by Hamilton Southam, had already approached the government with a proposal to separate the orchestra from the National Arts Centre. In these alarming circumstances, Alain Gourd, the man in the middle between Masse and the cultural agency, decided to become active again ("Always at arm's length," he later insisted),[13] and he phoned Harold Clarkson, the orchestra manager, and invited him to his office for talks. Informing none of his colleagues, Clarkson went.

Gourd was on friendly personal terms with DesRochers, and he had frequently intervened to try to soften the director general's roughshod approach, especially in the case of Chmura's contract. The deputy minister had also been a close friend of Chmura and his wife since their arrival in Ottawa and had cautioned DesRochers, in vain, not to terminate the conductor. Now Gourd opened talks on the orchestra's future without informing DesRochers. "We have to do something about the NACO," Gourd told the orchestra manager. "A number of us think it might be best if it were 'divorced' from the NAC, and this might also address Yvon's concerns."[14]

This idea—that the orchestra should be a separate entity from the NAC, though resident there—had been discarded at the very first meeting of the National Arts Centre board in 1966. Now Southam offered not only to put up some money but to be chairman of an orchestra board. Clarkson was sent to see him, and they met several times, together with others who were also interested in the suggestion, including Mitchell Sharp and Bertram Loeb. Clarkson "enjoyed the process enormously,"[15] as the meetings invariably involved drinks or a meal at the gracious Southam's home or club. Clarkson, with all the Music Department's financial figures at his fingertips, was able to work out a budget for the proposed enterprise. It included a place for Maestro Chmura, who was party to the talks and who, it was thought, could be kept on to lead the orchestra.

The group initially thought that DesRochers would be glad to get the orchestra off the NAC's books, but that proved emphatically not to be the case. In April, when he became aware of the plans, he was tentative at first but soon became enraged when he learned from his finance officer, Ron Blackburn, that, if the orchestra left, its share of the government subsidy would likely go with it. He berated Clarkson for giving out NAC numbers to private individuals, even though the figures were readily available in the annual reports filed with the government. DesRochers had never really trusted Clarkson, and now he fell out with him completely. With negotiations for a renewed contract with the orchestra under way again, Clarkson was pulled off the file and, by June, had been fired. With no prospect of subsidy, the Southam group dropped its plans. DesRochers, having found no solution in privatizing the orchestra, now determined to curb its demands in another way. He hired a new orchestra manager, Jack

Mills, from the Winnipeg Symphony to take Clarkson's job, and a new hard round of contract talks commenced.

As the early months of 1989 unfolded, matters deteriorated further. In February the news broke that French theatre director, André Brassard, had given notice that he too would leave at the end of the 1989–90 season. He could no longer produce new work in the cash-starved Theatre Department. The lack of resources was taking its toll elsewhere too. Theatre Ballet, which presented its work at the NAC and had enjoyed the patronage of Mila Mulroney, was losing its artistic director, Larry Gradus, for whom the company had been created by the Canada Council.* It was just eight years since the first gala performance at the NAC. In the current circumstances, however, the company was no worse off than many others in the country. Canada Council grants had been frozen, and the ever-diminishing dollar's buying power was having a terrible impact on the arts. The Canadian music community was decidedly anxious over Chmura's contract not being renewed, and the national music press still kept close track of the story. Labour relations with the orchestra would soon bring the Arts Centre to the brink of disaster and national focus of the worst kind. For now, though, DesRochers turned his attentions to the energetic pursuit of his dream—television.

The National Ballet's Celia Franca and Russian dancer Rudolf Nureyev backstage during a tour to the arts centre. High art continued at the NAC even during difficult times. Photo © Jean-Marc Carisse.

---

*Gradus's replacement as artistic director was the dancer Frank Augustyn. He changed the company's name to Ottawa Ballet and worked hard to puts its finances in order. He resigned in 1994, and the company suspended operations soon after.

TELEVISION: THE
LONGED-FOR PANACEA

Robert Landry and Yvon DesRochers carefully crafted a new strategic plan, "The Third Decade and Beyond." It gave respectful acknowledgement to the NAC's past accomplishments but argued that it was essential now for the Arts Centre to revise its mandate and assert its national character if it was to survive. Tucked away in four neutrally drafted passages on the last page of the document were references to broadcast technology— the key, both men believed, to the centre's future in reaching its national audience.

The newest technology of all was high-definition television, HDTV—a format that was already in operation in Japan but still in the experimental stage in Canada. Its appeal to DesRochers was not only its intense, sharp pictures but also a possible interactive dimension, which he thought could be used in educational projects such as master classes. At the core of his concept was the beaming of live performances from the stages of the Arts Centre to audiences in special theatres, equipped to receive the high-definition signal, across the country. DesRochers was so enamoured of the technology that he had announced, soon after his appointment, that the NAC would have it on air by July 1, 1989—in time to broadcast the opening of the Canadian Museum of Civilization, across the river in Hull.

His plan was linked to an agreement he had struck with Telesat Canada. The Canadian satellite company was involved in a two-year development project designed to test the feasibility of delivering HDTV's high-quality images by satellite. The NAC as a test product had glamorous appeal for the satellite company. DesRochers brought Telesat vice-president Linda Rankin to the NAC board meeting on July 6, 1988, to explain to the trustees the potential of an NAC/HDTV network. The trustees were impressed, particularly at the mention of potential multi-million-dollar profits if the system worked. They swiftly approved "up to $500,000" to pursue the NAC's "electronic touring" initiative,[1] and DesRochers set off on a whirlwind cross-country tour to sell the idea to provincial cultural and educational ministers and other arts leaders. Initially, he had imagined twelve locations for the project, at least one in each province, which would receive programming "beamed live from the stages of the National Arts Centre." But his enthusiasm was rebuffed. Many of the arts officials he met were preoccupied with finding funding to create basic artistic work and were baffled, even angry, at the tangent he seemed to be pursuing. It was clear that it would take longer than a year to get the project up and running.

Despite troubles in Theatre at the NAC and storm clouds gathering again around the orchestra,[2] DesRochers focused his attention on television. In the spring of 1989 he turned for help to one of the more recent additions to the NAC staff, dance producer Jack Udashkin. An unconventional and free-wheeling individual, Udashkin had worked as a manager/producer with the small Margie Gillis Dance Company before joining the NAC. "Very creative and always up to a challenge,"[3] he was open to new ideas for presenting the arts and not afraid of bending the rules. His position at the Arts Centre would expand into being head of the Dance and Variety departments and, eventually, of Dance, Variety, and Special Events. Suddenly, "somewhat to my surprise," he recalled, he found himself a member of the NAC senior management team.[4] He got along well with DesRochers, and the director general handed him the television file.

A year earlier, Udashkin had served on a Canada Council jury selecting dance companies which wanted to do video projects. There he had run into a young former dancer and now television producer/director, David Langer. In May 1989, at DesRochers's request, Udashkin contacted Langer, who had moved from Toronto to Los Angeles. Langer remembered the phone call as a conversation about "the insane notion of the National Arts Centre getting involved in high-definition television and broadcasting live from its stages."[5] Nevertheless, he was soon on a plane to Ottawa. By July 1 he and Udashkin were engrossed in preparing a detailed working paper on this television potential. Langer enjoyed the experience immensely: "Out of Jack's office window you could look at the Rideau Canal. Inside we were having bottles of wine and working like crazy." At times DesRochers, Landry, and their wives would come by and encourage the two: "Not only were they extremely helpful and nurturing but it was just an immense hot-house." By the end of the summer the paper was ready, and, Langer declared, "everybody thought it was fabulous." By September he had moved his family to Ottawa and been given carte blanche to proceed.

DesRochers had a lot riding on the arrangements. He had already committed the NAC to an HDTV seminar planned at the centre for mid-November in collaboration with the Banff Centre for the Arts, where he intended to demonstrate the new medium's potential. Langer was responsible for ensuring that happened. "It was Yvon's style to have an idea and say immediately, 'We're doing it,'" Langer said. "Feasibility came after."[6] With Langer now on contract, the two men flew to Banff in September to promote the HDTV plan with television directors and producers. Langer recalled the enthusiasm for making arts programs in the country, but the prohibitive costs meant that no single producer could go it alone. Co-productions were a necessity. The appearance of the NAC on the scene as a potential co-producing partner with real money whetted the appetites of many in the television industry. Among those who approached Langer at the first Banff meeting was Rhombus Media, the leading production company for arts programs. The encounter would lead to some fruitful work with the NAC.

Telesat was also heavily involved in planning for the HDTV demonstration, investing millions of dollars on the technical side, providing a mobile unit with cameras and videotape machines, and flying in several Japanese consultants to participate. The seminar went ahead in the Studio at the NAC from November 21 to 23, using a scene from the Ottawa Great Canadian Theatre production of *Cold Comfort* for demonstration purposes. The event was fascinating for "techies" wanting to learn more about the lighting, cameras, and other technical aspects of the new format, but the reality was that, for now, there was no consumer market for HDTV and the expensive high-end receivers it required. Although the program was successfully beamed to Banff, the results cut little ice with anyone outside the television industry. On the contrary, DesRochers and the NAC were coming in for increasingly harsh criticism for imagining that people would leave their homes at night to go to a theatre to watch a live television performance from the National Arts Centre.

DesRochers engaged the former broadcaster Peter Herrndorf, now publisher of *Toronto Life*, as a private consultant to advise him on the idea's feasibility. Herrndorf believed the HDTV plan "was a mug's game from beginning to end," although he put it more tactfully to the director general. He advised DesRochers that "the content had to be sufficiently unique to get people out of their homes," and the only kind he knew that was not already on existing North American television was "closed-circuit heavyweight championship boxing fights or the Metropolitan Opera."[7] It is ironic that, eighteen years later, the Metropolitan Opera under Peter Gelb initiated its hugely successful HDTV broadcasts of live performances to commercial movie theatres across the country, proving both DesRochers's vision and Herrndorf's observation to be correct. For now, the NAC's problem seemed obvious: the product it could put out on the HDTV system was not sufficiently unique to be financially viable. DesRochers ignored the advice and pushed on.

Langer soon discovered that he, too, was a full member of the senior management team: he was required to wear a suit and tie to meetings, where he found himself talking about not only television but also the NAC's other operations and revenue streams, including the Catering Department and the parking garage. DesRochers wanted to reorganize the entire structure at the Arts Centre. Despite the existence of artistic directors in Theatre and in Music, he offered Langer a position over them both as director of programming. When the astounded Langer explained that this responsibility was far beyond his capabilities, the two men agreed that he would concentrate on television, and DesRochers created a new department for him to head.[8]

Meanwhile, serious problems, specifically with the orchestra and its negotiations, had been heating up all summer and were now set to boil over. In this round the NAC Orchestra was determined to achieve the gains it had sought the year before, but DesRochers was equally determined to maintain a hard line with the musicians. Chmura, despite his lame-duck situation, was still music director, and, early in the summer, he tried to communicate with the board, writing a passionate memorandum that set out the situation from the musicians' point of view. He gave the memo to DesRochers, who read it but did not pass it on to the trustees because, in his view, it was "full of false accusations." Chairman Landry concurred, commenting later that the board was too busy dealing with financial matters to bother with the conductor's "hysterical intrusion."[9]

By summer's end, relations between management and the orchestra had collapsed and, in an unprecedented development, the musicians voted to go on strike. On the day that should have marked the opening concert of what was now Chmura's last season, the maestro and others recalled a poignant morning rehearsal together in the final hours before the strike began. "They came to me and said, 'Maestro, we need something emotional,'" the conductor remembered, "so we have chosen Beethoven's Seventh, which was not even on the program. We played in the rehearsal hall, not for the public, just for ourselves."[10] When the rehearsal was finished, the musicians put down their instruments and moved to set up a picket line outside the Arts Centre. It was a bitter moment, and the strike would unleash a storm of criticism aimed largely at NAC management.

The musicians were widely supported both locally and nationally. The initial issues focused on pay and length of season, though a new negotiator

The strike by orchestra musicians in 1989 was a "first" and a painful time for everyone. Photo © Wayne Hiebert/Ottawa Citizen. Reprinted by permission.

on the management team soon discovered that there were deeper concerns. Jack Mills had joined the Arts Centre as the new music producer, the de facto head of the Music Department. His exhausted predecessor, Joanne Morrow, had left in July after the final performance of that year's summer opera, *Don Giovanni*, but also because of a prolonged and growing discord with DesRochers.* Mills would eventually be renamed managing director of the NAC Orchestra.

Mills said he came to the Arts Centre because he had the idea he could bring management to realize what a valuable asset they had in the orchestra. When he took up his post in September 1989, however, DesRochers's first comment to him revealed his enmity to the NAC Orchestra. By Mills's recollection, "it was something to the effect that you and I have to teach these musicians a lesson and teach them that they don't run the whole show here."[11] With the orchestra's contract negotiations now under way, Mills was shocked when he sat down at the bargaining table to hear the NAC's lead negotiator blithely propose to the union that, to save money, the number of musicians be reduced by four and the orchestral season be shortened. The proposal, in his opinion, showed how little management understood about the dynamics of an orchestra and its sound. These questions, as well as the coming departure of the music director, Gabriel Chmura, would become central in the bitter struggle that ensued between NAC management and its musicians.

As the strike wore on, alarmed high-profile figures from Canada's music world, including Louis Applebaum and Maureen Forrester, made public pleas for a return to normalcy. Other orchestras also weighed in. The Toronto Symphony, whose management had complained so often about the NACO's alleged privileged status, wired a strongly worded message in support of the musicians along with a cheque for the strike fund. Artists and arts groups across the country who usually liked to gripe and complain about the Art Centre's special benefits came out in support of the NAC as a "centre of excellence" for the performing arts. On October 10, 1989, the NAC Orchestra played its gala twentieth-anniversary concert, not in the Opera hall as planned, but in an Ottawa high school auditorium. The musicians continued to walk the picket line around the main building through the increasingly cold late autumn weeks.

Backed by the powerful union, the American Federation of Musicians, many other musical events were cancelled at the centre. The conductor Trevor Pinnock, who had travelled to Ottawa with his orchestra, the English Consort, for two scheduled concerts remained holed up in the Château Laurier Hotel, refusing to cross the picket line. Only a few popular performers slipped through, mainly because they were "rentals" (an outside presenter had booked the hall) and not NAC presentations. Singer Rita MacNeil

*Mills and Morrow essentially traded jobs: she joined the Canada Council as music officer, and he came over from the Council, where he had received a bird's-eye view of the growing problems in the Music Department at the NAC.

put on a popular show as did the country/blues singer k.d. lang, although lang, with her well-known anti-establishment views, came in for sharp press criticism for doing so. Through it all DesRochers remained obdurate.

When the HDTV seminar took place in November, the orchestra had been out for over six weeks. DesRochers's style in managing the situation came in for particular attack that, to some, was "almost stunning in its ferocity."[12] He was blamed not only for the strike but for a host of other related issues. Much of the anger was aimed at the expenditures on the new television project. Even the former minister Flora MacDonald, now out of office after her 1988 election defeat, took a swipe at DesRochers: "He should be called to account for the new directions in which he trying to send the National Arts Centre," she opined.[13]

In a well-organized campaign by the NAC's traditional supporters, Hamilton Southam now weighed in. He denounced his successor as director general, describing him as "lacking in sensibility and ability to deal with artists."[14] DesRochers fought back, blaming his troubles on "seven years of no financial growth at the NAC"—and Landry reinforced him: "The NAC is slowly starving because of decreasing federal support."[15]

In terms of maintaining its previous work, that was true. Despite a federal subsidy that was nearly $16 million in 1989–90, the organization used every cent it brought in and was still running a deficit, which was starting to grow again. Landry warned that the annual shortfall in the budget of $1 million would rise to $3 million within two years. He even alluded to the fact that the board might have to address some private fundraising to make up the difference—though that was against his principles. He acknowledged that DesRochers might have "overstressed" the potential for HDTV, which was clearly a long way from operational in North America, but the role of television, even conventional television, he believed was essential for the NAC's future.[16] It remained at the forefront of the thinking of the two men.

While other programs continued to suffer cost-cutting pressures, David Langer's annual budget of $500,000 remained intact. That was a modest sum in terms of television, but Langer now set out to create some programs while his bosses pondered what to do next. They would soon seize on the audacious idea that the National Arts Centre should apply for its own television licence in the expanding new satellite/cable universe that the CRTC was about to open up to specialty licences. The orchestra strike was settled at last in December, but not before a brutal bruising of the parties involved that would never entirely disappear. The new year would bring an uneasy truce—along with controversial new initiatives.

Although DesRochers had his own vision for the Arts Centre and understood clearly that, without change, the organization could be lost, much of the bad blood that was circulating in and around the Arts Centre was aggravated by his way of dealing with people. Warm and close to family and friends on a personal level, he could be harsh and autocratic, even crudely spoken, in his professional capacity. Once settled in the director general's office, he made it clear that what he said would rule, and his abrasive manner extended into the board room. There, Landry, a skilled chairman, ran interference for his CEO. At the staff level, things were not so easily managed. Richard Lussier, DesRochers's senior financial officer, described him as "a tough guy ... who could talk like a street thug at times," and, although he wanted people around him who would make tough decisions, "he did not take suggestions well, he wasn't a great listener, so basically all of us in senior management became quasi 'yes-men.' It was his way or no way."[17] This confrontational approach evoked what many referred to as "an atmosphere of fear" at the corporate end of the workplace.[18] It was graphically demonstrated in the locks on doors which were introduced between departments, and by the orders to shred financial documents after meetings.

At the board level, Landry also introduced his own new methods. Rather than the long and sometimes discursive board minutes that had been characteristic of previous regimes, board reporting was now pared down to the minimum. "I learned in the private sector that what you record is the decisions, not a record of the discussions," he stated.[19] And the board, although concerned, was shielded from much of the turmoil within the Arts Centre. Landry himself stayed close to DesRochers, advising him where he could. "I spent a lot of time with Yvon counseling him ... he had this great vision, and an ingredient in getting his vision was the way in which he was bringing about the vision tactically ... he had a very sharp temper. It was tough."[20] Still, Landry remained convinced that they were on the right course with television. Two new trustees, former television newsman Ron Collister and Vancouver financial consultant Mel Cooper, had joined the board, and they soon became important allies in its pursuit.

An uneasy truce reigned at the centre in the early months of 1990. The orchestra set off on what would be a well-received U.S. trip under the baton of Maestro Chmura—his last tour with the NAC Orchestra. They travelled together up the eastern seaboard from Florida, ending with concerts at Washington's Kennedy Center and a well-praised final performance at Carnegie Hall in New York. Halfway through the tour, Jack Mills was called back to Ottawa for a special meeting. While Landry and DesRochers pondered the NAC's financial quandary, an unexpected "angel" had arrived on the scene.

Impresario Garth Drabinsky, in casual encounters with Landry and DesRochers, had proposed a most unusual idea, and they were meeting to formalize it. In a move that would lead to even more controversy, the NAC was embarking on the "Phantom Phenomenon"—a commercial theatre project that would come to occupy a lot of space in the program schedule and further enrage many of the traditional supporters. It also would put some money into the NAC coffers.

By 1990 the Canadian production of the American musical *The Phantom of the Opera* had become a legendary musical success. The Toronto show was set to run for years at the Pantages Theatre, but there was wide public demand to see it elsewhere in the country. Its producers, led by Drabinsky, decided to create a touring version of the production, and they turned to the Arts Centre in Ottawa for help. The NAC was the only place in the country that had the workshops, the stagecraft crews, and the space to build the new show.

Yvon DesRochers liked popular musical theatre, and he had no qualms when Drabinsky arrived to make the deal with the NAC. There was no doubt that the new project would take up time and space at the centre. Other activities, and in particular the orchestra, would have to be pushed off their traditional main stage to make room for it. The new show would be built on the vast Opera stage, and it would eventually have a lengthy run there. NAC finance officer Rick Lussier alerted Mills—"Jack, you've got to be here or there is going to be a twelve-week hole in the middle of the orchestra season."[21] Mills flew in from the tour in Tampa, Florida, in mid-February to be part of the negotiations.

Mills was discouraged going into the meetings, knowing that Landry and DesRochers badly wanted the *Phantom* project even at the cost of the NAC's regular musical activities. After protracted discussions, Drabinsky recognized that the NAC Orchestra was the stumbling block and, according to Mills, "basically inquired what it was going to cost for the orchestra to find something else to do while the *Phantom* came to the Arts Centre."[22] The idea of an extended national orchestra tour that would justify the orchestra being out of the city was touted, and Mills named a substantial figure for the tour's costs, throwing in a request that Drabinsky bring his musical show *The Music of Andrew Lloyd Weber* to Ottawa as part of the NAC Pops concert series for good measure. The impresario readily agreed, and the deal was struck. Both Landry and DesRochers were thrilled. Not only was there money for the NAC in exchange for its services but it would also have a slice of the show's profits when it performed at the Arts Centre. In addition, they intended to use the *Phantom* for some first-time fundraising of their own.

In the spring of 1990 they approached one of the Ottawa's leading volunteers, Karen Slipacoff, an experienced fundraiser and self-named "Gala Queen." In principle, Landry was against going to the private sector for funds, believing that such a heavily subsidized public institution should not compete with less-fortunate arts companies for funds. But DesRochers, said Slipacoff, "could see the handwriting on the wall." Once convinced that any money raised "would be used for artists, and not for new red carpets for the centre," she agreed to organize "the Phantom Gala" that marked the opening of the show's first extended run in Ottawa on April 26, 1991.[23]

The press took a harsh view of the Landry/ DesRochers plans, especially when the commercial musical Phantom of the Opera displaced the orchestra. Cartoon © Alan King.

At the root of much of DesRochers's thinking was a populist view of the arts. Both Landry and he had a strong streak of anti-establishment Ottawa in their attitude. DesRochers saw no reason why the public should not have access to popular commercial theatre as part of the NAC's programming, along with what was often commented on as its otherwise "elitist" product. Landry shared this view and also thought that privileged Ottawans wrongly saw their financial problems as different from those of anyone else. "Ottawa tends to be a bit provincial in the way in which it looks at these things," he said. "If you are in Montreal or Toronto or Vancouver, you don't run to politicians. You solve things for yourself."[24]

The *Phantom* would stir up another angry debate over just what it was that the National Arts Centre should be doing. Much of the resistance was organized by the same supporters who had backed the orchestra so fiercely during the strike and who now decried the orchestra's apparent dislocation in favour of the popular commercial show. Slipacoff laughed later that the attitude to *Phantom* and what she set out to do was definitely considered "déclassé" in some Ottawa circles: it was the old debate about "elitist" versus "popular" art.

Within senior management, the *Phantom* and the handful of other big commercial musicals that came later to the NAC were seen as engines for profit, and not everyone inside the centre was unhappy with the arrangement. The IATSE stage crews, which included not only the stagehands but the skilled prop-makers and set-builders at the centre, had been seriously underused since the collapse of the operas and the reduction of in-house theatre production. The union was pleased to be part of this big new show, although, in a letter to management, it decried the loss of the "glory days" of opera and theatre when the NAC created its own productions. Later, some of its well-trained staff would go on the road with the *Phantom* when it set off to tour the country.

✳

By Christmas 1989 the HDTV idea was clearly unworkable, but DesRochers directed Langer to build a body of television work that could be used either on HDTV or sold to more conventional television. The aim was to develop the Arts Centre as an important co-producer of arts programs for both the Canadian and the international television markets. The visual excitement of modern dance was ideal for this purpose. Jack Udashkin had an intimate knowledge of the dance scene around the world, and, after consulting him, Langer selected *Le Dortoir* as the first project. An ingenious dance-work by the Montreal company Carbone 14 (Carbone Quatorze), it had been created by the company's director, the avant-garde and internationally respected choreographer Gilles Maheu.

The television show was directed by Francis Girard, who later went on to direct opera and films, including *The Red Violin*. The work was co-produced with Rhombus Media, with help from the CBC and Radio Canada, and shot in the spring and summer of 1990 in the NAC Studio—a facility originally designed for television production. The result was exquisite—and it won many national and international awards, even an Emmy.

It was a promising start to the NAC's role in television production. Unfortunately, despite general cooperation from the in-house unions—IATSE was keen to have its members involved in television and was working out a deal with DesRochers in that direction—*Le Dortoir* was almost the only program of this type produced at the Arts Centre. Adapting live performances for television on the premises was costly, and other programs, including director Robert Lepage's play *Tectonic Plates*, a delightful production of the Ottawa Ballet's *Tin Soldier*, and various programs for the Youth Television network, would later be produced in television studios outside the Arts Centre—some in Ottawa, but mostly in Toronto or Montreal.

The television initiative produced some interesting programming. The NAC's production Le Dortoir *won an International Emmy. Left to right: TV director David Langer, Yvon DesRochers, and special events producer Jack Udashkin delighted in the award. Photo © Allan de la Plante.*

The termination of Maestro Chmura, the collapse of the HDTV project, the seven-week orchestra strike, and the plan that sent the orchestra out of town as it was replaced by big commercial entertainment had all created disquiet in powerful official circles. After much behind-the-scenes prodding, the Parliamentary Committee on Culture and Communications, under the chairmanship of Conservative MP Felix Holtmann, convened hearings on June 13, 1990 to examine the situation at the Arts Centre. The clever Holtmann, who delighted in his regular press attribution as "a pig farmer from Manitoba," had already made national headlines stirring up the Canadian arts community and many Canadians generally with his public attacks on the National Gallery's purchase of an abstract expressionist painting, *Voice of Fire*, by the American artist Barnett Newman. Now it was the NAC's turn for some vigorous questioning, not only from the chair but from the opposition culture critics, Sheila Finestone for the Liberals and Ian Waddell for the NDP.

Relying on the work of an independent consultant who had researched the matter at the request of the parliamentary committee, the MPs were well informed about the problems at the Arts Centre, and they sent the board of trustees a list of forty-six questions for response. These questions ranged over the full spectrum, from the NAC's structure, management, and mandate through plans for improved summer programming to how best to serve the thousands of ordinary Canadians who poured into Ottawa each year on vacation.

A parade of witnesses was called before the parliamentarians. The most prominent was Hamilton Southam, who turned up to blast Landry and DesRochers and call for their resignations. He accused them of betraying the NAC's mandate and questioned whether the board of trustees really knew what was going on. In a swipe at the decision to install the *Phantom of the Opera* for an extended run at the NAC, he asked: "Is the board even aware that giving a visiting commercial company priority over the last remaining resident company is a contradiction of the mandate?"[25] Speaking for many of the orchestra's supporters, he criticized the plans of the incumbent leaders to de-emphasize the orchestra and invest in new television technologies. Other Ottawa heavyweights backed his comments, including former Liberal Cabinet minister Mitchell Sharp, the distinguished public servant Gordon Robertson, and former National Ballet director Celia Franca. They were all members of a new group calling itself Friends of the National Arts Centre. Franca, who was married to an orchestra musician, described the atmosphere at the centre to the MPs as "a frigid prison ... no longer a people place."

Critical that the committee witnesses had been stacked against them, Landry and DesRochers came out swinging when it was their turn to appear before the parliamentarians. They declared that the Arts Centre was being judged on the past, forcefully

Yvon DesRochers took a tough line in appearances before parliamentary committees, defending his actions and harshly pointing out the NAC's lack of resources and government inaction. Photo © Wayne Hiebert/Ottawa Citizen. Reprinted by permission.

labelling much of the previous testimony as "propaganda" and "baloney." DesRochers told the MPs that "it's ludicrous for me to be sitting here talking to you about keeping up a level of excellence and the same numbers of performances after seven years of zero financial growth!"[26] The realities of the present included a parliamentary grant that had decreased in real terms nearly 25 percent in the previous ten years.

DesRochers aggressively asserted that while the NAC prided itself on its orchestra, its cost was 45 percent of the entire government subsidy. Landry backed him up, telling the committee that "the NAC orchestra is no longer immune from the cost-cutting that the centre must endure if it is to survive." He suggested that, to meet the orchestra's expectations, the centre would have to "abandon all other in-house production"—something he and DesRochers so far "had refused to do."[27] The two men dismissed charges that the board had been in the dark about their manoeuvres and, in any case, insisted that booking the *Phantom* was an independent management programming decision that had nothing to do with the trustees.

The hearings were inconclusive, but they laid bare the opposing forces struggling over the NAC's future. While many defended the values and principles on which the NAC had been founded, the centre's new and pragmatic leaders were addressing the dismal state of affairs for support to the arts in Canada in an unvarnished, unsentimental fashion. Management's counter-offensive raised questions in some journalists' minds—whether the parliamentary committee was getting all the facts it needed or even whether the right questions were being asked—but the *Ottawa Citizen*, in an editorial on June 16, returned to the nub of the problem: "What is the NAC? A national theatre or a rental hall? A showcase for Canadian talent? Or a profit-oriented showcase for popular international entertainers?" It urged parliamentarians to consider answers to these questions as they prepared their report.

The report was tabled in the House of Commons on September 26, 1990. NAC management had received wind that its findings would be harsh. In a pre-emptive move from

DesRochers's office, the Arts Centre released its earlier correspondence with the committee that had complained about the way the hearings were being conducted and the selection of witnesses. Holtmann was shocked by the release of the letters and implied that it challenged MPs' parliamentary privilege. "I have never witnessed such a clear protest to committee activities," he declared.[28] It was no surprise when, throughout the report, the constant thread was direct and implied criticism of the board and the senior management at the NAC. When the report considered the NAC's financial plight and recommended that the government provide a $3 million one-time grant to wipe out the deficit, for example, it also stated that the NAC should receive no new funds until it responded to the committee's twenty-two recommendations. The MPs called for a permanent end to the HDTV project, better relations with the NAC Orchestra, and even suggested that the orchestra change its name to the National Orchestra of Canada.

Overall, the report avoided singling out DesRochers and Landry individually for their management practices, although some committee members were clearly shocked at the NAC management style. As Ian Waddell told a news conference, "You can't run this NAC like you run a tank battalion. They've blasted everyone who came in their path. I think they should listen to other people's recommendations once in a while. If they are not prepared to listen they should get out."[29] The politically savvy and steel-nerved Landry publicly played it down, saying only that "this report does not represent government policy."[30] The responsibility now lay with Marcel Masse, and the NAC would await his opinions. By law, the minister had 150 days to react.

When Masse did finally respond months later, in February 1991, this notoriously hands-on minister used the arm's-length principle to avoid involvement in the NAC mess. There was considerable irony in his position. Since returning to the portfolio in late 1988, Masse had demonstrated that his views on culture were much more in sympathy with the past and present French culture ministers, André Malraux and Jacques Lang, respectively. In this respect he had put himself in tune with his colleagues in Quebec, where many senior cultural officials and politicians were actively questioning the arm's-length principle that prevailed in the rest of Canada. Lise Bacon, the Quebec minister of cultural affairs, in an interview in early 1989 openly questioned the independence of the Canada Council. "These people aren't government ministers," she said; "they aren't politically accountable to the public." She also commented that she expected Quebec artists to remember "their responsibilities from time to time," implying their responsibilities to support the state, and said that the government should remind them of this role.[31]

English-Canadian commentators had no difficulty identifying Marcel Masse with this "Gallic definition of culture as a vehicle for social architecture."[32] Many anglophone writers despaired at what they observed as the erosion of the arm's-length principle, which had begun under Gérard Pelletier in the Trudeau years. Most of the officials in Masse's department, which was heavily staffed by francophones, saw no harm in the new approach, especially as their own departmental budget was growing to provide more funding of culture directly from the ministry.* On his return to the Communications portfolio, Masse had been named chair of an allegedly powerful new Cabinet Committee of Cultural Affairs and National Identity, intended to hold the line for culture during the free-trade talks. He also remained a member of the inner Cabinet—an honour that suggested some political clout for culture. He would make breakthroughs on issues of principle, such as the status of the artist legislation, but he seemed powerless or disinclined to shore up the dwindling financial resources for cultural crown organizations—the Canada Council, the CBC, and the National Arts Centre, for example—in the face of the financial strictures being demanded by Finance Minister Michael Wilson.

When Masse finally issued his reply to the raft of recommendations on the NAC that the Parliamentary Committee had sent him, he showed how politically nimble he could be. While remaining in step with a government-wide exercise under way that was "rethinking federal and provincial powers," his response to the NAC report was generally "hands off"—indicating that all but four of the recommendations dealt with matters under the sole discretion of the NAC board. Although he urged "circumspection" because of the costs associated with ideas like the HDTV project, he declined to intervene in any of the other complaints that had swirled around management.

By now Masse was fully occupied by one of his other pet projects. The same week that he responded to the NAC problems, he announced the creation of a $45 million Montreal-based Institute for Research on Cultural Enterprises, a controversial proposal that seized the headlines away from any news of the Arts Centre. A brief statement issued by an NAC spokesman confirmed that DesRochers had been "very pleased" by the minister's response, while the Liberal opposition's new culture critic, Mary Clancy, angrily dubbed Masse's actions as "a prosper and be damned approach." The centre was effectively left to proceed on the course chosen for it by DesRochers and the existing board.

The artistic fallout from the political and financial turmoil surrounding the NAC would be profound. In the face of the boardroom battles, the artistic staff continued their

---

*Most of his staff had applauded Masse's bumptious stance when he turned up at the Hollywood Oscar Award ceremony in April 1989 to accept an Oscar on behalf of the National Film Board in recognition of its fiftieth anniversary while two mute senior NFB officials stood at his side. Many inside the NFB were furious, on the grounds that politicians were supposed to keep at arm's length from culture.

Theatre director Robert Lepage came to the NAC as director of French theatre with big dreams but was disillusioned, resigning at the end of his three-year term. Photo © Wayne Hiebert/Ottawa Citizen. Reprinted by permission.

work. The relentless demands of filling the Arts Centre's three main stages and planning adequately ahead for the future, all in a climate of acute financial uncertainty, taxed the imagination of the most creative members of the team. It is surprising that, despite the evident dysfunction through much of management, the NAC still made two remarkable artistic "hires" in this period. The exciting young Quebec theatre director Robert Lepage agreed to replace André Brassard as director of French theatre, and, after another protracted search, the English musician and conductor Trevor Pinnock was designated the next music director, to replace Chmura. He would be the third music director in the NAC's history.

The twenty-nine-year-old Lepage was already recognized as a theatrical "wunderkind." As Brassard expressed it, "I consider him a real man of the theatre, a genuine innovator. The theatre community is lucky to have him."[33] An actor, playwright, and director with a growing international reputation, Lepage came to the centre with high hopes. Fluently bilingual, he announced at once that he wanted to work with the English theatre producer Andis Celms on possible co-productions between the NAC's French and English sections. DesRochers "crowed" over the appointment, which fell in line with his plans. "I think it's marvellous not only for the National Arts Centre but for the development of theatre in the country. Robert Lepage strongly believes that the regions have a lot to offer and that the National Arts Centre can play a supporting role in that development."[34] Many years later, Lepage would sadly note that his appointment to the NAC had been "full of illusions."[35] Although his own reputation would soar around the world during his time there, and he was able to introduce some innovative work at the centre, his choice of plays on the stages at the NAC did not appeal to local theatre-goers. French theatre's much-vaunted subscription successes under Brassard would plummet during Lepage's tenure to the lowest levels until then at the NAC.

When he signed on, Lepage carried the same vision that Jean Gascon had brought to Ottawa. "I didn't have any hang-ups about working with people from English

Canada," he said. "On the contrary, it was a very exciting moment with all the English-language directors and writers up and coming."[36] He thought the NAC was unique in the country, a place where French and English professionals worked under the same roof. Excited by the innovative work he saw outside Quebec, he declared publicly, "We're going to merge this country's talent whether French or English."[37] His choice of Ottawa was dissonant to some ears. When asked by La Presse Canadienne how he felt about leaving Quebec to come to Ottawa, his reaction was startled. "Leave Quebec? I'm one of those Quebecers who thinks English Canada is very different with a very separate cultural identity, but I am not moving to England! I'm still part of this country."[38] Lepage imagined the Arts Centre as "the shop window of what is good in art and what is happening in art in Canada," and he thought that his job there would be "the fast-track for touring productions and co-productions both around Canada and internationally." He was initially intrigued by DesRochers's talk of television. "I was interested in the new technology, to see how recorded performances and live performances could actually live together," he said. Later he came to realize that "once you start bringing TV people into the live performance world, there's always a clash in technology, a clash in language and dialogue and intensions."[39]

Lepage's first season at the NAC was a success for him. Like Brassard before him, he delighted in all the resources the place had to offer. "My first production there I discovered the creative potential of that tool which was the National Arts Centre in those days. The greatest costume shop, the greatest set shop, the greatest prop shop. The 'savoir-faire' of the place." The first play he directed was *La Visite de la Vieille Dame*—the same opening play presented by the star-crossed first director of French theatre, Jean-Guy Sabourin. The rest of the season was mainly productions by other francophone companies or co-productions with them.

Lepage admitted that he was initially shy about presenting his own work, and it was not until others on the artistic team persuaded him that some "original Lepage" was wanted that he began to work on his own creations there. Among them was *Tectonic Plates/Les Plaques Tectoniques* as well as development work on his astounding one-man show *Needles and Opium*, which would later travel the world. Lepage saw the excellence of the facilities at the NAC as an advantage not only to himself but also to smaller companies from the regions which, given the opportunity to co-produce or appear at the NAC, would have an experience with theatrical excellence otherwise not available to them. "Conceptually, even though the whole country was turning inward, the place did offer opportunity that I didn't see anywhere else in Canada." As time moved on however, much of what he attempted at the centre would be hampered by the soon-made discovery of "this illusion that there was a lot of money and a lot of open-mindedness and a lot of possibilities."[40]

In music, the search committee created to find Chmura's replacement included the usual luminaries, along with the managers of the Montreal and Toronto Symphonies, Zarin Mehta and Walter Homberger, respectively. Jack Mills replaced Joanne Morrow as the NAC's management representative, and concertmaster Walter Prystawski was once more among the orchestra representatives. It was not until the NACO's 1990 European tour, nearly two years after Chmura's announced departure and several months after he had officially left the building, that a choice came clear.

Violinist Pinchas Zukerman, who had replaced Chmura as conductor for the European tour, was a leading candidate for the permanent music director's job. After he met with DesRochers, he also became interested in the proposed TV development there. Given the NAC's troubles, which were well-known, the maestro had been sceptical that the tour would actually take place, and his agent insisted on upfront payments and guarantees before he agreed to participate. The European tour manager, Hans Ulrich Schmidt in Germany, also queried Jack Mills when he arrived in Hamburg to settle the orchestra's tour programming. He wanted a signed contract, this time with Zukerman's name on it, before setting up the final arrangements for the concerts. Mills was able to oblige, and Schmidt, who knew the orchestra well,[41] reassured concert hall managers across Europe that the NAC Orchestra would not only show up but also play good music.

As the musicians left Ottawa to fly from Mirabel to Europe, Mills convinced DesRochers to turn up to see them off. The director general boarded the bus, where he told the musicians: "This tour is going to be memorable. Fantastic. It's going to show Canadians where you really should be."[42] Given management-musician relations, many of the players wondered if that meant somewhere other than the Arts Centre. It was clear, Mills said, that a period of healing was badly needed by everyone after the strike, and the appointment of the right music director was critical. During the strike, at the suggestion of Christopher Deacon, Mills had approached Trevor Pinnock, the English conductor and harpsichordist, to sound him out on the position. The decision not to cross the picket line in Ottawa had caused serious financial damage to Pinnock's small English Consort orchestra, but the NACO players loved him now for his loyalty as well as his musicianship. Although Zukerman was an appealing candidate, there was still talk of the difficulties that had occurred during his previous musical directorship at the St. Paul Chamber Orchestra in Minnesota. He had also told Mills that while he wanted very much to work with the orchestra, he would rather not be involved in the hirings and firings and other administrative and programming duties that came with the music director's job. At the tour's triumphant final concert in London's Royal Festival Hall, Mills invited Pinnock to join him in the audience. When the concert was over and they went backstage to congratulate the players, Zukerman turned to a colleague and said, "There goes your next music director."[43] Although it was still some weeks before the matter would be settled, he was right. Mills was concerned about DesRochers's reaction to the recommendation, given Pinnock's close association with

English conductor Trevor Pinnock took the music director job with high hopes but found the internal struggles within the arts centre a painful experience. Nevertheless, his stewardship brought calm to the difficult situation. Photo © John Major/Ottawa Citizen. Reprinted by permission.

the musicians, but this time the director general did not resist, and he reported the appointment to the Board of Directors. On March 13, 1991, the NAC announced Trevor Pinnock as the new NAC music director, starting in the fall of 1991 for a period of three years. Altogether he would stay for five years, through to 1995.

Pinnock would later describe his time at the National Arts Centre as "one of the most painful periods of my life, because morale was so low," but his presence was a critical component in restoring the orchestra to a semblance of health and stability. Pinnock believed strongly in "the firm framework" an orchestra needs to function well, and he admired what Bernardi had created during his years there. "My task became to re-establish that firm framework" within the orchestra, he said.[44] His approach also helped to rebuild the jaundiced Ottawa audiences that had fallen away through the various orchestral crises.

For Pinnock, the job was a chance to broaden his own experience. His main short-coming was his limited repertoire, which was largely confined to the baroque. Mills and the Music Department solved the problem by arranging for the German-born, Montreal-based conductor Franz-Paul Decker to handle some of the orchestral duties. Decker had appeared many times with the orchestra, and he now provided an excellent support partner for the larger repertoire that included big works by Beethoven and Brahms. "I was largely a specialist in baroque music, and I knew I could not be trapped in that one sphere of music all the time," Pinnock recalled. "The National Arts Centre Orchestra, of all the orchestras I conducted, was one which I felt very easy with musically … and it provided me with the opportunity to do a wide range of repertoire, including the newest repertoire."[45]

New music was an area where the maestro really shone. Early in his tenure, he established the first ever composer-in-residence at the Arts Centre. After listening to the work of "a lot of different young Canadian composers," he settled on Linda Bouchard, a Canadian composer who had been born in Val d'Or, Quebec, but received most of her musical training in the United States. Pinnock found her music "technically superb. It uncompromisingly followed a sort of 1960s tradition of modern music-making." He soon discovered that both Ottawa audiences and the musicians themselves sometimes found this new music hard to take. Nevertheless, he stuck loyally behind her as she developed and took on a project to record her music. "I don't know if I ever managed to win them around fully, although just before I left they were playing it superbly," he said. "We recorded a lot of her music. Even the local music critic praised that record very highly, which was a great surprise to me."[46]

Like Lepage in theatre, Pinnock also had a view of his position as music director. "The real job of a music director is to be part of the community, to spend considerable time building the orchestra, to take care of the educational aspects which are part of any orchestra's life nowadays." He too had high hopes of working at the NAC on joint projects with the other departments. This goal was to prove as illusory for Pinnock as it was for Lepage. Both men were young and had little experience with the type of internal problems that were wracking the NAC. As Pinnock put it, "I didn't realize until I got there quite how far apart the orchestra and management were. At the beginning, trust seemed to be out of the question. So I found myself in the middle of having to deal with it and having to sort of broker elements of trust."[47] He took his administrative duties seriously, dealing with sometimes painful personnel issues in the orchestra but also arranging for some brilliant "hires"—the flautist Joanna G'froerer and principal oboist Charles (Chip) Hamann, both of whom added musical lustre to the ensemble. Pinnock was proud of his role in these appointments.

Despite these and other successes, the ever-worsening financial situation exacerbated matters everywhere at the centre. Personal relations with the board and management caused both artistic directors deep unease. Pinnock found himself "very, very affected by the atmosphere. I wasn't at that time equipped to sit between those two seats of unrest."[48] Lepage was on better terms with DesRochers—"He was always very sympathetic, very generous to me"—but a curious exchange over lunch one day altered the theatre director's perception. "I was doubting if I would do a second season and he wanted to convince me to stay." DesRochers urged Lepage to remain, on the grounds that he himself was "a winner." "I don't know anything about music, opera, theatre or dance … but I am the director general here!" he told the startled Lepage, implying that, if Lepage stuck with him, he could be a winner too. It was a revelation to the artist. "I really understood then that we were in a different world. This was not a man of the arts. It was obvious … that this was not about art at all." Lepage concluded: "This man did not have an ounce of hypocrisy. He did not say things he did not believe. It's just that he wasn't in the right place."[49] Lepage would stay on to complete three seasons at the centre, but his interest in the possibilities began to fade from that point on.

By his second season, it was evident to Lepage that he would have little money to realize his personal vision. His solution was to accept more and more work outside the NAC, using his base there to springboard him into the highest international circles of theatre. In 1992 that included an invitation to direct a radical version of Shakespeare's *Midsummer Night's Dream* at England's National Theatre in London, an event that created much buzz in theatre circles on both sides of the Atlantic. While credit accrued back to the centre, it provided little to the development of the Canadian theatre of which he had dreamed. While his Ottawa seasons involved interesting new versions of his works, including an English-language version of *Polygraph*, based on the cruel story of the murder of an actress friend but inspired by the coming down of the Berlin Wall, as well as reworkings first in French and then in English of his play *Les Plaques Tectoniques/Tectonic Plates*, his ability to create other new works was limited. There was still room for some adventurous experiments, however.

The French *Les Plaques Tectoniques* opened the 1991–92 French theatre season, Lepage's second, and was presented not at the Arts Centre but in an old stone commercial warehouse on an island in the Ottawa River close to the centre of the city and alongside the Chaudière Falls. With the audience seated in a circle around the action and a large pool of water in the middle, the play's dream-like symbolism and shifting disjointed scenes reflected the important nature of human relations. The play left theatre-goers sometimes baffled but intrigued, and the piece, a visual tour-de-force, was later put on film for the collection of television productions the NAC was creating.

While Lepage was planning his third season at the NAC and Pinnock was undertaking the first full season for which he was responsible, new and disturbing financial news again rattled developments. As the spring 1991 board meetings approached at the end of May, finance officer Rick Lussier circulated a memo to the staff that spelled out the details of the dismal financial situation. The previous September, Lussier had been projecting a break-even position, with the prospect of additional funds approved by the Treasury Board for both the current and the next fiscal years to take care of the NAC's potential deficits as well as add a cost-of-living increase and some additional benefits for the staff. Just two months later a new round of cuts began, precipitated by initiatives in federal government policies. All federal departments and agencies were asked to contribute. At the NAC, that meant $200,000 to help fund Canada's contribution to the Gulf War, over $475,000 for financing the government's elimination of the federal sales tax, and another $320,000 for a catch-all federal plan labelled "deficit reduction initiatives."

To cap it off, the local Ottawa regional government was terminating its annual grant, now totalling $230,000. While the Arts Centre was expected to keep operations going at the same level, it was losing half-a-million dollars for its coming season and nearly $800,000 in the following year. The NAC trustees as well as senior management were adamantly opposed to a deficit, and Lussier sharply pointed out in his report that the "the focus of future reductions must impact directly on the programming."

By the time the trustees met in May, extensive reductions had already been made in the dance program, and the meetings confirmed that both the English and the French theatre seasons in the coming year would be reduced from five plays to four, each focused on co-productions or rentals. These latter would include a play from the Shaw Festival, for which the NAC offered only its stage and its facilities. A recommendation to eliminate the workshop, prop shop, and costume department was also on the table. This proposal elicited an outspoken reaction from the NAC Local 471 of IATSE. In a letter to the trustees, union president Claude Desvoyault complained there was "too much management at the centre while the stages were going dark." A similar letter from the NAC Orchestra Players remonstrated, "This is not the time to begin dismantling the National Arts Centre." Senior management responded that the reorganization of programming was only part of a much larger reorganization and restructuring plan. DesRochers later commented to the press that dwindling ticket sales told him that "the supply of programming at the NAC exceeds the demand," and that he intended to correct this imbalance.

With the exception of Andis Celms, who was a member of senior management and part of its meetings, none of the artistic directors were consulted about these measures. This neglect particularly angered Lepage, and he commented in public. He described his own shock when the ever-recurring rounds of budget cuts finally closed down the props and costume workshops he admired so highly and outsourced what they had done. "Ironically," said Jay Stone in the *Ottawa Citizen*, "these were the departments that had produced the magnificent outfits and props as well as the spectacular sets of the *Phantom*, the show that seemed to be the symbol of the NAC's future." Administrative offices now moved into these workshop spaces.

It was the NAC's involvement with the big American musicals that most upset Lepage. "They got involved in doing *Phantom* and *Les Miz*. That really scared me. Not only is 'the shop window of Canadian culture' producing these big Broadway hits, and obviously with lucrative intent, but they did not originate in Canada." Lepage was always embarrassed by Canadian culture attempting to imitate American art, but now "suddenly, my own seasons were competing; my own ticket sales were competing, within the National Arts Centre, with these big block-buster musicals coming from America—built, rehearsed, and produced at the NAC and then touring out to all the big cities in Canada. Suddenly you are not fighting a good idea that goes wrong, like HDTV; you're fighting the whole American vision of what live entertainment should be. That was very, very tricky."[50]

None of the severity of these cultural measures was occurring in a vacuum. All across the country, cultural activity was being reduced in the face of hard economic times. Book sales in Canada were reported down by 30 percent; recorded music sales by 25 percent. Theatre companies everywhere were reducing seasons, and many were threatened with closing, while most experimental and risky work was disappearing off Canadian stages. The *Globe and Mail* music critic Robert Everett-Green noted that "the drama being played out at the NAC marks the end of a 21-year experiment with the European model of complete state subsidy at major cultural organizations." The underlying subtext among most of the governing Tories, according to the journalist, was, "if art doesn't make a profit, it can't really be any good."[51]

The bitterness of the budget cuts were not yet at an end. Scarcely ten months later in another explosion at the centre, full-time staff layoffs again rocked public perceptions about the organization. This time the main target for "restructuring" was a recently rearranged marketing department, but it was the particularly cruel and brutal way in which the cuts were made that burned itself into people's memories. On March 3, 1992, a group of thirty NAC employees were called out of their offices and told to report to the Lord Elgin Hotel directly across the street. In what was later described as "the most up-to-date personnel practices,"[52] the group was divided in two and sent to different floors. Members of the first group were told their jobs were safe; those in the second group were dismissed—immediately. They were escorted back to the centre by security staff to pick up personal belongings; during their short absence, their computers had been unplugged and their office locks changed.

While personnel experts blithely referred to the exercise as a "clean surgical strike," most observers found it deeply dehumanizing and reflective of the mindset prevailing at the centre. Among the dismissals was the in-house expert trained to operate the computerized notice-board, the only identifying symbol of the Arts Centre on the city side of the building. Three days after his departure, the sign jammed, never to function properly again. Robert Lepage, with members of his own support staff among the dismissed, remembered the black day nearly twenty years later. Not surprisingly, the outcry led to another parliamentary committee appearance for DesRochers, this one a much more low-key affair. DesRochers was unapologetic for the action and told the MPs "there was no easy way to do it."[53]

Meanwhile, one department at the Arts Centre continued to progress. Under David Langer, the Television Department was working to assemble a series of programs. *Tectonic Plates* was among them, part of a series, Stage on Screen, being produced by the independent production company Primedia that was run by television producer and impresario Pat Ferns. Undeterred by his failure with HDTV, DesRochers hung tenaciously to the concept that television was the key to the NAC's future. Although Peter Herrndorf, his private consultant, had nixed the idea of HDTV, he did support the notion that conventional television could be a valuable asset in establishing the NAC's national identity. DesRochers began to drive hard for a new objective: the NAC should obtain its own television licence to broadcast arts programming across the country.

Refreshed by the board's unanimous decision in November 1991 to renew his contract for a further five years, DesRochers made a forceful pitch to the trustees at the next round of board meetings in February 1992 for what he was now calling "TV Canada." A month later, his greatest ally, Robert Landry, was reappointed as chair. DesRochers's rationale to the trustees was detailed. He argued that the lack of federal government support was due to the failure by previous administrations to establish the NAC as "national." With the devolving of federal powers now under way in the Conservative regime, only those organizations that could aggressively show they were providing benefits to the country as a whole were likely to get support. Conceived as a national centre of excellence based in the capital, the perception, however untrue, that the NAC only served an Ottawa audience had been a serious drawback. The solution was a television licence on basic cable which would, for example, develop programming in collaboration with universities and serve the francophone community outside Quebec. To support his argument, he drew on the succession of federal consulting reports--Applebaum-Hébert, Hendry, and even the Caplan-Sauvageau Report on broadcasting,[54] all of which had called for the televising of Canada's arts.

DesRochers painted a sorry picture of performing art companies all across the country. He estimated the combined deficit of the country's eleven performing arts centres at $11 million, and stated that ticket sales of live performances were down on average 25 percent. In Quebec alone he claimed there was a 40 percent reduction in programming and a 20 percent fall in attendance during the previous year. In Ontario, Stratford had cut three plays from its roster, and the Avon Theatre season was being shortened by two weeks, with fifteen actors cut from the company. "TV Canada," he told the trustees, would present "Live from the Stage" at the NAC. It would not only expose performances nationally but would provide actors and performers with long-term work. The NAC would get into television production in partnership with independent producers, and the ad-free programming would run every evening from six until midnight. DesRochers saw no reason why organizations such as the lobby group the Canadian Conference of the Arts or even the Parliamentary Standing Committee on Culture and Communication could not tap into the channel to broadcast their proceedings. Provided the NAC specialty channel could obtain a place on the basic cable tier, it would have an automatic share of the consumer dollar. The problem of revenue for operating the NAC long into the future would be solved.

DesRochers believed completely in this vision, and, initially, he was able to bring almost his entire board with him. An exception was Joyce Zemans, director of the Canada Council and, therefore, an automatic ex-officio board member. Zemans wanted to work out a strategy for the hard-pressed theatrical community, and she had grave misgivings over the dismantling of the production facilities at the NAC. She tangled openly with DesRochers again and again over this issue and managed to set up a task force at the board to examine the state of affairs for theatre in the country.

CBC Board president Gérard Veilleux, also an ex-officio board member, believed initially that the talk of television was merely "blue-skying," although he raised questions about the role of the CBC in any broadcast initiative. DesRochers aggressively reminded board members of the Nielsen Task Force proposal to privatize operations and turn the building over to the National Capital Commission—an idea that still lingered in the wings. Further cuts would force privatization of some operations, he warned, or lead to the sale of the Arts Centre to private owners and an abrogation of the *NAC Act*. All these considerations justified the quest for a television licence—the all-important "licence to print money."[55] If the NAC could obtain a licence for a "non-discretionary service on the basic tier … revenues could be as high as $7 million a month for the NAC."[56]

DesRochers had good reasons to worry about the NAC's conventional subsidy. In February 1992 the House of Commons Standing Committee on Communications and Culture published its report, "The Ties That Bind," which reflected Conservative government policy. The move was on, as part of a revision of the constitution, to transfer cultural responsibilities to the provinces. Although the government intended to retain the national cultural institutions, little attention was given to the means by which they were to be sustained, especially financially. Moreover, further "across the board cuts" were said to be coming,[57] and, in addition, the forthcoming labour negotiations with IATSE and the public service union, PSAC, would be sure to have an impact on the NAC budget. The fixed costs involved merely in keeping the Arts Centre open were now "a huge problem," as they were for all the large performing arts centres in the country.[58] Inflation and deficits had eaten deeply into their sustainability.

Even rental shows were looking elsewhere for more economical accommodation as costs continued to rise at the NAC. Some acts, such as Céline Dion, opted to play at Ottawa's Congress Centre, where tickets could sell for as little as $3 versus nearly $8 for the same show at the NAC. The "tenuous nature of the centre's financing," DesRochers warned the board, "compelled the search for more diversified sources of funding."[59] He therefore insisted that the trustees support his request that he develop a detailed plan for a television licence application. Communications consultant Richard Paradis was hired by DesRochers to prepare the application over the summer.[60] The board consensus was that providing universal access to Canada's performing arts through TV would "preserve the arts heritage for the future."[61]

Not everyone in the boardroom was happy with this initiative. Veilleux confirmed later that he thought the CBC was responsible for broadcasting the arts and that the NAC should at least work in consort with the corporation. He was also not convinced that the idea of an arts channel was financially viable. Until he could see a business plan that set out in clear terms the revenues such a channel would produce, he would not support the idea. Robert Landry disputed this view: he maintained that the Arts Centre had long wanted to work with CBC, but it could get nowhere with the negotiation. "We just could not penetrate the CBC. They showed absolutely no interest. They were doing their own thing," he remembered. He had decided "that was not going to work, so we had to look at other alternatives."[62] Some NAC trustees expressed concerns about spending too much money on the television idea, about the quality of what might be presented, and about the need to protect the NAC's reputation. Otherwise, there was little resistance to DesRochers's plans. His forceful personality influenced board members even when some of them were anxious about his aggressive manner. Marie-Claire Morin, a trustee appointed by Flora MacDonald, recalled that "Yvon was a combination of extremes. Everything was huge. He was capable of accomplishing great things. Yet many of us were dismayed by his behaviour. He was championing a vision of the centre. He was very driven, relentless."

There was one achievement that Morin later remembered with pride—the Governor

General's Performing Arts Awards. Conceived as lifetime achievement awards for
Canada's finest performing artists, they were modelled on the American Kennedy
Awards presented annually in Washington. This grand idea emerged from the synergy
among many parties, and was championed by Governor General Ramon Hnatyshyn
and his wife, Gerda.

The national awards had been preceded by the successful Toronto Arts Awards,
created and administered by the Toronto Arts Foundation under the skilful leadership
of its president, Peter Herrndorf. His successor in Toronto, the independent television
producer Brian Robertson, agreed to pursue the national project in Ottawa. "It needed
four things" Robertson remembered. "A venue, a broadcaster, sponsorship, and credibility at the highest level."[63] When the Prime Minister's Office showed no interest,
Robertson made his way to Rideau Hall, where he found that Hnatyshyn was excited
by the idea and ready to lend his prestige to it. The gregarious Hnatyshyns enjoyed the
arts. They had already approached the Arts Centre to inquire if the orchestra would
play in the grounds of Rideau Hall in a summer concert series, and DesRochers was
on good terms with the vice-regal couple. Once the governor general championed the
awards, everything else fell into place: the National Arts Centre became the venue,
the CBC/Radio Canada signed on for national broadcasts of the event in both official
languages, and Bell Canada agreed to be the lead private sponsor.*

The timing of the awards was ideal for the Arts Centre. Not only would it host the
gala concert but "this star-charged cultural event" would provide a perfect opportunity
for it to demonstrate that television productions could emanate from the centre. David
Langer fell quickly into partnership with Robertson and played a key role in developing the stage show, making multiple exploratory visits to the Kennedy Center in the
process. Finally, on November 22, 1992, Canada's first Governor General's Performing Arts Awards came off with great panache. The Arts Centre had never looked more
beautiful, its grand staircase mezzanine and Opera hall laden with lavish sprays of
flowers and draped with banners in ruby and gold. Mindful of the needs of television,
the vice-regal party eschewed the state box set off to the side of the stage and sat in
plush red armchairs in the front row of the first balcony, with the honoured recipients
by their sides. The sweeping cranes of the mobile television cameras could easily cap-
ture the images they needed there as well as the action on the stage. Opening with a
specially composed trumpet fanfare and the swirling arrival of a Scottish pipe band,
the evening was an extravaganza of Canadian talent, from pop singers to ballet

---

*In that first year, 1992, one other key ingredient helped to launch the awards: the celebra-
tion of Canada's 125th anniversary. Just as the Centennial Commission had made common
cause with the Arts Centre on the cultural front in 1967, the 125th Anniversary Committee
now provided some money for this new cultural event. This infusion helped to trigger the
generous private lead sponsor, Bell Canada.

dancers, wittily hosted by Canadian actor and Hollywood star Donald Sutherland. The proceedings were recorded and, in a variety of year-end programs, the splendid gala event was broadcast nationally on the CBC network across Canada.

Inside the Arts Centre, specific plans continued to be developed for the application to the CRTC for a performing arts channel. The reports of all the many investigations to which the NAC had been subjected in the previous decade had emphasized the importance of television as a tool for distributing its arts product. Reports like the Hendry Task Force had urged that the centre apply for additional funds for such an initiative. In the climate of the times that was clearly impossible for the Landry/DesRochers regime, and the two men began to divert funds from the hard-pressed operating budget for this purpose. A new Conservative minister, Perrin Beatty, took over the Communications portfolio from Marcel Masse in 1991. Initially he was pleased that the NAC team had not come whining to him over a lack of money but, rather, seemed to be developing an intriguing new plan that would help the NAC raise some of its own funds, Beatty later recalled.[64]

With the prospect of a vast array of television channels made possible through the use of satellite-to-cable technology, the Canadian cultural bureaucracy focused on ways to guarantee the survival of Canadian content in this new "100-channel universe." Many Canadian broadcasters challenged by the technology voiced fears of "death stars" that would rain hundreds of foreign channels down on unsuspecting viewers in competition with their own signals. Other officials, such as Keith Spicer, the chairman of the CRTC, embraced the new world order. "One realistic method for dealing with this competitive threat for our Canadian system is to offer more distinctively Canadian alternatives," he told a Commons committee. "In a marketplace where positioning is key, offering unique, high-quality Canadian content is not a burden; it is a marketing advantage."[65] Everything seemed to dovetail with DesRochers's plan to reach out to a national audience through "conventional and alternate television programming," as the Hendry Report had put it in 1986.

By August 1992 the Arts Centre had prepared a detailed working paper to present its idea for TV Canada. It assumed a network that would have national coverage, be ad free, and an obligatory part of the basic cable. It would consist of two services, one in English and the other in French. Given that much of the performing arts product was "linguistically neutral,"[66] the assumption was made that much of the same product would appear on both services.

The CRTC began to pave the way for the process that would lead to the new specialty channels by announcing hearings on structural change to the television industry on September 3, 1992. The NAC trustees had "resolved that the management of the

National Arts Centre proceed with the necessary development for proper intervention to the CRTC on TV Canada,"[67] and a working paper was circulated to a wide range of interested parties invited to be part of an NAC Working Group. They included not only board members but others such as Francis Fox, the former communications minister; Francis Macerola, the former head of the National Film Board; and Nini Baird, a member of the Hendry Task Force who now was programming director for British Columbia's Knowledge Network. David Langer, Peter Herrndorf (now chairman of TV Ontario), and W. Paterson Ferns (president of Primedia Productions Limited) were also invited to be part of the group.

In the fall of 1992 Landry and DesRochers sought and received legal advice that they were on sound ground in terms of the NAC's legal mandate in pursuing a television licence. Three prestigious Canadian law firms—Stikeman Elliott, Martineau Walker, and Gowling, Strathy and Henderson—gave considered opinions that, so long as the service was structured correctly, it was possible for the NAC to proceed under its existing act. On March 18, 1993, DesRochers, accompanied by David Langer, made an intervention at the first round of CRTC hearings in support of the new specialty channels. Officials within the Communications ministry did not intervene in any way, either to offer potential financial help to DesRochers or to discourage his plans. Rather, they kept a close watching brief on developments, as if waiting to see who would be the successful contender for the arts channel licence.

Within the NAC boardroom, however, a fierce quarrel had begun, especially between DesRochers and CBC president Gérard Veilleux who saw the NAC proposal as a clear broadcast challenge to the public broadcaster. Landry later claimed that the NAC had tried to collaborate with the CBC, but that these efforts "had gone nowhere."[68] Veilleux, also known for his quick temper, was particularly upset at what he described as DesRochers's "bullying the board all the time." He was also concerned about the diversion of funds from the NAC budget into the TV project. He considered the whole enterprise, whoever undertook it, lacking in a sound business plan. It was "stupid, costly, potentially ruinous," he said, and the Arts Centre was "beyond its mandate and spending money not authorized by Parliament."[69] He did, however, ask his officials to try to find a way that the NAC and the CBC could work together on a proposal. Besieged by other problems at the CBC, he decided to boycott the NAC board meetings himself, convinced that he could make no headway with the headstrong DesRochers and adamant that he was wasting his time.

When word of DesRochers's high-handed approach to staff and trustees reached Minister Beatty, he called Landry to his office and asked him to rein in the NAC chief executive. Landry listened politely but made it clear that the trustees had already agreed to renew DesRochers's contract for another five years—a decision over which the minister had no control. All the while the Arts Centre continued along the critical path of its strategic plan for the licence application—analyzing artistic data, devising programming alliances, developing a support campaign with the help of the working group, and generally preparing its formal CRTC application for the public licence hearings expected in early 1994. Veilleux, although absenting himself from NAC board meetings, made sure that senior officials at Treasury Board, the Department of Communications, and the Privy Council Office were aware of his opposition to the NAC's pursuit of a television licence.

In April 1993 the NAC received a first warning that, despite the legal opinions it had obtained, Denis Desautels, the auditor general, intended, in his report on the Arts Centre, to come out against the NAC's plan as being contrary to its mandate. This opinion was critical, and Landry went personally to meet with Desnautels. But the auditor general had formed his own idea and was not to be shaken from it. His contrary view, when it was formally issued, seriously affected the thinking of the trustees and eventually the final outcome. The CBC's late involvement in another application for a specialty arts channel, called Festival and chaired by the distinguished dancer, choreographer, and independent producer Veronica Tennant, introduced more complexity into the quest for an arts channel.[70]

The end of 1992 had brought more bad financial news to the Arts Centre. It received word from Treasury Board that the operating budgets of all the cultural corporations would be permanently reduced by 3 percent in the coming year—the result of an economic statement by the minister of finance in the House of Commons on December 2. Everything else was frozen or reduced by up to 10 percent. The government's stated aim was to reduce its operating costs by over a billion dollars, rising to $1.7 billion by 1994–95. The Treasury Board missive acknowledged that the reductions would lead to a deterioration of service at all levels of the public service. This information was soon followed by another announcement in April 1993, this one declaring that government restructuring would take a further $3 billion out of government operating costs. The constant hits made financial planning impossible in a volatile arts institution where artists had to be booked sometimes years in advance.

In the new year, the NAC trustees continued to cast about for other ways to raise money. The idea of a gambling casino was considered for a while, then dropped as being not feasible under the mandate. Early 1993 also brought the news that Robert Lepage was resigning at the end of his three-year contract. He would create one modest last production for the Arts Centre, the bilingual play *National Capital/Capitale nationale,* co-written by francophone Jean-Marc Dalpé and anglophone Vivian Laxdal and performed in the Studio. All about Ottawa, it had some clever and interesting visual effects but received lukewarm reviews. Its opening night coincided with the televised Youth Awards in the NAC Opera—the event of choice that evening for both the chairman and the director general.

Despite the pressures weighing down on him, DesRochers remained fully focused on the television licence for what was now renamed the "Performing Arts Network." In his reports to the board through the spring, he was able to confirm a growing group of outside supporters. In the face of the new cuts, he now proposed a radical restructuring of NAC management, cutting senior management from nine to three people, among them a single director for programming and operations, and a director of commercial activity who would handle all the revenue-generating efforts. About forty more permanent staff positions were scheduled for elimination. In programming, the number of concert series would be reduced and some musical activities moved off the Opera stage to smaller venues to make room for revenue-generating shows. The traditional dance and theatre seasons were to disappear, to be replaced by block programming in the spring and fall with a more interdisciplinary approach.

Overall, the plans were a rationale for an untenable situation, but obvious unease crept into the board's observations. The vice-chair, Madeleine Panaccio, had already registered her reservations over the plan for the Performing Arts Network, expressing grave concerns about any further reduction of programming. Other board members shared her concerns. As a changeover in board members began to occur, the board split into factions—a development that would have a decisive influence in the months to come. Although Minister Beatty had no say in the choice of the CEO, he could influence appointments to the board. He was now firmly opposed to the NAC's drive for a TV licence and began to add trustees who had some understanding of his views. Nevertheless, DesRochers announced a new strategic plan and continued to solicit supporters for the Performing Arts Network. The plans called for it to be a wholly owned subsidiary of the NAC, and DesRochers began to send out invitations to prospective board members for it. Pat Ferns would chair the board, and others were approached to become directors.

In September, after winning board support for his restructuring plans, DesRochers announced them to NAC staff. While trying to put a bold face on the announcement, he informed them that more extensive layoffs were coming and pointed out that an estimated $1.6 million was disappearing permanently from the NAC's budget. The accumulative effect of all the government cuts would be approximately $4.9 million in the coming four years. When asked why he would be laying off so many more staff, DesRochers told the press, "We have decided to take the brunt of this total cut early."[71]

The accumulative effect of all these reductions and changes plunged the NAC further into the vortex. DesRochers wistfully told Jay Stone of the *Ottawa Citizen:* "Once you've done the major reform that was needed in this institution, you would expect to get in return better recognition for your efforts,"[72] but his own impatient, often angry management style stressed matters. Despite the loyalty that senior staff had shown him through all the difficult times, events were about to reach their limit. Financial officer Richard Lussier, who had generally got along with DesRochers and been willing to carry out his orders, was becoming disillusioned by DesRochers's autocratic treatment of both the staff and the board. Consistent with his personality, DesRochers had acquired a strong proprietary sense of the NAC. "It was *his* art centre," Lussier recalled.[73]

A single moment stood out. On the evening of October 3, 1993, the French-language leadership debate was broadcast live from the NAC Theatre, just days before the October 1993 federal election. There were strict orders that no one other than CBC technical staff and the participants would be allowed into the Theatre during the debate. DesRochers refused to accept that this order applied to him and, when he was prevented from entering, he raged in public at his own box-office manager, who had no control over the situation. Lussier and other senior staff witnessed this incident. In that instant, Lussier resolved that, for the sake of the NAC, DesRochers had to go.

From his financial contacts within the government, Lussier knew that the NAC would get no further help as long as DesRochers was at the helm. Despite the risk to his own position, he talked the situation over with Jack Mills, who was effectively DesRochers's number two man, and they decided to contact selected members of the board who they believed would be sympathetic. They were correct. Slowly the players worked to piece together a common front of trustees who would force DesRochers's departure. A secret meeting of board members was arranged in Montreal approximately a month later. Robert Landry was not aware of the gathering, but Lussier and Mills drove down and were subjected to intense cross-questioning by the assembled trustees. After an extended period of discussion while the two men waited outside, the door finally opened and they were informed of the decision to remove the director general. Careful planning ensued in the following weeks in preparation for the board's next full meeting on January 14, 1994. In the meantime, DesRochers continued to move energetically ahead with his television plans, preparing for the CRTC public meetings that were to begin on February 14, 1994.

As the board members gathered on January 14, Vice-Chair Madeleine Panaccio asked Chairman Robert Landry to take the meeting "in camera." With a majority in favour, Landry complied, although he had no idea of the reason for the request. Senior personnel were asked to withdraw, including DesRochers, who was annoyed because he allegedly had the right in his contract to be present during policy discussions of the board and believed they were going to discuss his television plans. Landry protested that they were not giving DesRochers a chance to speak to the matter, and at least one other ex-officio trustee who was relatively new to the board, Yves Ducharme, the mayor of Hull, agreed. "It was a slaughter!" he would later recall. "The guy didn't get a chance to defend himself."[74]

Lussier and Mills had made careful preparations for the *putsch*. A locksmith was standing by to change the locks on DesRochers's office; his car and driver were waiting for his departure from the building. The anxious Lussier, overcome with stress, absented himself from his own office, leaving orders with his secretary to call him if he was needed. A little more than an hour later, Landry and Panaccio left the meeting, met with DesRochers in his office, and secured his resignation. He was immediately escorted from the building. At noon a staff meeting was held in the NAC Salon to announce that DesRochers had departed and that Jack Mills had been appointed acting director general of the Arts Centre. The DesRochers era was over.

DesRochers was gone, but the TV initiative was not yet dead. In a rear-guard action designed to save the project, Landry sent a long and detailed letter on January 27, 1994, to the new Liberal minister responsible for culture, Michel Dupuy—a cultured and well-respected former diplomat who was now head of a newly named Department of Canadian Heritage.* The letter summarized the television licence application from the NAC's point of view. Landry told Dupuy that, the previous June, deputy minister of communications, Marc Rochon had written "an alert" to the NAC that, "on the 'basis of preliminary discussions' with the Department of Justice, a broadcast undertaking by the NAC in the form of a satellite to cable service for the performing arts would most likely be legally problematic." A change of heart had occurred at the government level towards the NAC initiative. The actual legal opinion from the Department of Justice did not arrive at the NAC until November 18, 1993. Landry stated that the NAC had "taken this signal very seriously" and it had asked for a supplementary legal opinion from its own lawyers.[75] They had concluded, wrote Landry, that "it was within our mandate to proceed with the NAC-sponsored application to the CRTC."[76]

Landry also cited another letter that had arrived at the NAC on July 27, 1993, this one from the chairman of the CBC, Patrick Watson. With just seven weeks to go before the deadline for submissions to the CRTC, Watson was proposing a collaborative CBC-NAC effort for a licence. A number of meetings at the highest levels between the two organizations had ensued, but the NAC had balked. It was offered a seat on the board of the CBC-sponsored project, Festival, if it would drop its own proposal, but CBC officials had refused to reveal details of the Festival plan to the NAC brass "for competitive reasons." Landry defended the NAC's position. "We were being asked to drop

---

*A Liberal government under Prime Minister Jean Chrétien had been returned to power in the election of October 1993. The previous Conservative government of Kim Campbell, in its measures to streamline the public service, had rearranged all the old Secretary of State files from parks to culture into one ministry: the Department of Canadian Heritage. Chrétien did not change this model—nor the name.

a very strong project, developed over a long period time with extraordinary support and assistance from the artistic and educational community across Canada, for a secret CBC plan only then being hastily developed."[77] With no resolution between the two national cultural organizations, the NAC filed its Arts Network/Le Reseau des Arts application as planned in September to meet the CRTC deadline. The other bombshell for the board's Audit Committee in November was the auditor general's formal opinion that the NAC was beyond its mandated powers in applying for a television licence. This opinion was received in letter form at the Arts Centre on January 6, 1994, four months after the CRTC filing.

The infighting between the NAC and the CBC over an arts programming licence was being monitored in the small tightly knit Canadian arts community. If the channel was designed to provide long-term funding and exposure for Canada's creative community, many feared that the squabbles between the two main cultural agencies would put the whole enterprise on the rocks. The distinguished Louis Applebaum personally wrote to Dupuy on December 20, 1993, copying both chairs, Landry and Watson. "We need such a channel now," the experienced Applebaum told the minister. "Canadian audiences, performers and creators need that outlet." He deplored the fact that "two agencies within your ministry" were competing with each other for the same project, both using scarce taxpayer dollars intended for the arts, and he urged the minister to help find a resolution to this "preposterous and self-defeating" situation. Applebaum's stated fear was that, unless the two organizations could merge their ambitions, the CRTC might respond by saying "a plague on both your houses" and give the licence to someone else.[78]

The guard had changed suddenly at the top of both cultural organizations. Not only was DesRochers gone but Veilleux had abruptly resigned from the CBC at the end of October 1993. After a thirty-five-year career that had taken him to the top of the public service, he accepted a post in private business with Power Corporation. CBC vice-president Anthony Manera was appointed acting chair and then confirmed in the job by Chrétien on February 3, 1994. These changes in leadership created a more conciliatory atmosphere, and friendlier talks occurred between the CBC and the NAC. Yet neither side would yield in dropping its own application. To his credit, Landry made a forceful case for the merits of the Arts Network application over the CBC concept in his January 27, 1994, letter to the minister. Ever since he became chair of the NAC board in 1989, he had been unwavering in his view that television was the key to the future both for the Arts Centre and for the Canadian arts community.

But time was running out for the centre. While there was talk of some funding from the Department of Canadian Heritage if either public organization won the licence, there were no money guarantees as required in the application. Strenuous efforts were made to secure regular bank loans, with some success. The Hong Kong Bank turned the Arts Network project down, but the Bank of Montreal indicated that it was ready to support it, providing the loan was guaranteed both by the National Arts Centre and by the Government of Canada. The NAC and the Arts Network team scrambled to keep the process going, but as the February public hearings came and went, it was evident that it could not be sustained.

By late April, deputy minister Marc Rochon wrote again to the NAC, this time in a lukewarm letter suggesting that the department might offer financial support if either the CBC or the NAC got the license, but indicated that it was up to the CRTC to make the decision. On June 6 the CRTC finally awarded a license for an arts specialty channel. It went to Bravo!, controlled by privately owned CHUM Limited. As Applebaum had feared, the chance to have a publicly funded arts channel that would support Canada's arts had been lost. The ungranted licence application, David Langer estimated in a memo to his bosses, had cost the NAC approximately $455,000 in "risk capital" over a thirty-month period.[79]

In July, Robert Landry resigned as chair of the NAC board, even though there was still a year to go on his term. His verdict on his years in that position was "disappointment—perhaps at not being able to manage the board better nor managing DesRochers as well as I should have." His mostly positive opinion of DesRochers remained intact. "He was highly principled, worked very hard, kept his eye on the ball; but the personal relationships which can sometimes, or most times, help get thing done were not his strength."[80] Robert Lepage summed up DesRochers's years in more Shakespearean terms: "He was acting like Macbeth. He was the best-intended man in the world at the beginning of the play—really sincere, generous-hearted, very strong person. But fighting the wrong people, fighting the wrong wars, really thinking he was bringing good stuff to the National Arts Centre. And the means, the kind of wars he fought, and the decisions he took, isolated him. He was in that fortress alone, and they had to send people to undo the door and take him out. That is Macbeth."[81]

Many agreed that those years at the Arts Centre were a sad, even tragic, tale.

Part Three
THE RENAISSANCE

Previous Page:
President and CEO Peter Herrndorf
reinvented Hamilton Southam's Arts
Centre to adapt it to the modern age.
Photo © V. Tony Hauser.

16

STUMBLING FORWARD

By the end of the DesRochers era, the overall impression in the country was that, with the exception of the orchestra, creative work had ground to a halt at the National Arts Centre. This was not quite true. The tenacious theatre producer Andis Celms continued to eke out what he could for the Theatre Department through clever co-productions and innovative use of the theatre spaces—the Theatre, the Studio, and the off-site Atelier. The period was marked by the first major work by an aboriginal writer produced on the mainstage at the Arts Centre—Tomson Highway's *Dry Lips Oughta Move to Kapuskasing*, a "co-pro" with Toronto impresario David Mirvish.

The controversial show—which featured some searing content and garnered lots of complaints to the NAC box office—had first been performed at Theatre Passe Muraille in Toronto and showed just how the NAC could take up a new Canadian work and assist it to become a larger-scale production. Working with the Mirvish Corporation, the Arts Centre developed an expanded version of the play, which began its run on the NAC's main stage before going back to the Royal Alexandra Theatre in Toronto. It featured a number of young native actors who would go on to major careers in Canada—Graham Greene* and Tom Jackson, for instance. Celms also commissioned other new Canadian plays, even more than the NAC had encouraged in the earlier 1980s. While many of these plays did not get beyond the workshop stage, the Arts Centre still showed leadership in developing many Canadian dramatists. "Page to Stage" was one series that showcased new work in the small and barebones facilities of the Atelier, where so much of the creative work in theatre took place.

---

*Greene would eventually receive an Oscar nomination for his role in the Academy Award–winning American film *Dances with Wolves*.

The Atelier was also an excellent venue in which actors from the local community could perform. Victoria Steele, the Theatre Department's administrator (and subsequently managing director), recalled that it became the first home for a serious theatre school in the city, the Ottawa School of Speech and Drama. When Nathalie Stern, its founder, approached the Arts Centre for help, Celms had no money to give the budding enterprise, but he offered her space in the Atelier. On the French theatre side, too, this eighty-seven-seat intimate theatre was the venue for ARTO—the Atelier de Recherche Théâtre Ottawa—which Robert Lepage established during his three-year tenure as artistic director. "I couldn't believe how brilliant his work was, on a shoe-string, in this tiny little space," Steele recalled. Like her theatre colleagues from the Wood era forward, she characterized the Atelier as "a wonderful place for the creation and exploration of work in English and French for older and younger audiences. It had never been an IATSE venue, so we had more flexibility. It was away from what we called 'the Big House,' with all its restrictions of times and rules."[1]

In music, Trevor Pinnock continued his role as music director with due diligence. With the uproar over DesRochers's departure, however, he felt he had to step away from the position because, he said, "in all honesty I could no longer fulfill the role of music director, but they needed two more years to sort things out."[2] He agreed to stay on during this turbulent period to maintain stability for the Music Department but assumed the title of music adviser and conductor instead. As both a participant in and an observer of the troubled times, he was in a position to give insightful advice, and he did so, as both a new director general and then a new chair of the board were appointed to the NAC.

The DesRochers debacle left the fate of the Arts Centre in serious doubt. Many in officialdom, including members of the new and restructured Heritage Department,[3] tilted towards putting the organization out of its misery and acting on the recommendation in the 1986 Nielsen Task Force report: to privatize the operations of the Arts Centre and turn the building over to the National Capital Commission.* The NAC operation was even shopped around in the commercial theatre world. David Mirvish was among those approached: "I thought it was the most ludicrous idea imaginable," he said. "There was no way to make it financially viable. There are many good reasons for the NAC, but they are all non-financial."[4] Before anything happened, the change of government in Ottawa brought a reprieve.

The minister named to head Canadian Heritage after the Liberal victory in October 1993 was Michel Dupuy, an experienced career diplomat who had taken one previous

---

*The NCC administered and maintained many federal buildings in Ottawa, from the Houses of Parliament to the Governor General's residence at Rideau Hall.

Former diplomat and foreign policy adviser to Jean Chrétien, Michel Dupuy became the new culture minister with the return of the Liberal government in 1993. Photo © John Major/ Ottawa Citizen. Reprinted by permission.

unsuccessful run for public office. He had been close to the new prime minister, Jean Chrétien, for many years, serving as his foreign policy adviser when Chrétien was leader of the Opposition. Now the Liberals were in office, he expected that he might be made foreign minister, but Chrétien gave that plum post to another long-time colleague, André Ouellette. Dupuy accepted Canadian Heritage, a ministry he later described as "a hodge-podge of files." He found himself dealing "not only with broadcasting but all the cultural agencies and programs. They were all agencies full of problems!" The short-lived Campbell Conservative government had split up the Communications Department, separating the technological delivery systems from cultural content. In Dupuy's view, this division was a fundamental mistake. He believed that the telecommunications sector "created pots of gold," and that some of this gold was needed to subsidize content. He was emphatic that "from a cultural point of view, content had to be subsidized."[5] It was the same view Southam had espoused in the NAC annual report twenty-five years before.

Once in office, Chrétien and his finance minister, Paul Martin, quickly realized they were confronting a financial brick wall, and they called for a new round of drastic budget cuts to attack the country's huge deficit. They received kudos for their action and managed to sidestep much of the flak by "leaving each Cabinet minister the dirty job of choosing what to cut in each department." Dupuy recalled. He had the misfortune to have within his department "the greatest number of subsidy programs of any department in government. There were small subsidies everywhere!" As he chopped away, he found himself alienating would-be supporters in almost every sector. "For example," he recalled, "when I made cuts to programs under the *Official Languages Act*, I lost the whole constituency."[6] The arts sector was no different.

When it came to culture, the problem in Dupuy's mind lay with the Constitution, where "the dividing line over what constitutes culture and what education (a provincial matter) is not clear." He had received early indoctrination in federal subsidy to the arts when, as a young public servant in the Privy Council Office, he worked with his senior colleague, Peter Dwyer, to draft the Canada Council legislation. Dupuy believed in the importance of culture in national life, but, in contrast to Prime Ministers Pearson and Trudeau, he felt that Chrétien was unsympathetic to it. Chrétien was certainly lukewarm about the CBC, which many Quebec federalists viewed as "being staffed by separatist artists."[7] Whatever the details, he had few of the essential "friends at court" he needed for support.

According to Dupuy, the Tories had already done much of the groundwork towards privatizing the CBC and other cultural agencies, including the National Arts Centre. Although Dupuy did not have the full support of the prime minister, he made it clear immediately that any move towards privatization would trigger his resignation. The Cabinet accepted his stand, but, in return, he was required to make deep cuts in the budgets of these national cultural crown corporations. Dupuy came to office in the last days of Yvon DesRochers's term. Marc Rochon, his deputy minister, enlightened him about the perceived illegality of the television initiative and all the internal feuding. With vacancies coming up on the board of trustees, Dupuy decided to clean house. "We had to get rid of the bellicose members and put in some new faces," he said. His personal dealings with DesRochers had been "correct, even pleasant," though he had told the director general that "there was no money for the foreseeable future for television."[8]

With DesRochers and Landry gone, Dupuy had to find both a new chair and a new CEO, even though the latter position was not officially in his gift. Nevertheless, he summoned an old Liberal friend to Ottawa, Joan Pennefather, the Canadian film commissioner at the National Film Board, and she agreed to allow her name to go forward for the top NAC management job. Her close connections with the Liberal hierarchy* ensured that she would be well considered for any senior position. Dupuy thought of proposing the long-time NAC loyalist and former Liberal finance minister Mitchell Sharp, now in his late eighties, for the chairmanship. Appointed as a $1-a-year adviser by Chrétien, the older politician would have liked the job, but when Dupuy informally approached the prime minister, the idea was scotched. "Sharp was Chrétien's soul and memory," Dupuy said later, hypothesizing that Chrétien wanted to keep the elderly Sharp by his side.[9]

Former NFB commissioner and well connected to the Liberal Party, Joan Pennefather was appointed NAC CEO in December 1994. Photo © Vero Boncompagni.

---

*Pennefather had once been married to former communications minister, now Senator Francis Fox.

While Jack Mills served as the NAC's acting director general in the intervening months, Joan Pennefather was selected and appointed CEO by the board of trustees on December 19, 1994, over four other candidates. Three months later Jean Thérèse Riley, a passionate arts supporter and the granddaughter of former Liberal Prime Minister Louis St. Laurent, was named chair of the board of trustees. Dupuy met her in a brief formal meeting just before the announcement—one of many such appointments he made at the time. When the subject of initiating some private fundraising was broached, Dupuy encouraged it, advising that "the Canadian Treasury would not be providing any more money." When badly needed repairs to the building were raised, he cautioned the trustees "to be careful about getting into real estate."* With the most immediate problems facing the Arts Centre seemingly settled, he turned his attention to other issues.

The two women now named to head up the National Arts Centre were both viewed as dynamic movers and shakers, though personally they were a study in contrasts. "John Godfrey [a Toronto Liberal MP] said we were like the white swan and the black swan," Riley laughingly recalled. "We were exactly the same age. She was as blond as I was dark, then. We liked each other." In Riley's view, her CEO represented the "consummate bureaucrat." She admired Pennefather's "kind of brainy ease with the authority that went with the job." While Riley had served on a number of arts boards, she had no experience of Ottawa or its bureaucracy, and, in any case, saw herself as "someone creative and risk-taking, someone who would have made a very bad bureaucrat."[10]

By the time Riley arrived at the centre in late April 1995, Pennefather had been in the executive suite for several months. Immediately, she set to work to mend the dysfunctional operations and broken morale of the place. "I did not know the depth of the tremendous turmoil going on

Jean Riley became the new NAC chair in March 1995. A passionate arts supporter, she was also Prime Minister Louis St. Laurent's granddaughter. Photo © Bruno Schlumberger/ Ottawa Citizen. Reprinted by permission.

---

*What Dupuy did not grasp in the short meeting was that the NAC Corporation did not yet have title to its building and, therefore, had no money for capital repairs—and could not initiate them on its own.

inside the organization," she recalled, even though as film commissioner she had been serving as an ex-officio member of the board. "I had enough experience under my belt arguing the case for public institutions at a time when that was being challenged," she said confidently. "It would offer me an opportunity to do something that I felt strongly about." She was also aware that she was moving away from films and television to the live performing arts: "I needed to know I had a no. 2 who really knew that score," she added. To that end, she soon recruited a former NAC employee, Joanne Morrow. She arranged meetings with the staff in large and small groups, and in intimate one-on-one sessions, and gradually she shored up confidence and won the staff's support. These encounters also allowed her to glean ideas, some of which had been around for awhile, and work out the possible opportunities that lay ahead. She had a clear sense of the need to move fast to re-establish the NAC in the eyes of both the Ottawa public and the politicians as "a meritorious national institution worthy of taxpayers' money."[11] Her plan for the future was well under way by the time Jean Riley came to town.

Pennefather claimed some credit for Riley's appointment. Her name had been suggested to Pennefather by one of the trustees, a Mulroney-appointed Montreal lawyer, George MacLaren, whose friendships extended beyond party lines.[12] Pennefather passed it on to the government's appointments secretary, Penny Collenette. In a government keen to appoint women to top jobs (but only after careful screening by both Mitchell Sharp and Jean Pelletier, the prime minister's chief of staff),[13] the appointment flew through the process and was announced on April 25, 1995.

While he was interim director general, Mills had been forced to work through the government's plan for deficit reduction, euphemistically called "Program Review," and had also been called upon to cooperate with a Department of Canadian Heritage special study "to privatize and fully commercialize" the centre.[14] The question became what parts of the NAC could be privatized? The concept was held partially at bay with the help of trustee George MacLaren, who insisted that privatization was a matter of public policy and could not be undertaken by the ministry without parliamentary approval.

Before the Riley appointment was announced, Pennefather was informed that a further 31 percent cut would be made in the NAC's operating budget—one of the highest cuts in the government, and well beyond the 15 percent the new CEO had anticipated. It was the eleventh cut to the NAC budget in just four years. Inevitably it would lead to radical restructuring within the centre as Pennefather moved to reduce staff and to reorganize internal workings. Many employees, including the senior financial officer, Richard Lussier, took the buyout packages that the government was offering in this downsizing exercise. Jack Mills moved sideways to be in charge of operations, a task that included overseeing the NAC's finances as well as the physical aspects of the building. It would not be a happy move. Still, in her first six months, Pennefather worked hard to devise a new strategic plan, and her approach began to win some public praise: "An experienced cultural bureaucrat, with a sunny demeanor, forthright style and a democratic approach that so far has earned her considerable goodwill," opined columnist Susan Riley in the *Ottawa Citizen*.[15]

While management matters continued to churn, the daily demands of the three performance spaces continued apace. The adept Andis Celms managed to book in a series of "one- and two-hander shows" that minimized costs of production but still brought plays of high quality to the arts centre.[16] Among them was David Mamet's *Oleanna*, directed by Martha Henry and featuring the brilliant young Ottawa actress Sandra Oh and veteran actor Rod Beattie in this play about sexual abuse.[17] There were also sell-out performances of a one-man show by Newfoundland comedian Rick Mercer, and a new show by playwright/performer Sandra Shamas, *Wedding Bell Hell*. French theatre continued in a generally workmanlike fashion. One of the highlights of the year, however, was Les Quinze Jours de la Dramaturgie des Régions—a series that welcomed francophone theatre groups from all over the country in May.

For the orchestra, a long-planned, seven-country, fifteen-city European tour from February 21 to March 12, 1995, under Trevor Pinnock's baton, gave the musicians a much welcomed lift. The tour was all about "musical ambassadorship," Pinnock told the press on the eve of their departure to the first concert in Vienna. He emphasized the special prestige of the orchestra, appearing in some of the finest concert halls in Europe and "demonstrating this country's artistic excellence abroad." The orchestra's management added that tours of this calibre usually led to higher fees and more and better recording contracts. The cost of the tour was not made public, but the Arts Centre contributed close to $400,000

Then-rising young actress Sandra Oh and actor Rod Beattie appeared in a searing production of David Mamet's Oleanna in 1995. Photo © Cylla von Tiedemann.

and the Department of External Affairs, $200,000. Performance fees took care of the rest. The well-oiled machinery moving the forty-six musicians and their instruments around Europe worked smoothly, and the concerts generally received top reviews everywhere they were presented, from Salzburg to London. The whole experience was an emotional boost for the musicians, and Pinnock recalled the tour as a highlight: "The playing of the music was outstanding," he said. "Away from the centre we could concentrate on music and functioning as a team."[18]

The tour included the NAC Orchestra's first ever concert in Paris, where the musicians were warned that the audience could be "cold." It was a delight, then, when Parisians, and in particular French cultural officials, pronounced themselves amazed to discover such a "well-honed instrument."[19] Both Joan Pennefather and Hamilton Southam, now resident in France, were in the audience to soak up the praise. These performances would be Pinnock's last on tour with the musicians, as his term at the NAC was drawing to a close.

The refreshed spirit around the Arts Centre emboldened the artistic directors. Andis Celms in English theatre, Jean-Claude Marcus in French theatre (a long-time member of the Theatre Department who now stepped in after Lepage's departure), and Jack Udashkin in dance all announced their seasons for the following year. Celms clearly

felt a fresh breeze and selected more classics with bigger casts in his choice of plays. Following *Oleanna*'s success, he decided to open the following year with another controversial work, the American play *Keely and Du* on the subject of abortion, to be presented as a co-production with the Manitoba Theatre Centre. He also proposed to end the season with a colourful and large-scale version of Edmond Rostand's *Cyrano de Bergerac*, using a translation by Anthony Burgess and starring the well-known Canadian actor R.H. Thomson. Twenty-seven actors were planned for the cast ("More than *Kiss of the Spider Woman*," Celms laughed),[20] and he organized a three-way

In 1996 R.H. Thomson played the title role in Edmond Rostand's Cyrano de Bergerac *for the first time. Photo © Trudie Lee, Calgary.*

Quebec actor Guy Nadon played the title role in Cyrano de Bergerac *in the French theatre season in 1997 and won an award for his portrayal. Photo © Jean-François Bérubé. Courtesy of Théâtre du Nouveau Monde.*

co-production, this time with Theatre Calgary and the Manitoba Theatre Centre, to make it possible.

Marcus announced his next French season a couple of weeks later. It was designed to please all tastes, with a mix of classic and contemporary drama ranging from Molière to Roch Carrier. He also scheduled *Cyrano* into the French season, starring francophone actor Guy Nadon in an NAC/Théâtre du Nouveau Monde co-production; Nadon later won a top French theatre prize for the role.

There was even news of a mini-festival for the summer, featuring a combination of new music, performances by classical pianist Angela Hewitt and violinist James Ehnes, and more light-hearted fare from soprano Mary Lou Fallis, whose spoofs of opera had already proved a hit. A free concert was planned to celebrate the seventieth birthday of composer Harry Somers, and an Ottawa presentation of Benjamin Britten's *Noye's Fludde* was scheduled in Christ Church Cathedral. This piece, featuring the Toronto Symphony Youth Orchestra and a chorus of eighty children, was part of Canada's celebration of the fiftieth anniversary of the United Nations. It was to be conducted by the venerable but still hugely energetic Nicholas Goldschmidt, with the peripatetic Mavor Moore playing the Voice of God. As spring approached, fresh air indeed seemed to be blowing through the NAC.

While the orchestra was out of the country, the NAC was the site for an Ottawa pre-budget rally of arts groups from across the country gathered to protest the impending budget cuts. Representatives from fifty-two national organizations reflected a militant mood among artists: they brandished statistics showing that more than 660,000 Canadians worked in what were now called the cultural industries, and that they had generated $24 billion of economic activity in 1992–93. With the free-trade agreement now in place, they attacked American intrusion into Canadian cultural activity. It was "American cultural hooliganism," declared Keith Kelly, executive director of the Canadian Conference of the Arts, the national arts lobby.[21] Liberal politicians at

the rally included Liberal culture critic John Godfrey and the newly appointed senator, actor Jean-Louis Roux, and they defended the government, citing its policies on
Sports Illustrated and other split-run editions of magazines. The defence cut little ice
with the delegates. Word that the government's program review intended to delete
nearly seven hundred positions from the patronage appointments list did not help,
especially when it was learned that the Liberals also wanted to amend the *National Arts
Centre Act* so it would appoint the CEO directly and not have to rely on the board of
trustees. Although this proposal eventually failed, it was symptomatic of the constant
desire by ministers to exercise more control over an organization they had to answer
for in the House of Commons.

In retrospect, Jean Riley said that she came to Ottawa with an idealized notion of
public service that had been instilled in her from childhood by memories of her grand-
father. In her first days there she used a battered old leather briefcase that had
belonged to Prime Minister Louis St. Laurent. She later realized that her early expectations had been wrong, even naïve. On her first visit to the NAC at the beginning of
May, she walked around the building and introduced herself. "I was shocked at how
isolated I thought it was when I first went into the building," she remembered. "It was
so dark and complicated architecturally, and people were so … I won't say obsequious,
but there seemed to be rituals to everything and a huge amount of protocol and not
a lot of real exchange."[22] She was used to working with smaller arts groups that were
urgently trying to raise money, and she felt that the audience in Ottawa "was completely disconnected. There was a huge amount of a kind of snobbery in the air that
made people removed, as opposed to involved and engaged."

While Pennefather concentrated on reorganizing the centre on the inside, Riley
determined to improve relations in the community. She used her network of social
connections for the task, among them her cousin Pat Lafferty, a senior partner in the
management consulting firm Coopers & Lybrand. A civic-minded Ottawan with a
keen interest in the arts, Lafferty was happy to oblige. Riley also began to work up
other contacts in town, among them the publisher of the *Ottawa Citizen*, Russell
Mills. He formed a clear first impression of the new chair: "It seemed to me she was
a very ambitious person. She certainly wanted to make a big splash in the arts."[23] Still,
Mills felt strongly that he should support her. As he said, "The NAC was so important
to Ottawa."

Riley and Pennefather soon became firm accomplices. Pennefather was proud of
the process she had initiated in her first six months. Once Riley arrived, Pennefather
turned to drafting her new strategic plan for the Arts Centre. Adept at Ottawa bureaucratic manoeuvring, she knew that the plan should also please the minister and reassure

him that affairs at the NAC were now in good hands. Critical to her scheme were ideas she had picked up from dance producer Jack Udashkin, who had developed a paper for Yvon DesRochers that proposed to break down the walls between the different disciplines at the centre and integrate their work into multidisciplinary seasons.

The proposal she prepared, with its complete strategic overview of the mandate, the responsibilities with the budget that went with it, and the decisions that had to be made seemed to receive endorsement from the staff. Riley read the plan through carefully and promptly put it on the agenda for the first board meetings she would chair, on June 6, 1995. Ex-officio board member Tony Manera, the new CBC president, had helped Pennefather with its drafting, and the trustees took the view that it was "the only direction, if the NAC was to survive."[24] With little discussion, what would prove an earth-shattering document was approved unanimously by the board. On June 15, 1995, the details were released to the public.

Called *Setting the Stage*, the proposal was filled with motherhood clauses that touched on all that was good about the National Arts Centre. At its core, however, was a proposed radical change in operations that was frequently described as a "bold move" intended to change the structure of the NAC and alter dramatically the way it did business. While the orchestra would remain intact, the separate departments of theatre and dance, even rentals, were to be eliminated. Instead, one overall artistic director would produce and coordinate programming, including two festivals each year, one in the spring and the other in the autumn—a mix of theatre, dance, and music. The regular subscription seasons, historically perceived as the backbone of earned revenues for performing arts centres, and the in-house artistic directors who planned them, would disappear. Shorter special programs, run throughout the year, would replace them. Directors, producers, and other artistic staff would be invited in on a project-by-project basis, and perhaps to organize short series of plays or a mini-dance series. As Pennefather optimistically explained to a CBC interviewer, the Arts Centre, given its $5 to $6 million cut pending, "intends to do more with less."[25] There would inevitably be staff reductions, but she was counting on the buyout programs, designed to downsize the federal government, for help.[26]

Pennefather seemed confident that audiences would perceive the new approach as offering more choice. The 1995–96 season was already subscribed in the traditional fashion, but everything after that would be different. The strategy spoke about the development of young talent, while at the same time calling for more commercial rentals to bring in revenue and fill in the dark nights at the centre. It also showed clearly that the NAC would be turning to the private sector for some of its financing, especially in regard to the festivals and the summer programming. Pennefather put a bright face on the new plan and, although there were some qualms, it was initially well received. Throughout the summer of 1995 she threw herself into its enactment, rearranging her management team.

Andis Celms's career at the arts centre spanned its lifetime. His cool and practical approach protected the theatre and the centre through some of its darkest times. Photo © NAC.

Within the artistic ranks, however, and despite the impression that the staff supported the new plan, there was enormous nervousness and dismay. When Celms first learned of the proposal during the spring, he had argued with Pennefather that "it was totally the wrong way to go for the Arts Centre." They arranged a dinner meeting, where "she faced me with the reality: it was her idea and this was the way she wanted to go." Celms got the message, although it was painful. "I had lived and died for the place, but now I understood what she was saying, which was I didn't belong there anymore," he said.[27] By the time he thought it through, he realized his time at the Arts Centre was ending. He was not surprised to find that the Human Resources department already had a resignation package prepared for him.

The other artistic heads—Jean-Claude Marcus in French theatre and Jack Udashkin in Dance—who barely six weeks before had been announcing their next seasons, also realized that their jobs were finished and that the 1995–96 season would be their last. Although it later emerged that Udashkin knew he was being hired back to run the festivals, partially his own concept, both he and Marcus left the centre, the latter going on medical stress leave. Celms, by now the longest-serving member of the entire senior NAC staff, remained at his post overseeing the last regular season that he had programmed. His own lips sealed about the NAC plan, he attended a PACT conference in Halifax three weeks before the public announcement. Colleagues who saw him there recalled that he revealed nothing about what was coming but had been "grumpy, grumpy, grumpy."[28] Practical and stoic as ever, he watched Pennefather reshuffle the staff, proposing new places for two of his own team: Victoria Steele, the theatre administrator, and Gil Osborne, the associate English theatre artistic director, were both invited to be part of the new administrative group that would come under the control of the incoming director of programming. Interviews for that post were under way by the summer, with Joanne Morrow tagged as the front-runner.

By the September board meetings, Riley had pushed ahead with energy and enthusiasm. She had persuaded Pat Lafferty and Coopers & Lybrand to run a community consultation that included an all-day information session and an elegant dinner for sixty of Ottawa's most prominent arts supporters. She also enticed the firm to sponsor the opening concert of the fall music season. This gesture was intended to be exemplary to others, as well as an opportunity to showcase Coopers & Lybrand and thank them for their help. With Riley and Pennefather seeming to move smoothly in step, the evening of September 20, 1995, was a return to some of the NAC's former glamour. The prime minister was in the audience, the famed Beauchemin curtain was lowered and raised for the evening ("a technical feat in itself"),[29] and both Pinnock and the orchestra were in fine form. A search committee to replace Pinnock had been launched, with Mitchell Sharp again among its key members. Ben Heppner had been named as winner of the 1995 NAC Award at the upcoming Governor General's Performing Arts Awards, and a surge of energy seemed to be flowing again through the centre. Sadly, within two months, the NAC world, at least with regard to its management, would turn upside down again.

By the November board meetings, a shocking reversal was again in progress. Riley had attended the awards, and she reported back to the board her outrage and dismay at their lavish expense. (She would later acknowledge a concern for the public purse that could border on zealotry.) She was amazed that $271,380 of the million-dollar-plus budget had been financed by the cash-strapped NAC itself, including a $50,000 value for the orchestra and a $150,000 outright donation. She was also annoyed that Sandra Fresco, the awards' competent executive director, occupied a rent-free office at the NAC. The ultimate insult was that both the local and the national press had labelled the event as "lavish and elite,"[30] an image associated with the NAC that it was trying hard to shake. She identified the television broadcast recording of the evening a particular problem, with the NAC shouldering "lots of costs with little control" over the event.[31]

Far more serious, however, was the financial reorganization under way as a result of Pennefather's plan. At the same meetings, Joanne Morrow, who had just taken up her post as senior artistic director, outlined in copious detail the ideas for the future. There seemed to be a lot of loose threads and, despite polite attention from the trustees, many questions still needed answers, especially regarding how the plan would be financed and how quickly it could get in place. Morrow had already expressed reservations about cancelling subscriptions before a clear new financing model had been instituted. The board had established a Finance and Audit Committee, manned by several of the more feisty trustees including businessmen Eric Charman from British Columbia and Larry Brenzel from Toronto. Both energetically engaged in the fine detail of the NAC's financial arrangements. The 1995–96 budget had been approved at the September board meetings with a deficit of over $1.1 million while things were being realigned. The auditor general had insisted that this amount be reduced. NAC managers had made adjustments, but still with alarming results. The financial figures were creeping up again towards a million dollar deficit for 1995–96, with ominous financial indicators emerging for the next two seasons. Board members complained that the deficit they had finally approved had now been altered upwards.

As Pennefather struggled to maintain control, she was blind-sided by the shifting financial figures being supplied to her. The uncertainty of the numbers severely alarmed Riley, and the trust between the two women began rapidly to deteriorate. At the board meetings, the spokesman for finances, Jack Mills, deferred to the executive director. As tempers flared over a "breach in protocol" in the changing budget figures and complaints that the trustees "could not go to Parliament with the numbers," the board's Audit Committee members expressed a loss of confidence in Mills. After intensive wrangling, he would finally part company with the Arts Centre with a settlement under the government's politely named Early Departure Program. In the meantime, Pennefather's situation became more stressed, and her relations worsened with the agitated Riley, who now had several heavyweight board members behind her. A short-term contract Pennefather arranged to assess private fundraising was criticized, and even her own expenses and outside commitments were labelled as "a further breach of trust between the chair and the executive director."[32]

Central to the issue was how the money that usually flowed from the annual subscription campaigns would be maintained under the new model. The traditional seasons were regularly planned and sold almost a year in advance, and there was still no evidence how the new programming model would replace that income. An aggressive board Management Committee consisting of Jean Riley and members of the Audit Committee—Eric Charman, Larry Brenzel, and George MacLaren—demanded a full board/management partnership in the decisions to handle these issues. The aroused trustees tried to cancel a tour by the orchestra to the United States as being too costly, although the director general struggled to point out that it was already 60 percent paid for by sponsors. The tour eventually went ahead in March 1996 with one of the first major private sponsorships—provided by Goldman Sachs—that the NAC would begin to secure. A domestic NAC Orchestra tour to Newfoundland had a worst fate. In what amounted to a direct order from a member of the board's Finance and Audit Committee, Chris Deacon was forced to cancel the trip.

Riley's acute anxiety over the financial figures infected the entire board: "Since the numbers weren't what we were told they were going to be, and the argument for cancelling all the subscription series was built on those numbers, then all of a sudden panic sets in. You start to think if you're not going to have subscription revenue, what are you going to have? You're putting the place in extreme danger," she commented later.[33]

On December 15, 1995, the board took delivery of a widely researched Coopers & Lybrand internal management review conducted with the staff throughout the previous months. The report was highly critical of overall management at the centre, though it identified the senior team in particular as lacking important skills in the planning and communications needed to deal with the challenges. It remarked that the closer one got to the NAC stages, the less dysfunctional were the employees. The report stated that the majority of the staff members were in "a state of suspended animation" while they waited to see what was going to happen next.[34] It was the final blow to Pennefather.

The veteran bureaucrat had never before experienced a loss of confidence of these dimensions. "I assumed confidence. I assumed, bottom line, that I would be more than happy to be corrected if I made a mistake. There was a momentum happening which I could not stop, a momentum to change, to not go ahead with me as the executive director." With hindsight, Pennefather remained optimistic that her plan might have worked if she had been given an extra couple of years. At the time, however, she opted to step away from the struggle with Riley and the trustees. "It was very painful and, at the end, I offered my resignation," she said. It was "graciously accepted"—and immediately she found herself again on good terms with Jean Riley. As she was ushered out the door on December 19, 1995, she recalled, "we clicked again and we were chatting about the next steps."[35] Her term at the National Arts Centre had lasted precisely one year. One day later, the loyal Joanne Morrow also resigned after scarcely two months in her new position.

As she surveyed the scene a few days before Christmas, Riley perceived it as "a real crisis."[36] Who should the board put in Pennefather's place? Riley's first instinct was to give the top position back to Jack Mills, but she was advised against it. Among her counsellors was Trevor Pinnock, who phoned to tell her that it would be best to disassociate the Arts Centre from figures associated with past problems. That left Andis Celms, who had already made up his mind to retire, as the lone member of experienced senior staff on the program side. Riley sat down with Celms on December 22 and discovered first hand that many of the program staff had never supported the cancellation of the subscription series. Calling again for help from Coopers & Lybrand with the management situation, she went home to Toronto for Christmas and, she recalled, "burned the clothes I'd been wearing for seven days."[37] When she returned on January 2, 2006, she named Celms and herself as co-chairs of a Renewal Committee made up of nearly two dozen NAC staff members.

Once again the innate professionalism of the core program staff at the NAC kicked in. The immediate job was to organize the next season, now eight to nine months behind the normal planning cycle. Andis Celms, who was trusted by his artistic team, took charge, and Jean-Claude Marcus returned from his stress leave to book the French theatre season. Celms worked furiously to put the next season in place and, within weeks, he had done it. "I was basically on stream programming the following year," he said, "as well as programming and overseeing my current season." The relieved trustees suggested that he might like to stay on, but Celms knew that "this was not the place I wanted to be any more. I was too old. I had just given too much."[38]

After his one final push to keep the NAC on the rails, the long-serving and highly respected theatre man left the centre in May for a new position in Vancouver, as deputy director of Vancouver Civic Theatres. The departing administrator was belatedly honoured with the M. Joan Chalmers Award for arts administration, a coveted accolade recommended by his peers. Joan Pennefather also found new employment soon after departing the Arts Centre. Like DesRochers before her, she was hired for consulting work with the Department of External Affairs and left for Paris for several months to work on a media project at the Canadian Cultural Centre in the French capital.

The big challenge for Riley and the board now was to find yet another director general. Serious approaches were made to several candidates on an interim basis, including some well-established members of the public service, but no one would touch the job. Simultaneously, the NAC was also searching for an interim financial officer and a new permanent chief financial officer. In this deteriorating situation, Riley rationalized that because she was already giving the Arts Centre a lot of management advice, she might as well step temporarily into the top job herself. Despite clearly articulated concern at the board over the dividing line between governance and management, she moved into the executive director's office in late January 1996.

By late February, the Arts Centre had managed to find someone for one of the most pressing priorities identified in the Coopers & Lybrand report—financial control. Cy Cook, a former accountant who had worked for the National Harbour Commission in Thunder Bay, was hired in the newly created position of chief financial officer.

Another charged matter pinpointed by the Coopers & Lybrand report was the alleged disproportionate place and future role of the orchestra within the National Arts Centre— a perennial problem that each new administration had to address. The study remarked that the orchestra monopolized the use of the Opera hall, effectively blocking it from being used for revenue-generating rental shows. It also noted that the orchestra had a block of unused time, according to its contract, and argued for a more efficient use of its services. These signals quickly mobilized supporters of the orchestra's traditional pre-eminence, although intense board discussions also occurred in the coming weeks over how the NAC Orchestra could be employed more efficiently and how its budget could bear part of the brunt of the cuts—something it had mostly escaped until now. There was even a proposal to reduce the NACO season to forty rather than forty-six weeks. Andis Celms, the acting senior artistic director, grumbled against it, saying that it would be "a business, not an artistic decision."[39] Trevor Pinnock, now artistic adviser, also argued at the board that this move would not serve the orchestra's artistic worth.

As negotiations opened for yet another round of contract talks, these issues were highly sensitive and needed careful handling by NAC management. Christopher

Deacon, who had become orchestra manager, told the trustees that the musicians were expecting a cut in the new contract, but they would far prefer a salary freeze to a cutback in their season. If the proposed salary cutbacks were introduced, the orchestra would still remain in the top three in terms of salaries paid in Canada, although they would drop back from first to third position. In an era where orchestras all over the continent were suffering from freezes and cutbacks, or even folding, the situation could easily have been worse, and this time there was no jealous grumbling from other parts of the country.

The question was simple: How best to maintain the NAC's overall artistic activity, yet give the orchestra as much as it wanted? The matter of five weeks of unused orchestra services was indeed a problem. The approximately sixty-five concerts scheduled each year in Ottawa absorbed the potential audience, but now there was no opera, very little touring, and few other activities to pick up the slack. And this renowned orchestra was loath to see itself as the house band for just any show that performed at the Arts Centre.

Pennefather had opened one other contentious issue in her plan which now came before the board: selling the Atelier. The free-wheeling and experimental work it had housed could just as easily occur in the Studio at the NAC, the argument ran, and the proposal gained even more force when the francophone theatre companies in the region started a campaign to buy it for their own use. The facility had been appraised by the Arts Centre at $150,000 for the downtown Ottawa land and $500,000 for the converted warehouse with all its improvements. At first the trustees summarily dismissed an offer of $250,000 from the francophone theatre group. Then lobbyists for the project went to work and, with the help of local Liberal member of parliament Mauril Bélanger, among others, the board was soon brought around to a more accommodating attitude.

Celms argued that the proposed purchase price was too low, but Riley cautioned the board that it was "a highly political issue."[40] The matter was referred to the board's Executive Committee and, a month later, the French theatre group's offer of $250,000 was accepted. The French theatre community was delighted, and the plan at least accommodated the programs for young people's theatre in French which the NAC had encouraged.

Another suggestion Riley put to the board—that Canada's national anthem be played before performances—was not accepted. Celms explained that it was a sensitive issue both for the orchestra and for French theatre, and the board made a compromise recommendation calling for its playing only on special occasions, such as at gala concerts.

The January to June 1996 season at the NAC still brought its highlights, despite the turmoil. On March 4 the orchestra gave a stellar concert in Avery Fisher Hall at the Lincoln Center in New York. Led by Pinnock and featuring soloist Jon Kimura Parker in Mozart's *Jupiter Symphony*, as well as "Vertige" by the in-house Canadian composer Linda Bouchard, the performance won a warm review from Anthony Tommasini in the *New York Times*. Back at home, the English theatre's *Cyrano de Bergerac* opened in April to rave reviews. R.H. Thomson's portrayal of Cyrano, his first performance in the role, received high praise.

Another unexpected bit of good news arrived with word that a lifelong orchestra subscriber, William Kirkpatrick, had left the Arts Centre $86,000 in his will. Like the first NAC donor, Miss Bouvier, with her $5 gift, Kirkpatrick had been a relatively anonymous figure on the Ottawa scene, serving as an unnoted middle-level civil servant whose last job had been as an assistant in the Department of Defence. His true passion had been music and, on his death, he left not only the bequest to the NAC but an exhaustive collection of classical music records to the School of Music at the Université d'Ottawa. This unexpected gesture cheered the trustees and was, they hoped, a harbinger for the future. The first year's interest of $6,000 on his gift was used to pay for extra musicians for a performance of Mahler's Symphony No. 4, conducted by Franz-Paul Decker.

In the highest echelons of government, Dupuy, after two short years and a couple of serious political pratfalls, was shuffled out of the Cabinet. He was replaced on January 25, 1996, by the outspoken and highly partisan Sheila Copps, whose opening gambit was a loud avowal that she was going "to stand up for culture" and that she intended to harness it to the cause of unity in Canada. While Dupuy had earned a reputation as "the invisible minister," Copps would be the opposite. She was a favourite with Chrétien and he also named her as deputy prime minister. Hopes rose that her views would not go unnoticed.

The most critical item for the NAC trustees remained the search for a permanent chief executive. At the March meetings, they met at length "in camera" to figure out the kind of person they were looking for and to devise a careful search process The Toronto-based professional head-hunting firm, Janet Wright and Associates, was signed up to help. A formal search committee was named which included both trustees and staff but also two prominent outside members: Martha Henry, the renowned actress and director, and William Breen, a prominent Ottawa businessman and former chair of the high-tech company Cognos.

Riley's decision to fill in as interim director general had been tacitly accepted by the board, but it caused a lot of unease, and she would be heavily criticized for it. "My biggest mistake," she recalled later, "was taking money for it." The board had agreed that paying her the usual per diem fee that trustees received for the long weeks she was spending in the executive offices and on the Renewal Committee seemed fair, but the public perception it created made her a lightening rod for complaints and concerns surrounding the centre. Behind the scenes she continued to work with passion on the principles and ideas she deemed critical to straightening out the organization. Crucial to her plan was some serious private fundraising, and she moved the NAC towards this unexplored territory. It was an area largely resisted in the past, but one that would open up to the Arts Centre in the future in a big way.

Riley's first efforts in this direction included trying to secure an unheard of $400,000 orchestra season sponsorship from the CIBC through her connections with the president, John Ferguson. While this attempt failed for various reasons, the NAC's new interest in corporate sponsorship caught the eye of another giant company—Bell Canada. Ruth Foster was the astute officer responsible for administering the company's sponsorships and philanthropic funds. She spotted an interview in the *Ottawa Citizen* with acting director Riley discussing the subject, flanked with a photograph that included the words in Foster's recollection, "your name here." Clearly the Arts Centre was open to corporate business. After consulting with her boss, Linda Gervais, the vice-president in charge of Bell's government relations in Ottawa, Foster tentatively called Riley to explore what the message meant. Bell Canada was a well-known supporter of hospitals and universities, but had only recently become aware of the potential of cultural events as valuable networking and hosting opportunities: it was now lead sponsor for the Governor General's Performing Arts Awards. In her long exploratory dialogue with Riley, Foster was interested to learn that there might even be "naming opportunities" in the future at the Arts Centre. As visions of the "Bell Theatre" popped into Foster's head, Riley cautioned, "We are not quite there yet"—even though the idea was already being explored by the trustees. Still, after all the administrative turmoil at the NAC, Bell officials were worried about the future of the centre itself. They were certainly interested in corporate sponsorship there, but they decided to wait until a permanent CEO had been appointed before they took any further steps. Riley had, however, laid the groundwork for Bell to become the first major corporate sponsor of the National Arts Centre.

Two other factors Riley deemed critical were complete transparency in operations and engaging a disillusioned public once again with the Arts Centre. She made some headway with staff when she was questioned at a meeting with them about the Renewal Committee and the cost of the Coopers & Lybrand study—the blueprint for turning the place around. She didn't hesitate to tell the employees about its $30,000 price tag. Her frankness with them seemed to win her a few yards.

Riley also used all her considerable social connections, persuasive wiles, and undeniable charm to gain the support of prominent leaders in the Ottawa scene who could affect the NAC's fortunes. Over lunch once again with Russell Mills of the *Ottawa Citizen*, a shrewd player himself, they worked up a scheme for a public forum that would allow wide-ranging discussion on what the NAC's future should be. Scheduled for June 20, 1996, to be co-hosted by the two organizations, it would give the public a chance to air its grievances and offer its ideas.

In unprecedented coverage for almost any Canadian newspaper, the *Ottawa Citizen* pulled out all the stops in preparing the ground for the forum, publishing a lengthy series on the National Arts Centre that ran every day for two weeks before the event. The series of articles included thoughtful pieces by the newspaper's own writers, including political writer Susan Riley, film critic Jay Stone, and arts writer Paul Gessell, and also by a number of guest contributors who brought views from outside Ottawa. Among them were Stratford theatre director Robin Phillips, composer Louis Applebaum, and Vancouver playwright John Gray, who wrote poignantly about "the wrong cultural cuts."[41] Taking the example of his own work, he recounted the success of his play *Billy Bishop Goes to War*, which, thanks to the NAC, had received four weeks of rehearsal, a week of technical rehearsals, and several preview performances before going on to a long, triumphant nationwide run. In contrast, another play, *Amélie*, had received less than half the time for preparation and had fallen by the wayside. The bottom line for Gray, speaking for many Canadian playwrights, was that neither play would have been produced at all without the NAC's involvement. Gray deplored the funding cutbacks that had occurred in all Canadian cultural organizations and the growing difficulty of having distinctive Canadian voices on the cultural scene. By the time the evening of the forum rolled around, the public was ready to speak out.

Riley had assembled a distinguished broad-based panel to speak at the forum. Among its members were the outspoken flautist and former orchestra member Robert Cram, now chair of music at the Université d'Ottawa, the local Liberal MP Mauril Bélanger, the private impresario David Mirvish from Toronto, and Hamilton Southam, who had returned to Canada from his home in France. Riley opened the forum by trying to disarm her critics, including Southam, whom she referred to as "a hero of mine." She got little thanks: in return, Southam gave her a public spanking, as he had in so many other public forums when he felt that the leadership of his beloved institution was off course. He bluntly told the capacity crowd in the NAC's Studio theatre that "this place is leaderless, it's adrift. At the moment there is hopeless confusion, and people feel it and they are depressed by it."[42] The audience, many of them long-time NAC supporters, called for a return of the glorious artistic achievements of the NAC's early days. When Riley pointed out how Torontonians had rallied to the support of Harbourfront, the performing arts centre in the Ontario capital, when it was in trouble, few in the crowd believed that the local community could raise the substantial funds that would be needed to make up the government shortfall in Ottawa. Riley recalled the entire experience as "one of the most painful of my life."[43] What the event really did was to provide the occasion for a great public venting of all the alarm local Ottawans had felt about the fate of the Arts Centre for a long time.

Riley chose to take the view that the charged evening was demonstrable evidence that the local community was finally re-engaging with the Arts Centre. But the reality of official Ottawa was very different. The National Arts Centre operated within the federal government context, and the government did not like controversy. Riley was courting great risk and exposure by organizing this public forum, and her public statements and overall quest for transparency went against the grain in senior government circles. Without knowing the details, Copps and her officials were also alarmed at the way Riley had stepped into management. A new vice-chair of the board, Ottawa lawyer David Hill, was parachuted in by Copps to try to keep a lid on things. Riley could not turn for help to anyone in senior government. Her "creative risk-taking" was the antithesis of how things were done in the capital and, once appointed, she had been left pretty much on her own with her board colleagues to attempt to figure things out. Few in officialdom wanted to become embroiled in the problems that continued to swirl around the Arts Centre.

As the dust settled from the public forum and Ottawa went into its usual summer hiatus, the search committee for a new director general hastened to make a decision. By summer's end they had found their man. In a conference call on August 29, 1996, they unanimously agreed that John Cripton, a fifty-three-year-old Montreal-born impresario with vast experience of both domestic and international cultural touring would become the next CEO. He would be the sixth director general of the National Arts Centre in its twenty-seven-year history.*

---

*Six CEOs, some of them acting, had come and gone in the previous three years.

A SHORT
RUN

"To guarantee the longevity of the NAC, my goal was to somehow make it indispensable across the spectrum," said John Cripton, recalling the early days of his appointment as the new director general. "My concern was to create an NAC that could pay for itself, eventually, but also had a great deal of credibility artistically."[1] The vast experience in the arts that Cripton brought to the National Arts Centre made him well equipped for the task ahead, and he was warmly received by the board. He had been interviewed for the position before, in 1988, but, like the other candidates at the time, had sensed that the decision had already been made in favour of Yvon DesRochers. Nevertheless, the top job at the NAC had never been far from Cripton's mind, and he perceived it as the pinnacle of his career. That career had taken him a long way in the arts, both nationally and internationally. His term from 1973 to 1980 as the first general manager of the Canada Council's Touring Office had given him an intimate knowledge of organizing shows across Canada and abroad, and he knew how to bring important international companies and artists into the country. From there it had been a natural stepping stone for someone with his entrepreneurial nature to move into the private sector, where he became a full-fledged impresario running a hugely successful business.

As an impresario, he had developed a niche market by bringing top Soviet talent such as the Kirov Ballet and the Red Army Chorus for tours in North America. Vernon Turner, Canada's ambassador to the Soviet Union from 1986 to 1990 and later an NAC benefactor, recalled meeting Cripton in Moscow in 1987. "Here was a living impresario!" he recalled, adding that it was intensely difficult to deal with the Soviet bureaucracy, "especially when it came to their cultural treasures." He enjoyed his encounters with Cripton so much that he invited him back to the embassy residence to meet his wife. When he learned of Cripton's new position at the NAC, he had

Arts impresario John Cripton attained the post of NAC CEO with the board's unanimous approval in September 1996. Photo © Chris Mikula/Ottawa Citizen. Reprinted by permission.

one immediate reaction: "This is a good appointment. If John Cripton can work with the Soviet cultural bureaucracy, he can work with this institution."[2]

Cripton combined his admiration for artists with a clear understanding of the mysterious shell-games needed to transfer monies from one pocket to another, and so arrange for performers to get onto the stage. An imposing, capacious physical presence, well-groomed with a handsomely trimmed beard and a soft-spoken manner of speech, he was persuasive and stabilizing in the intense milieu of artistic production. Among his many business interests, he had developed a specialty in international cultural expositions where Canadian talent was on view. This experience had given him intimate knowledge of the various places where money could be found in the federal purse—knowledge that would be an invaluable resource for the National Arts Centre.

"From the beginning he bubbled with ideas," said choreographer Brian Macdonald. "He had a multitude of ideas."[3] Cripton's prime intention was to rebuild the Arts Centre artistically on all fronts, re-root it both locally and nationally, and find new ways of fundraising that would make all this development possible. The vision he sketched out for the board was ambitious—and one the trustees enthusiastically endorsed. He did not promise overnight results; rather, he indicated that, in his perception, it would take up to five years to rebuild the organization and establish it on sound footing.

Before launching his long-term plans, Cripton was faced, like every incoming director general before him, with the immediate problem of how to pay for the orchestra—the NAC's creative element that absorbed such a large proportion of the overall budget. Negotiations for a new contract for the NAC Orchestra had been under way for several months before his arrival, with little progress, and he quickly found himself in dispute on several issues with the musicians. While money and the length of the season were being hotly discussed, two other matters arose that were symptomatic of the differing views between management and the musicians. First, when the orchestra was founded, it was expected not only to perform at its own series of concerts but to be available as a pit orchestra for visiting shows. But some players now resisted this role as house band. Cripton disagreed with them—and so he began his tenure at odds with many of the musicians over what their role should be at the Arts Centre. The other matter was the use of the Opera hall, which was often blocked from lucrative rentals and other NAC programming because the orchestra was using it for rehearsals. One of Cripton's first moves was to cut back by a day the orchestra's rehearsal time on the Opera stage, sending them back to their regular rehearsal hall. "This of course did not sit very well," Cripton recalled.

While recognizing the orchestra's essential importance to the NAC, Cripton was operating in an environment where the entire public service had experienced zero growth in the immediately preceding years. All departments at the Arts Centre except the orchestra had suffered substantial cutbacks and salary freezes that had endured for more than five years. The new director general, supported by a board directive, felt that some sort of adjustment had to be made to the orchestra budget. But that proved difficult. Within three months of his arrival, Cripton was skating perilously close to another orchestra strike, in part because of his insistence that the orchestra must shoulder some of the pain of the Art Centre's difficult financial position. In the end he managed to secure a small symbolic reduction in the musicians' salaries, but the members would accept a shortened contract for only two years. It meant that the whole cycle of negotiating the next contract would begin again almost before the ink was dry on the current one. "It was very painful for both sides," Cripton remembered. Settling the orchestra situation was essential for all sorts of reasons—including the fact that the NAC's principal supporter in government, Mitchell Sharp, "never let anything go as far as the orchestra was concerned."[4]

Shortly after his arrival, Cripton, accompanied by board chair Jean Riley, met with Sharp to explain to the elder statesman what he was trying to do. Cripton went so far as to ask Sharp to refrain from interfering in the orchestra negotiations because he felt it was having a negative effect on management's role at the centre. Perhaps it was a tactless step, given that Sharp's goodwill was very important to the overall good health of the Arts Centre. Sharp had his own sources of information, primarily through the concertmaster, Walter Prystawski, and long-time political supporter Elizabeth (Liz) Waddell, who had managed public relations for the orchestra since 1988 and particularly through the 1989 strike.

Aside from these negotiations, the other pressing issue for the orchestra was to find a new music director. By the fall of 1996 the search process was again stretching into years and, while a long list of potential contenders, including many Canadians, had been scrutinized, it was time to resolve the matter. The small size of the orchestra meant that many good conductors were not interested in the NAC's chamber-size ensemble.

The 1996–97 orchestra season was arranged to bring in a wide range of guest conductors, and a string of promising candidates passed through Ottawa for a tryout on the podium. For various reasons—often the orchestra's simple dislike of a given conductor—nothing had yet worked out. Cripton had one clear notion: "to bring in someone who had such a high profile that immediately we would start the touring process and the recording process."[5] This desire would bring the name of Pinchas Zukerman eventually to the top of the list.

Through contacts with the arts manager Zarin Mehta, who was now in the United States but still interested in Canadian affairs, arrangements were made for Albert K. Webster, a musical consultant and former general manager of the New York Philharmonic, to aid the search committee's deliberations. Webster immediately became involved and, after several other candidates had been considered and discarded, the search committee made an approach towards the end of 1997 to conductor Keith Lockhart, the lively and personable young music director of the Boston Pops.

Cripton and orchestra manager Christopher Deacon travelled to Boston to meet with the maestro, and he was invited back to guest conduct a special concert with the orchestra—which went very well. The Arts Centre made an offer to Lockhart, who discussed the appointment with his wife and seemed on the verge of accepting, when, suddenly, a better proposal came his way from the Utah Symphony. It included the opportunity to work with the Utah Opera—and Lockhart accepted. The NAC search committee was deeply disappointed, but Webster quickly stepped in and firmly steered the members towards Pinchas Zukerman. As Cripton remembered, "Webster endorsed the idea very, very firmly that this was the right decision for us."[6]

On a visit to New York some time before, Deacon had made casual inquiries about Zukerman working with the orchestra and had fortuitously booked him to conduct a pair of concerts in Ottawa in February 1998. These concerts provided an opportunity for members of the search committee who had not seen him conduct to observe him in action. The evenings were enthusiastically received, especially by the musicians. Prystawski told Deacon after the concerts, "Now, there's a conductor!"[7] Serious negotiations were opened with the renowned violinist.

Jean Riley at once set out to establish a personal relationship with the maestro in lengthy telephone conversations, which roamed over both the NAC's problems and Zukerman's interests. While Zukerman was in Toronto for a concert at Roy Thomson Hall, the various protagonists met for lunch at Riley's home. She prepared her NAC team for the encounter by inviting them to imbibe some bee's royal jelly before the maestro arrived—an experience allegedly designed to sharpen the senses. It was clear that the beleaguered National Arts Centre might not be able to meet Zukerman's price, but the conductor's own long-felt desire to work with the NAC orchestra and his apparent personal attachment to Canada (his parents had once found a haven in Montreal) weighed in. Riley believed "he was also personally at a crossroads in his own career, and this was a wonderful opportunity for him. So we ... in a very informal way ... arrived at an agreement."[8] Deacon made a point of riding back in the taxi with the maestro to reinforce what had been decided and to head off any post-lunch misgivings that might unravel matters before they had jelled.

Cripton launched the formal negotiations for the contract, although Riley continued to claim a special chemistry with Zukerman. As she said, "The agreement between Pinchas and me was that it was going to be affordable because he knew that I was completely obsessed at not putting the Arts Centre at risk."[9] With her well-grounded concern over the use of taxpayers' money, she was extremely hesitant about his substantial price tag, though she knew he could bring in audiences to the NAC. Still, "there were cautioning voices" around the maestro's previous history as music director at the St. Paul Chamber Orchestra in Minnesota, as well as questions about his limited taste in repertoire and his skills as a conductor.[10] For these reasons, she said, "we did not want to make a too long commitment and not for too much money."[11]

When Cripton brought the proposed formal contract to the board, it was for a five-year term. "Years One, Two and Three were very generous on Pinchas's part, and Year Four was assuming good news," Riley recalled, "but Year Five was on another planet in terms of what he was to be paid." She personally baulked and managed to persuade her fellow trustees not to accept the risk of the fifth-year commitment management had negotiated. "To John Cripton's credit he protected me and the institution," she later acknowledged, and the NAC settled on an initial four-year contract with the Israeli-American. There was no doubt in Cripton's mind that having Zukerman at the helm would highlight the orchestra's ability to attract money, recognition, and opportunities. "It would give us the ability to be seen as a major cultural centre in North America and in the world," he said, "because the orchestra would tour a great deal and recordings would happen."[12]

Throughout the process, there had been the usual push for Canadian content in the appointment. Cripton had a broad view of the arts—"my feeling about the arts in general is that there are no national boundaries"—and he planned to forestall the nationalist critics by establishing an

In 1996 celebrated violinist Pinchas Zukerman was appointed the fourth director of music after a long association with the orchestra. Photo © Paul Labelle photographe inc.

associate conductor position that would be earmarked for a Canadian.[13] He also decided to create the position of conductor laureate—and hoped that it would first go to Mario Bernardi as conductor emeritus. In that way he could honour Bernardi's seminal work at the NAC, salute the orchestra's cultural origins, and appease many of NACO's traditional fans—among them Mitchell Sharp, who had been lobbying for Bernardi's return.

Finding the new music director was only one of the challenges facing Cripton as he tried to restore the artistic integrity of the National Arts Centre. "While I was concerned about the orchestra," he said, "I was also trying to create a balance. My job was to improve on French and English theatre and all the other artistic elements."[14] He began to gather around him a team of skilled professionals to rebuild the NAC's artistic life. To his surprise he found an old friend and mentor already present on a temporary basis—the well-known *festivalmeister* Nicholas Goldschmidt, who had arranged "Canada Sings!" at the centre in July 1996. Goldschmidt was starting work on another festival for the following summer, but Cripton had bigger plans—a full-blown Festival Canada in the old style. With his consummate showman's instincts, he understood Goldschmidt's value to the centre and offered him a permanent post as "senior Festival adviser"—although he also gently told the veteran musical man, now nearing his nineties, that he was also going to hire a "senior artistic adviser," someone to oversee the entire range of artistic activities needed to revitalize the NAC.

Besides a renewed Summer Festival, Cripton wanted the Stratford theatre company to come back to Ottawa. He was also thinking of creative liaisons with Charlottetown's Confederation Centre, the original home of Canadian musical theatre, and with the Banff Centre, including perhaps some opera co-productions, as ways of opening the Arts Centre once again to the national scene. Although no fan of mega-musicals himself, he was even thinking about creating big commercial theatre projects at the NAC, along the lines of the *Phantom* or *Les Miz*, which would perhaps even make their way to Broadway.

The man he had in mind to oversee these artistic endeavours for the NAC was Brian Macdonald, the highly skilled choreographer and dance and opera director who had been responsible for a string of commercially successful Gilbert and Sullivan productions at Stratford. Cripton and his wife, theatre director Linda Sword, went to Stratford and told Macdonald, "We need you."[15] Macdonald readily agreed to come. The fact that Cripton came from the private sector and that Macdonald had produced commercial theatre successes created some initial suspicious among some in Ottawa who were loath to countenance any effort to "commercialize" the NAC, but, aside from that mild carping, Macdonald's appointment was well received. Rounding out the team,

Cripton engaged Michael Tabbitt, a long-time friend and associate, as producer of special events—a position intended to give Cripton a reliable, experienced, and familiar colleague in carrying out some of his ambitious dreams.

The big dream of re-establishing the summer Festival Canada was at the forefront of Cripton's plans, and he had myriad ideas on this score. Building on Goldschmidt's work, and buoyed by Cripton's vision for the future, the trustees enthusiastically endorsed the plan. A grand launch, some would say a relaunch, of Festival Canada was planned in the Studio on April 8, 1997, to announce the details of the coming summer.

The press conference was choreographed by Brian Macdonald and produced by Michael Tabbitt. It was a spectacular "taster" of the lavish festival menu ahead that proposed events not only at the Arts Centre but at venues all across the National Capital Region, and included everything from opera singers to circus acrobats. Cripton was exploring many pockets of government to support the event. The circus at least, which performed in Jacques Cartier Park on the Quebec side of the river, was funded by the federal government's sponsorship program, and demonstrated Cripton's skill at finding financial resources in unlikely places.[16] A striking sunflower logo was devised as the Festival trademark, and everything from posters to T-shirts to coffee mugs, and even the Café waiters' aprons, bore the logo. Bell Canada had stepped up as the first significant corporate supporter for the revitalized Arts Centre, and it now signed on as presenting sponsor for the Festival—a first in the NAC's history. Credit for this achievement went to Jean Riley and her determination to attract corporate sponsorships to the Arts Centre. "We were so proud to be associated with it," said Bell's representative, Ruth Foster. "We were very excited by what was happening at the Arts Centre!"[17]

Before the Summer Festival, another art installation took place at the NAC. Like Riley before him, Cripton had been dismayed at the drab grey concrete walls in the public areas when he first walked into the building eight months before. "It felt like a mausoleum," he recalled. "This had to change. It was an ideal opportunity." Cripton made contact with the Canada Council Art Bank, the vast repository of contemporary Canadian art that is collected for rental and display in Ottawa and other government buildings around the country.[18] In due course, a massive and colourful exhibition of paintings, drawings, and sculptures was installed throughout the building. This first installation began a fruitful and long-term relationship with the Art Bank which has resulted in many more displays by Canada's visual artists at the centre.[19]

On June 18, 1997, Festival Canada opened a lavish and eclectic month of events. It began with three performances of Berlioz's oratorio *L'Enfance du Christ* under the baton of Mario Bernardi, and brought back Felix Mirbt's dramatic life-size puppets to help illustrate the story of the Holy Family's flight into Egypt. The figures baffled some observers: *Ottawa Citizen* publisher Russell Mills remarked, "Those strange puppets moving around. I thought that was an odd thing."[20]

The Festival went on to feature more than 100 performances in which some 1,500 Canadian and international artists were presented in forty separate shows. They ranged from an original new Canadian opera, *Gianni*, produced in collaboration with the local opera company Opera Lyra, through English and French theatre, to cabaret and multiple recitals—many of them Goldschmidt's favourite chorale works presented in Ottawa-area churches. Both Ben Heppner and Richard Margison were featured artists, along with jazz singer Diana Krall in her first appearance in cabaret in the Studio. The sprightly Goldschmidt had the main hand in the programming and delightedly told the press: "The Arts Centre was established to present and promote Canadian artists. What pleases me most is that, when you look through the program, except for some of the international choirs and a few soloists, these are all our own people."[21]

The $1.4 million budget set aside for the Festival was reinforced by some of the special funds that Cripton had managed to extract from the government, although the NAC's regular budget was still subject to government cuts. The variety of choice was devised in part to respond to critics who had complained so often that the thousands of tourists who visited the National Capital Region each summer rarely had a chance to see their own tastes on the stages at Canada's national performing arts showcase. Even so, selections for this first renewed Summer Festival were markedly high toned, sometimes to the point of esoteric, and much of it did not respond to the lighthearted summer fare that many MPs and others had wanted. When the Festival was over, the audience figures were disappointing, with many empty seats at some of the most prestigious presentations. Significant shortfalls in revenue put the whole event seriously in the red. Planners put it down to the short timeline they had been given to organize and market the Festival.

Cripton was unperturbed and already planning for the years ahead. He told the press that "no festival in its first year is going to be as satisfying as it is ten years down the road in terms of audience development,"[22] and he confidently announced that arrangements were well under way for the next summer. He had many ideas for expanding the Summer Festival, and he projected an eventual overall Ottawa Festival Network that would overlap and collaborate with other already existing festivals in the city—including jazz, blues, chamber music, and fringe theatre festivals.

At the board of trustees, the disappointing numbers rang a cautionary note. Their excitement over the renewed Festival Canada was tempered with their ongoing concern over the finances. The loss made them nervous, but they still endorsed the plans for the next summer. That following year, 1998, would mark the fiftieth anniversary of the United Nations Declaration of Human Rights, and, Cripton noted, the Department of Canadian Heritage had already announced an initiative to celebrate historic events in Canadian life. He intended to tap into that synergy and to build many of the Festival's activities around that worthy theme.

If the National Arts Centre was really going to rebuild its in-house creativity in areas other than music, it needed to find a new director of English theatre. The interim artistic director, Gil Osborne, had kept things going after Andis Celms's departure but was now leaving the centre to move to Texas. When the experienced actor and theatre director Marti Maraden came to Ottawa in January 1997 to work on a co-production of Carol Shields's *Thirteen Hands*, both Macdonald and Osborne pressed her to apply for the NAC job. As Maraden later recalled: "I and the entire world knew that there was change afoot at the Arts Centre—that John Cripton was essentially part of a renaissance here. There was a sense of renewal, adventure, and risk—of real energy coming into the building."[23] A few weeks later she returned to Ottawa for a long interview with Cripton and others on the theatre team—and then she heard nothing for five weeks. When she bumped into Cripton and Riley at the opening night of the Stratford Festival, they urged her to "be patient."[24] In July she was invited again to Ottawa and, while expecting another interview, Cripton told her she had the job. "I accepted," she said. "I'm always keen to scare myself, and this was the last bastion of scariness that I could think of in life."[25]

Running the English Theatre Department would be a challenge, but she was impressed by the warm welcome she received not only from the inside theatre and production team but also from members of the local Ottawa theatre community, including Micheline Chevrier, the director of the Great Canadian Theatre Company. Maraden acknowledged that the NAC had "a very poor reputation in the country at large at the time, but what was getting through to us was a sense of change." She had also "played here as an actor three times and had directed here … with truly one of the best productions teams in the country, rivalling and equalling, sometimes even surpassing, those at the two great festivals, Stratford and Shaw."[26] She was excited about the physical attributes of the Theatre, especially its thrust stage, and she had a strong sense that Cripton was urging his new artistic team to think big dreams. She would commit herself fully to the organization and, for the next eight years, be a seminal force in re-establishing the English theatre program at the Arts Centre.

Within a year of taking over at the NAC, Cripton's creative and entrepreneurial skills had him advancing on all fronts to maximize the resources at the centre and make it once again a well-grounded performing arts venue. In dance, for instance, David Lui, a leading dance impresario from Vancouver, commented that few dance tours in the country would get off the ground without the NAC. Cripton began to look actively for projects in all areas of the performing arts that would have a life beyond Ottawa and also be money-makers for the Arts Centre. With Brian Macdonald at his side, he saw plenty of potential. He also visualized possibilities in the arrangements that Yvon DesRochers had created with Garth Drabinsky. "We can build big shows more cheaply here," he told the *Financial Post* in April 1997, though he hastened to add that "all these commercial endeavors are designed to generate money for other things. At no time will we loose our artistic orientation."[27] These collaborations with commercial shows could, he thought, develop jobs for Canadian actors, dancers, musicians, and stagehands and, at the same time, ensure that the NAC was the top arts centre in Canada, its resources fully used.

To this end, Cripton proposed to the Departments of Canadian Heritage and External Affairs that the Arts Centre become the official producer for all of Canada's cultural outreaches internationally. As entrepreneurs in the private sector, he and Michael Tabbitt had previously teamed up to organize the cultural component of numerous world fairs and exhibitions for the federal government. Now Cripton proposed that this lucrative service industry become part of the NAC's mandate, with the income derived used to enhance its coffers. The idea gained some traction in official circles. He continued to extend his network within the federal government, sitting on various interdepartmental committees and forging close ties with Sheila Copps's office in the Heritage Department.

In the Ottawa community, he jumped into several local projects and established contacts with prominent local leaders such as Jean Pigott, a former National Capital Commission chair and now head of the Ottawa Congress Centre.[28] In this way he involved the NAC in a long-dreamed urban plan known as "the linkages project."[29] He urged the federal government to renovate the old downtown railway station, which had been converted into the Government Conference Centre but now sat empty,[30] and began to explore how it could be revamped as an additional NAC-run performing arts venue. He even hired an acoustics expert to assess its potential for music and other activities. At the same time, there was still talk in certain quarters of privatizing some of the NAC's activities—of finding "alternative delivery mechanisms," in the language of the official documents.[31]

Cripton told friends that, when he was appointed, "the government had made it clear that he was to get involved in serious fundraising."[32] During Riley's custodial period as CEO, she had made a tentative start on some fundraising, and she now warned Cripton not to try to get any more money from the government. Although the centre did prepare a new application for public funds, Cripton decided to focus on the private sector and he hired the NAC's first real development director, Kim McCuaig, who had recently retired from a senior position in the Carleton University Development Office. McCuaig's new job was to oversee the NAC's marketing endeavours and get the first fundraising efforts under way.

Cripton set in motion a series of fundraising initiatives designed not only to raise money but, with their glamour and prestige, to heighten the profile of the Arts Centre.

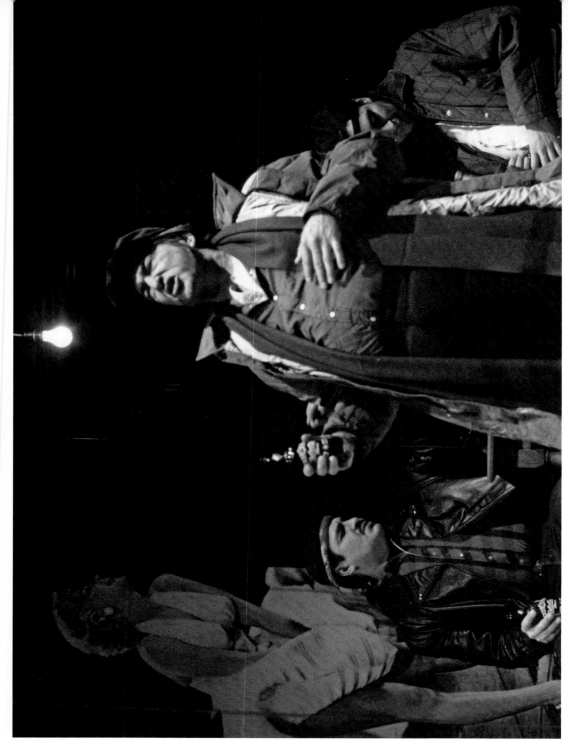

Tomson Highway's
Dry Lips Oughta
Move to Kapuskasing
had a searing run and
starred aboriginal
actors (left to right)
Ben Cardinal,
Graham Greene, and
Billy Merasty. Photo
© Gordon King.

Martha Henry has both acted and directed at the NAC. She starred in Michael Frayn's internationally acclaimed play Copenhagen, *which went on to an extended commercial run in Toronto. Photo © SWD Photography/NAC.*

Marti Maraden's Shakespeare productions were enthusiastically received. Featured in Love's Labour's Lost, *2005, were (left to right) Patrick McManus, Ben Carlson, Nigel Shawn Williams, and Brendan Murray. Photo © Andrée Lanthier.*

Denis Marleau's Dors mon petit enfant, *with (left to right) actors Ginette Morin, Paul Savoie, and Céline Bonnier. Photo © Richard-Max Tremblay. Courtesy of UBU compagnie de création.*

Wajdi Mouawad's Forêts—*Canadian audiences benefited from this play's ten European (and two Quebec) co-producers and over six months of rehearsals in France. Photo © Marlène Gélineau Payette.*

Avery Saltzman in the 1998 Summer Festival's The Mikado, *richly designed by Susan Benson. With its tour cancelled, the production failed to recoup costs. Photo © NAC.*

Cellist Amanda Forsyth and dancer Rex Harrington in A Pairing of SwanS, *produced for CBC Television by Veronica Tennant. Photo © Bruce Zinger/Veronica Tennant, from the film* A Pairing of SwanS, *Veronica Tennant, director/producer.*

Choreographer Édouard Lock's Amelia, *with dancers Mistaya Hemingway and Jason Shipley Holmes.*
Photo © Édouard Lock.

"Alberta Scene" 2005 was headlined by the new Canadian opera Filumena, *composed by John Estacio, libretto by John Murrell. Photo © Don Lee/Banff Centre.*

Pinchas Zukerman's love affair with cellist and orchestra member Amanda Forsyth culminated in their marriage on the beach in Anguilla in March 2004. Photo © Mike Byalik.

Raising money for an arts institution that already received nearly $25 million in government funds was a public-relations challenge. Brainstorming with his staff, Cripton developed the idea for an annual benefit concert that would feature a big-name internationally known classical artist. At the same time, the event would have the side advantage of absorbing some of that troublesome unused time in the orchestra's contract. The star, they agreed, "had to be the best in the world."[33] In early 1997 the internationally renowned black American soprano Jessye Norman filled that bill. The NAC booked her for the first fall gala concert and dinner, scheduled for October 4, 1997.

Raising private funds and running arts galas was virgin territory in Ottawa. Audiences were accustomed to seeing top-class artists at the NAC at bargain rates. Cripton approached his old friend, ambassador Vernon Turner, and invited him, along with others, to join a gala committee.[34] Turner attended the inaugural meeting and agreed to become its chair. "Until then," he recalled, "I had just been an ordinary subscriber to the orchestra concerts."[35] NAC support staff assisted Turner with a select committee of important local citizenry, among them Diana Kirkwood, the socialite and real-estate agent; Adrian Burns, a western-based CRTC commissioner making a big splash on the Ottawa social scene with her communications lawyer husband, Gregory Kane;* and, for added prestige, the balletomane Celia Franca, now living in Ottawa. In deference to Franca and her prestige as an artist, Turner insisted on making her the committee's official vice-chair.

Cripton expected the prominent group to promote and sell the event, and a careful timeline was laid out that counted down to the gala evening. In the tradition of gala committees, members sampled potential menus devised by NAC executive chef Kurt Waldele for the grand feast that would be set out on the Opera hall stage after the concert. "We selected ostrich, which we thought terribly daring!" Turner laughed later. The financial target for the gala evening was set at $250,000—an ambitious figure for Ottawa. Although Bell Canada was already on board, Cripton decided not to take chances, and he hired the Toronto fundraising firm of Nina Wright to seek out other benefactors.

The gala evening unfolded in the glowing environs of the red-plush Opera hall. It set a sparkling precedent for Ottawa, a glamorous fall event at the National Arts Centre which continues to the present. The orchestra was resplendent in best white-tie turnout, and the evening's chief entertainer, the gloriously impressive Jessye Norman,

---

*Burns and Kane would prove to be long-term staunch supporters of the NAC, serving in time as chair of the gala themselves. Despite her Calgary connections, Burns was eventually appointed to the NAC board as vice-chair in 2002 (ostensibly as the "Ottawa" member), and she became a valuable cheerleader for the centre both in Ottawa circles and, as it extended its connections into western Canada, in recruiting many of her wealthier friends to support its activities.

Fundraising loomed large in the NAC's life. A first fall gala featuring soprano Jessye Norman didn't raise much money but it did put the idea in the limelight. Photo © Julie Oliver/ Ottawa Citizen. Reprinted by permission.

won over the black-tie audience of high-ranking ministers, ambassadors, and such other "glitterati" that Ottawa could muster.[36] There were only a handful of opera aficionados in the audience, so, after singing her way through several beautiful opera arias, Norman humoured the crowd with an amusing encore of a hummed version of "Amazing Grace." After the concert, the NAC's stage crews and kitchen team demonstrated the skills honed so well in earlier years of large-scale opera and theatre productions and extravagant state dinners. Within forty-five minutes the massive Opera stage was transformed into a beautifully appointed dining wonderland, serving an elegant hot three-course dinner to over 800 guests. The evening ended with after-dinner dancing to music provided by Peter Appleyard and his ensemble. While Norman did not stay for dessert, her short appearance at the after-concert party made the splash that Cripton had sought. Buzz about the Arts Centre resonated through corridors in the highest circles in Ottawa and was picked up in social news across the country.

While the event scored on the artistic and public-relations front, the financial results were disappointing, reaching just $112,000—less than half the targeted figure. It was "entirely respectable under the circumstances," remembered Turner.[37] While Bell Canada had chipped in early, Nina Wright had not been able to secure a single sponsor. It was thanks to last-minutes efforts by Jean Riley that the A&E Network stepped in to help. The rest of the money came mainly from local pockets. Hard cash might have been short, but the whole experience, in a town averse to private fundraising, opened many people's minds to the fact that the NAC now needed to raise private funds. Turner and his wife were not the only ones who began thinking that they ought to consider some annual giving to the centre. Cripton's government masters at the Department of Canadian Heritage, particularly Minister Sheila Copps, were delighted at this first indication of new sources of income for the Arts Centre.

The evening inspired other efforts too. An outside group soon approached the Arts Centre, volunteering another benefit concert. Again building on the available services of the NAC Orchestra and the sponsorship of Bell, this next evening was conceived in a more light-hearted manner, as a midwinter "picker-upper," and offered the free services of Peter Jennings, the Canadian-born anchor of the American ABC news

Others stepped forward to help. ABC news anchor, Canadian-born Peter Jennings, made his "operatic debut" at the NAC in a spoof concert of The Merry Widow. *Funds raised were dedicated to music and opera at the NAC. Photo © Dave Chan/Ottawa Citizen. Reprinted by permission.*

network. All the singers and the conductor, Timothy Vernon, also provided their services for a modest honorarium. On February 21, 1998, Jennings made his "operatic debut" at the NAC as the narrator in a concert version of *The Merry Widow*, using a libretto by the playwright Tom Stoppard written for the Glyndebourne Opera in England. Ottawa was Jennings's hometown, and he began his network television career there with CTV. His return for the evening was a triumph, and he had the time of his life, even receiving the key to the city. The concert achieved two important objectives for the centre: first, Cripton shared the proceeds with the local opera company, Opera Lyra, whose efforts had kept the missing opera art form on the NAC stages after in-house opera had been cancelled in 1983; and second, the NAC demonstrated that it actively supported and intended to work closely with the local arts community.

This time the event provided a seedbed of corporate sponsors. Many small and medium-sized Ottawa companies contributed. After these initial donations, many firms went on to become bigger supporters at the NAC. Corporate sponsors included the hockey team, the Ottawa Senators, and all five of the large chartered banks, none of which had any previous record of giving to the Arts Centre. While their sponsorships were modest on this first occasion, it set their names on the roster of new donors. The evening netted nearly $150,000—a healthy amount of money at the time—and established another tradition. In subsequent versions, known as the "Black and White Opera Soirée," it has become an amusing antidote to the hard Ottawa winter and the other bookend to the fall event. Both evenings remain the two most important fundraisers in the NAC's annual calendar. Key to their impact was their ample demonstration that the NAC could help itself—and that the public was prepared to support it.

Behind the scenes, however, Cripton and his team were working on a far more lucra-tive and spectacular donation, one that would set the NAC's name in lights in terms of gift-giving to the arts. Sadly, it was also a donation that, ultimately, would have an equally spectacular but unhappy flame-out.

On his arrival in Ottawa, Cripton had scanned the horizon for practical help for the Arts Centre and, before he hired McCuaig, had brought in a local freelance marketing promoter, Patrick Reid. Cripton gave him an office, calling cards, and a parking pass and agreed to pay him a commission for any funds he raised. Reid, who had ties to the Ottawa Senators, the local NHL hockey team, as well as the Corel Centre where the team played, came up with a brilliant idea—an arts-sports partnership.[38] It all hinged on a young Russian hockey star named Alexei Yashin, who was playing for the Senators. Alexei had come to Ottawa as the first-draft pick of the team in 1992. His parents, also sports professionals, and his brother, Dmitri, had joined him in Ottawa. The Yashins, a cultivated family with wide cultural interests, were already known on the Ottawa artistic scene as regular attendants at the opera, and their sons often joined them at classical music concerts and performances after hockey practice. Far from home, the cultivated Russian family was making a new life in the city.

Alexei Yashin, who had played a brilliant previous season with the Ottawa Senators, was now having public-relations problems as he held out for more money from the wealthy team. The Senators had been cast as a "blue-collar" organization, and Yashin's desire for more money had both public opinion and the local sports press raging against him.* Reid's idea was simple: Yashin would make a million-dollar gift to the National Arts Centre, demonstrating his love of the arts as well as sport and cementing his affec-tion for his adopted city. The arrangement would include a role for his parents in what was to be a newly created Alexei Yashin Foundation for the Performing Arts.

When Kim McCuaig arrived as the full-time director of development at the NAC, he terminated Reid's freelance contract and the promoter left the centre, leaving behind the carefully worked out arrangements for the creation of the Yashin foun-dation.** As usual, the foundation was required to submit an application to Revenue Canada to establish it formally and allow it certain tax benefits. Normally the approval process took about six months. Reid claimed that everything was ready when he left, including the Revenue Canada application forms, though they needed to be completed.

The sports-arts connection was a marriage made in heaven for the National Arts Centre. The trustees were thrilled at the prospect of a million-dollar donation and, for

---

*Several other hot young NHL hockey stars at the time were also negotiating hard for more money, in particular Paul Kariya with the Mighty Ducks of Anaheim. The Ducks' owner, Disney's Michael Eisner, obliged, but the Ottawa team owners were not prepared to do the same.

**Many well-paid young hockey players and other professional sports players have similar foundations run by family members, directed to the charities of their choice.

Hockey fan Pinchas Zukerman conducted the Hockey Night in Canada *theme to celebrate the Alexei Yashin gift. Photo © Pat McGrath/Ottawa Citizen. Reprinted by permission.*

several practical reasons, the pressure was on to make the news public as soon as possible. The announcement was delayed twice, first because the world's major sports media were preoccupied with the February opening of the Winter Olympics in Japan, and then because of the local opening of Ottawa's Winterlude. Finally, on March 3, 1998, at a spectacular press conference in the Opera with the full orchestra on stage, the happy news of Yashin's gift was released: "the largest gift by a single donor to the NAC in its 29-year history."[39] While the incoming music director and self-confessed "hockey nut" Pinchas Zukerman led the orchestra in a rendition of the *Hockey Night in Canada* theme,[40] Minister Sheila Copps showed up for the occasion and hauled on an Ottawa Senators hockey sweater. As Cripton took delivery of a blown-up version of a million-dollar cheque, Alexei Yashin was publicly lauded, described as someone who had grown up in a world filled with culture as well as sports. "My parents knew the importance of arts in a child's education and development, and I wanted to make sure that every young person has the opportunity to appreciate the arts as I did," the young player was quoted as saying.[41]

In the pledge agreement to be established with the Alexei Yashin Foundation, two items were highlighted: the donated funds would be channelled through the NAC towards educational programs in the performing arts, and some of the money might be used to bring Russian artists to Ottawa "for the enjoyment of the Canadian public."[42] A small side-bar requested that, when Yashin's funds were used to bring in visiting, presumably Russian, performers, a portion of the revenues be used as a fundraiser for the Ottawa School of Dance. This item appears to have been a small salute to Russell Mills of the *Ottawa Citizen,* who had agreed to become a director and chair of the Alexei Yashin Foundation but was also chair of the dance school.* John Cripton did not meet personally with the Yashins until the mock cheque was handed over on the NAC stage, but his former connections with Russian cultural authorities had resonated with them.[43]

---

*In an April 2008 interview, Russell Mills, now chair of the National Capital Commission, recalled that Patrick Reid had originated the idea for the Yashin gift. Among other events, Reid had organized the *Ottawa Citizen* Indoor Games for twelve years, and Mills had nothing but praise for the skilled sports and marketing entrepreneur.

The million-dollar gift to the arts by hockey player Alexei Yashin created a worldwide sensation. Photo © Pat McGrath/ Ottawa Citizen. Reprinted by permission.

The exciting news sped around the world. Daily newspapers from London to Reykjavik carried the story. NHL hockey was a global industry, with players in the league from an array of countries. Swedes, Finns, Germans, and Czechs were intrigued with the announcement, along with Americans and Canadians. One Italian newspaper editorialized that its soccer players should emulate Yashin.

The gift was to be paid out over five years, and the first $200,000 had already arrived at the NAC on January 29, 1998. NAC staff, who had no previous experience in a venture of this kind and magnitude, were still fretting over details with regard to the tax receipt and other aspects of the pledge contract. Far beyond the money, however, the promotional potential of the gift was unheard of in artistic circles and focused instant attention on the NAC. Even the Senators hockey team souvenir program *Bodycheck*, published for fans at home-team games, featured an extensive interview with Maestro Pinchas Zukerman of the NAC Orchestra. "Zukerman with a violin is what Alexei Yashin is with a puck," the magazine explained to its readers. "A true artist capable of creating magic."[44] There was also a double-page picture of the full NAC Orchestra, and sidebars on each hockey player's page associating him with music. The page describing Alexei Yashin included details on the life and work of Russian composer Peter Ilyich Tchaikovsky. The whole affair was a public-relations coup of enormous proportions.

While these high-profile developments unfolded, Cripton, now in his second year at the helm, was still spewing out ideas in all directions—artistic, administrative, and financial. In the spring of 1998 the NAC teamed up with an Ottawa independent film company, Sound Venture, to produce a new six-part television series for the Bravo! network hosted by classical pianist Jon Kimura Parker and featuring the NAC Orchestra under the baton of music director Pinchas Zukerman. The year before, Parker had won the NAC Prize for mid-career work at the Governor General's Performing Arts

Award gala.[45] Cripton had also participated in a trade mission to Italy organized by Sergio Marchi, the international trade minister. When questioned by an Ottawa radio station, Cripton explained that culture was an important component in any trade mission. Moreover, he said, the trip would give him the opportunity to get to know important Canadian corporate leaders and to educate them about the value of the arts. And, while abroad, he would search for international opportunities for the NAC, and especially for the orchestra.

Nothing reflected the cultural context of the times better than the founding meeting of the International Network on Cultural Policy that Sheila Copps hosted in Ottawa in June 1998. It brought together cultural ministers from countries as far afield as Senegal, Armenia, Poland, and France. The only absentee at the talks was the United States, which lacked a minister of culture, but U.S. observers were present. The group was designed to counter the long-held U.S. position that culture was just another commodity when it came to trade. Copps would make this initiative one of her priorities in the balance of her time as minister.

On the administrative front at the Arts Centre, Cripton instituted new and badly needed financial reporting procedures, though not quickly enough for the board, which was still unsatisfied with the financial information it was receiving. As in the Pennefather period, Riley again became suspicious of the financial figures being provided, and questioned whether Cripton had sufficiently divested himself of his private companies. She also worried that "he appeared to be hiring a lot of people he already knew."[46] "I knew so many people in this country that, with almost anyone I hired, I could be accused of cronyism," he quipped later.[47] Whatever the differences between them, and many of them revolved around finances, fissures began to open up between the director general and his board. Cripton's management style and hiring practices, which tended to place people on contract rather than going through the usual rigorous public service hiring processes, contributed to the climate of suspicion and unease that was developing.

Some of Cripton's other management initiatives also made his chair, Jean Riley, uneasy. A suggestion that the NAC could entertain a casino within its confines was frowned on by board members as unsuitable, but the discovery that Ontario provincial tax laws contained exemptions from property tax for non-profit theatres over a certain size was more promising. The origins of the exemption were obscure, though perhaps they had been designed to give a break to large theatres in Toronto that were bringing in the crowds and filling up restaurants and hotels as well as their own seats. Nevertheless, it held out the possibility that the NAC could retain millions of dollars that it was now handing over in property tax levies. There had been positive discussions with both the Heritage Department and Treasury Board over the proposal, but Riley, who perhaps did not fully comprehend the idea, was uncomfortable with it and concerned about the good relations she had established with the municipalities. When the report on the negotiations was brought back to the board for consideration, the initiative was not encouraged.

A special audit of the National Arts Centre, requested by the Board of Trustees, was completed by the Auditor General's Office in the spring of 1998 and formally presented to the trustees on June 29, 1998. While much of it was boiler-plate commentary, it specified the need for a better strategic plan to tie artistic programming more closely to revenues. It also listed hiring and general financial reporting practices among the deficiencies. In response, in intense sessions with the board at its early summer meetings, Cripton tried to come to terms with what his trustees required.

Meanwhile, the second Festival Canada opened in Ottawa on June 30. Despite the poor houses the summer before, hopes ran high for the new season.[48] The theme revolved as promised around the fiftieth anniversary of the Declaration of Human Rights, and organizers pulled out all the stops to mark the occasion. The opening performance featured a stunning rendition of Beethoven's Ninth Symphony and its famous "Ode to Joy," under the direction of the Czech conductor Zdenek Macal, with the widow of John Humphrey, the Canadian who had drafted the UN Declaration of Human Rights, in the audience. A wide variety of other performances ensued aimed at satisfying every taste. For the high-brow crowd, there were concerts by classical soprano Denyce Graves and of Anton Dvorak's *Staber Mater*. For the middle-of-the-roaders, there was everything from Jazz under the Stars to the Cirque Parasol in Jacques Cartier Park. The popular singer Rita MacNeil performed at the NAC, but ticket sales for her show in the Opera hall were astonishingly low. A new, small-scale opera, *Elsewhereless*, presented in the NAC Theatre also bombed at the box office. Composed by Rodney Sharman with lyrics and direction by filmmaker Atom Egoyan, it had received mixed reviews at its premiere in Toronto yet still had attracted a lot of interest there. Fortunately, the remounting of Brian Macdonald's Gilbert and Sullivan show *The Mikado* was a huge success. First performed in Stratford in 1982, it had toured all the way to Broadway, where it had won two Tony awards. Now, after the summer, the NAC planned to take the show on tour again and had pumped generous sums into this new production, including beautiful sets and costumes designed by Susan Benson, which had been crafted in the reopened workshops at the Arts Centre.

Events around the Festival included an intellectually high-powered and star-studded international symposium, The Artist and Human Rights, hosted by Adrienne Clarkson, which brought together international thinkers from around the world. New technologies and their ability to aid or abet artists and human rights were at the centre of the discussion, with speakers ranging from Canadian Nobel Prize–winner John Polanyi to Nigerian playwright Wole Soyinka and a live video hook-up with South Africa's Archbishop Desmond Tutu. Co-organized by the Arts Centre and the Université d'Ottawa, the proceedings harked back to the 1970s Arts and Media Conferences that had been a feature of the early years at the centre. In every respect but one, the NAC seemed to be settling itself back on the firm footing of its first days.

The continuing fly-in-the-ointment was the uncertain state of the NAC's finances. Despite its lofty intentions, Festival Canada again turned in disappointing financial results. An optimistic forecast by Cripton to the board before the summer had predicted a small surplus. By summer's end the overall loss was verging on $1.7 million, although just under $390,000 of this amount was tagged as production costs for *The Mikado* and would be amortized over the next two years while the show went on tour. Ever the risk-taking impresario, Cripton was unruffled, confident that he could pull money from sources to alleviate the deficit. "In my life there have been many projects I started without knowing where I was going to get all the money until I got to the end," he noted years later.[49] He had the goodwill of Minister Copps on his side, the Department of Heritage had agreed to provide a million-dollar grant for the Festival's expenses—and he had fair expectations that there would be even more money available for future festivals.

But the poor results of this second Festival were a major disappointment to the trustees, whose timidity over running deep deficits at the NAC had been forged in the dreadful years before its fortunes began to turn under Cripton. Riley's sensitivities over financial matters again went onto high alert. In the rocky days of her interim directorship, the management-board division of powers had disappeared. That dividing line still remained murky, despite the fact there was now an experienced professional CEO in charge. But Cripton's sensibilities were perhaps more attuned to the flexibility of the private sector, and his frustration mounted as he tried to respond to the ever-increasing interventions by the board.

In most arts organizations in the country, boards of trustees had an aggressive fundraising role, and people joined boards with this expectation. By contrast, an appointment to the NAC board was generally a reward for past services. Its members might be responsible and well intentioned, but few had experience in the arts. In any case, they met together only four times a year and rarely saw each other otherwise. In the interim, the small Executive Committee kept tabs on things. As Cripton looked at the broad picture and tried to create new financial support for the NAC, he openly suggested a change in board structure: "I said, on a number of occasions, that this board should reflect the kinds of arts boards that exist throughout the country," he recalled. The suggestion did not sit well with the trustees, who saw their role primarily as guardians of the public interest. An inevitable clash between board and management loomed.

First, however, the NAC's second Fall Gala rolled around again. On October 2, 1998, the sensational American soprano Kathleen Battle was the renowned star. A controversial figure in the opera world, Battle had been banned from the Metropolitan Opera by its general manager, Joseph Volpe, after repeated misbehaviour at rehearsals. Her reputation as "the bad girl of opera" had proceeded her to Ottawa, and an NAC music staffer was assigned to shadow her closely. There were no difficulties. She sang

The NAC gala was established as a "must-attend," high-toned social event. Future NAC vice-chair Adrian Burns greets chair Jean Riley at the Jessye Norman concert. Photo © Julie Oliver/Ottawa Citizen. Reprinted by permission.

magnificently and behaved impeccably, lingering on into the early hours of the morning as she socialized with the guests. Once again the gala, chaired this time by Adrian Burns, attracted the cream of Ottawa and raised just under $125,000. Cripton was a prominent presence throughout the evening and graciously accepted congratulations, including personal good wishes from Prime Minister Jean Chrétien and his wife, Aline.

Back at the Board of Trustees, the continuing financial shortcomings had led to another wave of anxiety in the fall, fuelled by Riley's suspicion of anything that failed to meet her exacting standards. A woman of integrity with great concern for the careful use of taxpayers' money, she nevertheless accelerated problems when a lighter touch might have been more helpful. Now she was bolstered by three strong new appointments to the board, including Senator Royce Frith, the former government leader in the Senate who had gained attention as Canada's high commissioner in Britain during the nerve-racking cod wars. When the Executive Committee met on September 18, it carefully examined Cripton's draft for his new corporate plan. Riley complimented Cripton on his quick response to the auditor general's report and his overall "transparency," and he promised to have a full strategy ready for the board by the November meetings.[50] In truth, however, Riley was well on the way to another "breakdown in trust" with her CEO.[51]

A number of things were troubling her, but they revolved around three issues: the continuing financial shortfalls, her disagreement with some of Cripton's hires, and, above all, her insistence that the Arts Centre needed a different artistic direction that would be less costly. The Executive Committee organized a series of private meetings away from the NAC in the boardroom of vice-chair David Hill's law firm nearby. None of the NAC's financial staff was invited. After heated discussion, the group agreed that, if Cripton would not adopt their position, he would have to go.

Matters boiled to a head a few days later at a meeting between Cripton and a few trustees who had stayed on after both the gala and the October board meetings held on October 1 and 2. Cripton was confronted about his hiring of a new management consultant who was expected to assist him in developing commercial entertainment opportunities. Riley had heard rumours that this individual had acted unethically in his previous job and wanted him fired. Cripton refused—and left the contentious meeting briefly to fetch a letter that would prove he had already acted on her information. By the time he returned, trustee Royce Frith, who was also a skilful lawyer, was ready for him. Cripton's refusal to comply in the first instance with Riley's demand was labelled as "insubordination," and his departure from the meeting as "constructive resignation."[52] Cripton stormed out and retreated to his Gatineau Hills cottage. Despite some attempt by David Hill to resolve the dispute, the gap between the two parties was unbridgeable. After financials terms were settled, Cripton was informed by telephone that the rupture was final, and, in the seemingly regular practice for departing NAC directors general, he was ordered not to return to the building. He insisted he certainly would, as a member of the public, but he never went back to his office, and his personal belongings were sent on to him. Cripton's contract was over, just two years into his five-year plan.

This time Riley had ensured she was ready for the breakdown. She had already contacted Elaine Calder, the former general director of the Canadian Opera Company, who had flown to Ottawa to meet with the board so she could step in if Cripton rejected the trustees' ultimatum. She had been party to some of the deliberations on Cripton's fate, and was briefed on the financial affairs at the centre. She was ready, and she quickly stepped in as acting director general.

Reflecting on these events, many officials and NAC staffers focused later on the immense artistic vision that Cripton brought to Ottawa and on the way he fired them up with his ideas. From her position as deputy minister at Canadian Heritage, Suzanne Hurtubise recalled her regular meetings with Cripton, as he kept the department apprised of his plans. She also remembered the frequent meetings he arranged with representatives of the other cultural agencies, especially the Canada Council, to discuss common problems. "He was putting out synergies everywhere," she said.[53] But it was also her sense that there were "cultural differences" between his style as an entrepreneur and the particular needs of a highly complex public institution. "There are issues of probity in the public sector," she remarked, "that you just can't take a chance with." As to boards of trustees and their chairs, she emphasized the potential danger in appointing people who are not familiar with the way of operating in Ottawa. Unfortunately, Jean Riley seemed to lack a full understanding of this complicated world.* In future years, the government would stress competence and suitability in all such governance appointments. For now, however, the promising Cripton era at the National Arts Centre had come to an abrupt halt.

---

*Elaine Calder commented in an interview in April 2008: "If Jean Riley took accountability and transparency more seriously than the government which appointed her, or how the game is played in Ottawa, I think she was well out of it."

18

UPSET AND
RENEWAL

The news of John Cripton's sudden departure hit like a thunderbolt and created an uproar in Ottawa. Very few people were aware of the board-management struggle. On October 8, 1998, the Kathleen Battle gala chair, Adrian Burns, wrote to Cripton thanking him for his help and cooperation for the October 2nd event. The very next day, the Arts Centre issued the terse public statement announcing Cripton's departure. The entire NAC staff, especially the artistic team, were deeply shocked. Neither of the new artistic directors appointed by Cripton, Pinchas Zukerman and Marti Maraden, had yet launched their first seasons. Zukerman was not scheduled to take the podium as music director until September 1999, but the first play in Maraden's season, a Vancouver Playhouse production of *An Ideal Husband* that she had directed previously at the West Coast theatre, was opening the following week, on October 15. Cripton phoned her and promised he would be in the audience.

Few staff members, even those who had attended board meetings, had any inkling of the crisis, though Maraden recalled that, in the days before Cripton left, she had sensed "there was something unhappy going on, and financial issues were being discussed."[1] As a member of the senior management team, she was dismayed that she had not been directly informed of Cripton's departure. Victoria Steele, the dumbfounded English theatre manager, was in a meeting with colleagues when a board member walked in and delivered the news. Steele immediately called Maraden at home, so she would not hear it first on the radio. The artistic director went straight to the NAC and, as she walked into the theatre department, bumped into the Criptons. Cripton's wife, Linda, had close ties to the Ottawa theatre community and knew the news would hit hard. "They came to talk to us directly and to make sure we would be alright. They did not come to create animosity," Maraden attested.

That day or the next, the new interim director general, Elaine Calder, and chair Jean Riley summoned the staff to a general meeting in the NAC's Panorama Room, once the site of the elegant Le Restaurant and now a meeting room reserved for upscale parties or business conventions. Once again Riley faced an angry crowd. Maraden recalled: "It was a very hostile crowd indeed. The artists, the technicians, and all the staff were so disheartened." The meeting heard "an outpouring of disillusionment and hopelessness that was profound." Very little of what was happening had anything to do with the primary purpose for the NAC, and when someone piped up "It's called the National ARTS Centre," there was wild applause.

Maraden was "not a believer in curtain speeches," but at both the preview and the opening night performances of *An Ideal Husband* she addressed the crowd. "I welcomed the audience, spoke a little about the play, then ended with acknowledgement of John Cripton, the man who had brought me there."[2] She explained how supportive he had been and said she wanted to honour him with this production. Like others, Maraden questioned whether she wanted to stay on and work in such a "dysfunctional and sick building."[3] Her commitment to and affection for the artistic staff, as well as loyalty to her own first season, persuaded her to remain. Similarly, Zukerman was contacted through his agent in New York. With his big plans for the NAC already well under way, he too agreed that he would stay the course.

Public reaction to the news was powerful. On the airwaves, in editorials and letters to the editor, a groundswell of support rose up around Cripton and the misfortune of his departure. In a lengthy personal letter to his former staff, he outlined the initiatives and accomplishments he felt they had achieved during his short term and bade them farewell. He gave his version of the efforts to bring the budget into balance, including the cutting, and the networking with potential corporate sponsors he had begun. He expressed his sorrow at not being able to carry through his vision, but warned his former colleagues that all would be lost unless they kept true to the dreams and plans that had been initiated.

Even Heritage Minister Sheila Copps weighed in, telling an interviewer on CBC Radio that "Mr Cripton was a fantastic impresario." "The game was cut short," she said, "and, frankly, that's disappointing."[4] Her dismay was echoed by other parliamentarians. NDP culture critic Wendy Lill, a playwright herself, championed a motion at the Parliamentary Committee on Heritage to call the NAC brass on the carpet once again to explain to MPs what had happened. "Why are we losing very good people like John Cripton?" was the question. A huge number of letters and messages from all over the country flowed in to Cripton personally and to the letters columns in the media, attesting to the impact that Cripton had made in his short time at the Arts Centre. Among the many "shocked, dismayed and frankly depressed"[5] correspondents from the arts world were David Haber, the NAC's first program director; Louis Applebaum, the indefatigable composer and arts statesman; Shirley Thomson, the Canada Council's

The Honourable Sheila Copps took over the now-named Department of Canadian Heritage in 1996 as a member of Jean Chrétien's Cabinet. She promised to be a "hand's-on" cheerleader for arts and culture. Photo © Dave Chan/ Ottawa Citizen. Reprinted by permission.

director; and Mavor Moore, the renowned author and playwright. Peter Herrndorf, in his position as president of the Governor General's Performing Arts Awards, thanked Cripton for his help and lamented that he would be not be able to complete his five-year mission.

By the beginning of November, as the saga played out in the columns of the country's newspapers, it was clear that the NAC Board of Trustees was on the losing end of the public-relations battle. In a carefully orchestrated appearance, a delegation of trustees led by Jean Riley and David Hill, the reliable and steady vice-chair, met with the editorial board of the *Ottawa Citizen* to try to redress the situation. They managed to defuse some of the heat coursing through the story when Hill told them that the Arts Centre was seeking more transparency and, among other things, now planned to open its board meetings to the public. Riley added her comments, telling the editors that, in her opinion, "Cripton had a good good ego!" and that "John had seen the board as a necessary evil. He didn't want to pay attention to us."[6]

Elaine Calder was the right leader to step in at this exceedingly painful period in the NAC's history. She "was a good dose of nice cold water that we all needed," Maraden recalled. "She was efficient, respectful, helpful."[7] A clear-headed, intelligent, no-nonsense individual, Calder was not the type to shirk from the hard decisions needed to redress the finances and try to get the organization back on the rails. Though some, including the press, could find her terse manner acerbic, overall she quickly won support for her businesslike approach to the situation.

Although she had witnessed the high drama surrounding Cripton's demise, she discovered, when she finally got into the substance of the job, that "it was not the catastrophe" she expected. "Really," she said, "it was mixed."[8] She easily understood the rationale for some of the issues that had bedeviled her predecessor, such as the charge that he had hired his friends. As Tom Hendry reminded her, "Cripton had needed friends when he started to put the NAC back on its feet, and he worked with the

Acting CEO Elaine Calder earned the credit for tidying up the mess at the NAC and preparing it for the new leaders. Photo © Mike Pinder.

people he knew."[9] She respected the strategic corporate plan Cripton had been working on, and decided that the central issue for her was to tackle the unexpected deficit that had flared up and get the budget again under control. She made a point of meeting individually with the key people at the Arts Centre.

Shortly into her new job, she met the development officer, Kim McCuaig, to go through his dossiers. There she came across the Yashin gift. "That's secure, right?" she asked. She was shocked with his reply, "Not exactly."[10] A close examination of the paperwork showed a confusing tangle of arrangements. Among the documents was a copy of an agreement with the Alexei Yashin Foundation for the Performing Arts that set out the terms for his gift. A second agreement between the Arts Centre and a company called Tatiana Entertainment Inc. allowed Yashin's parents to provide consulting services for fees "up to $85,000" on Russian artists who might come to Canada.[11] Both documents had been signed by Cripton, but the file copies had not been executed or counter-signed by the Yashins. It was very different from the original proposal for the foundation which Pat Reid had conceived. According to that plan, Mrs. Yashin might serve as a director or even as one of a foundation's paid employees—an arrangement entirely legal under Revenue Canada rules—but one needing up to six months for approval. The haste with which the Yashin gift was announced appears to have precluded the proper arrangements being made. The "Tatiana" agreement bore Cripton's penciled notation that McCuaig should witness it, but McCuaig was away on holiday at the time. The witnessing was waived and the agreements were sent back to the Yashins for signature. Finalized documents were not to be found in the NAC's files.

McCuaig informed Calder that there was a dispute over the second $200,000 instalment of the Yashin donation: it would not be handed over until an invoice for $85,000 for consulting services requested by Mark Gandler, Yashin's Russian-born New Jersey agent, was paid. A dismayed Calder took the documents to Jean Riley, who turned immediately for legal advice to Scott and Aylen, an Ottawa law firm. In a formal opinion issued by David Scott, its senior partner, the firm advised the Arts Centre that the consulting agreement, given its close proximity to the Yashin donation, was illegal and unenforceable. Shocked NAC officials decided to reason with Alexei

Yashin in an effort to hang onto the donation, while not contravening Revenue Canada rules that gifts could not come with strings that benefited the giver.

Much was riding on the outcome. Extensive plans were already under way for further collaborations between the Arts Centre and the hockey team. Numerous meetings and conversations ensued. Even Maestro Zukerman, who was on good terms with Yashin, was asked to help out. He flew in to Ottawa, and accompanied by his assistant, Liz Waddell, met the young athlete for a private lunch at the Château Laurier hotel in the hope that the maestro could appeal to him on a personal basis. They showed Yashin the legal opinion the NAC had received and explained that the consulting arrangement for his parents could not proceed. Sadly, the meeting did not have the desired result. Yashin's lawyer wrote a letter stating that his client "had been deeply embarrassed and upset" by the information and believed that his parents were being maligned and accused of doing something illegal.[12] There is no doubt that, in the preamble to the Yashin gift, particularly given Cripton's close association with the Russian cultural scene, there had been enthusiastic conversations with the Yashin's representative that led the family to believe that they would actively contribute to the cultural life of their new city by helping to bring some Russian artists to Canada. Part of the gift was specifically dedicated to this purpose. When the first year of the gift had brought only a single Russian pianist to play at the Arts Centre, they were already disappointed.

The fallout from the bungled arrangements was huge. For almost a year, plans had been in progress for a celebratory concert to mark the handing over of the second instalment of the gift: an event called "Pucks and Tux" at the Corel Centre hockey stadium scheduled for January 30, 1999, with both Zukerman and Yashin conducting the NAC Orchestra. Now its fate hung in the balance. In a further effort to forestall the collapse of the pledge, Calder wrote Yashin a friendly note in early January, wishing him a happy new year, thanking him for his support, and inviting him to call the centre if he or his family wanted tickets to any of the forthcoming performances there. Aware of Yashin's interest in dance, she especially recommended the National Ballet of Canada's new production of *Swan Lake* coming to the NAC in May. In response, the disaffected Yashins informed the NAC that they were revoking their pledge, as the agreement permitted. In a brief press release, dated January 19, 1999, the Arts Centre made the news public: the largest single contribution in the history of the NAC, and all the potentially exciting activities surrounding it, had evaporated.

Two days later, Jean Riley, with the cool-headed Calder by her side, set out in a well-attended press conference the NAC's version of what had occurred—and another firestorm exploded over the centre.[13] David Scott had advised the board that it did not have to inform the media of all the details, but the decision by Riley and Calder to go public with the facts eventually produced a wide range of results for the National Arts Centre. To begin, it immediately tainted Cripton's reputation, just at a time when he was courting other job offers in Ottawa. A subsequent forensic audit initiated by the board

and kept securely "in camera" confirmed that there had been weaknesses in hiring practices as regards public service rules, but there had been no malfeasance on Cripton's
part. But the damage was done and he would have a difficult time finding future work
in Canada's art sector. The scandal also ended Riley's term as chair of the Board of
Trustees. Although her appointment had been renewed for a further three-year term
the previous April, Jean Pelletier, the chief of staff to the prime minister, called her to
his office and advised her to resign. No minister ever wants to be forced to stand up
in the House of Commons to answer for any controversy at a crown agency. And
Sheila Copps had now had enough of the furor at the National Arts Centre.

In the meantime, the Yashin camp countered with its own press conference, this one
at the Corel Centre, intended to clean up the mess from the hockey player's point of
view. The principled young athlete continued to insist that neither he nor his family
had done anything illegal, but so far as most of the media and the public were concerned, the matter was finished. Just as the news of the donation had led to an upsweep
of goodwill for Alexei Yashin, now the local sports press turned on him. The atmosphere in the city was poisoned for him, and, soon after, he left to play for the New
York Rangers.*

In retrospect, Riley perceived herself as someone "who had been mandated by the
government without having any government support."[14] It was true that, once given
the NAC chair, she was left to her own resources with little counselling from experienced people in government, and she had scant previous practice for the job's political
intricacies. Although she had a highly idealistic view of public life, she had no real
knowledge or understanding of the complexities of political Ottawa, and she went
beyond her depth. "She was well connected, but she did not have the experience," said
Russell Mills, the published of the *Ottawa Citizen*. "It was not a time for amateurs."[15]
Towards the end of her term, some senior officials, including Copps's deputy minister,
Suzanne Hurtubise, tried to give her sage advice, but Riley's personal sense of outrage
at what she perceived as wrong-doing overrode her ability to listen.

Before the affair was over, Riley was called back again, in February, by the Parliamentary Committee on Heritage, accompanied by fellow-trustees Royce Frith, David
Hill, and Andrew Ogarenko—all three Liberal Party stalwarts. Elaine Calder and
Rosemarie Landry, an opera singer who had reluctantly joined the board in 1996,
were also part of the delegation. In light of this latest disaster, the Liberal-dominated
committee seemed primarily interested in muting the uproar, and it refused to enter
into debate over the rights and wrongs of Cripton's departure. Instead, it simply chastised

---

*The Yashin family was personally hurt by the whole affair. While the parents remained living
in Ottawa, both their sons moved to work in the United States. Dmitri, who had been a top
student at Ashbury College, went into the financial business in New York, and Alexei continues
to play hockey for the New York Rangers.

the organization for its problems. Riley was not so fortunate: she reported a truncated attempt within the minister's office to question her own personal expenses. Despite the solid work she had done in re-engaging the community and helping to initiate corporate fundraising, it was made clear to her, she said, that she "had lost the confidence of the minister and also Mitchell Sharp's support."[16] After establishing yet another search committee to find a new CEO again for the centre, she left Ottawa, her dreams of making a mark on the national arts scene thwarted.

With razor-sharp precision, Elaine Calder set about cleaning house at the National Arts Centre. In her public report to the January press conference, she had summarized recent events. Three members of senior staff had departed since her arrival on November 2, 1998.

Brian Macdonald, Cripton's "eyes and ears" and adviser on artistic matters, had voluntarily followed his former boss out the door when he realized that opportunities for producing shows like *The Mikado* would not be forthcoming in the straitened financial situation. Personally, too, he was furious at the treatment meted out to Cripton and never forgave Riley and the trustees for their actions. Calder insisted that Macdonald return to the Arts Centre—and he did. Plans were already afoot for the workshop in February of a new opera, *Erewhon*, based on a Samuel Butler story, that had been commissioned by Nicholas Goldschmidt, with Louis Applebaum as composer and a libretto by Mavor Moore. Macdonald was also scheduled to stage an Opera Lyra production of *Tosca* at the NAC in April—an event partially underwritten by the NAC in its ongoing support to the local opera company.

The second casualty was Kim McCuaig, the senior director of marketing and development, who was shown the door in December. The prime reason cited by Calder was the high cost of fundraising associated with his work. The eighty-cent cost for every dollar raised was "unacceptable by any standard," pronounced Calder, adding that his response to the directives of the government's special audit had also been inadequate.[17]

The third departure was Denise Perrier, the senior cultural official on loan from the Department of Canadian Heritage, who had served as deputy director to Cripton. Calder caustically commented to the press conference that "there was a breakdown in confidence between us … and so she left."[18]

Calder then turned to a spirited defence of what had been happening on the stages of the NAC. Her vivid description painted a hopeful picture for any sceptical observers: "Last night as I walked through the backstage area to reach the Opera for Anton Kuerti's marvellous performance with the NACO," she said, "the public address systems were broadcasting the opening performance of *Les Nuits de la Liberté*, a co-production with Les Trois Arcs of Montreal in the Studio, and the preview performance of *Skylight*, produced here in partnership with Edmonton's Citadel in the Theatre. Tonight we open "Destroy—Punk Graphic Design in Britain" as part of U.K. Accents [a show brought in from England by the British Council]. Earlier this week we heard legendary pianist Radu Lupu, and on Saturday afternoon Boris Brott will be conducting and hosting one of his sold-out Young People's Concerts in the Opera."

She was right to point out the obvious—that, despite all the *sturm und drang* that had again swept through the board of trustees and the upper management at the NAC, the centre was still in business, putting out artistic work night after night. And, evidently, its audience was growing again. She reminded reporters that, "fortunately for the centre, for the citizens of the National Capital Region, and the taxpayers of Canada, we have immensely gifted and dedicated artistic, technical, and management staffs" producing a huge range of activities.[19] The coming months would demonstrate what she meant.

This press conference report was a skilful performance on Calder's part, one in which she positioned herself as a simple general manager, quite different from the exciting and risk-taking impresario John Cripton had been. She called upon the community, local and national, not to abandon the Arts Centre. And, amazingly, the national publicity that had swirled around the upheaval at the NAC now had a most unexpected result.

"Out of the blue," a surprised Jean Riley recounted, "two people we didn't know telephoned and offered us financial pledges. And the rest of the public joined them."[20] Toronto financier Grant Burton was one of those callers. While driving to work that grim February while the Parliamentary Committee hearings were in progress, he picked up a CBC Radio arts report that detailed some of the more disappointing aspects of the Yashin gift. He stopped his car by the roadside, called his wife, and they decided on the spot to help the National Arts Centre. When he arrived at his office he telephoned Elaine Calder. "I remember it was just before lunch on a Friday," she recalled. "He said he was prepared to put up $400,000 if we could match the money within six weeks."[21] Within days, the NAC Challenge Fund was launched.

The first cheque to actually arrive on Calder's desk after the fund's announcement was from the classical pianist Anton Kuerti. He had played a recent concert at the NAC and sent along a thousand dollars. Others followed, among them Ottawa high-tech financier Michael Potter, who was angry and ashamed when he heard on the news the NAC's version of the Yashin affair. He called up spontaneously just a couple of hours after Burton and agreed to give the Arts Centre $500,000, of which $100,000 was sidestepped for Opera Lyra, the arts company providing opera to the NAC. Donations, large and small, were soon flowing into the NAC's coffers. David Scott recalled that "people felt the whole Yashin thing was so tacky, we had to come to the rescue of the institution."[22] His firm chipped in $100,000, and other wealthy Ottawans also gave money.

With the help of the *National Post*, the NAC's plight was publicized across Canada, and the campaign received funds from every province and territory in the country. Calder called up many of her friends in the arts world and asked for their help. Many leading artists who had appeared at the NAC gladly gave their testimonials on the value of this performing arts centre. Even the gambling casino across the river in Hull, Quebec, kicked in, providing a lavish fundraising dinner. While it couldn't give money, it let the NAC keep the proceeds. Within weeks, Burton's challenge had been matched, and then some, leading the wealthy Torontonian to double his pledge. When the final tally was in, the Challenge Fund had raised $2.1 million. It was not only a concrete sign of the place the NAC held in the hearts of Canada's artistically minded citizens but it opened the way for the new world of private financing that would soon become firmly established at the National Arts Centre.

As she pruned and shaped the institution in those months, Calder also oversaw the reawakening artistic life. She was not exempt from the ritual faceoff with the NAC Orchestra that all directors general faced. The truce contract that Cripton had settled was over, and the musicians and their union felt the time had come to move their salaries upward again.

As negotiations proceeded, they chose a graphic way to get the message across. Zukerman, by now the music director–designate, had yet to formally take office, but he was booked for concerts at the Arts Centre. The most significant was a two-day series scheduled for November 18 and 19, 1998. Apart from a July 1 concert, it was the maestro's first formal appearance on the NAC podium since the announcement of his appointment. The concerts were also planned to mark the fiftieth anniversary of the State of Israel—"Israel at Fifty"—and Zukerman invited one of his protégés, Israeli violinist Ariel Shamai, to appear as soloist. Also on the program was the Canadian premiere of the "Los Alamos Suite" by the conductor's close collaborator and friend, the American composer Marc Neikrug. The orchestra musicians got their message across clearly by playing the first concert and then going on strike for the second. The gesture lasted only a few days but was sufficient.

Calder "found it fascinating" how quickly Treasury Board was able to find funds to meet the musicians' demands.[23] Once again Mitchell Sharp intervened behind the scenes to solve the problem. Minister Copps, whose job it was to manage requests for funds in the cultural sector, recalled that "Mitchell's love was primarily the orchestra. Not that he didn't love the Arts Centre, but when I got calls from Mitchell … the dollar-a-year man for Mr. Chrétien who was … important to the prime minister … I would try to accommodate him."[24] In the years ahead, Mr. Sharp's influential position within the Prime Minister's Office would often play a valuable role in the life of the NAC.

The ability of the artistic team to continue to put good work on the NAC stages spoke volumes about their resilience and tenacity in this, the NAC's thirtieth anniversary, season. Despite all the uncertainty in senior management, the show went on. Music reported a 9 percent growth in subscribers in the orchestra's regular season, which saw the newly designated conductor emeritus, Mario Bernardi, come back for a celebration concert with soloist Itzhak Perlman and the return of many other well-known musicians who had performed at the Arts Centre. Most important were the first inklings of the activities that Maestro Zukerman was planning there.

The summer season featured a first NAC Young Artists Program, which brought fledgling musicians from across Canada and abroad to the centre to work with instructors Martin Beaver and Patinka Kopec, the latter a close friend and associate of Zukerman from the Manhattan School of Music in New York. The summer also featured a Great Composers Festival, with performances by singer Ben Heppner, pianists Anton Kuerti and Janina Fialkowska, the debut performance of Isabel Bayrakdarian at the Arts Centre, and a joint concert with the NAC Orchestra and the National Youth Orchestra of Canada. Zukerman quickly got the orchestra back into the recording business with two new compact discs—a recording of Vivaldi's "Four Seasons" (which was to get plenty of play in Zukerman's future programs) and another of chamber music with Martin Beaver and NACO musicians Joanna G'froerer playing flute and Amanda Forsyth the cello. Forsyth was also forging a closer personal tie with the maestro and would eventually become his third wife.

Starting in the fall, Marti Maraden's first English theatre season unfolded with one well-received play after another—five on the main Theatre stage and three in the Studio—including collaborations with a diverse group of Canadian companies and artists. Her second offering in November was her own fine production of *A Man for All Seasons*, which she had staged for the Stratford Festival the previous summer to great success. Among her initiatives were shows for young families during the holiday season, beginning with the production of *The Secret Garden* at Christmas time. Sales for English theatre were up significantly among subscribers and single ticket buyers, and an after-show poll instituted by the staff revealed a 94 percent approval rate for what was appearing on the stage.

On the French theatre side, Jean-Claude Marcus put in a solid and creative season, demonstrating once again the well-grounded work that characterized this department.

Denis Marleau, Michel Lemieux, and Victor Pilon were among the creative visionaries cited in the annual report for bringing new work to the centre in the Découverte Series, which enjoined Quebec, French, and American co-productions. The NAC French Theatre Department was nominated for numerous awards at the francophone Soirée des Masques, a Quebec event. Marcus also presented the usual co-productions with Canadian francophone theatre companies. In particular he organized Les Quinze Jours de la dramaturgie des régions, a special theatre festival that brought hundreds of theatre artists from outside Quebec to the National Arts Centre.

The Dance and Variety Department, now headed by producer Michel Dozois, with Jack Udashkin as a consultant, "remained faithful to its mission of encouraging the creation of new works and making dance known to the widest possible public."[25] The Ottawa audience was receptive to dance, and the producers organized four series that presented sixteen works in all. Among them was a new work by Édouard Lock for La La La Human Steps and a co-production with modern dancer/choreographer Marie Chouinard, *Les Solos 1978–1998*. Visiting avant-garde companies from Holland and Israel presented the very latest in modern dance from around the world. The Canadian classical ballets all took their turn, with a new *Carmina Burana* choreographed by Fernand Nault for Les Grands Ballets; James Kudelka's contemporary version of *Swan Lake* for the National Ballet; and two new ballets, including a version of Bram Stoker's *Dracula*, from the Royal Winnipeg Ballet. Other well-established foreign companies, both classic and modern, as well as works from several rising new young choreographers, rounded out the thriving dance program.

There was no summer Festival Canada in 1999. That annual event was now cancelled. When all the reports were in for the 1998–99 season, they showed that, although overall attendance figures had dipped slightly from the previous year, ticket revenue was up significantly in all the disciplines. Despite all the administrative turmoil, performance at the Arts Centre remained strong.

Most encouraging of all, two new men had arrived to lead the National Arts Centre into the new century: Dr. David Leighton, a distinguished business director and educator, had been appointed chairman of the Board of Trustees in May; and Peter Herrndorf, the former chairman and CEO of TV Ontario, was named as director general and CEO in July. Another new era was about to commence at the NAC.

19

THE ROAD
TO RECOVERY

The Ottawa that awaited the new NAC leadership was a long way from the 1960s capital in which Southam and his colleagues had undertaken their dream of the Arts Centre. The country, and its artistic life, had changed dramatically. The roller-coaster ride for the National Arts Centre through the intervening years had seemed for a long time to be on a permanent downward slide. That had been halted with the election of the Chrétien government in 1993. While forward progress since had been fitful, there was no question that, when the two new men arrived in town, the centre was ready to move ahead. The terms and conditions under which the new chair and CEO would perform their work were stricter and more complex than those that had prevailed in Southam's day. "Art for art's sake" in the world of government was an ideal of the past. Now these federal arts organizations were expected to serve not only the arts but also the specific purposes and national goals of the government of the day.

When Chrétien's government took power, it retained the reorganized department that had been initiated during the short-lived regime of Conservative prime minister Kim Campbell. It was now known as the Department of Canadian Heritage, and had a firm grip on the management and financing of the cultural sector. When he appointed Sheila Copps to the portfolio in 1996, Chrétien advised her that, despite his apparent indifference to the arts during the previous years of strenuous budget cuts, he really thought that "arts and parks" were the hallmarks of a good government. "Nobody cares about them as far as the normal scheme of government goes," Copps said he told her. "But they are the things that last forever and really make a difference."[1] He also made it abundantly clear to her that Heritage was not a "constituency" portfolio. "People are not going to vote for you because you invested in the arts, and they are not going to vote for you because you expanded the parks systems." "Sad, but true," Copps commented later. But now that the deficit was under better control, the government's purse strings were loosening a notch. Chrétien gave Copps the job of pulling the department together and putting it fully into the national cause for Canada It was a challenge she relished.

As the latest blow-up at the NAC simmered down, a new deputy minister, Alex Himelfarb, was installed at the Heritage department. He replaced the competent Suzanne Hurtubise, whose first love was economics, and who now moved on to become Canada's ambassador at the Organization of Economic Cooperation and Development in Paris. During his short term of just two years at Heritage, Himelfarb would play a seminal role in pulling together the powerful energies and intelligence that resided in the cultural Crown agencies to make an impact on the government. His connections and interest in culture would continue when he moved up in 2002 to become clerk of the Privy Council and secretary to the Cabinet—the most senior and powerful position in the public service.

Board and other appointments were still in the hands of Penny Collenette, Chrétien's appointments secretary, and she had turned up an unexpected yet worthy candidate for the position of chair at the Arts Centre. Dr. David Leighton, at seventy-one, was a quiet-spoken, widely experienced, astute professor emeritus at the University of Western Ontario's Ivey Business School who had served on the boards of over eighteen national and international companies.* In addition, he had a solid and broadly demonstrated love of the arts and, for thirteen years from 1970 to 1982, had been president and CEO of the Banff Centre—an appointment many credited with saving the centre as a formidable force for the arts in Canada. Under Leighton's leadership, and thanks to the support of Alberta premier Peter Lougheed, the Banff Centre expanded from a summer operation to a year-round program for the arts and, subsequently, business seminars as well.** Arts and business rubbing shoulders would become a Leighton specialty. He accepted an influential appointment as the founding chair and CEO of the Organizing Committee of the 1988 Calgary Winter Olympics, and helped to ensure that a significant cultural component was included in those festivities. Above all, Leighton had written what was generally perceived as the definitive book on good board governance—a hot topic in the business world, as appalling tales of misgovernance in companies such as Enron were hitting the news. The same concern applied to government, and it was soon agreed that appointments to public boards had to be

---

*Educated at Queen's University and then at Harvard, Leighton's board appointments included Nabisco and the international mining company Rio Algom Ltd. A principled man, at the latter company he instituted a responsible environmental policy at Rio Tinto for its South American operations.

**Lougheed later credited the intervention of his arts-loving wife, Jeanne, with having allowed Leighton to make an unprecedented direct presentation to the Alberta Tory Cabinet on arts matters and the Banff facility and to make the case for the Banff expansion.

far more effective.* A small *L* liberal, though no Liberal Party partisan, Leighton, with his wife, Peggy, brought tailor-made credentials to the fraught job of NAC chair. Together they would play an important part in the centre's regeneration.

Leighton had been invited once before to Ottawa in connection with the NAC, in 1988, when he too was interviewed by the trustees for the post of director general. The couple were known as a working partnership, and Peg Leighton recalled being asked if she would want her own office at the centre. They soon realized, however, that the interview was a *pro forma* exercise and that the job was going to Yvon DesRochers. Now, before accepting the government's offer, Leighton wanted to learn more about the situation and flew to Ottawa to talk over the job with Mitchell Sharp, the prime minister's right-hand man. Sharp had personally telephoned Leighton to inquire if he would be interested in the job.**

While waiting in Sharp's office in the Langevin Building, opposite Parliament Hill, to see the elder statesman, a curious incident revealed to Leighton a great deal about the way life was conducted at the NAC. Sharp's secretary handed him a set of files on the centre to peruse while he waited. A quick skim of the sheaf of memos and letters demonstrated a communications pipeline between concertmaster Walter Prystawski, Liz Waddell, and Sharp that extended back over several years, including throughout the threatened 1996 strike period when John Cripton was struggling to establish relations with the orchestra and to rebalance the resources available to all the disciplines at the NAC. In the case of the more recent symbolic one-day strike, it was Sharp who had been a key factor in securing the funds from Treasury Board that allowed the matter to be settled in a manner that seemed, to Leighton's eyes, almost incidental to senior NAC management. Leighton recalled that, in that short waiting period before he hastily handed the files back to the secretary "as something I should not be seeing, I got a very quick early lesson on how communications and the decision-making structure of the government worked. It was something that was very handy to know later on."[2]

A good pipeline to power, when it existed and functioned, was crucial to the success of the National Arts Centre. Without it, the organization invariably foundered. From the earliest days, Hamilton Southam's ability to pick up the telephone and reach the prime minister directly had been essential to the institution's very creation. As Leighton discovered, and would later gladly acknowledge, it was the presence of

---

*Co-authored with D.H. Thain, *Making Boards Work: What Directors Must Do to Make Canadian Boards Effective* (Toronto: McGraw-Hill Ryerson, 1997).

**Some months before, the Leightons had visited Ottawa on the invitation of Brian Macdonald, the NAC's artistic director, to attend the first gala with Jessye Norman. There Dr. Leighton had run into an old friend, Walter Waddell, husband of Liz Waddell, both of whom were active Liberal Party members and very close to Sharp. It's likely that it was Liz Waddell who put Leighton's name into the system for the position of chair of the board.

Mitchell Sharp, as the NAC's distinguished champion, that helped to enable many of the new dreams for the Arts Centre to flourish.

Before accepting the offer of the chairmanship, Leighton checked to ensure how he could do his best work in the position. Through his invaluable network of old friends and colleagues in the senior civil service, including Gordon Osbaldeston, the high-ranking and well-informed former deputy secretary to the Treasury Board, he learned that he would never have more power than the moment just before the official announcement of his appointment. That was the time, advised Osbaldeston, to ask for everything he wanted. Leighton had no difficulty with partisanship in appointments, but he had strong ideas about the kinds of qualifications needed to provide good governance. While the position of trustee might be an honorific, it was no sinecure but, rather, a responsible job to which the appointee should make a commitment. The message of good qualifications for board appointees became a dominant theme in his seven years of service as NAC chair and, under his leadership, a proper job description for the post was developed. As a condition of accepting the chairmanship, he obtained an unprecedented assurance from Prime Minister Chrétien that no political hacks would be parachuted onto his board, and even got the promise in writing from an exceedingly reluctant Sheila Copps. The formal announcement of Dr. David Leighton as new NAC chair was issued by the government on May 6, 1999.

The prime task now for the new chair and his board was to find a new CEO. The acting director general, Elaine Calder, had expressed an interest in staying on but was not favoured by Mitchell Sharp, who indicated to Leighton (even though the appointment was not his to make) that she should not be considered. Calder sensed the mood and withdrew any idea of her candidacy, eventually taking her considerable management skills to a new challenge as managing director of the Hartford Stage—a regional theatre company in Connecticut. In the meantime, she continued diligently to clean up the mess at the Arts Centre. In her surgical style, she earned full credit for cutting and clearing out financial problems and leaving a relatively clean field for her successor. The outgoing chair, Jean Riley, left as her parting gift a well-formulated CEO Search

An expert on governance, Chair Dr. David Leighton devoted his talents and time to the NAC. Photo © Jim Cochrane.

Committee, led by the seasoned vice-chair David Hill. The board engaged a competent Ottawa-based head-hunting firm, Robertson-Surrette, to conduct the formal search.* After a thorough-going review, the system turned up a remarkable candidate.

Peter Herrndorf was the child of German nationals, a Protestant father and a Jewish mother, who left Germany in the mid-thirties and met in Holland before the war. As tensions mounted, the couple sailed for Indonesia but were forced to return to Holland, where Peter was born in Amsterdam in 1940. In the postwar period, as former German citizens, they became stateless persons and went, first, to the United States. But lacking some of the needed documents to settle there and with a family connection in Winnipeg, they moved to the Manitoba capital, where Peter grew up. The city at the time was a hotbed of creativity and would produce an astonishing array of artists, public servants, and other talented individuals who served Canada well in the ensuing decades.**

Herrndorf attended the University of Manitoba and then obtained a law degree at Dalhousie University. His passion for politics and public affairs led him straight out of university into the CBC, first as a reporter and editor, then as a television producer in Edmonton,*** and finally to network headquarters in Toronto. After stepping out to take his master's degree in administration at Harvard in 1970, he returned to the CBC and began a stellar career that took him up the ladder in programming to over-see some of the most innovative and challenging programs on the air—*The Fifth Estate*, *The Canadian Establishment* (based on the book by Peter Newman), and important special documentaries such as *The October Crisis* and *Connections* (a two-part series on organized crime). Program colleagues such as CBC journalist David Halton remembered him as a knowledgeable, engaged, and supportive executive producer. After becoming vice-president and general manager in 1979 of CBC's English Language Radio and Television Networks, he moved the English-language *National News* back to 10 p.m. and introduced the acclaimed national public affairs program *The Journal* to the CBC network. Unfortunately, differences with top CBC management, led by president Pierre Juneau, led to his departure from the corporation in 1983, though his work was characterized as "superb," a man who delighted in putting the best

---

*The author was named to the committee as the Ottawa community representative. Besides Dr. Leighton, local theatre director Gilles Provost and staff member Robert Asselin were among its members.

**Theatre director John Hirsch, playwright Tom Hendry, diplomat Allan Gotlieb, and financier Jim Pitblado were among many Winnipeggers from this era who went on to influence Canadian public life.

***There he produced a revealing television portrait of Peter Lougheed, the soon-to-be Alberta premier. Lougheed would later become a staunch supporter of the NAC, when Leighton and Herrndorf began to push its interests in the West.

As the new president and CEO, Peter Herrndorf worked himself and his staff hard. Photo © Jim Cochrane.

people on a team and clearing the way for them to get on with their work. He would amply demonstrate these qualities when he came to the National Arts Centre.

After the CBC, Herrndorf worked for a time as publisher at *Toronto Life* magazine before going on to become chairman and CEO for three terms at TVOntario, a post he was leaving when the NAC came calling. Along the way he had been touted as a possible president for the CBC, a job he was said to desire and for which many CBC activists had lobbied.* When the NAC Search Committee contacted him, he saw it as a job that might have all the problems of the CBC, as a national cultural organization, but with perhaps more fun. Herrndorf met with the NAC Search Committee in Ottawa on June 25, 1999, and was intrigued, though he did not readily accept. It took several weeks and the skilful intervention of Dr. Leighton, along with the essential behind-the-scenes help of Mitchell Sharp, before the matter was settled. Leighton and Herrndorf hit it off immediately and spent many hours discussing what they could do with the place if they got together. With a deal finally struck, Peter Herrndorf took over as president and CEO of the National Arts Centre on September 1, 1999.

When Southam left the National Arts Centre in 1977, he had described it as "just like a well-tuned Rolls-Royce. Anybody could drive it."[3] The intervening years revealed how wrong he had been, and how very difficult to run and how vulnerable the highly tuned organization really was. Now the Leighton/Herrndorf team set out to re-establish

---

*Halton indicated that there had been some suggestion at the time under the super-sensitive Liberal government that Herrndorf had a latent tie to the Conservative Party, dating from 1979, He had made the documentary of the Alberta Conservative premier Peter Lougheed, and Halton thought this slight connection might have worked against him. In 2008, the former deputy minister Alex Himelfarb indicated that Herrndorf had been offered the CBC presidency. For complicated reasons the appointment did not proceed. The CBC president, Robert Rabinovitch, a former deputy minister in the Department of Communications, was then reappointed.

it in a political, cultural, and social context that was vastly different from the conditions that had prevailed in Southam's day.

Herrndorf chuckled later about the day he first arrived at the NAC and was shown down the long windowless corridor to his office. "You realize this is known as Death Row?" commented the helpful staffer who ushered him in. Herrndorf smiled and told her, "We should put an end to that," but he later used the incident in his opening press conference as the kind of gallows humour that prevailed at the abused organization. In his view the Arts Centre needed "to have both trust and optimism rekindled," and he set out to tell everyone to "calm down, relax. It is going to be okay."[4]

In his early months, Herrndorf met and talked with everyone he could in the building—the ones who had kept the place running through all the traumas. While he had regular meetings in his, or their, offices, he also walked the halls, hung around outside where he shared cigarettes with similarly nicotine-challenged staffers,* and took his meals in the informal backstage Green Room cafeteria, listening intently to everyone he spoke to. It confirmed what he had instinctively believed: "My sense had always been that Hamilton's vision was, in fact, the right vision for the National Arts Centre and that it was national in scope and one of the artistic leaders in the country—it would have an impact across the country and would be a showcase for the best work from the various parts of the country," he recalled. "I thought that was the right vision for the place. It was a big, ambitious, meaty, quite romantic vision, and that was very appealing to me."[5] As Herrndorf found his feet, and with Dr. Leighton's support, he began work on a new strategic plan that, when it was finally presented, was not accidentally entitled "Restoring the Vision."

The two men had an innate respect for each other and quickly worked out a mutually supportive *modus operandi* that allowed them to settle down to the serious work of repairing the organization. "David was the perfect person to reshape the board and the role it played," said Herrndorf. "He was very good at getting the board to calm down. It had been far too involved in the inner workings of the place. With his knowledge of governance, he persuaded them that they should be engaged in the big issues of strategic conceptual planning and policies, and stay out of an organization that was far too complicated for a board to run."[6]

At the same time, Leighton played an important personal support role for Herrndorf, serving as his invaluable behind-the-scenes sounding board while the CEO worked out his strategies and plans for the NAC's recovery. "We liked and trusted each other, in a way that I have not seen elsewhere between a board chair and the CEO," Herrndorf remembered. The two men worked back to back, and Leighton even took a small apartment in Ottawa, devoting the majority of his time to the NAC job in the early years. He showed little inclination to get directly involved in management, but

---

*Herrndorf gave up smoking after a couple of years on the job.

Chair David Leighton, playing at a Christmas concert for the Snow Suit Fund with concertmaster Walter Prystawski and second violinist Donnie Deacon, was a good-humoured supporter.
Photo © Fred Cattroll.

"he was full of views and ideas which he shared, with restraint," his CEO later recalled with a smile. In truth, Leighton became a champion for a number of issues, including taking up the cause of opera and improving relations with other local arts groups, and he undertook a vigorous though ultimately only moderately successful attempt to link up the NAC with programs at Banff, and an unsuccessful effort to forge a permanent tie with the National Youth Orchestra. When they had differences of opinion, they kept them behind closed doors. In public, Herrndorf confirmed, "we were essentially interchangeable, which was a great strength," given the heavy workload of reorganizing the place.[7] Together they developed a comprehensive view of the future, and Herrndorf was free to get on with it.

At the core of Herrndorf's approach were the same ideas which had worked well at the CBC and later at TVOntario. His specialty as a manager had become "the art of running large, sprawling, and difficult creative organizations, usually dominated by complicated, ambitious creative figures," and he worked with the guiding principle that "they were the ones to be helped, unleashed, and supported." While his first step at the NAC was to create "a sense of optimism and trust so that people should feel good about working there again," his central move was to put the artistic leadership, "the heart and soul of the place," back at the core of the organization and then "put together the best management team available to properly guide and support the NAC."[8]

Herrndorf had been schooled in these management ideas by working with creative people such as broadcasters Barbara Frum and Peter Gzowski and particularly the great theatre director John Hirsch. Herrndorf claimed Hirsch as a close friend and said he learned a lot from him about "the struggle of artists trying to work within large organizations with the kinds of necessary resources they needed to achieve the bold vision they were seeking."* He applied this experience as he started to work on the first pillar of his new strategic plan: artistic expansion and innovation on the stages at

---

*Herrndorf later remarked, "I've often said to Pinchas that I owe an enormous debt of gratitude to John Hirsch for making me able to work for eight years with Pinchas Zukerman."

the NAC. Building on the first-class creative team that Cripton had begun with Pinchas Zukerman in music and Marti Maraden in English theatre, Herrndorf soon added the renowned Denis Marleau as the artistic director of French theatre and Cathy Levy as the producer of dance—an appointment that would finally put dance into full prominence among the four performing arts disciplines at the NAC.

The outgoing occupant of that position, Michel Dozois, who had previously worked closely on the dance program with Yvon St. Onge and Jack Udashkin, moved over to become producer of a creative new program in the space on the Elgin Street side of the building that had degenerated from the originally planned commercial shops into an in-house party room. Here, with Herrndorf's full encouragement to improve relations with the local artistic community, Dozois oversaw the creation of the Fourth Stage—a new performing space at the centre that would be open to all local artistic comers. It soon proved to be an enormous success.

Herrndorf's optimistic style of leadership infused the centre and its employees. The process of participation that he instilled in the staff was marked by another new and useful innovation. From November 1999 forward, he ensured that the detailed *CEO's Report*, a comprehensive summary of events from the proceeding quarter that he prepared for meetings of the Board of Trustees, was posted on bulletin boards throughout the centre for all the employees to see. This meticulous record signalled to the staff the attention Herrndorf was paying to details in every department as well as the importance he put on transparency within the organization. While generally characterized by upbeat and positive items, the reports also recorded deaths and other affecting events in the life of the centre. They reflected the loyalty that Herrndorf felt towards his staff, but also the loyalty that he expected from them.

An early gesture that helped to cement the sense of inclusiveness he was trying to engender was the January 27, 2000, renaming of the Opera hall after the NAC's founder, Hamilton Southam. The event not only paid tribute to the values of the glorious past Herrndorf was trying to rejuvenate but was a touching gesture to the venerable Southam,

Peter Herrndorf raised morale by participating in all events, including an informal Christmas concert in the NAC foyer. Photo © Ashley Fraser/ Ottawa Citizen. Reprinted by permission.

with whom Herrndorf had established a close personal friendship. Southam affirmed in his remarks that he now felt that "his" institution was coming back into safer waters at last. At the gathering to mark the occasion, Herrndorf had ensured all the other previous directors general who had struggled through the intervening years to keep the NAC afloat were invited, and nearly all of them attended. It was a gracious acknowledgement and was followed soon after by the mounting of photographs of all the previous NAC chairs in the vicinity of Southam Hall. The pioneer work of the first chair, Lawrence Freiman, was recognized when the laneway leading down to the entrance of the NAC was named Freiman Lane. The names of long-serving employees at all levels were also mounted on one of the public walls. Herrndorf's conciliatory approach to all the hurts and injuries of the past helped clear away many of the old wounds, although there would be plenty of new challenges to confront.

Besides the well-grounded artistic teams, the CEO tapped other in-house talents. They included a finally reliable financial office led by chief financial officer Danny Senyk,* as well as other competent senior managers ranging from executive chef Kurt Waldele, who was listed as part of the creative team, to such experienced hands as the long-time production director Alex Gazalé and the director of operations Gilles Landry. From the outside, Herrndorf brought in Jayne Watson, a fluently bilingual and well-connected Ottawa operative, as his new director of communications.** Watson came from the Export Development Bank, where she had a network of excellent local and national business contacts that would prove invaluable as the NAC got into the quest for new sponsorship funds. She was also on friendly terms with everyone in the national and the local media, and her positive, energetic personality was an excellent foil and support to the hard-working, focused Herrndorf. The NAC also hired a competent new human resources director, Deborah Collins, who brought tough-minded professionalism to the ongoing negotiations with the various well-entrenched unions at the centre.

By the time the new strategic plan was announced publicly in 2001, a gifted and widely respected creative team was in place, supported by a sound management group. Before the full flowering of their talents could occur, however, the organization had to be placed on more sound financial footing.

---

*In fairness, the previous financial officer, Cy Cook, who had retired at the end of his contract, had suffered from the antiquated financial systems being used at the NAC and which had been part of the problem in providing updated and current financial information to the previous board and CEO. Danny Senyk and his staff now benefited from the new computer practices that had been put in place.

**Jayne Watson's brother, Jim Watson, had served on the NAC board as mayor of Ottawa and was now an MPP and Cabinet minister in the Ontario Liberal government.

The new strategic plan started with excellence and innovation in artistic creation, but it also contained three other important thrusts. The second was to put the "national" back into the Arts Centre's activities. "Our goal is to make a difference in the performing arts throughout Canada—by working with artists and arts organization, and by bringing NAC performance to Canadians wherever they live." The third objective was "a greater commitment to youth and education activities," and the fourth—the key to them all—called for "a dramatic increase in our 'earned revenues.'"[9] This last aim would be essential in underpinning the work that lay ahead. It would also provide the dramatic and fundamental difference between the way the NAC had operated over the previous decades and the way it would function in future.

The goal, by 2010, was to invert the fundraising model that had prevailed since the days of Hamilton Southam. In the early years, more than 60 percent of the NAC's funding could be expected from parliamentary appropriation, while the balance came from box office, special grants, and other incidental revenues from commercial and other activities. There was little or no fundraising from the private sector. Within ten years, the new team aimed to reverse that equation and have earned revenues account for at least 60 percent of the NAC's total funds—with a significant portion of that to come from private fundraising.

Although parliamentary funding had stabilized after the painful program review cuts of the early 1990s, it was Leighton and Herrndorf's view that much of the new artistic vision would have to be funded by earned revenues. A new entrepreneurial ethic was being introduced at the NAC. While it was Herrndorf's intention to increase already existing revenues from activities such as the commercial parking garage (which saw almost immediately a long-overdue increase in parking fees), and possibly in catering, the biggest innovation would be the establishment at last of a formal, properly staffed Development Department to raise new money for the Arts Centre.

With the exception of the artistic directors, no new appointment received more care and attention from the CEO and the board than the search for a new executive director of development—a position that would spearhead the NAC's march into the highly competitive and intense world of professional fundraising. Even before he came to the centre, Herrndorf had worked out that "what was needed was a sophisticated new revenue strategy that would release the NAC from the financial trap in which it had been caught for so long." Unlike the Southam years, where the ethos held that the government should largely foot the bills, the new leader "had no difficulty, philosophically, with the idea that we were going to be a 'not-for-profit' that blended fundraising, earned revenue, and government support. It had always been natural to me that you would use all these tools and that they would complement each other." His chairman, David Leighton, fully agreed, and the two worked hard together to devise the new model. Herrndorf asked a long-time colleague and friend, Janet Wright, president of a well-respected head-hunting firm in Toronto, "to go out and recruit the best fund-raising person she could find."[10]

The job at the beleaguered Arts Centre was "perhaps not the most appealing in the arts fundraising field,"[11] but Wright turned up an unusual candidate. Darrell Louise Gregerson had been working at the Hospital for Sick Children in Toronto as part of the major disbursement team. While she had been in fundraising for nearly twenty years, she was a musician by training and had played the oboe in several orchestras. Quiet and intense, she was also relentless and passionate about the arts—a fact that quickly drew Herrndorf's interest to her. Music director Pinchas Zukerman, also concerned about the fundraising plans for the new projects he was already working on, advised Herrndorf that "oboe players are known as very determined and stubborn people"[12]— useful talents when tapping donors for money. After nearly eight weeks of discussion largely devoted to persuading Gregerson's husband, a Toronto architect, on the merits of a move to Ottawa, Darrell Gregerson joined the team. She would soon turn her unequivocal commitment to theatre, dance, and especially music into a fundraising money machine for the organization.

"Unlike most fundraisers, her message is visceral, not cerebral," Herrndorf later commented, and her commitment sharply focused the NAC's fundraising efforts. Hired on July 17, 2000, within months she had launched and become the first CEO of a new National Arts Centre Foundation—the fundraising arm of the National Arts Centre. The idea might have been old-hat in some artistic organizations, and certainly for most philanthropic efforts at Canadian hospitals and universities, but it was a brand-new concept at the NAC. Gregerson set herself and her team an ambitious target—to bring in $10 million a year for the NAC within ten years.

Gregerson's previous experience showed that institutions like hospitals or universities, also funded by government, had no difficulty raising money to "expand the edge of excellence." Although she knew it would not be easy, she anticipated something similar at the NAC. To her surprise, she found that although people felt very proprietary about the centre, the concept that they had a role to play as donors was in its infancy. Her biggest challenge would be to change that perception among the public. It also meant a considerable adjustment within the organization. "Staff needed to learn about having donors and investors in their lives, and the accountability and the responsiveness and timeliness that required," Gregerson noted.[13] Setting ambitious goals, and with a development staff that grew rapidly, she was soon firmly launched on a new campaign to recruit supporters for the NAC from all across the country, leaving her boss to sort out the internal practices that the new development program imposed. Herrndorf and Leighton had begun to acclimatize the staff to the idea, but the level of accountability and detail, and the demands on staff time required, was intense and just becoming apparent.

By the time Gregerson arrived, the Challenge Fund campaign had been a great success, and she saw as one of her first tasks the need to inform people what had happened to their money. That fall the NAC Orchestra under Pinchas Zukerman was embarking on an important Middle East and European tour, and some of the funds were dedicated to it. A million dollars was also being used to provide starting funds for the new foundation. NAC donors heard all about these plans in a first newsletter from the NAC development office. The aim was not only to tell donors what was being done with their money but why. The quest for this information sometimes raised consternation in-house, as Gregerson and her team tried to fathom from the artistic teams not only what they were doing but why they were doing it. With the exception of Pinchas Zukerman, who was immediately intrigued by the question, others were initially affronted that their work was being "queried." But that was not how Gregerson saw it. Drawing from the creative staff what they specifically wanted to accomplish, and then going out and persuading donors they could make a difference in achieving those specific goals, was key to her approach.

The development work would not all be about money but also about implanting the idea of the National Arts Centre in people's thinking from coast to coast to coast— that it was national, that it belonged to all Canadians, and not just to Ottawa. Soon, an ingenuous series of new initiatives would begin to drive this point forward.

20

THE REBLOOMING
OF THE ARTS

Reports from the artistic side at the National Arts Centre began to carry a more optimistic tone, as evoked in the quarterly *CEO's Report*. A sense of the crackling new
energy flowing through the centre's artistic activities was reflected in the news that
Peter Herrndorf brought forward as early as November 1999: overall subscription revenues for the next season were substantially up over the previous year (6.9 percent)
and, in terms of total dollars, were the highest ever in the thirty-one seasons of the
NAC. Local audiences at least were taking note of the new action at the centre and
seemed eager to participate. Given the dynamic and demanding presence of Pinchas
Zukerman, the news was dominated by reports from the music side, but the other disciplines were also re-establishing their mark on the artistic scene in a remarkable way.

In English theatre, Marti Maraden had embarked on a fascinating artistic journey.
Thanks to her peerless leadership during her tenure, the centre would see not only the
classics return but a whole new world of Canadian theatre emerge. Her efforts brought
an attentive and faithful audience back to the NAC, and the theatre community across
the country became attuned to its work. "Marti had good credibility as a director," said
theatre administrator Victoria Steele. "The selection of an artist of her calibre …
signalled to the rest of the country, Wow! the NAC is back in business and ready to
offer artistic leadership." While Maraden had some administrative experience, "her
chops were first and foremost as a director and she was well regarded," added Steele.
"That spoke volumes."[1]

Initially, Maraden was a little in awe of her prestigious new post. Her second night
on the job, she found herself playing host to Robert Lepage, whose play *Elsinore* was
opening that evening. Lepage was not performing in the production, but had turned
up for the festivities. "Here I am with this iconic, much-admired, virtually 'worshipped-

by-me' great director," said Maraden as she recalled sitting beside Lepage at dinner. She found the young francophone director charming and easy to talk to. "The headiness of having to do that," she said. "For the first two weeks of my job I was 'acting' at being an executive, because I couldn't actually be this person!"[2] Those opening weeks of her time at the NAC revealed to Maraden the richness that awaited her. Andis Celms had programmed the first season she oversaw. "We did an *Othello* from Edmonton's Citadel Theatre, directed by Michael Langham, which starred Megan Follows and her partner, Stuart Hughes," Maraden said. She recalled a conversation with the legendary Langham, the former director of Stratford, as "an enormous highlight of that season." The production immediately opened to her the potential for the thrust stage that was available in the Theatre, and she determined that it must again come into regular use.

She also grasped the significance of the co-production model that had kept the NAC's theatre functioning during the recent difficult years. From the perspective of an artistic director, however, she realized how important it was to plan them carefully so as to avoid, as much as possible, the unfortunate compromises such arrangements could impose. In the future, she insisted that such collaborations would be initiated and created at the Arts Centre, and then shared with another company, or, conversely, started elsewhere with the NAC's help and then toured into Ottawa. Either way, her aim was to help in devising the best possible creations artistically and presenting them in Ottawa and elsewhere. From the beginning, she worked hard to reconnect with the theatre community across the country in order to make that happen. "Marti had the personality and talent to be able to go out and listen and communicate well," Steele recalled, "both to our audience, who loved her, and to theatre people across the country."[3]

New partnerships had to be built. It would be the quality of work on the stage that determined how well the NAC established its credibility both with its audience and especially with the country's artists. Maraden had no illusions that the Arts Centre could pretend to call itself Canada's national theatre. "We don't have a company," she stressed. "I'm not saying that it can't be, but at that point it was not viable at all." Instead, she defined the NAC theatre as "a catalyst for the national theatre and a home to it. I was saying, 'Anyone in Canada who practises theatre should be able to consider this as a potential home and venue.'"[4] This attitude, and her ability to supply support quickly, led to good relations with a number of exciting new enterprises. Albert Schultz and Susan Coyne, who were getting Toronto's Soulpepper Theatre Company under way in Toronto, immediately came to Maraden for help in producing a play. Maraden was not able to make it happen until her second season, when she began the first of several projects with Soulpepper in 1999 with *The Play Is the Thing*. The approach from her colleagues, and their trust in her ability to help them, cheered her immensely.

In Ottawa, the Theatre Department opened itself up in two ways. Early on, at Steele's suggestion, Maraden ran two evenings of meetings with the NAC audience. Subscribers

Theatre director Marti Maraden took on the challenge of renewing theatre and rebuilt both the audiences and the art. Photo © Stephen Fenn.

came and told her both their frustrations and their hopes for the future. The result was an immediate loyal following that soon morphed into the Friends of English Theatre—a group that became the focal point for everything from season launches through pre-show chats and talk-backs to a support group for other initiatives that the department undertook. For decades the orchestra had been able to count on a loyal support group of volunteers, but this one was a first for theatre, and it would produce remarkable results—including a core group of supporters for a fundraising campaign that Maraden would soon initiate for refurbishing the Theatre itself.

One highlight of each new season's launch was an invitation to the Friends, and others, to hear what the theatre would be offering in the coming year. These events rapidly became little performances in themselves, led by Maraden and usually presented in the Studio. "Marti is such a great storyteller," said Steele. "She would be in the Studio, usually on the set of a show we were doing, and she would talk magically about the work—it really engaged audiences."[5]

For in-house productions, Maraden knew that a strong local artistic community was key, and she set about to engage and encourage actors and other theatre professionals in the National Capital Region to participate in her theatre enterprise. "Marti made a real commitment that we would look at hiring Ottawa artists and put them on the main stage here," noted Steele, something that "had not really happened much in the past."[6] Many of the performers had worked in the Atelier, but few had been given opportunities in "the big house." Maraden set out practical programs to help them hone their skills: she devised professional development opportunities, such as inviting Stratford's David William to Ottawa for a workshop in advanced Shakespeare technique. The practicalities of being able to rely on a good local talent pool were obvious, particularly when she began to direct her own productions of Shakespeare at the centre.

Maraden did not neglect talent elsewhere. One of the privileges of her position at the NAC—to offer opportunities and help develop Canadian talent—meant that she travelled constantly, seeing plays and auditioning artists. Although she had broad experience at both the Shaw and the Stratford festivals, she found these trips to other regions of the country a real eye-opener, and, on her return, she often enthused to Steele about the wealth of good people she was finding in other parts of the country. "When I came to the job, I felt I had a healthy understanding of who the best actors, designers, and directors were. My crisscrossing of Canada taught me how foolish I was. I was really profoundly ignorant of the talent there was across the country and how innovative some smaller companies were."[7] Direct results from these sorties included hiring the young Alberta actor Tom Rooney to play his first Hamlet in her production at the Arts Centre, and also producing *The Coronation Voyage*, an original work by Quebec playwright Michel Marc Bouchard, translated by Linda Gaboriau, that Maraden saw at the Calgary premiere in February 2000 by Alberta Theatre Projects. Set on a ship, the play portrays a group of Quebec Canadians crossing the Atlantic en route to the coronation of Queen Elizabeth II—and in the process it investigates themes of sacrifice, forgiveness, and the need to throw off the colonial relationship. Maraden mounted her own production of the play at the Arts Centre that fall. "I'm seeing plays, I'm seeing directors, I'm seeing actors who I didn't dream existed and came to greatly admire," she said, "and I eventually brought them to the National Arts Centre."[8]

These encounters and discoveries led the NAC to become an important partner in one of the most creative new developments in Canadian theatre in many decades: the establishment of the annual Magnetic North Theatre Festival, now a regular fixture of the Canadian theatre world. Theatre staff at the Arts Centre had talked extensively among themselves about creating a national theatre festival, but when they arrived at the annual PACT meetings in Charlottetown in 2000, they discovered that a group of other theatre professionals had the same idea. At first it seemed logical that the Arts Centre, with its extensive facilities and financial resources, should simply take over and "own" the festival, but it soon became clear that although English theatre at the NAC was earning new respect, the theatre community at large was still sceptical. "It was a great idea," Maraden recalled. "We had to find a way to make it happen, with the National Arts Centre having a significant part in it … but not insisting on ownership."[9] In a move that intrigued everyone, especially fund-granting bodies such as the Canada Council and Canadian Heritage, the planners decided to devise the festival as a separate entity that would have a strong partnership with Ottawa. Billed as "Canada's National Festival of Contemporary Canadian Theatre in English," it was launched with great fanfare by the newly appointed festival director, Mary Vingo, at the NAC's Fourth Stage in 2002.

The model was unique: the festival would travel, appearing in a different Canadian city every other year and returning to Ottawa's Art Centre for the in-between years. Within six years, it had been presented in Edmonton, St. John's, and Vancouver as well as three times in Ottawa. The Arts Centre was ideally placed to give it the muscle-power and facilities it needed to get under way, without taking it over. Maraden's tact ensured that happened. Theatre staff helped to set up its roster of exciting new Canadian plays, and theatre companies included works for young people and a bevy of forums for exchange among theatre people who sometimes worked a continent apart. The initiative was an ideal expression of Herrndorf's vision for the NAC: giving the arts everywhere in Canada a hand while not trying to dominate them, yet helping to ensure the highest standards. Maraden recalled: "For me that was the pinnacle in terms of our outreach, nationally. Over 50 percent of the plays produced in the first four seasons had further lives, and we now have regular attendees from international companies all over the world who go to this festival. Plays have travelled abroad, our voices are getting out, and they are enduring."[10]

During Maraden's eight years at the Arts Centre, she presented a total of twenty-one new works on her programs, some of them produced by far-flung companies, including *Brilliant*, produced and presented by the Vancouver Electric Company, all the way to *Tempting Providence* by the small but vibrant Theatre Newfoundland Labrador. On the Verge, a new play-reading festival that operated out of Ottawa, provided the laboratory for experimentation which helped to replace the lost Atelier. The aim was to find new plays and give them some workshopping and read-throughs in front of an audience—both important stages on the road to production. "Although there was not a lot of money," Maraden remembered, "we used what we had to seed projects both across Canada and locally to make things happen."[11]

The rebuilding of relations with Canada's English theatre community led back to the stages of the Arts Centre, where a cornucopia of plays unfolded that established, as never before, the NAC as a fine place to experience theatre in the English language. Maraden developed projects with new and established companies, including Glynis Leyshon at the Vancouver Playhouse, Albert Schultz at Soulpepper, and Bob Baker at the Citadel Theatre. Rather than coming to the NAC by rote (as often occurred with Canada's three classical ballet companies), the regular returns to the NAC by these theatre troupes were based on the merit of the creative projects they planned together. Maraden helped Martin Bragg of Toronto's CanStage to realize a long worked on and much-awaited *Pélagie*—a piece of musical theatre based on the novel by Acadian writer Antonine Maillet.

Starting with her own production of *A Man for All Seasons*, which she had directed at Stratford, Maraden reforged relations with the Stratford Festival. Still, it was not until her final year as artistic director that the two groups put together a co-production: James Reaney's horrific and powerful trilogy *The Donnellys: Sticks and Stones*. Under Maraden's direction, there were beautiful versions of Shakespeare's *All's Well That Ends Well*, *Love's Labour's Lost*, and a handsome production of *Twelfth Night* which played on the twelfth night of Christmas in the Studio. The "Shakespeares" tapped into all the rich talent and resources of the NAC stagecrafts that had lain semi-dormant for so long. Her love for children and children's theatre was expressed in many productions, but never more beautifully than in her version of *The Secret Garden*, mounted in her second season and using the young talent available to her from the local Ottawa School of Speech and Drama. It proved so popular that it was remounted again two years later.

There were many other highlights in the Maraden years. A production of the powerful international hit *Copenhagen* by Michael Frayn, originating at the Neptune Theatre in Halifax, directed by Diana LeBlanc, and starring Martha Henry, Michael Bell, and Jim Mezon, went on to a seven-week commercial run with the Mirvish Productions in Toronto. Locally, she maintained an interest in actor Pierre Brault's one-man show *Blood on the Moon* until it became a repeated hit. These were all hallmarks of the Maraden era.

As she handed the reins over to Peter Hinton in 2006 and left to become part of the artistic leadership of the Stratford Festival,* it was clear that English theatre at the National Arts Centre had again become an important and influential player. As one critic wrote, it was "a place where artists can go and grow their work ... on a par with the best of any Canadian company."[12]

In hiring Denis Marleau to be the new director of French theatre at the National Arts Centre, Peter Herrndorf knew he was getting one of the brightest contemporary stars of the French theatre world. Marleau's own theatre company, UBU, based in Montreal, had created a sensation at international theatre festivals, a circuit where Canadian francophone artists in theatre and dance were well represented—in part because of the financial support provided by both federal and provincial sources. As always at the Arts Centre, the French theatre operations were entirely different from the other disciplines—especially English theatre.

Before and during John Cripton's short-lived directorship, artistic administrator Jean-Claude Marcus had helped to restabilize French theatre and had reasserted the centre's presence in francophone theatrical life throughout the country. His own roots in the regions predicated his views. As a young professor of theatre at the Université de Moncton in New Brunswick, Marcus had been hired in 1979 by Jean Herbiet and Jean Gascon to come to the NAC primarily to work on children's theatre and to take care of the successful travelling troupe L'Hexagone. When André Brassard succeeded Herbiet as head of French theatre, Marcus worked closely with him, taking charge of projects for young audiences and working on a program aimed at helping companies in francophone communities outside Quebec. A non-Quebecer, he understood well

---

*This artistic triumvirate maintained itself for only a few months before it blew apart over artistic differences as to the role of the Stratford Festival in Canadian theatre.

the thirst for their own theatre felt by groups outside the main francophone province and, when he succeeded to the top French theatre job himself, he adhered to these same priorities. Marcus had left the NAC on sick leave at the time of the Pennefather regime, as he disagreed profoundly with the operational model that was being devised— "I fell into a depression and took sick leave before I was fired!"[13]—but he returned to the Arts Centre to assist when Andis Celms stepped in to save the 1996–97 theatre season. After Celms's departure, Marcus assumed the title of artistic adviser for French theatre, first in an acting capacity and then as a permanent appointment in 1996.

Marcus understood that money could not simply be thrown at projects with the expectation of overnight results. In some cases he knew it would take a generation to build up companies in isolated pockets of the country, but it was the consistency of his approach that won him the admiration of francophone theatre practitioners, especially outside Quebec. Among his accomplishments were the establishment of the francophone theatre festival, the Quinze Jours de la dramaturgie des régions (which later became the Festival du théâtre des régions), where a special award was eventually named in his honour, the Marcus Prize, intended to acknowledge "those who distinguished themselves in the development of French Canadian theatre."[14] "I lived many years outside Quebec and was preoccupied by the 'Quebec/other' view of culture," he said. "The NAC was an excellent way to be part of the culture of French people across Canada."[15] Internally, the work was seen as the NAC interpreting its national mandate, although delicate political arrangements meant that Québécois theatre companies did not generally participate in the "regional" initiative or characterize themselves as French-Canadian companies.

From a "plays presented" point of view, Marcus's work was restricted. It was here that he provided important support for Quebec-based companies, although, because of the fragility of the NAC as it tried to rebuild, his choice of work generally erred on the safe side from the audience point of view. His ability to inject money into these "co-pros" with companies that included Montreal's Théâtre du Nouveau Monde, Le Carrousel, and Les Deux Mondes; Quebec City's Théâtre du Trident; and, on the more daring side, Lepage's Ex Machina and the radical Montreal-based company UBU was invaluable. NAC financial support was an important aid in raising the standard of works to international levels and particularly in the important area of theatre for young audiences.

Unfortunately, the lack of any real in-house production at the NAC during the Marcus period meant that no clear artistic personality or voice was identified with the centre as there had been in the glory days of Herbiet, Brassard, or even Lepage, although some good and interesting productions were presented. It was fortuitous for all concerned, then, when Marcus's wife was assigned to an international post in Belgium and, by mutual consent, he left the NAC in 2000—opening the way for a new leader for the French side of theatre.

A star on the international French theatre circuit, Denis Marleau brought lustre to the NAC as director of French theatre. Photo © NAC.

Efforts to replace Marcus with a really challenging theatre figure were stalled until French theatre administrator Fernand Déry met with Herrndorf to explain the dilemma. Herrndorf was direct, telling him that there were three criteria: "artistic, artistic, and artistic."[16] In this regard Déry had Denis Marleau at the top of his list. The decision to hire Marleau meant that a clear and emphatic artistic vision would be identified with the new director of French theatre at the NAC. The announcement of his appointment in the fall of 2000 brought widespread and excited response from the theatre community and especially the cultural press.

Marleau's love of theatre dated from his school years. After CEGEP, he had enrolled in Quebec's Conservatoire d'art dramatique de Montréal, training as a professional actor before leaving to study in France. There he immersed himself in theatre forms of all types. "What interested him was what he called 'the historical avant-garde of the twentieth century,'" recalled Paul Lefebvre, who would later become his associate artistic director at the NAC. "This included the Dadaists, the Surrealists, and the Russian Futurists."[17]

This grounding fed directly into Marleau's own future work. Back in Montreal, although a man not noted for his patience, he began carefully to build up his own creations and, with others, to found the theatre company UBU. As early as 1981 he had caused a sensation by staging *Coeur a gàz et autres textes Dada* at the Musée d'art contemporain de Montréal. Marleau was a minimalist, and his distilled creations were the antithesis of the very broad and emotional work that characterized much Quebec theatre. Through the 1980s he specialized "in the European avant-garde collage productions" and "developed an acting method based on vocal work where actors de-emphasized text and focused on resonance and actual sound."[18] Was the work even theatre, some debated, or some strange kind of weird cabaret? His successes included a production of a work by the surrealist poet Kurt Schwitters, a collage entitled *Merz Opéra* (1987), produced in collaboration with the Goethe Institute, which later toured to the Centre Georges-Pompidou in Paris.

From that period, many of his productions began to tour worldwide, Marleau was perceived as "a director with a unique theatrical vision." He became interested in the works of the symbolist Maurice Maeterlinck and also began to explore multidisciplinary collaborations, working with the sculptor Michel Goulet on several shows. By introducing video projections into his presentations, he even questioned the notion of the actor's presence, such as in the hugely successful *Les Aveugles*, a Maeterlinck play that premiered in Montreal in 2001.[19] It went on to be presented at many international theatre festivals, and later at the National Arts Centre, where it appeared in Marleau's fourth season as theatre director. At the moment when the National Arts Centre approached him for the French theatre job, Marleau was wondering whether he should stay in Montreal or move to Europe, where there were so many important opportunities for him.

The insightful Déry* knew he was observing a peculiar type of theatre in Marleau's creations, but understood its essential importance to French theatre in Quebec and internationally and realized that the appointment would put the NAC in the front rank. He persuaded Marleau that the Ottawa job could offer him "the possibility of sharing his own experiences, and help other creators to develop in a milieu where artists could have a serious exchange."[20] That was exactly how Marleau liked to work, and he accepted the post—with many provisos. He would not give up his Montreal-based company UBU, which he "had spent twenty years building up"; he would not move from Montreal to Ottawa to conduct his work; and he would be free to travel and work abroad. Déry's supple and supportive administrative collaboration with the director ensured that there would be interesting outcomes for the NAC from the decision. Whereas Robert Lepage had come to the NAC as his brilliant career was going upward, Marleau's reputation was already well established, and he brought that prestige to the Arts Centre.

From the outset, there were specific areas he was interested in, and others not. He met early on in Montreal with his theatrical colleague Paul Lefebvre and Déry to hammer out what he wanted the French theatre at the Arts Centre to be—a "force vive" (cutting-edge) for Quebec and a platform from which "to dialogue" internationally. He quickly understood how difficult it would be to produce these kinds of shows in Ottawa, particularly given the dearth of good francophone actors in the capital, so he planned to rehearse them in Montreal and bring them into the NAC. Once on site, he would have full access to the excellent stagecraft and production facilities the NAC offered, which would allow him to experiment fully with many of his more challenging technical ideas. This process "often gave the production team gray hairs" as they struggled to satisfy his demands in the short timeframe he allotted for rehearsals in Ottawa.[21] Marleau opened his first season with a vibrant production of *Au coeur de la rose*, which attracted enthusiastic response in Montreal and Ottawa. The season also

---

*Déry had broad experience in Canadian francophone theatre. He had been hired as theatre administrator during Marcus's time after stints in the Quebec Ministry of Cultural Affairs and a tour of duty as a French theatre officer at the Canada Council.

featured sold-out performances of a new one-man piece by Robert Lepage, *La face cachée de la lune/The Far Side of the Moon*, which was also presented in the English theatre season.

During this first full year, Marleau established two projects that he valued highly. The first was Les Laboratoires du Théâtre Français, which brought participants from across the country to take master classes with the renowned French and Russian translator André Markovicz. Marleau felt strongly about bringing this great and internationally known translator to Ottawa because he felt it was significant for the NAC as an organization and also for the language issue in Canada. "It was very important, and *judicio*—proper,"[22] he declared. Issues of multiculturalism were raised, particularly as many of the participants, some of whom were neither English nor French, were not able to work in their first language, although they were all professional artists proficient in French.

The second project was the creation of an elegant new theatrical review, *Les Cahiers du Théâtre Français*, a publication edited for the theatre department by Paul Lefebvre and containing erudite articles and critiques designed to improve and deepen communication with the French-language audience. The booklet* was circulated not only to local theatre-goers but internationally and served as a kind of calling card about the work that Marleau was devising and producing at the Arts Centre. Pre-show talks were also introduced to try to connect with the audience in Ottawa.

Marleau was less active in some of the other projects of the NAC's French Theatre Department and, while Déry worked with him on the administrative side, Marleau had turned to his long-standing Montreal friend and collaborator, Paul Lefebvre, and asked him to join him in Ottawa as his associate director. Lefebvre, a director, and scholar of Quebec theatre, took over the programs for francophone regional theatre and for young audiences. While Marleau, who did not speak English, remained mainly in Montreal, Lefebvre found himself, as one of the few fluently bilingual members of the French theatre department, based at the NAC and taking care of many of Marleau's artistic duties there.**

"The important part of my job," he said, "was the development of the theatres in the regions"—a delicate role because Quebec companies did not wish to be seen as part of this regional group.[23] Lefebvre developed an encyclopedic knowledge of all the companies that existed and played in French anywhere in the country, from Saskatchewan to Winnipeg, through Toronto to New Brunswick. Thanks largely to his

---

*The publication continues today in with a different mandate and an expanded format under new French theatre artistic director, Wajdi Mouawad.

**Apart from his regular duties, he was frequently consulted on issues of translation and on written materials for brochures and other publications—including those for the Communications and Marketing departments.

efforts, an important theatre festival, Le Festival Zones Théâtrales, was set up and flourished during the Marleau period. While he strongly endorsed the initiative, Marleau was less directly involved and generally preoccupied with other matters. The festival was dissimilar from the Magnetic North Festival developed for English-speaking theatre because companies from Quebec's two main cities, Montreal and Quebec, were excluded from the festival's mandate and it served only francophone companies coming from elsewhere. Companies from the two large Quebec metropolises had their part at the NAC as producers of the majority of the plays put on there—it was virtually impossible to put on a French play at the NAC without the help of these producers. Marleau's own productions were co-produced with UBU. This relationship led to co-productions by the National Arts Centre with European companies, as the centre was able to attach itself to the "Denis Marleau international network" and have the organization's name associated with important productions on the international theatrical scene.[24]

Home audiences in Ottawa, who preferred more conventional theatre fare, sometimes found it difficult to relate to much of this work. Lefebvre recalled that some of Marleau's more avant-garde pieces, such as his November 2002 production of *Quelqu'un va venir*, a modern play by Norway's playwright John Fosse, and originally written and presented in Norwegian in 1996, "sent Ottawa audiences out of the theatre in droves" and initiated phone calls and letters of complaint. The play, the first original NAC French theatre production in eight years, created in collaboration with UBU, was a minimalist contemporary drama. "It was received with surprise, even stupefaction!"

Le Moine Noir *(The Black Monk) galvanized audiences. Left to right: Sébastien Dutrieux and Anne-Pascale Clairembourg, both actors from Belgium. Photo © Richard-Max Tremblay.*

Marleau recalled with a laugh later, a response that amused him.[25] His preoccupation was to produce new and challenging work. And he retained a high regard for Peter Herrndorf, "who," he said, "gave me a lot of freedom to do what I believed was the best strategy for the French theatre."[26] He wanted to offer a diversified program and bring exciting new artists and works to the NAC, such as Gabriel Arcand with le Groupe de la Veillée, and the sizzling new plays of the fabulous but relatively unknown theatre creator Wajdi Mouawad. The highly artistic work he offered did not always serve the wishes of the general audience, and with his absence from Ottawa, "he did not build up the strong relationship of trust with local audiences which is needed."[27]

Yet Marleau was challenging the art of theatre with his new forms of expression, and associating the NAC's name with this work. That was enough to satisfy top management and the Board of Trustees, and they were proud to have him on the roster for the six years he retained the artistic director title at the Arts Centre. Throughout his tenure he continued to garner awards—local, national, and international—for productions touring throughout Europe as well as being presented in Ottawa and Quebec. While he finally bent sufficiently to direct a heralded but muted and drab production of Shakespeare's *Othello*, he continued to challenge his local audiences to the end with such avant-garde plays as *Oxygène* by Russian playwright Ivan Viripaev, directed by the Bulgarian Galin Stoev for the Belgian company Cie Fraction. Whether it was appreciated by the public or not, Marleau remained consistent in presenting his own "technological phantasmagorias," among the most challenging and cutting-edge international francophone theatre. By 2005 the French theatre department was able to invite the French Théâtre National de la Colline of Paris to play in Ottawa, where it presented two plays, including *E, roman-dit* by Quebec playwright Daniel Danis, before it went on to the Festival de Théâtre des Amériques in Montreal. It was the first French national company to visit the NAC since the Comédie-Française in 1970.

The theatre *laboratoires* (master classes) remained an important focus for Marleau and the regional theatre festivals, which had morphed by 2005–06 into the Festival Zones Théâtrales (FZT) under Lefebvre's guidance. At the end of 2005, however, Marleau announced he was leaving. His own view was "that a new NAC artistic director with a new vision should happen around every five years."[28] Lefebvre summed up the period: "The Marleau years were very positive because they re-established a standard of quality."[29] As in the case of Maraden and the subsequent appointment of Peter Hinton to English theatre, the Marleau era paved the way for the next director of French theatre—the up-and-coming theatrical "wunderkind," Lebanese-born director and writer Wajdi Mouawad. In the view of the newcomer, "it is Denis Marleau who set the bar for French theatre at the NAC, and he has set it at a very high level."[30] This new and daring popular artist, whose plays, such as *Incendie/Scorched*, are presented in both French and English, declared he was "delighted to follow in the footsteps of Denis Marleau."[31]

�֍

Dance was the only art form at the National Arts Centre that used all three main performing halls, and Cathy Levy, the incoming producer of dance, found this abundance
a special challenge as she began to revitalize the dance program there. Her stated
goal was "to fight for an identity for dance in the building,"[32] including space for it to
perform. She brought outstanding credentials to the task. Her contact with the Arts
Centre dated back to the late eighties, when Yvon St. Onge, with other leading figures in the dance world such as the Canada Council's Monique Michaud and Barbara
Laskin, as well as Gordon Pearson, the general manager at the short-lived Ottawa
dance company Theatre Ballet, co-founded the Canada Dance Festival at the NAC—
an outgrowth of dance events previously held at the annual Dance in Canada
Association conference.

When the association foundered, the Arts Centre and the Canada Dance Festival
formally signed on to be co-producers of the Canada Dance Festival. It turned into,
and continues to be, a central element in Canadian dance life, as the gathering presents the best in Canadian dance every two years at the NAC. "The organizers wanted
to make something of significance and importance to Canadian dance," Levy recalled,
a vision she wholeheartedly endorsed. She became the associate to the festival's first
producer, Mark Hammond, in 1987 and, three years later, took over the festival herself. Subsequently she was appointed in 1992 as dance producer at Harbourfront's
Dance Series in Toronto. With the Festival International de Nouvelle Danse, run by
Chantal Pontbriand in Montreal, these three events became Canada's important dance
showcases, bringing an extraordinary range of national and international dance groups
and artists to the attention of the Canadian public. Levy's two jobs allowed her to
develop a good working relationship with the Arts Centre.

Jack Udashkin's term, as Levy's earlier predecessor at the Arts Centre, had coincided with an explosion of contemporary dance in Canada, much of it happening in
Montreal, where he had his roots. A lot of this new work, including that of companies
such as Carbone 14, Édouard Lock's La La La Human Steps, and Margie Gillis's
company (which Udashkin had managed), established an impact on the international
stage. When Udashkin came to Ottawa, therefore, he brought with him a strong dance
background that helped the NAC to connect with some of the world's most interesting
dance, both national and international.

"Jack and I started to work together from the get-go," Levy recalled. "I partnered with
him on projects that allowed both organizations to do more. I was less a balletomane
and more a contemporary dance lover, and it was one of the only places, thanks to
Jack, where one could see what was going on at the forefront of the development of
dance—and especially contemporary dance outside Canada." When Udashkin left
the NAC and moved back to Montreal (although remaining on for a while as dance

consultant while his friend and former colleague Michel Dozois filled his place), Levy was approached for the NAC job. At the time she felt conditions were not right for her. She had returned to live in Montreal, was pregnant, and had a husband "with a good job at Le Cirque de Soleil."[33]

In the early summer of 2000 she was contacted again, this time by Peter Herrndorf himself. He invited her to lunch. "I was very attracted to Peter, extremely excited about what he was doing," she reflected. "He had been there only about eight months, but everyone was observing what he was doing."[34] For Levy, who was still contracted to both the Canada Dance Festival and Harbourfront, as well as having a small presenting company of her own, the appeal of combining all she was doing into one job was irresistible. Now she would be working with different-sized facilities all under one roof, putting experimental new dance into the 250-seat Studio, bringing the big ballet companies with a full orchestra into the 2,300-seat Southam Hall, and putting everything else in the 750-seat Theatre. Moreover, "with a decent budget … and an opportunity to invest in the creation and development of new work"—something she was deeply committed to since first starting at the Canada Dance Festival—she could expand her "own horizon as an impresario/producer-type person in the dance field."[35]

As with Denis Marleau, Herrndorf did not insist that she move to Ottawa. It was more than possible, even an advantage, if she could orchestrate much of her work from Montreal, which remained one of Canada's most important centres for new work in dance. In return, Herrndorf obtained a dance organizer with not only the highest qualities but the added bonus of a proven record as a producer—skills he would press into service for other projects designed to enhance the stature of the NAC in the eyes of the public.*

---

*Within weeks of her arrival, Levy was assigned to help the NAC produce a gala for Prince Charles, the Prince of Wales, in Toronto at the request of Mr. and Mrs. Galen Weston, the prince's hosts in Canada. The obliging Herrndorf, who had fielded the request from Weston, readily accepted the challenge of producing the gala at Toronto's Roy Thomson Hall. He was confident he could rely on his top-class NAC production team, led by Cathy Levy and the experienced and highly competent technical producer Alex Gazalé. He was right, and a stellar evening ensued, presented in a matter of weeks with a smooth professionalism that left a good impression with the non-Ottawans involved. The NAC had some hope that Prince Charles might also become a patron of its budding Youth and Education Trust, which the Development Department was setting up. Though protocol advisers in the Department of Canadian Heritage blocked this plan, the evening helped put the NAC back on the radar as the arts organization in Canada best capable of producing these high-toned events. The centre would be soon called on again by the government for a repeat performance when Queen Elizabeth visited Canada for her fiftieth anniversary, and another concert was held in her honour in Toronto. These events helped in the careful repolishing of the NAC's image which management was undertaking.

When it came to dance at the centre, Levy did not hesitate to credit the ground-work that St. Onge and Udashkin had laid down—and which made it possible for her to undertake the ambitious programs she wanted for the art form there. The developing network of international contacts ensured that a great deal of the most cutting-edge work from Europe and Japan was seen in Canada, although the ability to bring in larger companies, especially from the United States, had been truncated by the weak state of the Canadian dollar and the ever-constrained state of funds. Still, with the demise of the private impresarios who had once toured dance, the NAC's leverage was helping to pull together key dance presenters in Canada, especially from Toronto and Montreal, but also from Vancouver, and creating a climate in which they could work together. There was also important NAC support for Margie Gillis's company and Édouard Lock's La La La Human Steps as they became established. These changes were significant, compared with what had occurred in the past. The NAC had become indispensable in bringing much of the best work to the public in Canada even before Levy arrived, and it was something that she would now expand. The best international dance companies were again persuaded that stops in Canada, at the very least in Ottawa, were worthwhile and, indeed, an important part of a North American tour.

Cathy Levy's arrival brought a fascinating flowering of dance at the Arts Centre. She characterized the Dance Department as "the little engine that could," because of the tiny team she had to work with; she described her first office as "a broom closet."[36] Levy coined the term "the World of Dance" as an informal slogan for what she was trying to bring, and Herrndorf gave her full support and complete autonomy. Wedging her work in between the much larger demands of French and English theatre, with which she had to jockey for space in both the Studio and the Theatre, as well as competing mostly with the orchestra in the scheduling of Southam Hall, was a constant challenge as well as a balancing act. Still, the results were the year-by-year growth of an astonishing dance program that became the envy of the entire country. The *Globe and Mail* senior dance writer, Paula Citron, attributed to Levy "astute taste, awareness of the established companies abroad, but also the new 'hot' companies and dancers too, and an ability to provide a mix in her programming at the NAC that encompassed all of these with recognition of the best dance companies in Canada, not only from Montreal but from 'TROC'—the rest of Canada."[37]

From 2001 forward, the highlights that flowed from Levy's work ranged from the newest and most exciting work from Canada's big ballet companies to the debuts and ongoing relationships with many promising young artists, such as the brilliant young British dancer-choreographer Akram Khan. He made his first appearance in a duo performance in the Studio in the 2001–02 season, returned with his Akram Khan Dance Company to perform in the Theatre in 2003–04, and then formed a co-production relationship with the NAC to produce a work with four dancers from the National Ballet of China. Levy perceived the international connection as vital. "I think this man is a fantastic artist," she said, "but I recognize that it is through making Akram and others like him aware of what the National Arts Centre has, and what Ottawa has, that somehow it … has ramifications elsewhere in the artistic world."[38]

Her efforts extended to the international dance giants as well. In November 2004 the legendary German artist Pina Bausch and her company returned to the National Arts Centre after an absence of more than twenty years. Levy's extended courtship persuaded Bausch to come back to Canada. Her reception in Ottawa was huge, attracting dance fans from all over the continent, including some who travelled to Ottawa on a special "Bausch Package" with Via Rail that was reminiscent of the long-ago opera train from Montreal. Bausch was amazed at the support she received, from the ecstatic response of the audiences to the personal backstage encounter with Herrndorf, who told her how important it was that she was there. At the end of the tour she remarked to Levy, "We will be back."[39]

This success was followed a year later by an exclusive North American visit from the Kirov Ballet, again applauded by dance fans who travelled from far and wide for its performances. These engagements were big financial risks for the Arts Centre. The NAC's growing Development Department, preoccupied with other financial demands within the NAC, left it mostly to the dance team to find the resources to underwrite them. At times Levy felt that dance still did not have the coordinated "multi-floor help of communications, marketing, and development" that the other disciplines could count on. Still, dance continued to make its mark, and it did not neglect the all-important support for Canadian artists which remained the NAC's *raison d'être.*

Since the late 1980s, the NAC had provided financial support for emerging artists such as Édouard Lock and had awarded him the Governor General's Performing Arts/ NAC Award in 2001 for mid-career success. In the 2002–03 season, as an internationally established artist, he made the Arts Centre the venue for the premiere of his latest work, *Amelia.* Other established and emerging Canadian dancers also continued to appear. In 2003–04 Marie Chouinard opened the season with the North American premiere of *Chorale,* with the NAC as co-producer. Chouinard also received that year's NAC Award at the Governor General's Performing Arts Awards. The season also presented a display in the NAC foyer, "Hommage to Jean-Pierre Perrault." Mounted in collaboration with the Fondation Jean-Pierre Perrault, it showcased the lifetime achievements of this brilliant innovator of Canadian dance whose work had been strongly championed by the Canada Council and others. Perrault died an early death from cancer in December 2002 but the NAC's preoccupation with his work, as well as a Governor General's Performing Arts Lifetime Achievement Award, ensured that his contribution was publicly documented.

There were other NAC "co-pros." In 2004–05 a show from the Vancouver company Kidd Pivot, performed by Canadian dancer and choreographer Crystal Pite and fellow Frankfurt Ballet alumnus Richard Siegal, was a hit in Ottawa. Another world premiere, *Cobalt Rouge*, choreographed by Ottawa's Tedd Robinson, which featured Lock's former muse, dancer Louise Lecavalier, created such a furor that a second performance had to be scheduled. In Levy's opinion, "with stars like Lock and now Pite, who will soon be an international superstar, we're going to have been there from the beginning."[40] While much of the NAC's role in this regard had been historically unsung, Levy moved to establish an associate dance artists' program to acknowledge the dancers with whom the NAC had a history. In return, she asked them: "When you travel as Canadian artists, wear the flag for us. So that colleagues, when you travel, understand what value there is in the National Arts Centre, in this country of very few dance centres." The work did not go unnoticed. Writers like Citron readily described "Ottawa dance fans as the luckiest in Canada."[41] Thankfully, over the years in Ottawa, an intelligent, well-informed, and intensely loyal live audience for dance had developed, providing the dance program with solid local supporters. While subscriptions were up everywhere in the Arts Centre, no department made more sensational progress than dance, as "the little engine that could" made its way.[42]

The NAC's renewed preoccupation for developing and showcasing Canadian dance talent now merged with its strategic thrust towards youth and education. By 2003 a new Youth Focus Group had been set up for dance which selected students from different dance schools for discussion groups on the future of this art form. In parallel, the NAC Youth Commission for Dance was established, a three-year partnership with the Canada Council to promote the creation of dance works for young audiences. The first $50,000 Canada Council grant went to Toronto choreographer Matjash Mrozewski. His work, *Break Open Play*, part of the NAC audience development project, emanated from focus groups with five dance students aged between fourteen and sixteen, and it eventually reached over 100,000 young people through school performances and the NAC's new Internet hook-up. Other commissions from this program benefited artists such as Hélène Blackburn, who used the work she created as an ongoing calling card that she is still touring.

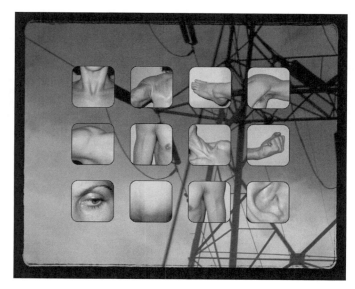

The Dance Department sponsored innovative youth dance programs. Among the first was work by Body Tattoo. Photo © Steven R. Gilmore.

Citron and others lauded Levy's NAC work. "She has the largest budget in the country to program dance, so it's a grave responsibility," the critic cautioned. "But what she does is all worthy. She uses incredibly astute judgment, and it reflects her enthusiasm and love of dance. And, above all, she wants to work with others. Her willingness to make partnerships is valued by everyone."[43]

Unlike the music and theatre sectors, the dance world in other parts of the country had never exhibited a burning resentment against the Arts Centre. The use of the NAC as the venue for the Canada Dance Festival was seen as "the absolute correct use of the centre—a good spot that has been well policed and well curated."[44] All this work helped to focus international attention, so that the leading international companies that made regular stops at the Brooklyn Academy, the Kennedy Center, or the Orange County Hall in Los Angeles now added Ottawa's National Arts to the first tier of performance halls. "To put it brutally frankly," Citron concluded, "it's Ottawa that is now the centre of Canada's dance world." From the dance partnerships through the programs for young people to the artistic excellence of dance performances on the NAC stage, this small department epitomized, as much as any, the new national identity of the National Arts Centre set out in Herrndorf's strategic plan. Even he acknowledged a new taste for dance that he had not previously discovered.

THE PINCHAS FACTOR

In contrast to the "little engine" in dance, the NAC had chosen a big engine when it came to music. Pinchas Zukerman, known primarily as a virtuoso violinist, was one of the biggest names in the world of classical music when he agreed to join the National Arts Centre as its director of music and conductor. "He's a big engine in a big landscape of music—for whom music is everything," recalled his old friend Eric Friesen, the CBC national music broadcaster.[1]

Friesen had worked in Minneapolis–St. Paul throughout Zukerman's seven years as music director of the St. Paul Chamber Orchestra in Minnesota. This ensemble had been Zukerman's first experience as a permanent conductor—a transition that many soloists would like to make but often fail to do. His years there had been tempestuous—but with interesting results. It wasn't only the music. His efforts "single-handedly," said some observers, delivered the orchestra a magnificent "acoustically sound" new concert space when he persuaded a local heiress to donate $25 million to renovate the Ordway Music Theater. Subscriptions shot up, the company's finances stabilized, and he left behind a valuable cultural asset in a community rich in such facilities. His whirlwind, aggressive, sometimes caustic way of doing things, however, had also inflicted some bruises. "Pinchas was a goad and a challenge," recalled Michael Barone, his radio producer for the St. Paul Orchestra. "He had the highest standards but was not one to be told there were any limits to a project." What he wanted "was often universally desired," Barone remembered, but his manner of going after things sometimes prevented them from happening.[2] When Zukerman left the orchestra, he said it was partly because the Board of Directors had refused him the additional musicians he wanted to enlarge the ensemble, and he couldn't realize his vision.

In the intervening years before coming to Ottawa, Zukerman had spent his time performing, guest conducting, teaching, and developing a budding enthusiasm for the use of technology both for performance and for music education. At the Manhattan School of Music, where he was a member of the faculty, the staff had at first been sceptical about his ideas for two-way teaching by broadband hook-up, but as the technology improved, largely through Zukerman's persistent demands, they were gradually won over. "Zukerman on a monitor was better than no Zukerman," recalled Manhattan School president Marta Istomin.[3] Zukerman himself was passionate about the potential of technology and thought of it as the wave of the future. "You can reach people in far distant places without the artist schlepping there! It's cost effective. Think of the Chinese. You can reach 50 million people for a dollar a performance 24 hours a day," he enthused. While he was prepared to concede that there was no substitute for the real thing, his own view was that "only 10 percent of the world comes to concerts anyway."[4] His continued interest in technology would be a boon to the NAC as it began to work again to position itself nationally.

Although rumoured to be coming to the NAC at a handsome price, friends close to the musician said his real reason for the move to Ottawa had less to do with money than with his thinking about his musical legacy. Zukerman said he came because "the chemistry with the orchestra was good. And I like Ottawa, the country, really because it still seems to represent values in art and education that I appreciate."[5] He opted from the outset not to maintain the "fly-in-fly-out-stay-in-a-hotel" model that is the practice of many musicians of his calibre; rather, he bought a house and made a home in the city—in time living there with Amanda Forsyth, the Alberta-born cellist who would eventually become his third wife.

The appointment of Pinchas Zukerman to the post of music director took the NAC by storm—and, in due course, caused many storms. Among all the new artistic leaders, Zukerman would have the greatest impact on the centre over the next several years, providing the flint for much of what occurred besides music. He would be a factor in some of the biggest changes and initiatives at the centre, and the orchestra would alter fundamentally under his leadership. The silver-haired, burly new maestro was a star, and his fame and celebrity would bring wondrous benefits to the Arts Centre, but, as with many such larger-than-life figures, "there's a huge brightness and then a dark shadow side," said Friesen.[6] His sometimes aggressive manner would cause friction and stress in a sedate Canadian institution that had not previously been exposed to the intense world of international classical musicians. As Peter Herrndorf would later note, "great arts institutions need great artists."[7] Zukerman was already on the scene by the time Herrndorf arrived, but if he wanted a great artist, he had one.

Once the Zukerman appointment had been confirmed, it was the job of the orchestra manager, Christopher Deacon, to start helping the new music director with his plans. Zukerman plunged in immediately, even before his formal appointment took effect, and began "to map out the new world order as he saw it here."[8] His working methods were a revelation to Deacon: "The first thing I had to get used to was his rhythm of working—which is, on a purely administrative level, very disruptive, because I am trying to get meetings done and odd stuff, and Pinchas will just phone me or drop in for an hour and a half."

The high-energy maestro was a whirlwind of ideas—and abrupt, impatient, and demanding when it came to getting action, which he wanted on just about everything, right away. Deacon had been forewarned by other orchestral colleagues who had worked with Zukerman that it was not always easy to follow the maestro's rapid, multilinear, and always passionate thinking, but he knew he "needed to understand what the new music director was saying and wanted." More than eight years later, he admitted with irony that he was still trying to digest the maestro's style. Zukerman worked extremely hard himself, and he expected the same from others. There was early burnout among some music staff at his blistering manner and pace. "It was a shock at the beginning," Deacon acknowledged.

The first demand was that the organization increase its professionalism—as one story reveals. Zukerman, an avid hockey fan, knew all the players and games. That had been an element that attracted him to come to Canada, and he soon became a keen Ottawa Senators fan and attended games, usually in VIP boxes supplied by friends. Yet when he first came backstage and found the stagehands watching hockey on a TV monitor before a concert, he was irked. Backstage he wanted quiet. Music-making was a serious business and before a concert there would be no distractions. The television sets went off; the backstage intercom that warned players of show-time was turned down and sometimes played an A note reminding musicians to tune their instruments. Some people missed the more laissez-faire atmosphere that had previously prevailed, but Zukerman rightly wanted the same standards he was accustomed to when he played with the great orchestras around the world. Deacon recalled: "Suddenly we had to pull up our bootstraps on a whole range of day-to-day issues in those first months."[9]

Pinchas Zukerman's fondness for hockey was a factor when he chose Ottawa. Photo © and courtesy of Senators Sports & Entertainment (McElligott, Teckles).

Zukerman's New York friend Marta Istomin,* who had known him since childhood, characterized his manner as that of "an Israeli-New Yorker"—a style that was right at home in that big brash American city but was a shock to Canadian sensibilities. His impatience and relentless drive to get what he wanted remained unaltered after his arrival in Ottawa, although he could turn on the charm when required.

The maestro recognized that he had to learn what the National Arts Centre was about and also the ways of Ottawa. He sought a trusted confidante who could be his guide through this maze and found her in Elizabeth (Liz) Waddell, who had worked as an effective public-relations consultant for the orchestra during the 1989 strike and still maintained a good relationship with the musicians. She was also politically engaged in Ottawa and knew Mitchell Sharp well. The maestro liked to operate through a small circle of close-knit and devoted advisers, and the NAC agreed to his request that she be appointed as his personal assistant. She worked tirelessly through Zukerman's first years, becoming "the filter and translator," explaining to Pinchas the world he was now operating in, conveying his thoughts about the vast array of ideas he was hatching to management, and simultaneously attending to his personal needs and wishes.[10] While her loyalties remained first with the maestro, she came to play a valuable role as the interface, often the shock absorber, between the music director and the administration, and pretty much the rest of the world trying to do business with him at the Arts Centre. Waddell was "the fixer"—the one who listened to the maestro's often lengthy late-night phone calls and conveyed to management his concerns. Herrndorf recognized her usefulness, including her political ties to the Liberals and Mr. Sharp. Early in 2001 he enhanced her position, appointing her director of government relations, moving her office down from the Music Department to the executive floor. Scarcely five months later she was abruptly felled by a debilitating stroke while working in her garden, sadly ending her career and service to the NAC.

One of Zukerman's most interesting characteristics was the speed with which he could make changes. "Whether it was because he was a celebrity or because he was a great artist or because he had a backbone of steel and was very pushy," Deacon reflected, "for whatever reason he got change that other music directors only dreamed of, and very quickly." A top item was that "the concert hall had to be fixed."[11] Zukerman did not pour cold water on the venerable Opera hall or recommend that millions of dollars be spent on rebuilding it. In fact, he quite liked the hall. He merely suggested that, with the changes in technology that had occurred, it could be made significantly better with an electro-acoustic solution. It was an interesting proposal

---

*Marta Istomin rose in the musical world to become president of the Manhattan School of Music. Jewish herself, she explained that many friends described Zukerman as a *sabra*, the name often used for indigenous Israelis, taken from the tough native Israeli fruit that is rock-hard on the outside but juicy and sweet inside.

from an artist seen as a purist who would not tolerate meddling with the art. Zukerman had experienced the system, which was made in Holland, and he had connections with the people who made and marketed it. Typical of his hands-on style, he telephoned the company himself and learned that the firm was thinking of a branch plant/laboratory/manufacturing facility in Nova Scotia. The NAC staff rightly calculated that there was a strong chance the federal government would pay for the sound system on the grounds that it was good not only for jobs in Nova Scotia but for marketing the products to potential clients throughout North America. With support behind the scenes from Mitchell Sharp, the $750,000 cost of the system was found in the government pockets available to the Heritage minister Sheila Copps, and it did not have to come out of the NAC's regular budget.

Orchestra members were thrilled at the initiative. It showed that Zukerman was taking an early interest in their welfare—the issue of injuries to players—and was sympathetic to making their life easier. That was especially important for string players, whose bow arms suffered when they had to reach for a bigger sound in certain acoustical conditions. Now making a beautiful sound would be so much easier.

Zukerman was impatient and wanted the system installed right away. When the company explained that it took six months to custom build, he argued that he had concerts coming up in less than three weeks. The company agreed to install a similar system being readied for another hall into the NAC on a temporary basis. It was an ideal arrangement, and allowed the administration to test run the system and try it out on possible critics. The amplification of orchestral sound might well have been a controversial issue. But the electro-acoustic solution went into place seamlessly and was equally well received by both the professional critics and the general audience. It was all part of the honeymoon period Zukerman enjoyed in the first years of his appointment.

Another project that benefited immediately from Zukerman's attention was a new piano. Buying a piano was a risky and expensive operation for all Canadian orchestras and was normally conducted by a visit to the showrooms of the Steinway Company, the premier manufacturer of concert pianos. At prices ranging up to $100,000, the new instrument might sound fine in a small studio but disappoint in a large concert hall. Zukerman wasted no time. Through his New York connections he contacted a company called Pro-Piano, which specialized in renting out Steinways to Carnegie Hall and music recording studios, and was accustomed to trucking pianos all over the eastern United States for professional engagements. The maestro wanted three samples, but the NAC could afford to pay the shipping for only two. These pianos were vetted in New York by Zukerman's pianist friend Emmanuel Ax before they were trucked to Ottawa. The NAC rented both instruments for two to three months, tried them out in real performance, and was able to make an informed decision on a piano that was less than six months old. Many of the outstanding keyboard artists who subsequently passed through the Arts Centre—Alfred Brendel, Yefrim Bronfman, Jon Kimura Parker,

Angela Hewitt, Louis Lortie—had nothing but praise for the new piano, deeming it "a magnificent instrument."[12] The Zukerman connection ensured only the best for the NAC.* Before the first concert in his first season, the new piano was in place and made its debut, along with the maestro, in the live concert broadcast by the CBC.

The third major innovation Zukerman helped to bring immediately to the Arts Centre was its work in music education—an outreach that would play powerfully into the NAC's new strategic plan with its emphasis on youth and education. Long before he came to the centre, at the long-ago lunch in Toronto with Cripton, Riley, and Deacon, Zukerman had sketched out his plans for what was one of his most consuming passions. He had told them then, "Here's what you've got to do if you want me. You've got to have a big summer training program for artists, and you are going to have artists from all around the world and there will be concerts, there will be training and a faculty."[13] None of them perhaps fully understood the depths of this bold vision or the maestro's determination that this project would indeed happen. But by the summer of 1999, as he officially assumed the position of music director, Zukerman had already arranged for ten young music students to come to Ottawa for the inaugural sessions of what would rapidly become the Young Artists Program. His colleague from the Manhattan School of Music, Patinka Kopec, and the Canadian violinist Martin Beaver joined him and, together, they worked for two weeks with the young musicians. "There was no budget, no plan, no anything," Deacon recalled. "It just happened. They came, they learned, they played. Suddenly the program was established."[14]

The public was permitted to sit in on some of the sessions, many of which were held in the Studio theatre. No one watching could miss the maestro's intense and friendly interest in the budding young artists, and he exhibited a warmth and patience that often could not be detected in other aspects of his work. Except for his glorious playing, which often graced the NAC stages, many felt that Zukerman was really at his best when dealing with young people. The Summer Music Institute, as the program became known, as well as the education outreach programs, which began to expand at the same time, were to become a vital and integral part of the NAC's new approach to its national role. Zukerman's personal championing of these endeavours was critical in garnering attention and support for them, especially financially. Within a decade the Summer Music Institute evolved from its spontaneous beginnings into a well-established and exciting young artists program, not just for players but also with workshops added for conductors and composers. By 2002 it had expanded to three weeks and, besides

---

*The instrument was reserved for NAC music programs and was not available for soloists with other orchestras, such as the Ottawa Symphony, except with special dispensation.

Zukerman and Kopec, was attracting distinguished faculty that included the pianist Anton Kuerti, Canadian-born cellist Gary Hoffman, and the maestro's constant companion Amanda Forsyth, the principal cellist of the NAC Orchestra.

The conductors' workshop started in 2001 and consisted of ten days of intensive instruction in a master class led for the first three years by the renowned Finnish conductor and teacher Jorma Panula, who had helped to bring many young Finnish conductors onto the world stage of music. Of the seven participants in the 2002 conducting program, four were Canadian, among them a twenty-one-year-old musician from Chicoutimi, Quebec, Jean-Philippe Tremblay—there for the second time. Tremblay had come to Zukerman's attention after studying at Tanglewood, where his conducting teacher, Robert Speno, had passed on his name to the Arts Centre. Zukerman, in one of his spontaneous gestures, abruptly created the new position of apprentice conductor for the young musician, giving Tremblay his first major break into the complexities of the professional conducting world and putting him into the public gaze.* He used the young conductor as his assistant and quickly put him on the podium in a light classics/pops concert just a few months into the NAC's 2002–03 regular season. It was a real challenge for the young maestro, as he had not only to conduct but also to host the evening in both French and English. By October 2003 Tremblay, with the Zukerman push, was listed in *Maclean's* magazine as one of "the thirty top Canadians under thirty"—a rare feat for a classical player. For Tremblay, "it was all a little like a fairy tale."[15]

The sizzle and excitement Zukerman created, especially around the Summer Music Institute, gave the NAC's burgeoning Development Department the tool to find the money for its financing. The ideas of Youth and Education connected strongly with donors and soon became a clarion call in the NAC's fundraising. By 2006 the institute's program brought a total of eighty-seven instrumentalists, conductors, and composers from eleven countries to Ottawa, with visiting faculty not only from Canada but from prestigious foreign organizations such as the Manhattan School of Music and the Chicago Symphony. Zukerman had contributed some of his own money** to get the young artists program started. By 2006 the National Arts Centre Foundation was raising nearly $400,000 from private and corporate sources for the annual budget. By then, 581 participants had come to Ottawa from all parts of Canada and thirty-three other countries. As Zukerman jetted around the world pursuing his own career, rising young musicians were brought to his attention as candidates for the Ottawa program.

---

*Zukerman immediately gave him half a Canada Day concert to conduct. Free summer concerts were conducted by Zukerman and featured artists from the Young Artists Program. The opportunity to conduct a piece of the concert quickly became a tradition for the young conductors coming in each summer to train.

**Zukerman contributed $25,000 a year, for a total of $100,000, to the Summer Music Institute in its first four years.

As a child, he had been plucked as a prodigy to come to New York to attend the Juilliard School of Music as the protégé of Isaac Stern and Pablo Casals, and now, in response, he wanted to locate and encourage new talent wherever he found it.

Zukerman had developed a passion for teaching and a sense of obligation to pass on his knowledge to the next generation. For those who sat in on his classes, that feeling was palpable. It was his aspirations that helped to push the NAC's Summer Music Institute towards par with the great summer music schools in the United States at Tanglewood and Aspen. "There is no place else like it in Canada," remarked Eric Friesen, whose own move to Ottawa to host the CBC's national network program *Studio Sparks* allowed him to observe Zukerman at work once again. "The quality of the teaching, the range of courses, and the experience for the young musicians who get to work with one of our best orchestras—it's fabulous and it's done because Pinchas is doing it."[16]

One of Zukerman's great skills was that, when he wanted something done, he never hesitated to go outside the proper channels. He went directly to the source. Whether it was sound systems, pianos, or airfares to fly in students, he called up anyone he knew and applied the chutzpah and charm to get what he desired—and he knew plenty of influential people. Those connections would benefit the NAC through the years— when he invited Yo-Yo Ma and Renée Fleming to star at the huge fundraising galas that were now an annual feature at the centre, for example, or tapped into big names from the corporate world, such as the cello playing World Bank president James Wolfensohn, to grace the philanthropic Roundtables that became associated with the Fall Gala weekend and brought key people to Ottawa to discuss questions that were challenging both society and the arts.*

Pinchas could be generous as well with his own talents in benefit concerts, often along with the beautiful Amanda Forsyth. Both donated their performances for a benefit gala at the Calgary Philharmonic on May 11, 2002.** Later, as Zukerman's wife,

---

*These annual Roundtable meetings harked back to the Arts and Media Conferences held during the Southam era. In recent years they have ranged over a series of fascinating topics, including the connection between medicine and the arts and the role of the arts in health.

**Zukerman had started a romance with the young blond cellist, who had previously dated the hockey player Alexei Yashin, shortly after he arrived in Ottawa. Their relationship became a source of much gossip and titillation, especially for the audiences, and in staid Ottawa there was some tut-tutting about the merits of a music director dating one of his orchestra musicians. But, as in so many other things, the maestro would not be denied. The couple eventually married on a white-sand beach in Anguilla in March 2004.

Forsyth would become a lightning rod, amid charges of favouritism and undue influence, in the orchestra's struggle over his leadership, but for now the couple's appearances added glitz and celebrity glamour to occasions where they appeared together, and they were part of the new exciting buzz around the NAC.*

Another benefit, in Victoria on November 18, 2004, arranged by former NAC trustee and fundraiser-par-excellence Eric Charman, netted $250,000 for the Victoria Conservatory and the Victoria Symphony. These gestures, along with the substantial education outreach programs that surrounded the orchestra when it went on tour, were invaluable in generating good will for the Arts Centre and in helping to improve its national image.

The extensive annual orchestra touring, both nationally and internationally, that had flagged badly in recent years was revived, now headlined by the famous Zukerman name. In his first 1999 season, Zukerman launched the orchestra back into touring in a big way by taking the musicians on a cross-country Canada tour that won plaudits. The maestro was upbeat about the tour: "Our mandate is to be a national arts centre, to show what can be done in Canada," he said. "I'm there to support that. In every community we hope to leave something that bonds with people."[17] The concerts invariably featured some of the virtuoso's own liquid-gold violin or viola playing. It all helped to thrust the Arts Centre back into the spotlight. "Life with Pinchas" was a whole new experience for the NAC.

An essential part of the first tour (and all subsequent ones) was the centre's first foray into its new program of musical education. A special teacher's kit featuring Vivaldi's "Four Seasons" had been prepared under the direction of the dedicated director of music education, Claire Speed. It was distributed to over 4,000 schools, and, for the first time, a website for children was established on the Internet. In Ottawa, the two concert programs planned for the tour played to full houses for the hometown crowd before the orchestra departed. The concerts were broadcast live on CBC, first on CBC Radio 2, and then aired "live-to-tape" the following night on CBC Television. There was also a CD recording of "The Four Seasons." Zukerman gave voice to the NAC's future plans "We want people to know that just because we happen to be 2,000 miles away from where they are, we can bond with them in different ways, whether that's through television, radio, or the web site. We want to bring music to each of them."[18] It was a harbinger of things to come.

The return to international touring was marked early on when a planned European tour was expanded into the Middle East. The board decided that it was time for the

---

*Forsyth's penchant for wearing glamorous versions of the regulation black dress of orchestral musicians, accompanied by her dazzling and seemingly endless collection of Manolo Blahnik shoes, never failed to produce a frisson from the audience every time she came on stage. Once settled to her instrument, Forsyth was a serious musician who paid rapt attention to the conductor.

orchestra to go back to Europe, and Zukerman suggested: "I would love to go to Israel with my orchestra!"[19] Before long, the idea had turned into a truly Canadian plan with the decision to straddle the Middle East and go not only to Israel but also to Jordan. For Zukerman, whose thinking was influenced by his friend Daniel Barenboim,* it was a thrilling opportunity. "The educational stuff had just started then," Deacon recalled, "and Pinchas said right away: 'I've got to do more than that. I want to be dealing with those rock-throwing kids in Ramallah.'"[20] The tour was well financed, not only by the money that the NAC had raised and set aside but also by generous grants from the Departments of Foreign Affairs and Canadian Heritage.

As in the past, the role of Canada's "national orchestra" took on symbolic proportions and several ambitious goals were set. Spearheaded by Maestro Zukerman, concerts with the full orchestra were planned in both Tel Aviv and Amman, as were extensive educational programs in both Israel and Palestine—including a visit to Palestine's national music conservatory in Ramallah where Zukerman himself would work with the young students. In every respect the trip exemplified the ways in which the NAC, and especially its orchestra, could serve Canada as a cultural ambassador, and many supporters decided to accompany the orchestra on the trip.

Among the enthusiastic camp-followers would be the senior statesman Mitchell Sharp, who at the age of eighty-nine had recently married for the second time. His new wife was Jeanne d'Arc Labrecque, a gracious and compliant companion whom he had met one evening at an NAC concert. The couple decided to join the musicians on the Middle East visit as their delayed honeymoon. Sharp, who had once served as Canada's minister of external affairs, had a keen sense of history, and he determined that he and Zukerman, perhaps even with the Israeli president Ehud Barak, would walk arm and arm across the Allenby Bridge that connected Israel to Jordan. Zukerman, who was fond of Sharp, loved the idea, and it quickly caught the imagination of all, especially the government. "It caught everyone's attention, and it made it somehow conceivable that we would play in Jordan," orchestra manager Deacon recalled.[21] Intense and detailed high-level diplomatic efforts ensued, and a delegation from the Arts Centre, led by Deacon and accompanied by Liz Waddell, flew ahead to the Middle East to plan the trip.

It was hard to imagine a tour that had more positive portents, and it was topped off by the decision of the Canadian film company Rhombus Media to send along director Niv Fichman to make a documentary about Pinchas's return to Israel and his visit to Palestine. The working title of the film was *Crossing Bridges*. The NAC Education Department was in close contact with its counterparts in both Israel and Jordan, and especially with the Conservatory of Music in Ramallah. "The level of excitement among

---

*An Israeli, Barenboim uses his musical credentials to improve Israel-Palestine relations, even accepting to become an honorary Palestinian citizen in January 2008.

the young Palestinian players that they were going to meet Pinchas Zukerman and learn about violin-playing from him—well, it was stunning," said Deacon. Talks between the Israel and Palestinian authorities were going well as the final preparations for the tour neared completion in June 2000, and the mood at the Arts Centre was "almost euphoric."[22] In Deacon's mind it was reminiscent of an NAC tour over ten years before when the orchestra played in Hamburg, Germany, on the eve of German reunification, and the following day went on to play in the former East Berlin. It was hard to escape the whiff of "destiny" sweeping through the project.

A week before the orchestra arrived in Israel, the pugnacious leader of the Israel opposition, Ariel Sharon, paid a provocative visit to Jerusalem's Temple Mount and, as so often happens in the Middle East, fighting immediately broke out again. Fichman, who was Jewish, remembered that "it was like *coup d'état*," as Barak was toppled from office.

The orchestra arrived in Tel Aviv and played to good reviews from the Israeli critics, but tensions mounted as to whether it would be safe for the musicians to go on to Jordon. As the situation deteriorated with the usual stone-throwing and exchange of fire, messages began to come in from Ramallah that parents and teachers felt it was not safe for their children to go out on the streets, and especially not en route to meet an Israeli-born conductor. Reports also began to circulate that there were student demonstrations in the Jordanian capital, outside the building where the NAC orchestra was to play. Matters remained top secret until the evening before the orchestra was to fly out to Amman.

As was his custom on tour, Zukerman was treating the entire ensemble to dinner, this time at a Tel Aviv Indian restaurant that was one of his favourites, when a call from the Canadian Embassy came through on Deacon's cell phone advising "that it was the Government of Canada's advice that it was too dangerous to cross the border. You can't perform in Jordan." Herrndorf quickly assembled a meeting in a side room with the embassy staff, pulling not only Deacon but Zukerman, Waddell, and Sharp out of the relaxed dinner to review the situation. After a briefing, each person in the room was consulted before Herrndorf concluded that the orchestra would not travel to the Arab side of the border. Zukerman was crestfallen. When the group stepped back into the main dining room and made the announcement, "it was like the air going out of a balloon." With the Rhombus Media cameras rolling, the chastened orchestra members slipped away. It was the eve of Yom Kippur, which left a single day to alter travel arrangements to get the musicians directly away to Switzerland.

Zukerman toyed with the idea of going to Ramallah himself but settled for a phone call with the director of the Palestinian conservatory. While the orchestra members left for the balance of their tour in Europe, Herrndorf and his wife flew to make a courtesy call on the Canadian ambassador in Jordan, where the elaborate preparations for the orchestra's visit, including a lavish meal, were now sadly gone to waste. The balance of the trip was successful, but nothing could salve the disappointment at the lost opportunity. One of those smarting the most was Niv Fichman, who had to improvise a documentary on the Middle East that was very different from the one he had imagined. To his credit, he made it to Ramallah, picking up video footage of the stormy crisis that was typical of the regular evening news, but at least allowed him to complete his documentary. The film of the tour was eventually broadcast on the Bravo! television network, its narration set to the powerful and poignant themes of Mozart's *Jupiter Symphony.*

The next international tour came in 2003, to Mexico and the United States, and once again it was connected to a political initiative—this time a celebration of the North American Free Trade Agreement. Again the education programs were a stellar part of the exercise, and this time they came off without a hitch, including a broadband hook-up of children playing and singing simultaneously in Monterrey in Mexico, Chicago, and Canada, with Zukerman prominently settled in their midst. In Zukerman's previous incarnation at the St. Paul Chamber Orchestra, he had widely explored the use of technology for videoconferencing and interactive programs for outreach, teaching, and performance He had become an expert, even a zealot, on the use of technology for "expanding the reach of the arts through the use of emerging and existing technology."[23] This passion would play into the Art Centre's expanding plans to make itself a real national presence, and he helped to open the door for more technological outreach.

The success of these tours prompted immediate suggestions to take the orchestra to Asia—including Japan and China—in 2007. Despite extensive planning trips by orchestra staffers, the fundraising, especially from government, fell behind what had been projected, and the project was postponed.

As more good things began to flow, the feedback from the orchestra in the early years of Zukerman's tenure was consistently positive. Even concertmaster Walter Prystawski expressed himself pleased, telling the orchestra manager that, although he had not always been impressed with Zukerman's skill as a conductor, he had now changed his mind. Zukerman included Prystawski in some of his new enterprises, such as having the older musician join him in a broadband electronic hook-up in a two-way teaching lesson with a student at the Manhattan School of Music. Zukerman was the champion for what, to some Canadians, was still new-fangled long-distance communication. He strongly influenced its expansion at the Arts Centre.

The improved acoustics, renewed touring, the excitement of television broadcasts and new recordings, the quickly developing outreach plans, and the new technology all combined to create an extended honeymoon period with the players—and with

Pinchas Zukerman's autocratic leadership would bring some tough changes to the orchestra and create schisms for a time. Photo © Fred Cattroll.

the audience too. In Zukerman's first season on the podium, the public responded by driving up the NAC orchestra subscription to a record 15,000, as local audiences feasted on having one of the world's greatest violinists on the NAC stage on a regular basis. Along with Zukerman came regular visits from many of his top-rank friends. Itzhak Perlman joined him the first year, in what was now the regular fall fundraising gala, followed by Renée Fleming and Yo-Yo Ma. He also became one of the NAC's best talent scouts, spotting such rising young artists as the Chinese pianists Lang Lang and Yuja Wang, who both put in early appearances at the NAC, as he continued to jet around the world as a star soloist and in occasional stints of guest conducting with other orchestras.

One of Zukerman's fundamental ambitions was to transform the orchestra into the instrument he sought to express the music he wished to play. The mature ensemble was now nearly thirty-five years old, and a dozen of its musicians had been with the orchestra since the beginning. To begin this revival, the maestro set up the Zukerman Musical Instruments Foundation, an independent charitable organization intended to locate and acquire better instruments, especially for the string players. "We want first-rate instruments … not the most expensive or most talked about. Just the best orchestral instruments that can be acquired. We will make great music together, and donors and friends from around the world who are contributing will hear the results."[24] The NAC's founding director, Hamilton Southam, was among the first to donate, giving $50,000 to help launch the foundation. NACOA, the long-established volunteer support group for the orchestra,* also presented the maestro with a $15,000 cheque, which was

---

*NACOA was also soon to undergo a change. An opinion poll showed that its name had diminished resonance with the public. Consistent with some of the other changes that were occurring with the orchestra, the volunteers' group voted to change its name to Friends of the National Arts Centre Orchestra.

applied towards the foundation's first purchase—"an exceptional violin made in 1785 by Italian violin makers Joseph and Antonius Gagliano."[25] A unique gift came from Mitchell Sharp, who was by now firm friends with the maestro. The old politician handed over a cello bow that had belonged to his first wife, Daisy, made by W.E. Hill and Sons of London—one of the finest bow makers in the world.

As the process of real change got under way, a gradual shift also began in Zukerman's relations within the orchestra, particularly with the older players who had kept the flame burning and protected traditions through the long dark years that preceded the renaissance at the NAC. In a pattern not uncommon with orchestras, the matter would eventually flare into a full-scale schism. The first sign appeared two years into his first contract when Zukerman addressed the question of "extra musicians." Historically, when the forty-six-member ensemble wanted to tackle larger works, it had on standby a number of freelance musicians. They were often lower brass or percussion players who did not usually feature in the pristine little orchestra that had originally been conceived and maintained at the NAC. There was no formal relationship with these additional musicians, who were basically players who tried to organize their calendars to be available when the orchestra needed them. Sometimes it could be a bumbling arrangement: administrators might forget to book the tuba player, and he would get a last-minute notice and have to scramble. On one occasion when Zukerman came to rehearsal, "his trombonist was not sitting where he was supposed to be" but was in Montreal for the week, doing a recording with Charles Dutoit and the Montreal Symphony.[26] That sort of arrangement was unacceptable to the maestro, and he commanded his orchestra manager find a way to make a regular commitment to these musicians. He also wanted to enlarge the orchestra.

In a matter of weeks, using a careful formula that identified those who did twenty-five weeks or more with the ensemble (which itself played approximately forty weeks a year), nine key musicians were given contracts that guaranteed them a minimum number of weeks each year with the orchestra. In effect, it quietly but also officially increased the size of the orchestra, slowly augmenting it to the sixty-one-member band it is today. In this way Zukerman achieved in Ottawa the size of orchestra he had been denied in St. Paul.

This slow change in the orchestra's size would become one of the bones of contention in the coming debate among the players. It still was not a one-hundred-member symphony orchestra, with all the costs associated with maintaining such a large ensemble, but it was expanding beyond the tight and fleet-footed group modelled on the "Mozart/Hadyn" orchestra that Beaudet and Bernardi had conceived, into an orchestra that could play the larger works of the musical canon. As Deacon noted, "Pinchas positioned the artistic centre of gravity from being the First Viennese School to being ... the mid-Romantics to the 1850s or so." In the process, he saw the maestro "giving the orchestra a broader palate."[27] Some observers had misgivings about the larger orchestra. A few cynics suggested that the real reason was to allow Zukerman to expand his own conducting experience to the big works by Brahms, Tchaikovsky, and Bruckner, so that he could conduct with larger symphony orchestras.*

One of the most contentious issues in the minds of some in Canada's music world was the NAC's commitment to Canadian musical artists and especially Canadian music. Zukerman had met casually in the summer of 1998 with a handful of Canadian composers in Ottawa, but there had been no concrete outcomes from that encounter. While Zukerman booked some fine Canadian musicians into his seasons, such as the pianist Jon Kimura Parker, he was less interested in ploughing through large numbers of Canadian scores to find something for the orchestra to play. Although he liked some new music, he was not prepared to countenance an incumbent for the composer-in-residence program at the NAC unless it was someone of the quality he deemed appropriate. To him that person's nationality was irrelevant. He had told *Globe and Mail* critic Robert Everett-Green in an early interview: "There's no such thing as Canadian content. Or Israeli content, or Arabic content. That's all b.s. It's either good content or bad content … if we find good Canadian music, I'll be the first to do it."[28] The Canada Council, which funded the "residence" program, didn't agree and, for a while, Zukerman's attitude posed a political problem for the organization. The Canadian League of Composers, which early on had taken a negative stance over the appointment because Zukerman was not Canadian, now engaged in major discussions over the issue of playing Canadian music at the Arts Centre. Letters of protest were written and, by late 2000, the NAC administration felt it could no longer ignore the matter. Once again one of the trusted advisers with whom Zukerman surrounded himself would help to unravel this knot.

The American composer Marc Neikrug had been a colleague and friend of the maestro since 1970, when the pianist Daniel Barenboim introduced them, and Neikrug subsequently wrote a cello composition for Pinchas's first wife, Eugenia. In the early seventies both men began to play together, Neikrug as piano accompanist and recital partner to the violinist. Over the years they had performed in hundreds of concerts as a team. Zukerman championed Neikrug's music, putting it onto his programs at the NAC, and at one point Neikrug reciprocated by arranging to program an event of music by Canadian composers at the Santa Fe Music Festival, where he was artistic director. If anyone understood Zukerman's single-minded and uncompromising quest for what he saw as "the best," it was Neikrug.[29]

The restrictions that required hiring or using Canadian talent meant only frustration in such a context. When Zukerman would or could not bend on the issue of programming Canadian compositions, it was decided that the trusted Neikrug would

---

*In 2008 Zukerman was named principal guest conductor with London's prestigious Royal Philharmonic after a short, successful tour in the United States the previous year.

do the first assessment, and large boxes of scores were forwarded to him from the Canadian Music Centre. Neikrug soon formed a clear opinion about the composing scene to the north which he shared in common with the maestro: "The protectionary system for developing composers in Canada works to their detriment," he opined. "It does not produce the best work."[30] He was referring to the steps involved in developing composers in Canada which Zukerman and he perceived as unrealistic in terms of what was really happening in the professional music world. Simply programming Canadian works routinely into the NAC seasons as a kind of tokenism was not the solution, and he supported Zukerman's approach: "His real intention was too improve the quality of everything the orchestra did," he reported. "That meant setting very high standards. How does that come into play with 'new' music?"[31] A system of quotas or protection for Canadian music ran directly contrary to the way the maestro saw things. "With Pinchas," who had been heard to refer to Canadian music in derogatory terms, "it was not a question of good or bad in terms of Canadian music," Neikrug insisted. "The system was getting in the way of playing 'the best.' We were interested in excellence for excellence's sake."

Still, the issue of how to get Canadian music into the Arts Centre in the face of protests, especially from the Canadian League of Composers, could no longer be ignored. To help find a solution to the impasse, Neikrug was hired as a consultant to work with NAC staffers Chris Deacon and Daphne Burt, a young American who had been hired from the Milwaukee Symphony to serve as Pinchas's artistic administrator and to help the maestro with programming. Together they developed a proposal for expanding new music and Canadian content at the Arts Centre.

Five or six pre-screened talented candidates were presented to the maestro, and three were selected for what was no longer a composer-in-residence position but a new and expanded New Music Program. The three composers—Gary Kulesha, Alexina Louie (both Toronto-based), and Denys Bouliane (from Montreal)—were each given a four-year $75,000 commission that required them to compose three works: a large orchestral piece, a composition for mid-size ensemble, and a chamber work.

The NAC would get its money's worth from its investment. All three composers worked to produce their commissions, and their music was rapidly integrated into the orchestra's programs, especially on tours. As part of their job, all three travelled with the orchestra and were pressed into service in the numerous and wide-ranging educational activities that were now an integral part of these expeditions. They also became involved at different times in the expanding Summer Music Institute and its new Composers Workshop. It was a concerted effort, led by its demanding music director, on the part of the NAC to try and alter the way composers are developed in Canada, and it was moving against the grain of accepted practices. In Neikrug's view, the program was "putting Canadian composers in the real world, and the National Arts Centre was the only place that this could be done."[32] As in the case of the Summer Institute, however, he felt it would take considerable time before this kind of approach would have a positive effect.

For the composers who had been selected, the results were mixed and very different. Alexina Louie, who worked as a freelance composer, finished all three of her compositions, although sometimes describing herself as labouring under tremendous stress as she sandwiched the projects between other demands on her time. On tours the NAC staff went out of their way to find her a piano and working space so she could continue to compose while fulfilling her other duties. She had written a piece for the cello, *Bring the Tiger Down from the Mountain*, which had attracted the attention of Amanda Forsyth, Zukerman's wife. Although only five minutes long, it received a good response every time Forsyth played it. Louie didn't get to know either of the celebrated musicians personally, nor did she ever meet Marc Neikrug, but she was one of the lucky ones whose music was programmed in the Santa Fe event, and she had positive memories of her tour of duty at the NAC. In due course she prepared an orchestral version of the cello/piano work—a tinkling, beautiful wash of music reminiscent of water falling which was featured during the NAC Orchestra's 2004 British Columbia tour. Her most recent piece, *Infinite Sky with Birds*, was included in the program for the orchestra's 2008 Western Canada tour.

Denys Bouliane had the opposite experience. He was not only a composer but an enthusiastic promoter and conductor of "new" music. He felt he had wide knowledge of its frequent technical difficulties, dissonant sounds, and different rhythms with which many orchestras and audiences are unfamiliar, and he believed that the only solution lay in having it played. On the music staff at McGill University, he had worked extensively both in Montreal and Europe conducting and introducing new music to orchestras and at music festivals. He came to Ottawa bubbling with ideas on how to promote and develop new music at the NAC. In a positive meeting with Neikrug, and also in discussions with Deacon and Burt, Bouliane's involvement in the early part of his commission was lively, with many talks about the possibility of more permanent projects at the Arts Centre. He even conducted one new music piece at an early NAC concert—a piano concerto with the pianist René Raymond—while Zukerman played and conducted the Mozart part of the program.

Bouliane was also actively involved in the Summer Music Institute, which was growing rapidly, helping to organize the Composers Workshop and conducting its concerts. When he first submitted his piece for mid-size ensemble, he forwarded a computer simulation of the work to assist the conductor in deciphering how to direct the very difficult technical text. The initial response came from Daphne Burt—that "it was 'fantastic,' very good."[33] Not long after, however, he began to hear that he needed to make alterations to the piece, and, when he travelled to Ottawa to discuss the score, Zukerman subjected him to a sheet-by-sheet criticism of the work and told him he should rewrite it—a proposal which, after reflection, Bouliane refused. When the piece came to be performed in October 2003, Bouliane felt that far too little time had been dedicated to its rehearsal. Zukerman abruptly announced in front of the orchestra one day that the work was unplayable and that he had decided to perform only an excerpt from it. Bouliane acknowledged that "there were real technical difficulties with the piece, the music was challenging," but he felt that, at the very least if the maestro did not want to conduct it, he could have asked the composer to do so instead. That didn't happen, and "75 percent of the piece was cut."[34]

Subsequently, Bouliane travelled with the orchestra on its November 2003 U.S./ Mexico tour and, although his piece was featured on every program, only the same single movement was played. Bouliane had debated whether he should even go on the tour, but he had worked closely with the education staff of the Music Department, who had laboured for over a year to prepare the ancillary portion of the trip, and he felt he would be letting them down if he dropped out. In the end, "that part went extremely well," Bouliane remembered. "I worked with thirty-five young composers, and that was top-notch."

After the tour, Bouliane heard nothing further from the Arts Centre. The balance of his commissions was not completed. One of his compositions involved a sonata for violin and piano, but he knew he could never give this work to Zukerman, and the large orchestral score remains to be composed. Bouliane continues to teach at McGill and is working with the Montreal Symphony, where its new conductor, Kent Nagano, has taken up his work. Bouliane maintains that Canada should follow the European system for new music—where a kind of artistic overlord works in the state-supported concert halls and ensures that conductors perform new works on their programs. "We lack this completely in Canada," he says.[35] What bothered him most in his relationship with Zukerman was the lack of respect between colleagues and the crude way in which he felt he had been treated. The failure of any sort of follow-up communication from the NAC told the story as far as he was concerned, and he has turned his efforts elsewhere.

Of the three composers, Gary Kulesha was most successful in sailing the tricky waters of the new music medium with Maestro Zukerman. As a result, all his new works were performed and he has established a stable and long-term relationship with the Summer Music Institute. A professor of music at the University of Toronto as well as a composer, Kulesha was not fazed by Zukerman's apparent unfriendly attitude to Canadian music. "He's an international touring artist," he cautioned. "He doesn't care where it comes from. He wants the best music."[36] Kulesha knew that Zukerman had strong contacts in new music—with Pierre Boulez, for instance—and that he played the works of Oliver Knussen, who had composed a piece specifically for him. He believed that Zukerman didn't program new music simply because it was not his taste—it was not the music that interested him.

Nevertheless, Kulesha supported a protectionist system to allow Canadian music to develop and was party to the "big discussions" within the Canadian League of

Composers, which was complaining so bitterly about the situation at the Arts Centre. Without knowing he would eventually be a candidate for a commission there, he travelled to Ottawa to meet with Marc Neikrug to figure out how they could reconcile the maestro's notion of only "excellence for excellence's sake" with the work of Canadian composers. He was surprised but pleased when he was selected as one of those first three composers. "It took me a year to know Pinchas's rhythm of working," he reminisced, "but once I figured it out I was able to work him. He is one of the great musicians in the world, and if you can learn to work with him he can be great."

Kulesha confirmed that, in his experience, working with the conductor had made his work better. He did not think Zukerman was always right in the way he played his orchestral piece, which was the featured Canadian work on the orchestra's 2005 Alberta/Saskatchewan tour, but when the *Globe and Mail* music critic Robert Everett-Green criticized its playing at one of the concerts conducted by Zukerman, Kulesha felt compelled to tell Green that he, as the composer, was delighted with the rendering. Kulesha lauded the NAC Orchestra as "one of the country's great orchestras" and found the "generosity of the organization in working with him tremendous."[37] He labelled the newly devised New Music Program as a tremendous asset to a mid-career composer. After travelling with the orchestra on an Atlantic tour as well as to the West, and continuing a close connection with the Summer Music Institute, Kulesha believed strongly in the value of the association with the NAC—when it worked. As the first cycle of four-year appointments ends, where the program goes next will attest to its merits.

Ultimately, the most controversial aspect of Zukerman's role as music director became his changes to the orchestra and their consequences in terms of its playing and its sound. It was his right as music director to revise the orchestra to his design, but how this would occur was a problem. In orchestras all over North America, strict union agreements, while they did not dictate where conductors could ask musicians to sit, did govern changes in players, auditions, the terms on which tenured players would depart, the ranking of musicians, and myriad other important if bureaucratic details— all of which was of little interest to the Zukerman temperament. As matters evolved, the NAC Orchestra's transformation turned into an extended struggle between the maestro and some of the ensemble's long-established musicians. It severely stalled musical matters for a time, causing a painful split of opinion within the orchestra that extended to its supporters in the audience and had a negative impact on subscriptions. And, as always in the orchestra's history, when concertmaster Walter Prystawski believed that the ensemble was at risk, he became the leader of the resistance. Matters were to be no different this time.

As in many orchestras, the debate centred largely on the recruitment of new players. With Zukerman at the helm, there was considerable interest in the musical world from players who wished to work with him. Joel Quarrington, considered the country's best bass player, joined from the Toronto Symphony specifically to work with Pinchas, and a number of other younger players were gradually brought in. One of these was Jessica Linnebach, a talented young Alberta violinist whom, at the age of seventeen, Zukerman had taken along as a soloist on the orchestra's 2000 tour to the Middle East. Subsequently, she was invited to join the orchestra, although she would endure a long and tortuous process to secure tenure. A number of other young artists were also gradually added, including Jethro Marks as associate viola, Donnie Deacon as principal second violin, cellist Timothy McCoy, and a new principal horn player, Larry Vine. Some of the older musicians chose retirement from the orchestra, but others found demands that they change what they were doing hard to accept. In one instance a successful grievance was brought against the maestro for the manner in which he had tried to enforce his will.

Although the renewal clause in Zukerman's contract had already been exercised, the orchestra's manager, Chris Deacon, observed that, by the fourth year of Zukerman's first term, there were signs of disaffection among the ranks. "Some individuals began to have experiences that did not fit with their picture of Pinchas. It's like, you know, there's a fly in my soup. It's a great soup, it's a great experience. But there's this one aspect."[38] In Deacon's recollection, "the trickiest part had to do with recruitment and the decisions being made about who would get to play in the orchestra." Careful audition committees were set up under the union rules that governed the orchestra and, while the maestro's contract allowed him to veto a decision, he was only one vote on the committee. This selection factor was of particular importance with string players. "If Pinchas had a fault," Deacon suggested, "it was that he would fall in love with people too quickly." While he could immediately see potential and a way of shaping a new player, the experienced musicians on the selection board were more cautious: "Not so fast. No experience. Too young," they warned. Zukerman quickly became exasperated with the process and tried to force things through the committee, but in this case he did not have the authority to impose his will. Moreover, "he could not compartmentalize," said Deacon, meaning that the maestro could not have a professional disagreement with his colleagues and then forget about it. Many players began to feel hesitant to voice their opinions publicly for fear of retribution, or at least being ostracized by the volatile maestro. What had been a collegial relationship now began to shift, and what had been historically a consensus method of finding new players turned into a secret ballot.

It was a clash of cultures between a world-sized musical personality and his players, an approach that might have had little effect in the New York Philharmonic but polarized views in the small and tightly knit NAC Orchestra. The protocol was little different from that in most North American orchestras, where the collective procedures and union agreements had been redrafted over the years to protect players and circumscribe the huge and dominant personalities of maestros of the ilk of Lorin Maazel, Kurt Masur, or even Charles Dutoit in Montreal, who was involved in a similar struggle with his players which contributed to his abrupt departure after twenty-five years of sterling service at the MSO. In Ottawa, Deacon noted, "Pinchas is not a congenial guy who is going to share decision making. So a lot of behaviour and practices had to change, some of it formalized in the collective agreement."

Nothing focused the issue more than the position of the concertmaster and who should replace him. Although Prystawski had enjoyed a friendly, even close, relationship with Maestro Zukerman in the early years, he became the central focus of much of the resistance confronting the music director. Historically, Prystawski had perceived his role through the years as that of protecting the orchestra in the face of adversity. He had injected himself into the political process in the capital, creating close ties with the orchestra's best political friend, Mitchell Sharp, and they had frequently worked together for the benefit of the ensemble. This time matters were different.

The orchestra's first big international tour to the Middle East and Europe had an enormous impact and meant a lot to everyone at the Arts Centre, but by the time the next big international tour came along to Mexico and the United States, "there were manifestations of discord," Deacon recalled. "It wasn't that the whole orchestra was unhappy, but the traditional leadership group was—the people who made the effort to meet with Herrndorf or me to complain." The growing disaffection between the maestro and the concertmaster led to more of these conversations in the senior director's office. A key factor playing out through this period was when exactly Prystawski would decide to relinquish his position. The man who had played such a pivotal role in the orchestra's life informed management that when he did so, he wanted a hand in picking his successor—or at least to have a strong influence over that election and, subsequently, to maintain a mentorship role that would help ensure his own legacy with the orchestra.

Behind the growing discontent by the players, the real question was the kind of orchestra it would be. "Was it going to remain a Mario Bernardi orchestra" with its clean, astringent sound, "or was it going to be this big warm Pinchas orchestra?"[39] "Who the concertmaster was would have a huge impact on that," Deacon declared. Shortly after the successful 2000 Middle East/European tour, Deacon had told Zukerman that he was going to lunch with Prystawski to discuss his retirement plans. The music director, in an expansive mood, was delighted "that there would be a conversation" and dispatched Deacon to the repast with an ambiguous message: "You tell Walter that, as long as he wants to play in this orchestra, I want him."[40] At the time there were many possibilities for a future mentorship, including the potential move of the National Youth Orchestra each summer to the NAC, and Prystawski seemed amenable to one or two more years in the concertmaster's chair and "was given the impression he would have a meaningful role in the selection of his successor."[41] But the arrangements for the Youth Orchestra fell through, as did Prystawski's other expectations—and the increasingly disgruntled concertmaster used the maestro's offer to extend his term year by year while he endeavoured to influence the proceedings. Prystawski's leadership role through the years had been immense, and he had unquestionably played a key role in the fate of all three previous music directors. As the NAC's third music director, Trevor Pinnock, had ruefully noted, "All concertmasters think it is their orchestra."[42]

Trial concertmasters came and went. Martin Riseley from the Edmonton Symphony (whose wife was a close friend of Amanda Forsyth) did not win over the entire audition committee and, as the union representative Michael Namer explained, "union rules applied."[43] Other guest candidates took the chair, including the principal second violinist Donnie Deacon, who was championed by Prystawski. For a time it looked as though the Quebec violinist Olivier Thouin had secured the job, but again the appointment was not confirmed. The impasse lay in the audition committee's protocols. While the maestro was not compelled to accept anyone the committee recommended, he could not foist anyone of his choice on the orchestra. To make matters worse, the outgoing concertmaster, Prystawski, was an active member of the selection committee. As the situation deteriorated, both management and the musicians' union agreed to suspend the selection process while everyone regrouped.

A new selection process was worked out. Prystawski would remain on the committee, but all ballots would now be secret. Although the union agreement stipulated that the maestro had the sole power to appoint the concertmaster, Zukerman made a significant and vital concession. It did nothing to improve his humour, but he was persuaded to agree that he would appoint the individual recommended by a majority of the audition committee. As the committee continued its work, the enmity between the two men struggling over their differing visions for the future—one holding on to the values and traditions in which he firmly believed; the other the instrument of change—became more inflamed, and the overall atmosphere in the orchestra deteriorated.

Prystawski, always a powerful force in the orchestra, had finally met his match. The cultural environment of the NAC had changed, competent management was in place, and the reliance on political friends and supporters to get things done had diminished. By mutual agreement, facilitators were brought in and began working with the maestro and the orchestra members on the internal schisms. As Robert Everett-Green noted in the *Globe and Mail*, "Other performing groups have made use of professional counselors to work out their problems," citing the rock band Metallica, which had hired a full-time psychotherapist and performance-enhancement coach to help its players get along together.[44] The NAC facilitation process extended on for nearly a year. While it did not settle all the differences within the ensemble, "It went about as far as it could go," Deacon recalled. "It succeeded in bringing some calm to the situation."[45]

A deal was struck at last for Prystawski's departure, an arrangement that was carefully orchestrated by chairman David Leighton and that ended with financial incentives heavily sweetened by the Arts Centre. The large sum published in the NAC's financial statements, and which came under the scrutiny of the auditor general, was deemed necessary to end the crisis in the orchestra. A pair of farewell concerts was scheduled for June 2006, at the end of the orchestra's season, for Prystawski's final performances with the ensemble. While these details were being tortuously worked out, the temperamental Zukerman remained upset with the seemingly disingenuous and infuriating concertmaster and declined to appear with him. Despite the turmoil under the surface, the orchestra embarked again on a widespread, lengthy, and successful western Canada tour, replete with the multitudinous associated education programs that were now its trademark and in which Zukerman was heavily involved. For the Ottawa audience, an October farewell pre-tour concert would be their last glimpse of the maestro for a while. Zukerman had no local concerts to conduct until the new year.

For an artist of Zukerman's stature and temperament, as well as the punishing work schedule he endured, the situation had become intolerable and exhausting. After returning from the western trip, the artistic director met with Peter Herrndorf and, to everyone's astonishment, the NAC announced just days before the Christmas break that Maestro Zukerman was taking an unpaid sabbatical from the music director's job. For the next six months he would leave the orchestra to play out the season on its own.

The news came as a shock and completely mystified the public. The official statement indicated that the maestro needed a rest, although he would fulfill his other extensive and lucrative concertizing commitments in the rest of the world. His wife, Amanda, was taking an extended sick leave and going with him. NAC management handled the matter as gracefully as it could. As the music staff began to fill in guest conductors for the concerts Zukerman would miss, both Herrndorf and Deacon were quoted in numerous press reports. "He is taking a well-deserved and much-needed break to rest and plan for the next exciting phase of the orchestra's development," said Herrndorf. And the media release elaborated: "There is no one in the world that has devoted themselves with such passion to the heavy demands of performing, conducting and teaching at such a high and sustained level."[46] Zukerman had already bowed out of the June 15 and 16 farewell concerts for Prystawski, and Mario Bernardi was booked to come back to the NAC to conduct those concerts. Deacon, who was fielding much of the practical fallout from Zukerman's sudden leave, echoed the party line by explaining: "Pinchas has no pause button. It's months since he's had a day off."[47]

❋

For all his foibles, the importance of Pinchas Zukerman to the revival of the NAC's fortunes was unequivocal in the eyes of the NAC's leadership. "Pinchas was the very person we needed to drive the strategy … the touring … the development and seeking of new funds … the educational component," recalled David Leighton.[48]

Early on, Leighton had tangled with Zukerman, but declined to become his enemy. They had argued angrily after the Arts Centre's agreement to work with two NAC alumni, Brian Macdonald and John Cripton, on an original dance and music version of Verdi's Requiem. Titled *Requiem 9/11*, the piece was Macdonald's testament to the September 11 tragedy. It grew out of his work with the dance program at Banff and included a mix of dance and visual effects as well as the usual orchestra, soloists, and chorus called for in Verdi's work. It was designed to tour and to engage local orchestras and choral singers as it went from city to city, though the dancers came from the Royal Winnipeg Ballet. In Ottawa, Cripton, with the cooperation of Peter Herrndorf, had booked the NAC Orchestra, for performances to be conducted by Mario Bernardi, for September 2002, before the orchestra's regular season started.

Zukerman was away on holiday when the arrangements were made. When he returned and heard about it, he was incensed, storming into in Dr. Leighton's office and demanding in the most forceful terms that the work not be performed at the Arts Centre. "He was furious. He said it was a sacrilege. I don't know if there was any religious connotation but he was just adamantly opposed to our doing it!" Leighton recalled. Personal reasons seemed to be driving Zukerman's emotions. He had lost a close friend in the 9/11 disaster and believed that this new production using Verdi's music was against the composer's wishes. It was true that Verdi had indicated that he never wanted the work staged. Macdonald knew there might be opposition to his version, but had been inspired by the music and felt he needed to create the piece as part of his own artistic response to the tragedy.

Zukerman told Leighton in no uncertain terms that "we must stop it!" Equally firmly, Leighton informed the irate maestro: "Pinchas, we are committed. It may not be your taste, it may not prove to be a great production but two out of the three people who are doing it, Brian Macdonald and Mario Bernardi, are members of the Order of Canada. We are committed to this team."[49] Zukerman continued to rage that he thought the whole affair smacked of opportunism on the part of the producers, and his remarks were tinged with his enmity for John Cripton, whom he still held responsible for the disaster of the Yashin affair. He left Dr. Leighton's office as angry with him as he was with everyone else connected with the project.

This was the first time that Leighton had been exposed to the kind of bullying artistic outburst others of Zukerman's colleagues commonly experienced. Though more than a little taken aback by the maestro's aggressiveness, and a little hot under the collar himself, the cool-headed Leighton kept calm and immediately met with Herrndorf. The two agreed that the music director could not be allowed to dictate what was presented at the Arts Centre, and they confirmed that the work would go ahead. Zukerman made his own feelings clear to his orchestra members at a rehearsal and hinted his displeasure if they worked for the project. He continued to let it be known around town how he felt, and the U.S. Embassy, which had agreed to a press conference to promote the occasion, cancelled out. Most of the NAC musicians went along with the maestro. When *Requiem 9/11* was presented in Ottawa—to critical success— it scrambled to find a pickup orchestra of musicians from the University of Ottawa, Montreal, and elsewhere. Cripton wryly noted later that the dust-up "added some thousands extra dollars to the budget."[50] The affair left Leighton on poor terms with Zukerman for a while. "I mean, that was the low point of our relationship. He didn't speak to me for the better part of a year after that, even if we passed in the hall."[51] Fortunately, the ill feelings did not last.

While Leighton still smarted from the exchange years later, he nevertheless came to revise his opinion of Zukerman completely. "I have to say, in subsequent years, I came around. While he has this great failing [of bullying], I had to put it in context." Leighton spent the next six years of his appointment watching the maestro and accompanying the orchestra, with his wife Peggy, on six separate orchestra tours both inside and outside Canada. "Pinchas does a lot of really wonderful things, far beyond the call of his job. I've come to respect the man immensely. I don't know another music director who is as generous with his time, with his ability, who is quite admirable in other ways."[52] Leighton also admired the skill with which the CEO, Peter Herrndorf, dealt with the maestro's moods. "Peter has to deal with Pinchas's almost daily wild thoughts and plans and dreams and all the things he wants. But he's learned to wait it out so that the ones that are unachievable are forgotten and a few pearls come through. Peter is very very good at spotting these, seizing them, developing them, and encouraging them—and the education programs are a wonderful example of that."[53]

In sum, Pinchas Zukerman was not only vital to the new strategic direction to put the National Arts Centre back on the map throughout Canada but in many ways he embodied it. When Herrndorf and Leighton took over, it was clear that the old way of doing things would change. In the orchestra, the traditionalists tried to maintain and protect what had worked so well in the past, but it was inevitable, said Leighton, that the old ways had to change—and they did. With the retirement of Prystawski, there remained both a divided orchestra and a disaffected local public, many of them still loyal to the past. Others had been put off by the apparent shenanigans and unorthodox behaviour that had swirled around the orchestra and been closely watched and reported in punishing detail by the press. Sadly, Prystawski's connections with the NAC, after thirty-seven years as concertmaster, were severed after his farewell concerts.* Leighton and the board worried about falling orchestra subscriptions, but the chairman, with his long years of marketing experience, again put the situation in the larger context of declining subscription audiences everywhere in the orchestra world. Complaints about repetitions in the repertoire that Zukerman presented each year were a source of frustration to the trustees, but that was not their responsibility. Herrndorf always treated his artistic directors as sacrosanct, and he never intervened in any way with their artistic choices. As time passed, Zukerman expanded the orchestra and, with it, the repertoire.

Negotiations for a renewal of Zukerman's contract had been ongoing throughout this period, and now a decision was required from the board. The Ottawa public speculated on what the outcome would be. As Dr. Leighton's term of seven years of intense service as chair expired, it fell to the vice-chair, Adrian Burns, stepping in as acting chair while the NAC awaited a new appointment, to preside over the discussion on the maestro's future. Public opinion among the capital's music lovers remained split, and Burns was peppered with advice as she moved through the social circles in the city. As it happened, Zukerman cut short his sabbatical after just five months and arrived back in Ottawa in time to perform a previously booked recital with Itzhak Perlman. He stayed off the podium for the remaining weeks of the orchestra's season, however, and allowed the final concerts for Prystawski to proceed without incident. Despite the negative public fallout from the orchestra dilemma, Herrndorf remained steadfast on the value of Pinchas Zukerman to the Arts Centre, and especially to its national role. Eventually, and to the surprise of some critics, the NAC's Board of Trustees, at the behest of management, confirmed the renewal of Zukerman's contract for a further five years. The maestro was booked to remain at the helm of the National Arts Centre orchestra until 2011.

Orchestra manager Christopher Deacon had worked long and hard with all the parties throughout the drawn-out struggle and remembered it as "one of the toughest periods in my professional career."[54] He held steadfastly to the view that the end result was going to be a better orchestra. In private conversations with small groups of musicians, it emerged that many relished playing music with the extraordinarily gifted Zukerman. Many of them welcomed the "warm, beautiful sound" that the maestro was creating with the ensemble. But critics and the public remained divided. Many long-time subscribers cancelled their tickets, and critics such as Robert Everett-Green remained sceptical about the Zukerman changes to the orchestra. While admittedly

---

*In late 2008, Prystawski was persuaded to help as a volunteer on a music history project at the NAC.

hearing the orchestra only sporadically, Everett-Green believed its expansion had altered it from a crystalline precision instrument that was among the best of its kind in the world to something that was more "mid-size conventional."[55]

Others argue that the development of the orchestra under Zukerman is still a work in progress. For Eric Friesen, an admitted Zukerman fan, "after forty years the vision for growth and change is a natural one and a good one. It's enriched the experience of going to the concerts."[56] Marc Neikrug, who remains a paid consultant to the Arts Centre, argued that "the institution now depends on a 'star' system" and laughed that "Zukerman may believe that the institution exists to serve him—like many great artists he has a healthy dose of narcissism—but the orchestra is infinitely better now. The level of musicianship is higher on all scores."[57] Zukerman has taken steps to maintain his new standards by ensuring that when he is away travelling, he puts in place guest conductors of a calibre who can maintain those standards week after week. "It's like having a fancy race car and going away. Who are you going to let drive it when you are gone? What Pinchas hears in his mind is always going to be the best," Neikrug asserts. The CBC's senior network music producer in Ottawa, Jill LaForty, who works and records the orchestra regularly, agrees. "He has brought in fabulous musicians that enrich the sound. They are setting the course of the orchestra for the next twenty years."[58] Richard Todd, music critic for the *Ottawa Citizen*, concurs: "It is a better orchestra now, although it is different."[59]

Zukerman's unbridled tongue caused him many problems with the press during the struggle for change at the orchestra, and he declined to be interviewed for this book. Colleagues describe his frequent frustration with the Arts Centre and the place of the orchestra as just one component within it. His preference, like others before him, would be to detach the orchestra from "the mothership," they say, and to have it operate on its own so he could devote all his energies to its benefit, and not to the other optics or substance of the centre.

For the institution and, in particular, Peter Herrndorf, Zukerman has delivered what the Arts Centre needs. "I was extremely keen about the orchestra being the initial driving force behind the NAC going national," he stated. "We've gone national, and international, and Pinchas has been the driving force behind that."[60] Herrndorf, along with informed outside observers, applaud the replenishment and renewal of the ensemble and the addition of the new and younger players who have joined it. "This is the basis for building for the future," he declares optimistically. "And the Summer Music Institute has broadened that future. It will be one of the characteristics of the National Arts Centre twenty years from now that hundreds and hundreds of music students from all over the world have come here, and it will be a place known to care about young musical talent."[61] This conviction has sustained Herrndorf through the difficult period in music at the NAC. Moreover, he said, "Pinchas is a great artist and, by definition, great artists aren't boring. He is really a terrific, fascinating guy to work with."

It was not until July 2007 that the NAC announced a new concertmaster for the orchestra. After a four-year search and consideration of some twenty candidates, the thirty-year-old New York-born violinist Yosuke Kawasaki, a former student at Juilliard whose parents were friendly with Zukerman, was appointed. In music at the NAC, the caravan had moved on.

The NAC is on the cutting edge with interactive technology in arts education and learning. Photo © Marnia Richardson.

22

THE ART OF
THE POSSIBLE

As the Herrndorf/Leighton leadership at the National Arts Centre gathered steam, Ottawa's senior cultural officials initially maintained a "show me" attitude. The organization "was operating under a kind of financial martial law when I arrived," Peter Herrndorf remembered.[1] The first step in debunking that perception was to ensure that there were no more embarrassing public crises for the minister in the Heritage Department to handle. The second and more important one was to re-establish confidence within the government and among the senior bureaucrats, especially those scrutinizing financial requests, that the institution was in capable hands, well run, and that its requests for funds would produce positive results.

The government's financial model for supporting culture was unrecognizable from the one that had operated in the days of Hamilton Southam. Financial requests from the crown agencies were now overseen by the large-scale cultural bureaucracy within the Department of Canadian Heritage, which also controlled several direct grants programs. It sieved and strained all requests and subjected the annual budgets of the agencies to close scrutiny before recommending them to the minister and the Treasury Board. At the Arts Centre, the new team worked step by step to win back this officialdom's trust.

Once they had re-established the first goal of artistic excellence in the departments of English and French theatre, Dance, and Music, Herrndorf and Leighton pursued the other objectives they had set out in their strategic plan for the NAC, especially the "national" part of its identity. Good relations with officials in the Treasury Board and the Office of the Auditor General were an important ingredient in this campaign, and improved financial reporting at the Arts Centre was an indispensable asset. New financial reporting systems were finally in place, and the corporation's ongoing financial status could at last be tracked on a regular basis with accurate and prompt reports provided by the senior financial officers. Financial oversight and support for management was significantly assisted by a strengthened board Audit Committee, as Dr. Leighton built up the competence on the Board of Trustees and put the individual trustees to work in well-organized board committees in the areas of finance, human resources, marketing, and governance—sectors that he clearly defined as board territory.

The board refrained from any further suggestions on artistic direction. That area was left as the exclusive purview of director Herrndorf and his staff, a division between "church and state" that greatly clarified operations at the Arts Centre. In some areas where there was a lack of personnel on the small NAC board, Leighton invited "outside board members" who were not appointees of the government to join the committees and to work alongside the trustees. These individuals added both bench weight and knowledge and included such experienced individuals as James Nininger, chair of the Conference Board of Canada, and William Breen, a former president and chair of the high-tech Ottawa firm Cognos Ltd. Breen, who had come forward once before to help the Arts Centre, could read a financial statement at a glance, identify trouble spots, and feed the information back quickly so that management could head off problems in their early stages. This advice was a great support to Peter Herrndorf as he worked to rebuild the entire organization.

As time went on, Leighton was able to secure stronger appointments to the board, some with solid business backgrounds. Montreal corporate lawyer Louis Lagassé, who had served on many boards, and Noel Spinelli, the owner of a successful Montreal Toyota franchise, joined the team. Others, such as the veteran arts volunteer Jenny Belzberg from Calgary, brought experience not only to the financial side but also in human resources, fundraising, and marketing. Adrian Burns had been installed as the new vice-chair, replacing David Hill, and brought with her high-level connections both in Ottawa and the West. Leighton cooperated with the government to ensure that competent trustees were appointed, and then worked them hard once they were there. While previous boards had not lacked people who cared about the institution, the trustees now operated as a team under a chair who had written the book on corporate governance. It did not happen overnight, but in striving to reinvent itself while staying true to its original vision and mandate, the Arts Centre gradually regained a firm foundation that brought it back in tune with the climate of the times that now prevailed.

In a country that had come a long way towards the "democratization and decentralization" model that Gérard Pelletier had first postulated in the late sixties, the National Arts Centre had to connect to the rest of Canada in an entirely different way from the days of Hamilton Southam. The challenge now was "how to be populist without 'dumbing down' the product; how to find 'something for everybody' but excellence at all times."[2] All the cultural agencies faced this same contemporary challenge, one that was closely calibrated to the ideas and attitude of the prevailing government of the day.

Just how the National Arts Centre would approach the rest of the country while maintaining its "creative heartbeat" was at the core of Herrndorf's problem—and he attacked it masterfully. No longer would the NAC view itself as bringing culture down from the mountain to the masses; rather, it would create new partnerships to improve the arts in all corners of the land, using the Arts Centre to enhance and highlight the best work to be found in Canada. At the same time, the centre's resistance to private fundraising was discarded as he introduced an aggressive approach to private and corporate fundraising. From governments, there would be no more increases to the subsidy, with the exception of one modest infusion of funds to the NAC's base budget in 2005 and automatic inflation increases for some, but not all, NAC salaries. All other government funds were strictly project based and, before being approved, were first scrutinized by Heritage ministry officials for their political and other advantages to the country. This process was arduous and often risky. "It was often a roller-coaster ride because you often didn't know until the very last minute whether the money was gong to come in," Herrndorf recalled, but the manner in which he framed the requests in terms of their public purpose—often heightened by an eleventh-hour urgency— usually got the job done.[3]

While the genesis of many ideas lay in the previous administration of John Cripton, an array of initiatives, both old and new, came to fruition under the skilful management of Peter Herrndorf and the top-flight management team he assembled. Leighton and Herrndorf split their responsibilities when they were dealing with the cultural mandarins. While it was often left to Leighton to work with Mitchell Sharp and the minister, Herrndorf also maintained a close relationship with Sharp and rapidly expanded his own contacts and network among the key cultural players in the capital. He had already experienced Ottawa to some degree during his several years as chair of the Governor General's Performing Arts Awards, but now he purposefully set out to work his way through the city's diplomatic and social circles as well as the corridors of power—in the crown agencies and departments where there were connections for the NAC and all the way up to Parliament Hill. "I spent a great deal of time telling the National Arts story to people in Ottawa, in the hope they would get interested, in the hope they would get excited, that they would become allies and champions," he recounted. "Put eight people in a room, and I would be telling them the story of the new direction of the NAC. In a capital, it is absolutely essential to do a lot of that, and it has to do with the comfort level that senior government people have in the CEO and the chair."[4]

Not since the time of Hamilton Southam had there been a chief executive officer who understood so well the need to identify and use the power and energy that was latent in Ottawa to enhance the centre's position. Herrndorf's voice was soon heard in the councils of federal cultural leaders, and he was genuinely impressed at the intellect and commitment of the individuals he was working with. One of those he befriended was Alex Himelfarb, the deputy minister in the Heritage Department. "I got to know him quite quickly after I arrived, and we became friends," he said. "I had a great admiration for his kind of entrepreneurial instincts within the government—that it wasn't about barriers but about opportunities."[5] Besides the predilection for smoking they shared at the time, Herrndorf also admired Himelfarb's "tremendous sense of optimism. There was a sense with Alex that 'Oh, for Christ's sake, let's just do this. Let's not worry about it. Let's not over-analyze it. It's a great idea. Let's make it happen.' It was an optimism that was almost American in its kind of enthusiasm for particular ideas and particular initiatives."

Those colleagues already fully versed in the byzantine ways of Ottawa came to admire how quickly Herrndorf grasped Ottawa practices and learned to work with them to the Art Centre's benefit. Dr. Shirley Thomson, the former director of both the National Gallery and the Canada Council, said that the head of every federal cultural agency had to master the political dimension—of bringing the deputy minister and the senior bureaucrats on side. "You sure as hell needed to talk to the guardians, and that is the deputies," she reflected. "It is critical to keep the lines of communications open, especially to the deputy ministers. Those guys at the top are always taking risks."[6] The work of these senior mandarins was dedicated to satisfying the political needs of the government while ensuring that effective public policy went into place—a daily tightrope they walked which absorbed considerable intellectual and physical effort

When Himelfarb moved up into the top job of clerk of the Privy Council and secretary to the Cabinet, he and Herrndorf continued their close friendship. Meanwhile, Herrndorf maintained a good relationship with Judith LaRocque, Himelfarb's tough-minded and capable successor. With these two top-level bureaucrats as well as Mitchell Sharp, the NAC had three powerful supporters in the highest echelons of government. Even so, Herrndorf felt it was not enough: "What you really need is an organization that has a very clear sense of where it wants to go and has the capacity to take you there. It has to have the creative and intellectual firepower to do it," he said. Central to all the strategies was the fact that "the federal agencies play not only a pan-Canadian role but a kind of nation-building role. If the National Arts Centre (or the National Gallery or the Canada Council) was not seen as an organization that had some impact in places like Regina and Prince George and Halifax, then it simply wasn't doing the job it was intended to do."[7]

Several items of unfinished business were finally attended to, among them the convoluted financial issue surrounding the payment in lieu of taxes, or PILT.* In this esoteric but financially important matter, federal government buildings in Ottawa paid the municipality calculated lump sums rather than the regular property taxes. The NAC building fell into this category because its title was still held by the Department of Public Works. However, this arrangement prevented the Arts Centre from taking advantage of an Ontario government tax exemption that gave non-profit theatres with more than 1,000 seats a tax advantage. Something had to be done to transfer the building's title into the corporation's name so it could benefit from this exemption.

When the idea had first been proposed during the Cripton/Riley period, it had been rejected by the board as too risky because of possible liability issues—although it turned out that these liabilities were already covered. It took several years to find a negotiated settlement that allowed the NAC to keep the PILT money. The feat was finally accomplished after extended federal-provincial-municipal talks: the city of Ottawa was included because it was its property tax base that stood to be affected. With the agreement came a federal government promise for additional funds from the treasury for the building's ongoing physical upkeep—money that would not eat into the NAC's regular operating budget.** Finally, in 2000, the ownership of the NAC building passed into its own hands and, as a result, approximately $5 million per year remained in the NAC coffers. This behind-the-scenes accomplishment was only one of many ways in which the Arts Centre was working hard to improve its financial situation.

The main task for the Leighton-Herrndorf regime was to establish the NAC's national identity in the life of the country. Herrndorf recognized the orchestra as his prime tool for getting the Arts Centre back into the nation's consciousness. To this end, after a gap of nearly seven years, he relaunched the orchestra tours—no year would go by without the ensemble travelling to one region of the country or another, and there would be important international tours as well. Having Pinchas Zukerman as the leader was invariably a star attraction for sponsors and audiences alike. In addition, the rich array of music education programs built around these tours became an essential

---

*The federal government paid the city of Ottawa a set sum of money for the use of city facilities rather than being taxed in the normal way for all its properties in the city.

**This idea had started under Cripton but, during the breakdown in trust between him and the chair of the board, it foundered.

The art centre's children's concerts are carefully crafted by the education staff and led by well-known Canadian conductor Boris Brott, principal youth and family conductor at the NAC. Photo © Fred Cattroll.

ingredient in demonstrating the NAC's value and concern for every community it visited—from downtown Calgary to Halifax, up through the coastlines of the Maritimes, into Quebec, across the prairies and mountains of Saskatchewan and Alberta to the West Coast cities of Vancouver and Victoria, and into the outermost reaches of First Nations reserves in the interior of British Columbia. These tours were rigorous for the musicians—they played concerts by night and fanned out in small groups during the day to visit different schools and communities. The schedule was demanding, but the response from the young students in the cities and villages the musicians visited was phenomenal. It was everything that the NAC planners could have hoped for.

From the earliest years of the NAC, youth and education had been part of its ethos, though it was normally expressed in visits to schools in the Ottawa region or in student matinees at the centre. The breadth and scale of the education program now being devised had never been tried before. Its prime architect was a young former teacher and music scholar, Claire Speed, who had joined the Arts Centre in 1994 as assistant artistic administrator in the Music Department. Although she was responsible for all the administrative details relating to visiting artists—meeting them at the airport and booking hotels—her true passion was music education, and she even had a master's degree in the subject. Her early duties at the NAC were split between her administrative duties and designing and producing original programs in music for students, children, and family audiences at the centre. It was "an odd mix," she remembered. Her early performance appraisals, she said, "often noted that sometimes my passion for education got in the way of my work!" She credited John Cripton for recognizing what she could accomplish in the education sector, but it was only when Herrndorf and Leighton adopted the youth and education objective in 1999 that her talents were unleashed. "Overnight," she enthused, "Peter made me education manager. He looked at me as a professional, gave me the title and gave me a salary to match." [8] The powerful trio of Leighton, Herrndorf, and Zukerman, all committed to the common

Graphic designers Ernst Roch and Rolf Harder of Design Collaborative created an enduring corporate symbol, a form repeated throughout the building. Photo © NAC.

education goal, opened the way ahead for Speed.

She immediately set to work with the maestro, cobbling together the first year's edition of the Young Artists Program in 1999. Then, once the annual touring of the orchestra was reinstated, she developed the concept of "the musicians being the teaching artists on tour."[9]

Together with a tiny team, she developed a Teachers Resource Kit, which was sent ahead to elementary schools to help teachers prepare students for the visit from the NAC musicians. Next came the idea for master classes, both in Ottawa and while the musicians were on the road.

The Debut Series, which introduced young artists to performance, was strengthened under Speed's aegis, with higher standards and live broadcast on CBC Radio. Speed did not favour pre-packaged shows for young audiences but concentrated instead on producing original young people's concerts and student matinées. The gifted talents of the well-known Canadian conductor Boris Brott were enlisted, and eventually he was formally appointed principal youth and family conductor at the Arts Centre. Though difficult and challenging to put together, these concerts were viewed as "essential for engaging young children with music, allowing them to become interested, to interact with classical music and its musicians."[10] These methods were highly effective not only in Ottawa but also when the orchestra travelled—and they soon attracted private supporters ready to help finance the work.

A complementary component in expanding its work in education was the NAC's interest in new media. The talented staffer handling this file was Maurizio Ortolani, who had started his working life as a concierge at Ottawa's Four Seasons Hotel, directing people to the arts facilities in the city. He had gone on to become program director for Ottawa's Tulip Festival and then director of the Ottawa Jazz Festival, before coming to the Arts Centre early in 1998 as an "internet communications consultant." There John Cripton gave him the task of figuring out how the NAC could have its own web page and make use of the Internet. His orders were "to get the Arts Centre into web space quickly." He had the first site up by June 1 that year, providing news on the Arts Centre's nine hundred events a year and information on purchasing tickets to them. After the purge of Cripton and his team, Ortolani managed to survive the "Calder house-cleaning" and was still on the scene when Herrndorf arrived in 1999. When Ortolani discovered that Herrndorf did not personally use a computer, he feared that the project would be quickly lost. However, he managed to give the new CEO his "elevator pitch for a New Media Department" a few weeks later. With Zukerman already at the Arts Centre and extolling the virtues of telementoring and other uses for new technology, Herrndorf swiftly grasped the possibilities. "The NAC as an Internet platform was a no-brainer," the delighted Ortolani reported.[11]

Ortolani soon realized that there were many opportunities to put the National Arts Centre in a leadership role with this new technology. Old connections with institutions like the National Research Council were renewed, and the Arts Centre became part of an important broadband research project. An NAC New Media Department was created, and a memo of understanding was signed with the Research Council that involved both public and private interests engaged in the research and development of a new broadband network.* Zukerman's commitment to technology helped drive the project, and the animated quality of music education was an ideal vehicle to test what the technology could do for long-distance learning. The interest of the Canadian government in the development of these technical systems, with their industrial and economic potential, ensured that funds were available, and Ortolani proved skilful at tweaking substantial amounts of money for his projects out of the Heritage Department. Demonstrations of the technology often included Zukerman working with children, hooked up with as many as three different cities during the orchestra's tours. Before long the new media was being used for several long-distance learning projects. The synergies that Herrndorf was interested in constructing worked in many different areas.

The NAC website soon shifted from being simply a corporate support service for programming into the Arts Centre's own webcasting and podcasting system that included features and interviews. Simultaneously, it launched Hexagon, an ongoing

---

*Broadband technology is not about the speed of transfer of information. Rather, it is concerned with the width of the "highway" down which information is travelling and, therefore, how much information can travel along that highway at one time. An analogy is often drawn between the width of a drinking straw compared to the width of a PVC plumbing line. More water can travel through the latter at one time than the former.

broadband research project designed to further arts education. The Music Department, under Zukerman's urging, was the first to seize the idea and was therefore ahead of the other departments in taking the major share of the opportunities the new media offered. Eventually dance, another art form well suited to graphic presentation on the Internet, gradually joined in and, later still, the Theatre Department began to see its potential as an educational tool.

The Arts Centre was soon among those at the forefront of performing arts content on the Internet. What is now called the "ArtsAlive.ca" site was "in the vanguard of education in the performing arts—the 'go-to' place both nationally and internationally, with a significant amount of the traffic outside Canada coming from Europe."[12] Ortolani credits Herrndorf with seizing the vision and running with it, along with the luck of having Zukerman as "the rock star" to champion and publicize it. As with all things on the Internet, the project is constantly evolving, but the NAC filled a communications gap largely abandoned by the national broadcasting services on their main networks, especially the CBC, which has continued to reduce and eliminate its commitment to Canada's high-art forms of music, theatre, and dance. Although only a small component of the Arts Centre's overall work, the tiny New Media Department continues to evolve. Ortolani's staff of six occupies a small, windowless space on the parking garage level at the NAC, two floors below ground. Even so, many staffers believe that if the NAC is to deliver its mandate to all Canadians, digital communication will be one of the indispensable and intrinsic ways that ensures it will occur.

One of the most effective and exciting innovations created at the revived National Arts Centre was the creation of a new series of regional festivals known as "Scenes." They would have a powerful effect in placing the centre back onto the national radar. These festivals had not been seen before in Canada, and the originator of the idea was none other than Peter Herrndorf himself. "It was very hard to communicate a sense of the place being national with just the existing programmed seasons," he remarked. "Forty concerts in Ottawa, a ten-play season in French and English—even when some of the companies and performers come from other parts of the country, it doesn't cut a lot of ice in Halifax or in Calgary or Vancouver."[13]

Herrndorf was inspired by the New Wave Festival held at the Brooklyn Academy of Music in New York which focused each year on a single country. He immediately envisaged that he could create a national focus for art from different regions in Canada and, when he pitched the idea to Alex Himelfarb over dinner one evening, the negotiations were speedy. "In about sixty seconds we had a deal. He said he would support it, and he ended up supporting it in a significant way," Herrndorf reported.[14] What was appealing to both officials, and eventually to Finance Minister John Manley, was the mix of public and private funds that would emerge to leverage each other. For Himelfarb, however, the greatest draw was the potential role of the National Arts Centre in his concept of nation-building.

As usual, Herrndorf brought in the best professional he could find, hiring Kari Cullen, a former colleague at TVOntario and a producer with a background in film and strategic planning, to help develop the concept. "Peter could see how the vast array of talent in each region could be turned into a national idea," Cullen noted.[15] Starting with Atlantic Canada, the festival would "ping-pong" across the country, going back and forth and focusing on a different region each time, taking Ottawa by storm with a mass of talent from one part of the country and giving it national attention.

The Scenes was an idea whose time had come, one that was in tune with the politics of contemporary Canada. Just as Hamilton Southam had hit the tenor of the times when he first set out to build the Arts Centre, so Peter Herrndorf's approach caught the mood of this now decentralized and democratized country. As the centre looked for ways to make an impact in communities across Canada, the festivals idea took shape. The notion was not to bring one or two performers to the capital for a guest appearance. Rather, Herrndorf declared, "We should showcase the best from the different parts of the country, and we should bring hundreds and hundreds and hundreds of artists in all disciplines to their nation's capital and do that in partnership with all kinds of groups." The funding model would be as innovative as the mass of performers: "partly federal government, partly provincial government, partly individuals, partly box office. You put all this together in this very interesting fragile coalition and suddenly you have all these artists streaming to Ottawa. It's a very different model from before."[16]

The first of this vast regional wave of artists began with the Atlantic Scene—a thirteen-day festival that featured "a stunningly diverse line-up of bold, fresh, and contemporary Atlantic Canadian art and culture."[17] Kari Cullen was given the task of producing this first effort, scheduled for spring 2003 in Ottawa. "Initially it was not an easy idea to sell. It took a lot of spadework," she remembered, "A lot of visits, a lot of credibility building. There was a lot of suspicion from the people out there that we were meeting, about why they would want to be involved in a two-week party in Ottawa."[18] It took persuasion to convince the would-be participants that there could be an ongoing payoff from the project for the artists in their region. When Cullen explained that they would be the ones selecting the best for this proposed national stage—and, furthermore, that "talent-buyers," arts presenters from both Canada and abroad, would be there to view the work for marketing elsewhere—"that was the big moment that everyone got on board."

Cullen also clicked with a CBC producer in Halifax, Jennifer Gillivan, who had the telling title of "executive producer in charge of partnerships." When she, in turn, vigorously sold the idea to her network bosses, the Atlantic Scene got national exposure on the CBC television network which reached an audience of more than three million viewers. The connections and partnerships that this first venture established became a model for further dividends in the future.

Staffers within the NAC also needed convincing about the merits of this new and different take on the centre's "national" role. Although Dr. Leighton and the board enthusiastically championed the idea from the outset, the culture within the organization had to change for this outreach program to be successful. The Atlantic event demonstrated the effectiveness of the new concept. On April 28, 2003, the Atlantic Wave hit Ottawa with four hundred artists and eighty-five events spread out across fifteen different venues in the city. Energetically launched with an opening performance by Newfoundland comedian Rick Mercer and billed as bringing "established and emerging artists" to town, the variety of performances ran all the way from the Nova Scotia Symphony to presentations of Maritime recipes prepared by Atlantic chefs at the NAC Café. From soprano Measha Brueggergosman to rapper Buck 65, the best that the four Atlantic provinces had to offer Canada came to Ottawa. At a closing "kitchen party" in the foyer of the National Arts Centre, IATSE stagehand leader Ron Colpaart left no doubt about how NAC insiders now felt about the idea when he told Cullen "This is the best thing we've had here in years."[19] Said Cullen: "The key to success was demonstrating to people what was in it for them, and showing that it could not happen without the NAC as a catalyst."

The next festival, The Alberta Scene, scheduled for 2005, benefited enormously from this first experience and became a more sophisticated version of the idea. For some these festivals were "a modern model for a modern world"—a demonstration that pooling and leveraging resources produced better results for all.[20] For others, they were a model for nation-building in Canada. "In Alberta, we began to get much more sophisticated about marrying the two elements of the national role," Herrndorf commented. "One is you bring all these artists to Ottawa, but at the same time you take the National Arts Centre Orchestra on tour in the same area that you're bringing the artists from."[21] The NAC arranged to do a centennial orchestra tour in Alberta and Saskatchewan concurrently with the Alberta Scene. "Suddenly you've got some synergy," he continued, "and that presents opportunities."

The Alberta Scene was broader and more developed because, by 2005, the management team that Herrndorf had built at the Arts Centre was beginning to reach cruising altitude in terms of its operating skills. Among these team members was Jayne Watson, his able director of communications, and the new executive producer of the Scenes, Heather Moore. The first step in readying the Scene was to arrange for both Watson and Moore to meet with the Tory Alberta caucus in Ottawa. "The conventional wisdom about the Alberta caucus of the Conservative Party," Herrndorf wryly noted, "was that this group was not terribly interested in the arts." But when they heard the NAC's pitch on the "incredible strength, variety, and success that artists have in Alberta," they swiftly bought in. When more than six hundred Alberta performers finally arrived in the nation's capital in spring 2005, the Alberta MPs were among their wildest supporters. In the meantime, they provided a valuable network of contacts for the NAC throughout the western province.

The pitch to governments was multifaceted, especially the idea that ongoing employment for artists might be one outcome of the exercise. The festival was spun not as an exercise of throwing money at the arts but, rather, as a business opportunity: "This is an investment, and we're going to get a payback from it," Herrndorf advised.[22] The Alberta government soon contributed $500,000 to the project. The other facet of support came from donors: the NAC's hardworking Development Department, led by the obstinate oboist Darrell Gregerson, had carefully cultivated the ground in the West, and an astounding $1.1 million in private money was raised for the Alberta Scene's budget.

Both Herrndorf's and Leighton's close Alberta connections paid off when they persuaded Peter Lougheed, the former Conservative premier of Alberta, and his wife, Jeanne, to serve as honorary chairs for the festival. With their enthusiastic support, the idea quickly spread through monied circles in Alberta that "this was just like going to a Grey Cup in the old days. People should come to Ottawa and cheer on the Alberta home team."[23] Peter Herrndorf laughed: "I loved the idea that the home team could be a bunch of artists." More seriously, the fragile coalition of partners that had first been created on the Atlantic coast was now a firm mix of "individuals, donors, companies, and governments, with a payoff for the artists that was incredible."[24]

The flock of Alberta artists that swarmed Ottawa from April 28 to May 10, 2005, revealed a truly startling depth and breadth of artistic work. The Scene ranged through theatre, visual arts, film, dance, and literature as well as country, jazz, blues, hip hop, and classical music. In Southam Hall the Edmonton Symphony played a free concert of exclusively Alberta-composed music to a packed house of concert-goers, which included young parents with children in strollers, students, and other irregulars as well as the usual music attendees. The festival had opened with the new opera *Filumena* by composer John Estacio and librettist John Murrell. Produced by Calgary Opera in conjunction with the Banff Centre, it was based on a true story of Italian immigrants to Alberta in the early twenties and the tragic consequences of their rum-running connections as they tried to find a place in their new world. Although an elegant and substantial work, the likelihood of it reaching audiences outside its home province would have been more problematic without the Scene.

Honorary chairs Peter and Jeanne Lougheed stayed in Ottawa for the entire run and attended events all over the city. In true western style, their reason for being there was straightforward: "My view of Canada is that we need to have strong national institutions," Lougheed said. "We're a small country, and these institutions need to be understood by our citizens. We are so glad that one of those institutions is the National Arts Centre."[25] Lougheed's view was echoed in the national press. Jamie Portman, the distinguished arts writer and critic for the Southam (now Canwest) chain of news-papers, stated in an article: "There is no chauvinism at this federal cultural institution on the banks of the Rideau Canal as it strives to showcase the best in Canadian arts and culture from coast to coast and to do its part to ensure that Canadians have a cap-ital city worthy of the nation. Some agencies for national unity do work in Canada: Alberta Scene is proof of that."[26] The formula for these regional festivals had proven successful and would go on next to spotlight Quebec, and then British Columbia, before starting to ping-pong back across the country again. They were emblematic of the new image the NAC was acquiring on the national stage.

As Dr. Leighton's seven-year term as chair moved to completion at the end of April 2006, the restored state of the NAC's financial health underpinned all its other work. In each of the previous six years before Leighton's departure, Peter Herrndorf and his highly competent management team had turned in a series of surplus budgets. That had been achieved in the early years with the fruitful assistance of Mitchell Sharp, who, as Prime Minister Chrétien's right-hand man, was always ready to intervene in the NAC's favour. Apart from the $5 million added to the base budget in 2005,* the rest of new government money came from other hard-won sources and on a project-by-project basis, as in the case of the orchestra tours to the Middle East in 2000 or to the United States and Mexico in 2003, when funds were forthcoming for reasons of the national political interest. Officials primarily at the Department of Canadian Heritage but also at Foreign Affairs or Finance and the Treasury Board, were charged with weighing and balancing the merits of everything in the context of the needs of their political masters and the interests of public policy. The same was true for bureau-crats at the provincial level when it came to endeavours such as the Scenes.

On March 19, 2004, Mitchell Sharp died in Ottawa at the age of ninety-two. For-tunately, his long-time support for the Arts Centre had been recognized at a special concert to celebrate what turned out to be his last birthday. The old political master was invited, alongside Maestro Zukerman and the concert's featured guest artist Yo-Yo Ma, to conduct an encore with the orchestra. Ma had also sustained a long relationship with the NAC, appearing there first as a young artist in the seventies. His humorous and generous personality was a perfect foil for the elderly warrior. Sharp, a man who was passionate about music as well as politics, acknowledged the

---

*It was the first extra funding added to the base budget in fifteen years. Shortly after the announcement, the government "clawed back" $500,000 of the money for other purposes—a move that led to extended negotiations between Heritage Department officials and Herrndorf, who had already allocated the new funds.

The Honourable Mitchell Sharp, a former senior federal Cabinet minister and political elder statesman, was a lifelong NAC supporter, especially of the orchestra. The NAC thanked him by inviting him to conduct an encore with Pinchas Zukerman and soloist Yo-Yo Ma at the 2001 Fall Gala, a moment Sharp recalled as a highlight of his life. Photo © Fred Cattroll.

concert as one of the highlights of his life.

The essential dynamic in the Arts Centre's financial health was the steady rise of the new Development Department under the guidance of Darrell Gregerson, who was charged with the private fundraising mandate. After decades of resistance to fundraising by the centre, this goal, set out in the strategic plan, had slid smoothly into place. Gregerson had pledged to Herrndorf that, within ten years, she would raise $10 million a year for the organization. It seemed a paltry sum set against the big donations that some cultural institutions in Toronto or Vancouver would come to enjoy, and for a federal public institution that was serving an entire fragmented country, it was a challenge. By the time of Dr. Leighton's departure, Gregerson and her team were well along the way to that goal. Once the National Arts Centre Foundation was created, it was soon peppered with prominent names from all over the country, and particularly from Alberta, Saskatchewan, the Atlantic provinces, and even Quebec, where the NAC had really made its presence felt through its aid to the local artistic scene and to regional artists.

Learning how to find and use money differently was part of "the art of the possible" at the Arts Centre. Figures compiled by the NAC's financial department showed that the amount of government subsidy to the National Arts Centre had peaked in 1978, at the very beginning of Donald MacSween's term as director general. In constant dollars, it would never reach that height again. After the difficult decades that followed, the level of recovery achieved after the Herrndorf/Leighton team took over was remarkable. As Dr. Leighton became chair, what had been called in financial circles "the numbing nineties" were over, and there would be no more government cuts. Elaine Calder, who stepped in as acting director general when Cripton was pushed out, had prepared the ground well for the incoming permanent team. She had not flinched in "making the crucial cuts" that the government had imposed, executing the tough job losses, terminating the money-draining Summer Festival, and starting to streamline the overhead. [27]

Subsequently, as new reforms were introduced—PILT and market-level parking fees that added more than $1 million a year to the coffers—it was evident that a new business approach to the centre's finance could produce solid results. From now on it was expected that the catering service would make some money, or at least break even, catering events both inside and outside the centre that ranged from state dinners to weddings to bar mitzvahs. By terminating the outsourcing of its information technology services, the centre saved well over $600,000 per year.

All fundraising, with the exception of provincial or government funds, was conducted through the National Arts Centre Foundation. In 2007 this ambitious team raised just over $8 million, and turned almost $7 million over to NAC operations. Over 60 percent of these donations came from the Ottawa area, demonstrating strong support from local corporate and private citizens, and the rest was drawn from interested philanthropists all over the country.

The Herrndorf/Leighton team's strategic business decisions were all factors in the centre's newfound good health. And these moves resonated well in high places. The successful project funding for the Scenes, the tours, the ArtsAlive web page, and other Internet projects were aided by grants from various sectors of the Canadian Heritage Department as well as other ministries. According to Danny Senyk, the NAC's senior financial officer, the common thread in the perception of all non-profit organizations such as the NAC was that, if there was a deficit, they were "incompetent." And too large a surplus meant they were getting too much. Herrndorf and Leighton were careful to keep their surpluses within a modest range to send the correct message. All these measures contributed to the extraordinary revitalization of the National Arts Centre.

At the centre of this remarkable makeover and extended renaissance at the Arts Centre was the leadership provided by the chief executive officer, Peter Herrndorf. While faithfully espousing the original vision and values of the founding director general, Hamilton Southam, Herrndorf signalled his own interpretation when he discarded Southam's old-fashioned title and replaced it with the more modern and masterly one of president and CEO—a moniker more in tune with the businesslike approach that would characterize his work. In Ottawa the term "director general" had come to apply to middle and upper-middle managers in federal departments, and it no longer connoted the top leadership post of a large cultural agency. These important distinctions, at least in the minds of beholders, would apply especially once the NAC began to move in the broad and high circles of corporate finance in search of support.

Herrndorf was a CEO suited to the times, and the times suited him. A "managerial man"* steeped in the principles taught at Harvard, he also brought with him to Ottawa a passion for politics and a seemingly insatiable willingness to work with the "stuff" of government. His approach differed from that of the Oxford-tinted Southam. Neither was he any more "resignation-proof" by means of a private income than Southam's immediate successor, Donald MacSween. But like Southam, he brought to the task the same exhaustive tenacity to realize his intentions. His affection and respect for the NAC's founding director informed much of what he did, but he was operating in a world far more complex and politically multilineared than had prevailed at the time when the Arts Centre was created. The current pluralistic world required much more patience. Herrndorf, whose family remained in Toronto, put in long hours both day and night at the NAC, and few of the copious minutiae that filled life at the centre escaped his attention. The work was a far cry from that conducted over the leisurely lunches, post-performance dinners, and visits to the Rideau Lakes in the simpler days of Hamilton Southam, but Herrndorf loved the job. "The most fun is being here at night," he enthused. "What is so interesting is that my colleagues in the day shift are completely different from my colleagues in the night shift, and I like the denizens in both these shifts. I think to do this job, to enjoy this job, you have to like both shifts. But you have to love the night shift."[28]

The CEO was expected to be seen at all the important performances as well as to toil long days, not only overseeing in-house operations but lobbying governments, travelling throughout the country beating the drum, and now raising funds for the Arts Centre. Perhaps it was not so different from the earliest whirlwind days of Southam, but it seemed to encompass more time and more intensity, with much more at stake. Herrndorf, with his hard-working tendencies as well as his ability to surround himself with equally diligent and loyal employees, ensured that a gargantuan amount of territory was covered by the NAC's operations—an amount that was not required, or even imagined, in Southam's period.

Like Southam, however, Herrndorf tended to stay above the fray, disliking conflict, although he had no Bruce Corder as a second-in-command to enforce the hard deci-

---

*A term coined by the renowned political writer Christina McCall and used in her description of Jim Coutts and the other Harvard-trained men who formed the Canada Consulting Group in the early 1970s. It was designed along Harvard principles to "meet the needs of top managers … with strategies to keep their organizations effective in a changing environment."

sions for him. Consequently, he tended to leave the scraps and disagreements to be fought out and dealt with by his subordinates, whether it was wayward maestros or the complexities of scheduling the centre's multiple halls. In the artistic domain, he interfered not at all, leaving the leaders he had put in place to determine what they would present to the public. These techniques sometimes drained his staff, many of whom had family and other responsibilities, but the effort he demanded of them forced the institution forward and upward. His regular weekly meetings of senior staff, whatever hard issues they faced, were remarkable for the good cheer and hearty laughter that emanated from them. As a morale booster and corporate cheer-leader, Herrndorf was in the first rank.

Fully aware of the importance of his presence, he perfected a delightful technique for attending performances that enabled him to attend as many as four different events in a single evening. His bald pate and imposing stature ensured that his presence was readily noted, honouring the performers and showing his support to the audience, but he had the gift of slipping away in a moment of inattention when all eyes were focused on the stage. Nor was there an occasion, whether a major roundtable of international philanthropists, a welcome for a new actor, or mourning the loss of an employee, that the CEO didn't attend, insistent always on a second round of applause. He drove himself and his staff hard but instilled in them a sense of devotion and commitment to high standards. Ever the optimistic general, he renewed in the staff a love for the institution along with a clear comprehension of its *raison d'être*—Canada's performing arts.

Herrndorf's all-encompassing commitment to the organization brought him associations and connections that he enjoyed to the full. Whether it was a gala concert for the Queen or Prince Charles, a round of golf at the annual NAC staff tournament, or a front-row seat from which to observe the rough-and-tumble political world, Herrndorf was at the top of his game. Above all, he recognized the value of the Arts Centre as the shop window in Ottawa to demonstrate its worth to those in power. As Leighton put it, "He understands the political process, he understands the power points, the pressure, the people who make things happen. He is extremely good at cultivating those people. He knows the route, the pattern, to get to power sources of influence."[29]

As the Liberal governments of Prime Ministers Jean Chrétien and then Paul Martin at last ceded to the Conservative minority government of Stephen Harper on February 6, 2006, there was soon another rapid succession of ministers of Canadian Heritage—first Bev Oda, followed by the Quebecer Josée Verner. Preoccupied with other issues, including the challenge of staying in power, no one in the new government showed much interest in matters at the NAC. In the deft hands of Peter Herrndorf and his team, the organization moved smoothly from one regime to the next as a new chairperson, Julia Foster, a Torontonian well connected to the Conservative Party, took Dr. Leighton's place, and the honorary chair position for the grand fall Gala passed from Aline Chrétien to Laureen Harper. While the prime minister himself was never to be seen in attendance at the Arts Centre during his first term in office, Mrs. Harper threw herself enthusiastically into the cultural role, actively involving herself in party arrangements at the centre, lunching with pals at the NAC Café, and turning up at special performances with the gallant Cabinet minister John Baird on her arm.

In his long years of studied neutrality, of cultivating and maintaining contacts, Herrndorf had plenty of connections in the new camp. Though the Harper government showed no particular passion for the arts, it did not yet appear to have any draconian measures in mind for the cultural institutions as had occurred in the days of Marcel Masse and the previous Conservative government under Brian Mulroney. In a gesture that Herrndorf took as a sign of good favour, the new government provided $56 million (spread over a number of years) to upgrade and repair the fraying physical structure of the building, which was now nearly forty years old.

The recovery of this single national cultural institution, after the years of devastation, was a testament to the solid values on which it had first been conceived and executed. It also spoke to the adaptability that was possible when the institution was placed in the hands of capable and dedicated believers. By defining a fresh purpose in the overall contemporary life of the country, it found its salvation at the hands of the political masters who govern it. Its uniqueness in the world—still the only bilingual, multidisciplinary performing arts institution of its kind—began and continues as a brave and audacious idea in a widespread, lightly populated country such as Canada. Its survival is testament to the place that excellence in the performing arts—music, theatre, dance, and opera—and even the culinary arts, retains in the creative imagination of the country.

Perhaps the stars crossed again when Herrndorf and his team arrived, and the time was ripe to recognize the tools that exist within the federal government which can help to bind Canadians together as a country. The National Arts Centre is but a small microcosm of some of the mighty programs of the federal government, but the performances it presents both in Canada's capital and elsewhere in the country are some of the country's best creative work. For the present team, the challenge to maintain and develop its national identity is a work in progress. As Herrndorf says, "we are still only a third of the way there."[30] Efforts continue to provide the organization with a stable and long-term future in tune with the politics of the country and the artistic climate of the times. As the journey proceeds, it remains "a wonderful stage for both artistry and the political dance."[31]

EPILOGUE

When Sheila Copps was appointed Canadian Heritage minister in 1996, Prime Minister Jean Chrétien told her that, even though he personally thought the arts were the mark of a great country, there were no votes in them. He was wrong. As the Canadian public went to the polls in October 2008, a subsequent prime minister, Stephen Harper, discovered otherwise. A chance remark he made about the arts during the election campaign in Saskatoon helped scotch his ambitions for a majority government in the upcoming vote. By suggesting that those who turned out for black-tie benefits to raise money for the cash-starved arts were somehow snobs, he raised the ire of Canadians everywhere, and especially in Quebec, where arts and culture are widely supported. Harper had perhaps forgotten that Gilles Duceppe, the leader of the separatist party in the Canadian Parliament, was the son of one of Quebec's greatest theatre people, the actor/director Jean Duceppe, and had known from his earliest childhood about the importance of support for the arts. Duceppe, whose Bloc Québécois party had been failing in the polls, seized the opportunity and surged back, making the arts and culture issue a factor that helped to doom the ruling Conservative regime to another minority government. Perhaps what politicians discovered during the 2008 election was that the arts do matter.

Nevertheless, the economics of the country, as well as the enormous financial difficulties that have swept across the world since that fateful fall, make it unlikely that the arts in Canada will be the beneficiaries of any significant new funds from governments in the immediate future. Elected officials will first have to deal with more immediate problems of poverty and urban disintegration.

In this harsh economic climate, the National Arts Centre will have an even greater challenge in maintaining and increasing the private resources it has tapped into in the past decade. While realistic about the tough task ahead, the NAC leadership is conscious that the institution is now firmly embedded in people's minds as a force in the country's cultural life.

One reason for optimism is the new generation of artistic leaders in place at the Arts Centre. Peter Hinton, artistic director of English theatre, has been recognized by his peers as one of the leading flag-bearers for Canadian theatre. He has been responsible not only for the first-ever all-Canadian theatre season at the Arts Centre but also for such projects as *The Penelopiad*, a collaboration with Britain's Royal Shakespeare Company of a production based on the Margaret Atwood novel that tells the Odysseus myth from the point of view of Penelope, the hero's wife. It is now set to tour across Canada.

In Wajdi Mouawad, director of French theatre, the centre has an artist following in the footsteps of the internationalist Denis Marleau and an actor/director who himself is a kind of Pied Piper for francophone theatre all over the world. Like the celebrated director Robert Lepage, he crosses over to English-language theatre too, where he has tremendous appeal to audiences. Dance, under Cathy Levy, continues its steady growth at the Arts Centre. The orchestra, still led by Pinchas Zukerman, will maintain its eminence, with the prospect of some exciting Canadians on the international scene ready to replace him when the time comes. The New Media department continues to expand its work, if not yet its staff, and now has agreement under the NACO musicians' contract to stream the orchestra's live concerts directly onto the website, giving it access to music lovers not only in Canada but across the world.

Among other projects, the NAC is a partner with the Toronto Symphony and with provincial, municipal, and federal governments in a long-distance project in Ontario's Niagara region, where a large music festival is planned to commence in 2012 on the 200th anniversary of the War of 1812. These types of outreach programs reinforce the NAC's national worth in the eyes of both decision-makers and public supporters.

After the centre's near-death experience, the trustees and other leaders now appointed to run this great national cultural institution fully endorse its nation-building role, whatever their political persuasion. When the last of the present top leaders moves on, a well-formed and well-grounded institution will remain in place for their successors. On June 2, 2009, the National Arts Centre will celebrate its fortieth anniversary since its doors opened that rainy but splendid night so long ago in Ottawa.

NOTES

Prelude

1. Hamilton Southam interview, October 29, 2004.
2. Gérard Pelletier, quoted in *Ottawa Citizen* from a TV interview with critic Nathan Cohen, June 18, 1969.

Chapter 1: Genesis of the Dream

1. Letter to Prime Minister Lester Pearson, November 8, 1963, National Capital Arts Alliance, Correspondence, Southam Papers, Library and Archives Canada [henceforth LAC], MG 31 D230, Vol. 12.
2. Southam interview, June 18, 2003.
3. National Capital Arts Alliance submission [henceforth NCAA], 7, Southam Papers, Vol. 12.
4. NCAA, administrative files, Southam Papers, Vol. 12.
5. Hamilton Southam, personal diary.
6. NCAA, administrative files.
7. *Ibid.*
8. *Ibid.*
9. Peter Dwyer, letter to Hamilton Southam, September 16, 1963, Southam Papers.
10. Aide-mémoire, conversation between Hamilton Southam and Mayor Charlotte Whitten, NCAA, administrative files.
11. Memo from Undersecretary Norman Robertson to Secretary of State for External Affairs Paul Martin, NCAA, General Correspondence.
12. NCAA, administrative files.
13. Memorandum to Government, August 28, 1964, NCAA, administrative files.
14. Memorandum from Peter Dwyer to the NCAA.
15. Memo from Undersecretary Norman Robertson to Minister Paul Martin, November 26, 1963.

Chapter 2: The Real Task Begins

1. Draft memorandum for secretary of state, June 23, 1964 (final version, November 27, 1964), from Office of the Coordinator, National Centre for the Performing Arts, Hamilton Southam, Southam Papers, LAC.
2. Mandate to Advisory Committee invitees, as described in the invitation to participate from the Canada Council.
3. Minutes, Advisory Committee on Music, Opera, and Ballet, National Arts Centre Archives [henceforth NAC Archives].
4. The O'Keefe Centre has since been renamed the Sony Centre.
5. Southam interview, July 18, 2003.
6. James Langford interview, July 17, 2003.
7. Southam interview.
8. Langford interview.
9. Southam interview.
10. *Ibid.*
11. Mitchell Sharp, as quoted by Arthur Kroeger, former member of the Privy Council Office.

12. Southam interview.

13. John Adjeleian interview, April 31, 2004.

14. *Ibid.*

15. NAC Archives, Minutes, Advisory Committee for the Visual Arts.

16. *Ibid.*

17. Telegram to Hamilton Southam from Arnold Smith, the Canadian ambassador to France, February 1964, Southam Papers.

18. William Teron interview.

19. Early draft, memorandum to Secretary of State Maurice Lamontagne from Hamilton Southam. By the time this proposal was in its final version for the secretary of state, the chairs of the advisory committees were recommending the "Stratford" concept—that the Art Centre's Board of Trustees be responsible for the artistic content performed at the centre.

20. The St-Adèle conference was perceived as a key gathering for the development of all future Canadian arts policy. John Hobday interview.

21. This lack of expertise had been noted at a Seminar on Architectural Requirements for the Performing Arts held in Ottawa on June 2, 1964. It recommended crash courses to train arts administrators and technicians to staff the new auditoria being built all across the country.

22. Memorandum to the undersecretary of state from Hamilton Southam, November 27, 1964, Files—Office of the Coordinator, NAC Archives.

Chapter 3: Making It Happen

1. Minutes, NAC Board of Trustees, March 8–9, 1967, NAC Archives.

2. *Ibid.*

3. Lawrence Freiman, *Don't Fall Off the Rocking Horse* (Toronto: McClelland & Stewart, 1978), 158.

4. Hamilton Southam, manuscript annotation, July 24, 2007.

5. Southam interview, June 24, 2003.

6. *Ibid.*

7. *Ibid.*

8. National Capital Arts Alliance minutes, May 3, 1963, Southam Papers, Library and Archives Canada.

9. Minutes, Advisory Committee on Music, Opera, and Ballet, NAC Archives.

10. Memorandum from Jean-Marie Beaudet to Coordinator, October 15, 1964, Office of the Coordinator files, NAC Archives.

11. *Ibid.*

12. Hamilton Southam to Dr. Ezra Schabas, January 4, 1965, Southam Papers; Dr. Ezra Schabas to Hamilton Southam, February 15, 1965, *ibid.*

13. Applebaum Report to Coordinator's Office, May 1965.

14. Walter Pitman, *Louis Applebaum: A Passion for Culture* (Toronto: Dundurn Press, 2002), 196.

15. Appendix to Minutes, NAC Board of Trustees, July 10, 1967.

16. Minutes, NAC Board of Trustees, September 5, 1967.

17. *Montreal Gazette*, quoted in the NAC Annual Report 1969–70.

18. *You Must Set Forth at Dawn* by Wole Soyinka, as quoted in the *Globe and Mail* review by Ken Wiwa, May 20, 2006.

19. Tom Hendry interview, April 12, 2006.

20. Southam interview, June 24, 2003.

21. Jean-Louis Roux interview, May 19, 2004.

22. Jean-Guy Sabourin interviews, various 2004–06.

23. Minutes, NAC Board of Trustees, December 5, 1968.

24. As quoted in Minutes, NAC Board of Trustees, July 5, 1968.

Chapter 4: New Regime in Ottawa

1. Marcel Masse, Conservative minister of communications responsible for culture in the Mulroney government, interview, August 15, 2006. Masse, who had been a Union Nationale member in Quebec, was scathing about this view of Quebec society in the Duplessis era.
2. Gérard Pelletier, as quoted in the *Ottawa Citizen*, May 29, 1969.
3. Minutes, NAC Board of Trustees, March 1969 meetings.
4. Mario Bernardi interview, October 21, 2003.
5. *Ibid.*
6. Ken Murphy interview, August 9, 2003.
7. *Ibid.*
8. Robert Oades interview, June 10, 2004.
9. *Ibid.*
10. Walter Prystawski interview, May 21, 2004.
11. Mary Jolliffe interview, October 22, 2007.

Chapter 5: Open at Last

1. Celia Franca interview, July 16, 2003.
2. Veronica Tennant interview, June 29, 2005.
3. Clive Barnes, article in the *New York Times*, June 4, 1969.
4. CBC Television, "Opening Gala."
5. Jolliffe interview, October 22, 2007.
6. Southam interview, July 24, 2003.
7. NAC Board of Trustees, Minutes, July 22, 1969.
8. Michael Namer interview, May 13, 2004.
9. Bernardi interview, October 21, 2003.
10. Public announcement or orchestra details by NAC.
11. Jolliffe interview.
12. Evelyn Greenberg interview, February 28, 2004.
13. *Ibid.*

Chapter 6: Growing Pains

1. *Time*, December 5, 1969.
2. Bernardi interview, October 21, 2003.
3. Critic Jacob Siskind in the *Montreal Gazette*, October 9, 1969.
4. Director General's Report, NAC Annual Report, 1969–70.
5. David Haber interview, March 22, 2004.
6. Southam interview, November 16, 2004.
7. NAC Board of Trustees, Minutes, February 13, 1970.
8. Editorial, *Ottawa Citizen*, November 10, 1969.
9. Gérard Pelletier, as quoted in *Time*, December 5, 1969.
10. Southam interview, July 9, 2006.
11. Southam interview, October 16, 2003.
12. Southam interview.
13. Haber interview.
14. *Ibid.*
15. Jean Herbiet interview, September 10, 2007.
16. Richard Dennison interview, July 14, 2003.
17. Michael Bawtree interview, n.d.
18. *Ibid.*
19. Dennison interview.
20. *Ibid.*
21. Annual General Report 1970–71, item 29.
22. Jean Roberts interview, September 25, 2003.
23. Dennison interview.
24. Herbiet interview.
25. Roberts interview.
26. Herbiet interview.
27. Annual Report 1974–75.

Chapter 7: Festivals and Financing

1. Hamilton Southam, memo to Board of Trustees, March 1968, NAC Archives.
2. Southam interview, November 16, 2004.

3. *Ottawa Citizen*, April 8, 1971, article by Betty Swimmings.
4. Bernardi interview, October 21, 2003.
5. Hugh Davidson interview, August 7, 2003.
6. David Currie (bass player) interview, November 6, 2006.
7. Southam interview, October 16, 2003.
8. Southam to reporter Tim Creery, Paris, June 5, 1972.
9. Mario Bernardi interview, October 21, 2003.
10. NAC Annual Report, 1972–73.
11. *Ottawa Citizen*, July 18, 1972, article by Lauretta Thistle.
12. Michael Gauvreau, *The Catholic Origins of Quebec's Quiet Revolution, 1931–1970* (Montreal & Kingston: McGill–Queen's University Press, 2005), 37.
13. D. Paul Schafer and André Fortier, *Review of Federal Policies for the Arts in Canada, 1944–1988*, published by the Canadian Conference of the Arts, 1989.
14. *Ibid.*
15. André Fortier interview, November 15, 2004.
16. Fortier interview.
17. Southam interview, November 16, 2004.
18. Gérard Pelletier, *L'Aventure de Pouvoir* (Montreal: Editions Alain Stanke, 1992).
19. Southam interview.
20. *Ibid.*
21. Canada Council, letter to Hamilton Southam, October 6, 1971.
22. Haber interview, March 22, 2004.
23. *Ibid.*
24. *Ibid.*
25. NAC Annual Report, 1971–72.

Chapter 8: Elegance and Operas

1. The Honourable Hugh Faulkner interview, October 30, 2006.
2. *Ibid.*
3. Pierre de Bon interview, October 31, 2005.
4. Southam, a theme repeated in many interviews and conversations over many lunches.
5. Robert Allen interview, March 22, 2005.
6. Dennison interview, July 14, 2003.
7. Claude Desvoyault interview, March 7, 2005.
8. Desvoyault interview.
9. *Ibid.*
10. Memo for Board of Trustees, "Festival Canada," April 25, 1973.
11. *Ibid.*
12. The National Ballet's Betty Oliphant, quoted in the *Globe and Mail*, March 10, 1973.
13. Brian Macdonald interview, May 11, 2007.
14. Southam, Memo to trustees, September 26, 1973.
15. *Ibid.*
16. *Ibid.*
17. Claude Corbeil interview, November 9, 2006.
18. NAC Annual Report, 1974–75.
19. Herbiet interview, September 10, 2007.
20. NAC Annual Report, 1973–74.
21. David Golden interview, July 9, 2004.
22. NAC Board of Trustees, Minutes, May 5, 1975.
23. Arthur Kroeger interview, November 17, 2006. Kroeger was a senior official at the Treasury Board at the time and a long-time top civil servant in Ottawa.
24. NAC Board of Trustees, Minutes, quoting official David Morley, July 22, 1975.
25. *Ibid.*
26. Bernardi interview, October 21, 2003.
27. "Opera in Canada," Charles Lussier in conversation with Douglas M. Leopold, *Montreal Star*, June 19, 1976.
28. *Ibid.*

29. *Ibid.*
30. Annual Report, 1975–76.
31. NAC Board of Trustees, Minutes, October 7, 1976.

Chapter 9: New Man in Town
1. *Halifax Mail Star*, December 17, 1977.
2. Donald MacSween interview, January 18, 2005.
3. *Ibid.*
4. *Ibid.*
5. *Ibid.*
6. *Ibid.*
7. *Canadian Encyclopedia of Theatre*, Robin Phillips entry.
8. MacSween interview.
9. *Ibid.*
10. Herbiet interview, September 17, 2003.
11. MacSween interview.
12. Annual Report, 1977–78.
13. Jean Gascon, quoted in an interview with Jamie Portman, Canadian Press, November 17, 1977.
14. *Montreal Star*, Myron Galloway review, November 29, 1977.
15. Jean Gascon, interview in the *Globe and Mail*, December 10, 1977.
16. *Ibid.*
17. *Halifax Mail Star*, December 13, 1977, reporter Mike Paterson.
18. Secretary of State John Roberts, as quoted in the *Montreal Gazette*, December 14, 1977.
19. Secretary of State John Roberts, *Globe and Mail*, December 31, 1977.
20. Herbiet interview.
21. Theatre critic Audrey Ashley, *Ottawa Citizen*, January 10, 1978.
22. *Ibid.*
23. John Wood interview, November 30, 2005.
24. *Ibid.*
25. Jackie Maxwell interview, February 2, 2006.

26. Andis Celms interview, August 12, 2003.
27. Wood interview.
28. Celms interview.
29. Maxwell interview, February 2, 2006.
30. *Ibid.*
31. *Ibid.*
32. Herbiet interview.
33. *Ibid.*
34. André Brassard interview, September 23, 2004.
35. *Ibid.*
36. NAC Annual report, 1982–83.
37. Denise Robert interview, June 29, 2006.

Chapter 10: A Cultural Investigation
1. MacSween interview, January 18, 2005.
2. *Ibid.*
3. *Ibid.*
4. Minutes, NAC Board of Trustees, January-April 1980.
5. *Ibid.*
6. The breakdown of the annual subsidy, and the way it was shared among the programming departments at this time, are interesting to note. Just slightly less than half of the annual government subsidy was going to programming at this time, and the net figures, after fixed costs were taken into account, broke down among the disciplines as follows:

Discipline	Net cost ($)	Percentage of work subsidized
NAC Orchestra	1,628,900.00	59.6
Theatre—English	1,413,000.00	49.9
—French	833,000.00	60.6
Dance	134,200.00	25.5
Festival	843,000.00	69.0

Source: Minutes, Board of Trustees, April 24, 1980. Salaries for permanent staff and fixed operating costs would not be included in these numbers.

7. MacSween interview.

8. The FAA—Financial Accountability Account—was the government's way of asserting control of the so-called independent agencies that reported to it. Historically, the cultural agencies resisted being placed under its measures on the grounds of freedom of thought. The government over the years would find other ways to tighten its grip, usually through the purse-strings. The result has been the diminishment of certain of the previously more powerful and activist cultural institutions, such as the National Film Board and the CBC. In 2006–07 the Harper government introduced the *Accountability Act*, which established stringent reporting procedures on expenses even for the cultural institutions.

9. William Littler, *Sunday Star*, February 15, 1981.

10. Currie interview, November 6, 2006.

11. Minutes, Board of Trustees, October 14, 1977.

12. Currie interview.

13. Bernardi interview, October 21, 2003.

14. Critic Jake Siskind, *Ottawa Citizen*, July 10, 1981.

15. Transcript, Applebaum-Hébert Committee proceedings, July 9, 1981.

16. Report of the Federal Cultural Policy Review Committee, Recommendation 43.

17. Walter Pitman, *Louis Applebaum: A Passion for Culture* (Toronto: Dundurn, 2002), 311.

18. Applebaum-Hébert Report.

Chapter 11: Change and Loss

1. Michael Aze interview, December 2, 2005.

2. *Ibid.*

3. *Ibid.*

4. MacSween interview, April 8, 2005.

5. Michael Aze interview.

6. *Ibid.*

7. *Ibid.*

8. MacSween interview.

9. Costa Pilavachi interview, April 4, 2006.

10. *Ibid.*

11. *Ibid.*

12. Aze interview.

13. MacSween interview.

14. Prystawski interview, May 21, 2004.

15. Namer interview, May 13, 2004.

16. Prystawski interview.

17. MacSween interview.

18. Hamilton Southam conversation, April 16, 2007.

19. *Ibid.*

20. MacSween interview.

21. Minutes, NAC Board of Board of Trustees, September 30, 1982.

22. *Ibid.*

23. Minutes, NAC Board of Trustees, November 25, 1982.

24. Minutes, NAC Board of Trustees, March 25, 1983.

25. Robert Rabinovitch interview, April 24, 2007.

26. MacSween interview.

27. Pilavachi interview.

28. NAC Annual Report, 1982–83.

Chapter 12: The Reality of the Plight

1. NAC Annual Report, 1982–83.

2. *Ibid.*

3. MacSween interview, April 8, 2005.

4. Marcel Masse interview, August 15, 2006.

5. *Ibid.*

6. *Ibid.*

7. *Ibid.*

8. MacSween interview.

9. *Ibid.*

10. As quoted in the NAC Annual Report, 1984–85.

11. NAC Annual Report, 1983–84.

12. NAC Annual Report, 1984–85.

13. NAC Annual Report, 1985–86.

14. NAC Annual Report, 1986–87.

15. *Ibid.*
16. *Ibid.*
17. Andis Celms, as quoted in the Annual Report.
18. *Ibid.*
19. *Ibid.*
20. Minutes, NAC Board of Trustees, January 29, 1986.
21. Tom Hendry interview, April 12, 2006.
22. "Accent on Access," press release, September 15, 1986.

Chapter 13: Rudderless Months
1. John Goldsmith, director of communications at the NAC, interview, August 10, 2007.
2. *Ibid.*
3. *Ibid.*
4. Minutes, NAC Board of Trustees, Steering Committee, November 14, 1986.
5. Minutes, NAC Board of Trustees, November 27, 1986.
6. Ian Clark interview, September 14, 2007.
7. As quoted in the *Ottawa Citizen*, November 10, 1987.
8. *Ottawa Citizen*, February 5, 1988.
9. As quoted in the *Ottawa Citizen*, February 5, 1988.
10. Hansard, Parliamentary Committee on Culture and Communications, as quoted by Hugh Winsor in the *Globe and Mail*, February 12, 1988.

Chapter 14: Times Get Tougher
1. Robert Landry interview, January 29, 2007.
2. As quoted in the *Ottawa Citizen*, March 25, 1988.
3. As quoted in the *Globe and Mail*, March 25, 1988.
4. Landry interview, January 29, 2007.
5. Yvon DesRochers, as quoted in an early interview as the new NAC director general, *Sunday Star*, July 24, 1988.

6. Landry telephone interview, October 15, 2008.
7. As quoted by William Littler in the *Sunday Star*, July 24, 1988.
8. Harold Clarkson interview, October 3, 2007.
9. Richard Lussier interview, April 25, 2007.
10. Clarkson interview, October 3, 2007.
11. *Ibid.*
12. Sarah Jennings interviewed Yvon DesRochers in his office at the NAC. The two had enjoyed a cordial relationship when DesRochers had worked in Francis Fox's office, and DesRochers had been an important source for the CBC reporter. His vitriolic attitude now towards the NAC Orchestra was a surprise to her, and she went out of her way to ensure that he really intended the harsh remarks he made about the orchestra before she published them. He confirmed that he meant every word he said.
13. Alain Gourd telephone conversation, October 12, 2007.
14. Clarkson interview.
15. *Ibid.*

Chapter 15: Television: The Longed-For Panacea
1. Minutes, NAC Board of Trustees, July 6, 1988.
2. The one-year interim contract that the NACO had agreed to in order to establish a cooling-off period with DesRochers was coming to an end and negotiations for a new contract were about to commence.
3. Michel Dozois interview, October 30, 2007.
4. Jack Udashkin interview, August 28, 2007.
5. David Langer interview, May 8, 2007.
6. *Ibid.*

7. Peter Herrndorf interview, October 17, 2007.
8. Langer interview.
9. As quoted in the *Ottawa Citizen*, November 18, 1989.
10. Gabriel Chmura interview, September 26, 2007.
11. Jack Mills interview, October 9, 2007.
12. Reporter Marsha Skuce writing in the *Ottawa Citizen*, November 18, 1989.
13. As quoted in the *Ottawa Citizen*, November 18, 1989.
14. *Ibid.*
15. *Ibid.*
16. *Ibid.*
17. Lussier interview, April 25, 2007.
18. Jack Mills interview, October 9, 2007.
19. Landry interview, January 29, 2007.
20. *Ibid.*
21. Lussier interview.
22. Jack Mills interview, October 6, 2007.
23. Karen Slipacoff interview, October 22, 2007.
24. Tickets were set at $1,000 per person, an unprecedented price for financially conservative Ottawa. Relying on her friends, especially in the Jewish community, Slipacoff devised an association of Friends of the National Arts Centre and sold out the grand dinner/performance event. Its huge success netted over $100,000 for the NAC and led to a permanent job for Slipacoff at the Arts Centre. After a thank-you dinner for gala supporters in May 1991, DesRochers hired her to become his new marketing director. Her efforts elicited the first steps towards a supporting Foundation for the NAC and laid down a fragile base for private fundraising in the future.
25. Hamilton Southam, as quoted in the *Ottawa Citizen*, June 13, 1990.
26. Hansard, Standing Committee on Culture and Communications hearings, June 14, 1990.
27. Robert Landry, as quoted in the *Globe and Mail*, June 15, 1990.
28. Felix Holtmann, as quoted by Stephen Godfrey in the *Globe and Mail*, September 26, 1990.
29. Ian Waddell, as quoted in the *Ottawa Citizen*, September 26, 1990.
30. Robert Landry, as reported in the *Ottawa Sun*, September 26, 1990.
31. As quoted in the *Globe and Mail*, April 8, 1989, from an interview in the Quebec magazine *Forces*.
32. Bronwyn Drainie, article in the *Globe and Mail*, April 8, 1989.
33. André Brassard, press statement, October 17, 1989.
34. Yvon DesRochers, as quoted in the *Montreal Gazette*, October 18, 1989.
35. Robert Lepage interview, October 13, 2006.
36. *Ibid.*
37. *Ottawa Citizen*, October 18, 1989.
38. Canadian Press report, *Toronto Star*, October 18, 1989.
39. Lepage interview.
40. *Ibid.*
41. Harold Clarkson, the fired NAC orchestra manager, had now joined Schmidt's staff in Hamburg and was able to inform him of the orchestra's quality.
42. As quoted by Jack Mills.
43. *Ibid.*
44. Pinnock interview, December 7, 2006.
45. *Ibid.*
46. *Ibid.*
47. *Ibid.*
48. *Ibid.*
49. Lepage interview, October 16, 2006.
50. Lepage interview, October 13, 2006.
51. *Globe and Mail*, October 7, 1989.
52. Gerry Stanton, outplacement expert, as quoted in the *Ottawa Citizen*, March 5, 1992.
53. As quoted in the *St. John's Evening Telegram*, May 26, 1992.

54. Testimony at Parliamentary Committee.
55. Roy Thomson, comment in the 1960s on the value of a television licence.
56. Director General's Report, Minutes of the NAC Board of Trustees, May 5–6, 1992.
57. Minutes, NAC Board of Trustees, May 5–6, 1992.
58. Chairman Robert Landry, Minutes of the Board, May 5–6, 1992.
59. Director General's Report, Minutes of the NAC Board of Trustees, May 5–6, 1992.
60. Paradis later became chief of staff for Lisa Frulla, minister of Canadian Heritage.
61. Minutes, NAC Board of Trustees, May 5–6, 1992.
62. Landry interview.
63. Brian Robertson interview, December 3, 2007.
64. Perrin Beatty interview, November 22, 2007.
65. Keith Spicer, comments before the Standing Committee on Communications and Culture, November 5, 1991.
66. Langer interview.
67. As quoted in letters, dated September 17, 1992, to individuals who had accepted the invitation to serve on the NAC's Working Group on TV Canada.
68. Landry interview.
69. Gérard Veilleux interview, November 23, 2007.
70. Tennant would be appointed to the NAC Board of Trustees in 2005 by the Liberal government headed by Paul Martin.
71. *Ottawa Citizen*, September 14, 1993.
72. *Ibid.*, September 18, 1993.
73. Lussier interview.
74. Yves Ducharme interview, November 8, 2007.
75. Landry, summary letter to Minister Dupuy, January 27, 1994.

76. As quoted in a letter from Chairman Robert Landry to Minister of Canadian Heritage Michel Dupuy, January 27, 1994, giving a summary history of the NAC's quest for a television licence.
77. *Ibid.*
78. Louis Applebaum, letter to Minister of Canadian Heritage Michel Dupuy, December 20, 1993.
79. Memorandum, November 22, 1993, from David Langer to Jack Mills, with a copy to Yvon DesRochers.
80. Landry interview.
81. Lepage interview, October 15, 2007.

Chapter 16: Stumbling Forward

1. Victoria Steele interview, December 28, 2007.
2. Pinnock interview, December 7, 2006.
3. The Department of Communications was broken up and its component parts redistributed under the short-lived Conservative government of Prime Minister Kim Campbell, who was engaged in an exercise designed to streamline government. The old Secretary of State's Department was permanently eliminated and the cultural agencies and other cultural programs, along with many others, from Canada's national parks to official bilingualism, were reassembled into a new department known as the Department of Canadian Heritage.
4. David Mirvish interview, February 7, 2008.
5. Michel Dupuy interview, January 18, 2008.
6. *Ibid.*
7. *Ibid.*
8. *Ibid.*
9. *Ibid.*
10. Jean Thérèse Riley interview, May 7, 2007.
11. Joan Pennefather interview, September 18, 2007.

12. MacLaren, who had campaigned for the Conservative Party, knew Jean Riley through Montreal connections. He would later become Quebec's agent general in London.

13. Michel Dupuy described Jean Pelletier in his 2008 interview as "a cultivated man. Rather like Cardinal Richelieu. Sometimes he was running the country. After the prime minister he was the most powerful man in Canada, but he made sure he left no traces." He was a man Dupuy admired.

14. Minutes, NAC Board of Trustees, November 3, 1994.

15. *Ottawa Citizen*, June 12, 1995.

16. Steele interview.

17. By 2006, Sandra Oh had made her mark in Hollywood, with an Emmy Award winning part in the intelligent television medical drama series *Grey's Anatomy*.

18. Trevor Pinnock, as quoted in the *Ottawa Citizen*, February 5, 1995.

19. As reported in the *Ottawa Citizen*, March 9, 1995.

20. The commercial musical had toured through Ottawa and played at the NAC with an aging Chita Rivera in the lead.

21. As quoted in the *Globe and Mail*, February 15, 1995.

22. Jean Riley interview.

23. Russell Mills interview, April 10, 2008.

24. *Ibid.*

25. Joan Pennefather, interview with CBC Radio's Jennifer Fry, June 15, 1995.

26. Similar job losses at the Canada Council and the CBC were in the news at the same time.

27. Celms interview, August 12, 2003.

28. Steele interview.

29. Minutes, NAC Board of Trustees, September 29, 1995.

30. *Ottawa Citizen* columnist Susan Riley, repeated in the *Globe and Mail*, as quoted at NAC Board meeting, November 23, 1995.

31. Minutes, NAC Board of Trustees, November 23, 1995.

32. *Ibid.*

33. Jean Riley interview.

34. Coopers Lybrand Report.

35. Pennefather interview.

36. Jean Riley interview.

37. *Ibid.*

38. Celms interview.

39. Minutes, NAC Board of Trustees, February 16, 1996.

40. *Ibid.*

41. *Ottawa Citizen*, June 12, 1996.

42. Hamilton Southam, as quoted in the *Ottawa Citizen*, June 21, 1996.

43. Jean Riley interview.

Chapter 17: A Short Run

1. John Cripton interview, May 9, 2007.

2. Vernon Turner interview, March 5, 2008.

3. Macdonald interview, May 10, 2007.

4. Cripton interview.

5. *Ibid.*

6. *Ibid.*

7. As quoted by Christopher Deacon.

8. Jean Riley interview, February 7, 2008.

9. *Ibid.*,

10. Zukerman's eight years as music director with the St. Paul orchestra had sometimes been chaotic. Although he had proved adept at raising funds for the orchestra, his musical administration was seen by many to have been disruptive, and few in Minnesota were interested in inviting him back.

11. Jean Riley interview.

12. Cripton interview.

13. Soon to be filled by a young trainee conductor, Jean-Pierre Tremblay.

14. Cripton interview.

15. *Ibid.*

16. Ultimately to be identified with Chuck Guité, a notorious public servant who

doled out sponsorship funds on directives, he alleged, from his political
bosses. Guité was finally charged and
convicted on the basis of breach of the
public trust.

17. Ruth Foster interview, March 5, 2008.
18. Since those days, Art Bank policies
have changed, and the private sector
can now also arrange to rent art.
19. The later regional "Scenes," developed
from 2001 on and still continuing,
are greatly enhanced by a visual arts
component featuring the work of
artists from the part of the country
being showcased at the NAC.
20. Russell Mills interview, April 10, 2008.
21. As quoted in the *Ottawa Citizen*.
22. *Ibid.*
23. Marti Maraden interview, June 8,
2007.
24. As quoted by Maraden, June 8, 2007.
25. *Ibid.*
26. *Ibid.*
27. *Financial Post* interview, April 5, 1997.
28. With strong Tory connections, Pigott
had been the appointments secretary
for a time in the Mulroney government,
responsible for patronage appointments. Her own reward came in an
appointment as chair of the National
Capital Commission in 1984.
29. Its intention was to join up a series of
downtown Ottawa buildings, including
the commercial Rideau Centre and
Ottawa's Congress Centre, through
underground tunnels that would see a
steady transfer of pedestrian traffic in
the bitter winter months.
30. The ill-fated meetings that had
surrounded the Meech Lake Accord,
chaired by former prime minister
Brian Mulroney, had been held there,
but after the collapse of the accord,
the Conference Centre had taken on a
jinxed air for many in government and
had sat idle and barely used.

31. Minutes, NAC Board of Trustees,
February 27, 1998.
32. Turner interview
33. Catherine Koprowski interview, March
12, 2008.
34. Letter inviting participants to join a
gala committee.
35. Turner interview.
36. Norman's singing credits included a
Bastille Day performance of "Le
Marseillaise" at the Place de la
Concorde in Paris the previous July.
37. *Ibid.*
38. Reid had helped to engineer the deal,
which saw the original name of the
hockey arena, the Palladium, changed
to the Corel Centre. The Ottawa high-
tech firm Corel, owned by Michael
Cowpland, bought the naming rights
for $25 million.
39. NAC press release, March 3, 1998.
40. *Bodycheck Magazine*, 1998–99
edition.
41. *Ibid.*
42. Memo, promoter Pat Reid to Kim
McCuaig of the NAC, with a copy to
John Cripton, January 23, 1998.
43. After Pat Reid had accosted Alexei
Yashin with the idea in the parking lot
of the Corel Centre after hockey practice, Yashin had arranged for his agent,
Mark Gandler, to meet with Cripton
that very day at the National Arts
Centre. A Saturday afternoon, the two
met informally, and Cripton was able
to reassure the Russian-born agent of
the merits of the Arts Centre.
44. *Bodycheck*, 1998–99 issue.
45. The NAC trustees had selected him
after a previous decision—to give the
honour to Céline Dion—had been
cancelled as being too commercial.
46. Jean Riley interview.
47. Cripton interview.
48. Houses for the 1997 summer performances had averaged only 42 percent

overall, and the financial loss was $1.8 million.

49. Cripton interview.
50. Minutes, NAC Board of Trustees, Executive Committee, September 18, 1998.
51. Jean Riley interview.
52. Royce Frith, trustees' meeting, October 2, 1998.
53. Suzanne Hurtubise interview, March 31, 2008.

Chapter 18: Upset and Renewal

1. Maraden interview, June 8, 2007.
2. *Ibid.*
3. *Ibid.*
4. CBC program *CBO Morning*, October 27, 1998.
5. Letter from David Haber, October 12, 1998.
6. Transcript, conversation with editorial board, *Ottawa Citizen*, November 14, 1998.
7. Maraden interview.
8. Elaine Calder interview, June 26, 2007.
9. As quoted by Calder, June 26, 2007.
10. Calder interview.
11. Agreement between Tatiana Entertainment Inc. and the National Arts Centre.
12. Letter from Yashin lawyer Fred Sellers to NAC lawyer David Scott, December 21, 1998.
13. Coincidentally, on the same day, John Cripton was fulfilling an earlier invitation to be a guest speaker at a luncheon at Ottawa's Rideau Club. Taxed with questions about the Tatiana side agreement after his formal remarks, he responded that it had never been his intention to pay out on it unless real services had been delivered. Many in the audience remained confused about the situation. Nothing was ever paid on the consulting contract.

14. Jean Riley interview, February 7, 2008.
15. Russell Mills interview, April 10, 2008.
16. *Ibid.*
17. Elaine Calder statement, press conference, January 21, 1999.
18. *Ibid.*
19. *Ibid.*
20. Jean Riley interview, February 7, 2008.
21. Calder interview, April 7, 2008.
22. David Scott interview, March 31, 2008.
23. Calder interview, June 26, 2007.
24. Sheila Copps interview, January 16, 2008.
25. NAC Annual Report, 1998–99.

Chapter 19: The Road to Recovery

1. Copps interview, January 16, 2008.
2. Dr. David Leighton interview, July 13, 2006.
3. Southam interview, October 16, 2003.
4. Herrndorf interview, July 19, 2007.
5. *Ibid.*
6. *Ibid.*
7. *Ibid.*
8. *Ibid.*
9. "Restoring the Vision," executive summary of new strategic plan, September 10, 2001.
10. Herrndorf interview.
11. *Ibid.*
12. Pinchas Zukerman, as quoted by Darrell Gregerson in her interview, January 15, 2008.
13. Gregerson interview.

Chapter 20: The Reblooming of the Arts

1. Victoria Steele interview, March 19, 2008.
2. Maraden interview, June 8, 2007.
3. *Ibid.*
4. *Ibid.*
5. *Ibid.*
6. *Ibid.*
7. *Ibid.*

8. *Ibid.*
9. *Ibid.*
10. *Ibid.*
11. *Ibid.*
12. *Ottawa Citizen*, March 30, 2005.
13. Jean-Claude Marcus interview, April 8, 2008.
14. NAC Annual Report, 1999–2000.
15. Marcus interview.
16. As quoted by Fernand Déry in his interview, July 11, 2008.
17. Paul Lefebvre interview, January 11, 2008.
18. *The Canadian Encyclopedia*, entry on Denis Marleau.
19. Marleau had joined the National Arts Centre by then.
20. Lefebvre interview.
21. *Ibid.*
22. Denis Marleau, interview with Catherine Palardy, Montreal.
23. *Ibid.*
24. *Ibid.*
25. *Ibid.*
26. *Ibid.*
27. Lefebvre interview.
28. Marleau interview.
29. Lefebvre interview.
30. Wajdi Mouawad, as quoted by Paul Lefebvre.
31. NAC press release on appointment of Wajdi Mouawad.
32. Cathy Levy interview,
33. *Ibid.*
34. *Ibid.*
35. *Ibid.*
36. *Ibid.*
37. Paula Citron interview, June 19, 2008.
38. Levy interview.
39. *Ibid.*
40. *Ibid.*
41. Citron interview.
42. Levy interview.
43. *Ibid.*
44. *Ibid.*

Chapter 21: The Pinchas Factor
1. Eric Friesen, as quoted in the *National Post*, October 2, 1999.
2. Michael Barone, as quoted, *ibid.*
3. Marta Istomin, as quoted, *ibid.*
4. Pinchas Zukerman, as quoted, *ibid.*
5. *Ibid.*
6. *Ibid.*
7. Herrndorf interview, May 20, 2008.
8. Christopher Deacon interview, October 3, 2007.
9. *Ibid.*
10. *Ibid.*
11. *Ibid.*
12. *Ibid.*
13. *Ibid.*
14. *Ibid.*
15. Jean-Philippe Tremblay interview, June 24, 2008.
16. Friesen interview, July 9, 2008.
17. Zukerman, as quoted in the *Ottawa Citizen*, September 27, 1999.
18. *Ibid.*
19. As quoted by Deacon in his interview, October 3, 2007.
20. *Ibid.*
21. Deacon interview, October 3, 2007.
22. *Ibid.*
23. From the mission statement of the company of MasterVision, a technology company of which Zukerman was the co-founder and artistic director in the United States and of which he had an interest when he came to the NAC.
24. Zukerman, as quoted in the *Ottawa Citizen*, May 12, 2000.
25. *Ibid.*
26. Deacon interview, October 3, 2007.
27. *Ibid.*
28. As quoted by Robert Everett-Green, *Globe and Mail*, n.d.
29. Marc Neikrug's term.
30. Marc Neikrug interview, May 21, 2008.
31. *Ibid.*
32. *Ibid.*

33. Denys Bouliane interview, June 26, 2008.
34. *Ibid.*
35. *Ibid.*
36. Gary Kulesha interview, June 24, 2008.
37. *Ibid.*
38. Deacon interview.
39. *Ibid.*
40. Zukerman, as quoted by Deacon, October 3, 2007.
41. Namer interview, July 4, 2008.
42. Pinnock interview, December 10, 2007.
43. Namer interview.
44. *Globe and Mail,* February 6, 2006.
45. Deacon interview, October 3, 2007.
46. NAC press statement, December 18, 2005.
47. Deacon, as quoted in the *Ottawa Citizen,* December 20, 2005.
48. Leighton interview, July 13, 2006.
49. *Ibid.*
50. John Cripton telephone conversation, undated (spring 2008).
51. Leighton interview.
52. *Ibid.*
53. *Ibid.*
54. *Ibid.*
55. Robert Everett-Green interview, July 3, 2008.
56. Friesen interview.
57. Neikrug interview.
58. Jill LaForty interview, July 4, 2008.
59. Richard Todd interview, August 5, 2008.
60. Herrndorf interview, August 23, 2007.
61. *Ibid.*

Chapter 22: The Art of the Possible

1. Herrndorf interview, August 27, 2007.
2. Dr. Shirley Thomson interview, July 18, 2008.
3. Herrndorf interview, May 20, 2008.
4. Herrndorf interview, August 27, 2007.
5. Herrndorf interview, May 20, 2008.
6. Thomson interview, July 21, 2008.
7. Herrndorf interview, May 20, 2008.
8. Claire Speed interview, May 22, 2008.
9. *Ibid.*
10. *Ibid.*
11. Maurizio Ortolani interview, May 2, 2008.
12. *Ibid.*
13. Herrndorf interview, July 19, 2007.
14. Herrndorf interview, May 20, 2008.
15. Kari Cullen interview, July 22, 2008.
16. *Ibid.*
17. Annual Report, 2002–03.
18. Cullen interview.
19. As quoted by Cullen in her interview.
20. Cullen interview.
21. Herrndorf interview, July 19, 2007.
22. *Ibid.*
23. Peter Lougheed interview, June 3, 2008.
24. Herrndorf interview.
25. Lougheed interview.
26. Jamie Portman writing in the *Ottawa Citizen,* as quoted in the NAC Annual Report, 2004–05.
27. Danny Senyk interview, June 3, 2008.
28. Herrndorf interview, August 23, 2007.
29. Leighton interview, July 13, 2006.
30. Herrndorf interview, May 20, 2008.
31. Herrndorf interview, August 23, 2007.

BIBLIOGRAPHY

Charest, Rémy. *Robert Lepage: Connecting Flights.* Toronto: Alfred A. Knopf, 1998.

Edwardson, Ryan. *Canadian Content: Culture and the Quest for Nationhood.* Toronto: University of Toronto Press, 2008.

Finlay, Karen A. *The Force of Culture: Vincent Massey and Canadian Sovereignty.* Toronto: University of Toronto Press, 2004.

Freiman, Lawrence. *Don't Fall Off the Rocking Horse: An Autobiography.* Toronto: McClelland & Stewart, 1978.

Gauvreau, Michael. *The Catholic Origins of Quebec's Quiet Revolution, 1931–1970.* Montreal: McGill-Queen's University Press, 2005.

Lebrecht, Norman. *Covent Garden: The Untold Story. Dispatches from the English Culture War, 1945–2000.* Boston: Northeastern University Press, 2000.

_____. *The Life and Death of Classical Music: Featuring the 100 Best and 20 Worst Recordings Ever Made.* New York: Anchor Books, 2007.

Manera, Tony. *A Dream Betrayed: The Battle for the CBC.* Toronto: Stoddart Publishing, 1996.

Massey, Vincent. *Speaking of Canada: Addresses by the Right Hon. Vincent Massey, C.H., Governor-General of Canada, 1952–1959.* Toronto: Macmillan Company of Canada Limited, 1959.

Pearson, Peter. "Entertaining Insurrection: My Life—the Movie." Montreal, unpublished manuscript, © Oro Films Ltd., 2005.

Pelletier, Gérard. *Years of Choice 1960–1968.* Toronto: Methuen, 1987.

_____. *Years of Impatience 1950–1960.* Toronto: Methuen, 1984.

Pitman, Walter. *Louis Applebaum: A Passion for Culture.* Toronto: Dundurn Press, 2002.

Schafer, D. Paul, and André Fortier. *Review of Federal Policies for the Arts in Canada (1944--1988).* Ottawa: The Canadian Conference of the Arts, 1989.

Setterfield, Gwenlyn. *Niki Goldschmidt: A Life in Canadian Music.* Toronto: University of Toronto Press, 2003.

Soyinka, Wole. *You Must Set Forth at Dawn: A Memoir.* London: Methuen, 2007.

ACKNOWLEDGEMENTS

Above all, thanks to National Arts Centre staff members at all levels, both present and past, who have been unstinting in their support and enthusiasm for this project. They helped in countless ways. Their trust and confidence cheered me and, without their practical assistance and insightful observations, this story could not have been told. While the co-operation of the National Arts Centre has been essential to this tale, it has had no editorial control and the interpretations the book contains are my own.

Thanks also to the more than 150 artists, politicians, officials, administrators, and other participants in the forty-year life of the National Arts Centre who gave their time, memories, and reflections in the research interviews. Most of their names and voices appear in this book, and all have agreed to the release of their recorded and transcribed interviews into the public domain. These interviews will be held at the National Arts Centre Archives and at Library and Archives Canada for future writers, students, teachers, and researchers interested in Canada's performing arts. Thanks to both institutions for their financial contribution towards collecting a portion of these interviews in return for these recordings, which will form the core of an oral performing arts archives.

On a personal level, thanks to NAC chair Dr. David Leighton, who originated the idea of a history of the NAC and asked me to take it on. G. Hamilton Southam helped start it all, and though he failed in his promise to be present at the book launch, he was able to read and annotate the chapters pertaining to his own era before his death at the age of ninety-one on July 1, 2008. Thanks to Rosemary Shipton, a superlative editor whose unflappable support and expertise explains her pre-eminent place among Canadian non-fiction editors; to Paul Lefebvre for his encyclopedic knowledge of francophone theatre in Canada and his willingness to share it; and to NAC staffers Doug Eide, Martin Jones, Gerald Morris, Jane Morris, Barbara Irving, Gerry Grace, Jose L. Hernandez, Luce Courtemanche, Diane Lemire, Nicole Milne, Peter Kealey, Gaston Roussy, Bob Asselin, Fran Walker, Agnes Lebrun, and many others, whose direct assistance has been immeasurable. Other trusted supporters include transcribers Joanne Beall and Kathy Bowie, photo researcher Vivian Hanwell, and friend Sheilagh D'Arcy McGee. Ana Maria Tavarez and Lobo Viejo kept the home fires burning.

Thanks also to the Ontario Arts Council for a Writers' Reserve grant, to the Ottawa Citizen Group Inc. for its generous corporate support for the photographs from its archive, to the Yousuf Karsh estate and the family of Malak Karsh who so kindly allowed their photographs to be used, to artist Alan King for the use of his wonderful editorial cartoons, and to the other photographers of NAC life who permitted the use of their images without fee. Thanks for other financial assistance from 40 Clarence Limited, Ashton Gate Developments, and Ian Johns.

Although an experienced journalist, I discovered as I wrote this text that producing a book is a new world unto itself. I am grateful for the confidence that my publisher, Dundurn Press, placed in this project at an early stage and for the support of its hard-working staff who have seen it through to the end. Their commitment to books that document our cultural life in Canada is unique.

INDEX

A page number in italics (e.g., *162*) indicates a photograph only. A page number followed by *n* (e.g., 153n) refers to a footnote on that page. The National Arts Centre is abbreviated as NAC.